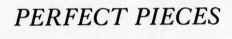

PERFECT PIECES

BY AARON LATHAM

Crazy Sundays: F. Scott Fitzgerald in Hollywood
Orchids for Mother
Urban Cowboy

PERFECT PIECES

◆ ◆ ◆

AARON LATHAM

ARBOR HOUSE   *New York*

Manufactured in the United States of America

10 9 8 7 6 5 4 3 2 1

Library of Congress Cataloging in Publication Data

Latham, Aaron
Perfect pieces.

I. Title.
PS3562.A7536P4   1987   814'.54   86-20669
ISBN 0-87795-871-8

Design by Laura Hough

To Lesley and Taylor

CONTENTS

♦ ♦ ♦

vii

JESSIE

It must be exciting being a reporter today.

ADAM

Yeah. He said suspiciously.

JESSIE

After all, you get a chance to try to keep the big guys honest. And you have fun trying to figure out which way the culture is headed.

ADAM

A friend of mine says that popular culture is to the society what dreams are to the individual. And so, if you can find out more about a person by analyzing his dreams, then you can also understand more about a society by studying things like music, film, junk food, health clubs.

—from the screenplay of *Perfect*
by Aaron Latham and James Bridges

INTRODUCTION: FALLING IN LOVE ON SATURDAY NIGHT

•   •   •

I've been lookin' for love
In all the wrong places . . .
—song in Urban Cowboy

For the past few years, I have been living that song, looking for love, sometimes in the wrong places, sometimes in the right ones. I have been looking for love stories to write about.

I like to use love stories to give structure and energy and emotion to my journalism. Whenever possible, I look for a couple whose romance illustrates the journalistic point I am trying to make.

I first tried this technique when I went down to Houston to write a story for *Esquire* on a huge honky-tonk called Gilley's. I walked into Gilley's—a place that frightened me, at first—looking for a love story that would dramatize the story of the saloon. After searching the honky-tonk's acres of indoor prairie for hours without success, I was getting a little discouraged. Then, sometime after midnight, I met a cowgirl whose marriage had been broken up by the mechanical bull at Gilley's.

I had the idea of basing a journalistic story on a love story years before I got around to trying it. Back when I first started turning the notion over in my mind—that would have been in the early seventies—I was an *Esquire* editor, *not* a writer. And I was editing and/or having long talks with such *Esquire* contributors as Gay Talese and Tom Wolfe, who were among the founding fathers of the New Journalism. Whether I was editing them or playing softball with them—*Esquire*'s team lost eight in a row in Central Park—I always asked them about writing the New Journalism.

Wolfe and Talese told me that the New Journalism simply meant applying the techniques of fiction to nonfiction. They said they tried to use the narrative voice. They attempted to write scenes whenever possible. They dramatized. They stressed the importance of using not just quotes but actual dialogue with people talking back and forth as in a novel.

As we discussed all these fictional techniques, however, I came to feel that they were leaving out an important one. Namely, the love story. One might quarrel with whether love is technique or theme or subject. But the fact remains that the love story is the engine that runs most fiction. Of course, there are a few exceptions, a few works of fiction that do not concern themselves with love—but *very* few. Most novels, short stories, movies, and plays are love stories. So to ignore the love story—when trying to copy the characteristics of fiction—might be to leave out the heart of the matter.

I carried this theory around with me for years without trying it out. It was like the cuff links you never wear. Like the phone number you keep in your wallet but never call. Like the tuxedo you buy but never have an occasion to put on.

I moved from *Esquire*, where I was an editor, to *New York* magazine, where I was an editor and writer. And I started writing all sorts of profiles, which I enjoyed. (I still do.) I created a furor with two pieces—one on Gay Talese and the other on Sally Quinn—that concerned themselves with the sex lives of my subjects. Of course, sex stories are similar to love stories, but they are not the same thing. Journalistically speaking—as I would eventually discover—love is better than sex.

Then I was dispatched to Washington to cover the growing Watergate scandal. The Nixon administration in its dying days offered few opportunities for telling love stories, so my thesis remained untried and unproven.

Although I wrote no love stories, I got caught up in one of my own. One evening, I telephoned the home of a young CBS reporter named Lesley Stahl and asked her if she could help me with a Watergate column I was trying to write. She rather rudely informed me that if I wanted to talk to her about business, I should call her during business hours at her office. I swore that I would never speak to Lesley Stahl again in my life.

But the next day, my reporting went even worse than it had the day before. I got more and more desperate—desperate enough to do what I had sworn not to do. I called Lesley Stahl at her office.

"Oh, hi," she said. "Want to have dinner?"

A few years later, we took a trip to Greece together. We had several fights because she always wanted to ask directions, and I never wanted to. One afternoon, this running argument developed into a crisis when I chose a road that would have been ideal for lemmings, since it ran right to the edge of a cliff overlooking the sea. I slammed on the brakes just in time to keep our rented car from making a spectacular dive into the waves. Lesley informed me that we were going to take a bus tour.

Although it seemed out of character for both of us, we climbed onto a bus with a lot of strangers and spent days traveling up and down the Greek peninsula. To make conversation, Lesley and I started asking our bus mates how they met. And we started hearing wonderful love stories.

For example, there was the ugly man with the beautiful wife. They had met on a blind date in college. For him, it was love at first sight, for her quite the reverse. She did like his dog (White Fang) and his car (the Black Duck), but she didn't like him because he was so unattractive. The date went so badly that she never expected—never wanted—to hear from him again. But he started calling her on the phone. And he was funny on the phone. And he wasn't bad-looking on the phone. They fell in love over the telephone. When they finally met face to face once again, she saw a completely different person.

Lesley and I wrote this love story and many others into our journal of the trip. By the time we got home, my interest in somehow finding a way to use love stories in my journalism had been rekindled.

Then I went to Gilley's.

While I was haunting Gilley's concrete badlands, another idea began to take shape in my mind. I scribbled in one of my notebooks: THE NEW SATURDAY NIGHT. For that was what I thought I saw at Gilley's. A new date night. A new dance floor for the never-ending mating dance. And the love story seemed the ideal vehicle for telling the story of the New Saturday Night. The article that I eventually wrote about Gilley's was a New Honky-Tonk Saturday Night Love Story.

I have been writing love stories set against the background of the New Saturday Night ever since. All sorts of Saturday Nights. The Health Club Saturday Night. Saturday Night in the New Speakeasies. The Four-Wheel-Drive Saturday Night.

Saturday Night is a fascinating window into the culture. It changes as we change. It tells us how we are entertaining ourselves, which tells us a lot about ourselves. It reflects the ebb and flow of the battle of the sexes, since so many sexual skirmishes take place on weekends. Saturday Night is when the pop culture is really popping. It is an energetic night, and I always look for pockets of energy in the culture. Where there is energy, there is usually a good story.

Sometimes I feel like a cultural prospector—lookin' for energy, lookin' for change, lookin' for love on Saturday Night.

PART ONE

◆ ◆ ◆

THE NEW
SATURDAY NIGHT

JESSIE
What kind of journalist are you?

ADAM
I guess I consider myself one of the New
Journalists. The idea is to apply the techniques of fiction to nonfiction, but I think
most new journalists leave out the most important thing in fiction. It's heart.

JESSIE
And what's that?

ADAM
The love story. That's what almost all fiction is about. So that's what I look for, especially when I'm doing a life-style piece, a
good love story.

—from the screenplay of *Perfect*

THE BALLAD OF
THE URBAN COWBOY

♦   ♦   ♦

Rupert Murdoch—who would be a villain in a black hat if life were a western—had just bought *New York* magazine, where I had been working for four years. As I wandered about dazed in front of the magazine's headquarters, a television reporter and crew caught up with me. The bright TV lights came on and I felt like a rabbit, paralyzed by headlights, about to be crushed by an onrushing car.

"What are you going to do now?" asked the reporter. "Are you going to stay or leave?"

I had been asking myself those same questions and coming up with no answers.

"I'm going to leave," I found myself saying. "I quit."

So I resigned on television. It seemed the modern way to go.

I quit because I didn't like Rupert Murdoch and his *New York Post* style of journalism. And because I did like Clay Felker, the founding father of *New York*. Murdoch's arrival meant Felker's departure—so I went, too.

I thought I would never be published again.

But a few months later, Clay Felker bought *Esquire* and I went back to work for him at his new address. And he had a new assignment for me. He told me he wanted me to write a story about a bar in Texas.

Clay knew about the bar thanks to a recent invitation to attend a publishing symposium—sponsored by *Texas Monthly* magazine—at Rice University. In agreeing to participate, he had struck an unusual bargain. He would act as speaker if the editors of *Texas Monthly* would act as guides and give him a tour of Houston. So he talked and then they took him out for a night on the town.

One of the places his guides showed him that night was a saloon called Gilley's that had a mechanical bull and a mechanical punching bag and four and a half acres under one roof and several thousand city kids dressed up as cowboys. The Texas editors looked out on this panorama and saw a good bar. The New York editor stared at the same indoor Big Valley and saw a good story.

When he got back to New York City, Clay gave me the assignment—largely because I had grown up in Texas. On the plane on the way to Houston, I began to wonder if this might not be a good time to try out my theory that a good boy-meets-girl story might be used to dramatize a work of nonfiction.

So my hatred of Rupert Murdoch in New York led me by a circuitous route to a search for a love story in Houston . . .

◆　◆　◆

Esquire, September 1978

Dew Westbrook is a big-city cowboy. The range he rides is a Houston honky-tonk saloon called Gilley's, which is as big as a ranch inside. The animal that carries him is a bucking bull. He straddles this dangerous beast right there in the saloon's south forty, where the landscape is dotted with long-necked beer bottles (in place of sagebrush) and verdant pool tables (in place of pastures). The bull is mechanized, but it bucks as hard as a real one, breaking an occasional arm, leg, or collarbone. Sometimes it crushes something worse. A honky-tonk cowboy has to risk his manhood in order to prove it.

Dew, the beer joint bull rider, is as uncertain about where his life is going as America is confused about where it wants to go. And when America is confused, it turns to its most durable myth: the cowboy. As the country grows more and more complex, it seems to need simpler and simpler values: something like the Cowboy Code. According to this code, a cowboy is independent, self-reliant, brave, strong, direct, and open. All of which he can demonstrate by dancing the cotton-eyed Joe with the cowgirls, punching the punching bag, and riding the bull at Gilley's. In these anxious days, some Americans have turned for salvation to God, others have turned to fad prophets, but more and more people are turning to the cowboy hat. Dew paid $35 for his on sale.

One way the Cowboy Code is transmitted to the new urban cowboy is through country-and-western music. How Dew sees his world is shaped by the songs he hears on the radio and the lyrics sung by the band at Gilley's. Country music is the city cowboy's Bible, his literature, his self-help book, his culture. It tells him how to live and what to expect.

Actually, the life story of Dew, the urban cowboy, sounds as if it should be set to twangy music and sung as a country-and-western ballad. Dew met Betty at Gilley's, *twang-twang.* Dew fell in love with Betty at Gilley's, *twang-twang.* They had their wedding reception at Gilley's, *twang-twang.* But they quarreled over the bull at Gilley's, *twang-twang.* And then Dew met somebody new at Gilley's, *twaaaang.*

A few months after the breakup, I made a date to go to Gilley's with Dew and his new girl friend. I knew his ex-wife would be there too. When the three of them met at the bullring, it might be like Frankie and Johnny.

Before we could go to Gilley's, Dew had to change clothes. He had curly hair the color of the beach at Galveston, worn a little long for a cowboy. His nose had a slight hump in it like a bull's back. And he had pale blue eyes that squinted. He was a good-looking cowboy who had had a hard, uncowboy day.

"The foam glass is eating me up," Dew complained. "It'll take the hide off you real quick."

Dew, who works six days a week, had spent his Saturday sawing foam glass, a form of insulation, at Texas City Refining. All of the maze of pipes and towers at the refinery needed insulation. At twenty-two, Dew has already spent over three years insulating petrochemical plants. It is hard, boring work. All assholes and elbows, as he puts it.

After work, the big-city cowboy had come home to his covered wagon: a mobile home. He lives in a trailer park that is built in a circle, so at dusk all the mobile homes really do look a little like a wagon train circled up for the night.

"I'll just be a minute," Dew said.

He was ready to turn into an urban cowboy. He exchanged his hard hat for a black felt cowboy hat with toothpicks stuck in the band and his name spelled out in small gold letters on the back. (No country cowboy ever decorated his hat with gilt lettering.) He traded dirty bell-bottom blue jeans for clean bell-botton blue jeans that had just been ironed. (No country cowboy ever wore anything but unironed, straight-legged jeans.) Then he swapped his work sneakers for cowboy boots with a flat, rubber heel designed for a range made up mostly of asphalt, sidewalks, and linoleum. (No country cowboy ever wore anything but high, pointed, leather heels designed to let a cowboy dig in his heels if he roped something mean.) And his workingman's T-shirt was replaced by a cowboy shirt with mother-of-pearl snaps and short sleeves. (If a country cowboy wore short sleeves, his arms would be scratched off the first time he passed a mesquite tree.) Now the urban cowboy was ready to mount his pickup truck and ride forth to Gilley's in search of adventure. He had his armor on. The cowboy has always been America's knight-errant. During the Middle Ages, dressing a knight in his armor was a solemnly important ritual. The dressing of the urban cowboy is no less so.

When a city cowboy dons his cowboy clothes, he dons more than garments: He dons cowboy values. These values evolved among people who lived fifty miles apart. While they were away from everyone else, they *had* to be independent and self-reliant. And when these people did occasionally see one another, they could not afford to waste time being anything but open and direct. And now these values, forged by people who lived too far apart, are serving people who live too close together.

When Dew puts on his cowboy hat, it temporarily drives from his head the memory of his job at the refinery. When he pulls on his cowboy boots, he can temporarily forget that he is a member of insulators' union local 22, which ties him to the city that he is always saying he is going to leave. His life is divided into hard-hat days and cowboy-hat nights. It is a way of coping. It may sound crazy, but it works. Or, as the band down at Gilley's sings:

> *I've always been crazy,*
> *But it's kept me from going insane.*

On the way to Gilley's, Dew drove his orange-and-white pickup fast and loose. He made it buck. Beside Dew on the pickup seat sat Jan Day, twenty-four, with whom he has lived ever since he broke up with his wife, *twang-twang*. Auburn-haired Jan possessed a porcelain beauty that made men want to save her from breaking. She was so fragile, in fact, that she sometimes fainted at Gilley's, which is no place for the porcelain-hearted. She wore cowboy boots, flared jeans, and a transparent top with nothing underneath. (No country cowgirl could afford to let her breasts roam free as dogies.)

"I'd never go to the Nesadel," Dew said of a joint down the road from Gilley's. "It's a rock place. A different set goes there. Sometimes there's tension between the two groups. I'd never go in the Nesadel without twenty ol' cowboys to back me up."

From the road, Gilley's Club looks like a little old shack. But when you walk through the door, you see that it is a great deal more. It's just a honky-tonk, but it looks about as big as the MGM Grand Hotel or St. Patrick's Cathedral. It has about forty pool tables, which makes it roughly equal to forty bars under one roof. On a busy night, this capital of the urban-cowboy culture has a population greater than most state capitals had during the heyday of the Old West. When Willie Nelson played Gilley's, 4,500 people crowded inside.

On our way to the dance floor we passed a gang of downtown cowboys gathered to pay a quarter to smash the punching bag just to prove how hard they could hit. A dial measured the force of each punch. If the honky-tonk cowpokes slugged hard enough, a siren went off. And most of them did hit hard enough. That part of Gilley's sounded like a firehouse. When the saloon cowgirls are watching, the saloon cowboys often hit the bag until their hands bleed and their knuckles break. At the end of an evening, there is often blood on the bag.

Jan and Dew tried to teach me how to dance the cotton-eyed Joe. You make a line and kick a lot. And every time you kick you yell: "Bullshit! Bullshit!" It is a perfect shit kickers' dance.

Then everyone danced the Shotess, which was followed by a crow's step, which was followed by a polka, which was followed by the whip. All the cowboys danced with their hats on. When they danced slowly, the cowgirls hooked the cowboys' belt loops with the fingers of their left hands. And the cowboys held onto the cowgirls' hair with their right hands.

When the band took a break, everyone headed for the bullring. It costs two dollars to ride the bull, and you have to sign a waiver saying you won't sue no matter how bad you get hurt. A cowboy on the sidelines runs the bull by remote control, making it buck according to his whim. One cowboy got so good at running the bull that he claimed he could throw off a cowboy's hat, turn the cowboy around, and then throw him on his hat.

Dew, who hadn't ridden the bull for some time, was apprehensive. He had brought two ace bandages from home. He used one to wrap his right knee and the other to swaddle his left wrist. Then he pulled a bull-riding glove onto his left hand.

"Why do you ride left-handed?" I asked. "I thought you were right-handed."

"I am," Dew said, "but that's what I make my living with." He held up his right fist. "I'm crazy to ride, but I'm smart."

He placed his cowboy hat on a chair in front of Jan like a votive offering. Then he climbed aboard the big, bad bull.

As the bull started to buck and spin, Jan took in a deep breath and looked worried. As I scanned the bullring, I noticed another intent face. It belonged to Betty, Dew's ex-wife. I knew she was still in love with the bull rider, *twang-twang*.

Dew's real name is Donald Edward Westbrook. The cowboys at Gilley's made a nickname out of his initials. Everybody at Gilley's has a nickname. There's Gator and the Hippie and Armadillo. . . . But Dew's family calls him Eddie. One night a couple of years ago, Eddie met Betty Jo Helmer at Gilley's. At the time, he was nineteen and she was eighteen. Betty and Eddie liked each other right away. It seemed like destiny. After all, their names rhymed the way the names of lovers in a good country song should. At the time, it didn't occur to them that all country songs have unhappy endings.

On that first night, Betty came to Gilley's with her girl friends. She wore pants, not having worn or even owned a dress for years. She had a turned-up nose, an adolescent pout, and long brown hair. She wasn't quite beautiful, but she was as cute as a picture on a T-shirt. Dew came up and asked her to dance. She accepted.

"Now you're stuck with him," one of her girl friends said.

But that was fine with Betty. She had been watching him dance, and she liked what she saw. An urban cowboy doesn't have to know how to brand or rope or hog-tie or bulldog . . . but he does have to know how to dance. Eddie took hold of Betty's hair, and she hooked her finger through his belt loop. They danced until closing time as the band sang good old honky-tonk lyrics like: "Help me make it through the night. . . ."

The next night, Betty and Eddie came to Gilley's together. And the next. And the next. Betty and Eddie were lovers.

One night after 2:00 A.M. closing time, Betty and Eddie went from Gilley's to Granny's all-night omelet joint. (There are more nicknames ending in "y" and "ie" in Texas than there are at an eastern girls' boarding school.) At Granny's, Eddie tickled Betty until she pinched his leg. He got mad and hit her right there in front of everybody. But Betty loved Eddie in spite of the pain, *twang-twang*.

They decided to get married. Eddie wanted to have the wedding at Gilley's. (Actually, there have been several marriages performed in the saloon. Judge West, a colorful old-time justice of the peace, comes over and joins the couples in matrimony.) But Betty refused to get married in a honky-tonk. She wanted a Baptist minister to perform the ceremony in church. So they compromised, agreeing to get married in church but to have the wedding reception at Gilley's.

The only dress Betty ever wore at Gilley's was her wedding dress. And she didn't want to wear it. She wanted to change right after the exchange of vows so she could go to her wedding reception in her Levi's. But her father insisted that he wanted pictures of his daughter dancing in her wedding dress. So another compromise was in order. Betty went to her Gilley's wedding reception in her wedding dress and danced just long enough for the photographer to snap a few pictures. Then she went into the ladies' room and took off her wedding dress. When she emerged to enjoy the rest of her wedding reception, the eighteen-year-old bride wore pants.

Betty had expected Eddie to want to stay until closing time. She was shocked when he suggested leaving early. They spent their honeymoon at the Roadway Inn, which is only about a mile from Gilley's. There was no place to stay any closer. The Roadway is built in the shape of a tower. Because the building is round, all the rooms are triangular. When they ordered breakfast on the morning after their wedding night, room service brought it up on a tray with plastic silverware.

Dew spurred the bull, even though he didn't really have spurs on his boots. He slammed his heels again and again into the machine between his legs. The mechanical bull bucked and spun. Dew was getting bruised and dizzy. He came up off the bull's back and thought he was headed for the mattresses that surround the bull, stacked two layers thick. But somehow Dew saved himself. He crashed back onto the bull's back, his sexual organs taking a beating. Dew winced in pain.

A honky-tonk cowboy named Steve Strange was manning the bull's remote controls. He made it spin first one way and then the other. Cowboys who have ridden real bulls say that in some ways the mechanical bull is harder to ride because you can't watch its head and tell which way it is going to turn. The treachery of the bull depends upon the treachery of the man at the controls. Steve, who was once badly hurt by a real bull, is treacherous indeed. He seems to believe that everyone should get mangled as badly as he did when a real bull gored him in the chute. He told me that as a result of his injuries he had a plastic bone in his leg, a plastic plate in his head, and a plastic testicle. I was not sure whether to believe him, so he knocked on his leg. It sounded like plastic. Then he knocked on his head. It sounded like plastic too. I was afraid he was going to keep on knocking, so I stopped him. Bragging about your injuries is another important part of being an urban cowboy. The more banged up you are, the more of a he-man you are.

Dew pitched forward on the bull, which is how you can get hurt the worst. I knew what he was going through because I had tried riding the bull myself a couple of days earlier. When I asked for instructions, one of the cowboys told me: "Put your left nut in your right hand and hang on." Armed with this advice, I crawled aboard. When the bull started bucking, I desperately wished I could think of some way to do what the cowboy had told me to do. I kept crashing into the rigging, which was supposed to hold me on but had become a hammer banging between my legs. A bell tied to the bull clanged maddeningly in my ears. I was frightened. Deciding it was time to get off, I began to wonder how you let go of a tiger. I looked for a good place to land. Then I felt myself flying horizontally through the air. I hit the mattresses with my right shoulder first. Stumbling to the sidelines, I sat down to record my impressions, but my hand was shaking so much I couldn't write.

Dew pressed himself back up into a sitting position, somehow staying aboard. The bull on which he rode had the heart of a pickup truck. A piston rather than sinews made it buck. The urban cowboy was trying to tame a wild, woolly machine. Which was as it should be because the urban cowboy knows a lot more about horsepower than about horses. He lives in a world where machines have replaced every animal but himself, and he is threatened. In his boots and jeans, the urban cowboy tries to get a grip on and ride an America that, like his bull, is mechanized. He can never tame it, but he has the illusion of doing so.

A sideline cowboy yelled, "Hurts your nuts, don't it?"

As Jan watched, she was obviously afraid the cowboy might be right: Had Dew hurt himself badly? As Betty watched from a greater distance, she was worried about something else: Could her former husband ride better than she could?"

Betty and Eddie spent much of their marriage at Gilley's. When they weren't honky-tonking, they both worked. Betty worked in construction, putting hardware in houses. Eddie insulated petrochemical plants and moonlighted at an auto racetrack.

Betty and Eddie are both second-generation noncountry cowboys. Betty's father works in construction like his daughter. And Eddie's father is an insulator like his son. Way back, one of Betty's grandfathers did have a trading post, but it doubled as a wrecking yard.

Eddie was born in a small Texas town named Longview. But he lived there only seven years before moving to the Houston area.

"I lived in a town on top of a mountain," Dew reminisced one evening in his trailer. "That's how the town got its name. I'd like to get back to Longview someday. Have my own insulation shop."

All the urban cowboys talk about going back to the great good country. In the meantime, they keep going to Gilley's, or some other honky-tonk. "It's like Peyton Place out there," Betty said one night at Gilley's. "Everybody's been with everybody." She even told me which cowgirls had given venereal disease to which cowboys and vice versa. Gilley's is a *very* small town in the middle of one of America's biggest cities.

While the Gilley's cowboys keep saying they are going home to a real small town someday, they grow more tightly bound to the big city, the union, and the petrochemical plant every day. They are ready to move at a moment's notice, but they don't move. They live in mobile homes that aren't mobile. Dew would need a semi to move his trailer. He lives in a home on wheels that has never rolled an inch since he moved in.

Dew has two pickups and used to have even more vehicles before he smashed up several cars. The driveways of the homes in his neighborhood are overrun with cars and trucks and campers. Everyone seems to have a herd of cars in his front yard. These car pokes have stored up all this potential mobility without going anywhere. As the band at Gilley's sings:

> *So many times these few dreams of mine*
> *Seemed hidden behind a mountain too high to climb. . . .*

Betty was born in the Houston area. The closest she ever came to real cowboy life was gathering eggs on a relative's farm. But if she is not part of a long cowboy tradition, she is part of a long Gilley's tradition. Back in the alleged good old days, her mother used to run around with Mickey Gilley and Sherwood Cryer, the creators of Gilley's Club. Gilley, the country canary who sings "A Room Full of Roses," gave his name to the honky-tonk, but he owns only a piece of it. The principal owner and real boss is Cryer. This king of the urban-cowboy business never wears anything but mechanic's coveralls. Betty's mother knew the two partners many, many dollars ago. Which makes Betty second-generation Gilley's.

The old honky-tonk has been around under one name or another for almost exactly as long as Betty has been alive: twenty years. It was originally called Shelley's which was what Sherwood Cryer's kids called him before they learned to say Sherwood. It started out as a slab of concrete to dance on and a small shack to lock the beer in. Eventually, Cryer, who was a welder by trade, put a tin roof over the slab. And then he got around to closing it in.

Meanwhile, Mickey Gilley was over on the good side of town playing at the Bell Air Ballroom and going broke. He couldn't even pay his band. So in desperation he went to Cryer and asked for help. Cryer asked Gilley if he would come back to the bad side of town and set up shop. Cryer even offered to name his honky-tonk after Gilley. Mickey Gilley came over and looked at the place and quickly saw it was no room full of roses. In fact, a rose wouldn't have a chance in a dump like that.

"Gilley said he'd come over," Cryer remembered, "if I bulldozed it and started over."

The man in the coveralls didn't go quite that far, but he did put in air-conditioning and paint some of the old chairs and put up the world's tackiest ceiling. So Gilley came on over. That was 1970.

Both Gilley's Club and Gilley's career started doing pretty well. The honky-tonk went from a place that would hold 500 to one that would hold almost ten times that many. Cryer kept tacking on tacky additions. As Gilley became better known, he started coming to the club less often because he was touring more. Now Gilley plays Gilley's only a couple of times a year.

When George Jones was playing Gilley's, the president of his fan club was murdered after she left the saloon. She was raped and beaten to death with a tire iron. The police suspected all the Gilley's regulars. Even Cryer had to take a lie-detector test. The case was written up in *True Detective*. Eventually, the cops arrested a local auto mechanic who seemed to fancy his tire iron as a six-shooter.

When Jerry Lee Lewis was playing Gilley's, Cryer himself got hurt. A woman hit a man over the head with a bottle of V.O. When Cryer went to the man's rescue, she cut the back of his head and neck with the broken bottle. His white shirt suddenly turned red, and he was terrified. The next day, he ran into the woman in a liquor store buying another bottle of V.O.

"She looked at me like she knew me," Cryer remembered, "but couldn't place me."

There is a local Monopoly-like game with a card that says not "go directly to jail" but "go to Gilley's and get stomped."

Cryer began trying to think of ways to cut down on the violence. So he put in the punching bag to give the honky-tonk cowboys something to hit besides one another. When the cowboys started lavishing more attention on the bag than on the cowgirls, the women cut the cord. But Cryer had it fixed. And he says the number of fights has gone down.

Then Cryer heard about the mechanical practice bulls used on the rodeo circuit. He thought a bull would go over in his shit-kicking honky-tonk. The bull was installed shortly after Betty and Eddie's wedding. The merciless machine was rough on the marriage. At first, Eddie did not want Betty to ride the bull. He said she would get hurt, but perhaps he was already worried she could outbuck him. Eddie even went so far as to order the man who ran the bull not to let Betty ride.

"I don't like anyone to tell me I can't do something," Betty told me one night at Gilley's. "To me, it's them saying I can't because I'm a girl. And I've got to show them I can."

She and her husband quarreled about whether she would be allowed to ride the bull. In the end, she decided she would have to show him. She had a drink to fuel her courage and to kill the pain. But when she got on the bull's back, she felt all too sober. When she got off, she was drunk.

The bull can be adjusted to buck hard, harder, or hardest. Betty kept riding it at higher and higher and higher speeds. Eddie rode the bull too, but he had a hard time keeping up. After all, a woman has an advantage over a man when it comes to bull riding. As the cowboys around the bullring put it: "A woman has nothing to lose." As strange as it may seem, bull riding is really woman's work. Poor Eddie.

Soon Betty wasn't only riding at higher and higher speeds, she actually started trick riding on the bull. She learned to stand up on the bucking bull's back. While Eddie had to hang on just to keep his seat, Betty was riding the bull like it was a surfboard.

Eddie found himself married to a honky-tonk Annie Oakley whose theme song seemed to be: "Anything you can do, I can do better. . . ."

After about eight seconds on the bull's back—long enough to qualify in a rodeo—Dew yelled that he had had enough. Steve pressed the bull's off switch. Sliding down, Dew staggered to the sidelines. He had lived up to the Cowboy Code, proving himself brave and strong, but it made him walk funny.

"That's the longest eight seconds I've ever seen," Dew said. "I'm shaking like a fucking leaf. Stand still, leg. My insides are going everywhere."

Jan handed him his hat.

"Were you worried?" he asked her.

"Just a little bit," Jan said.

Then the women took over the bullring. Jessie LaRive, a nineteen-year-old barmaid at a pool hall, rode the bull wearing jeans and a halter top. Her breasts bucked along with the animal. Standing up on the heaving back, she taunted all the men who had gathered to watch.

"Get up here and ride," Jessie challenged. "It's tame. I done tamed it. I'll ride with you. That's bad, lettin' a girl outride you. If I can ride with no hands, you can ride with one."

When she finally jumped down, Jessie came over to the cowboy running the bull. She had a favor to ask.

"Would you put this on my ass?"

She held out a Band-Aid. He agreed to help her out, and she lowered her jeans partway. The bull had rubbed a blister.

The next rider was Rita Sharp, a twenty-six-year-old waitress at the Red Lobster. She too challenged the men. If she could ride it, why couldn't they?

"I can ride her," called out one honky-tonk cowboy.

"I'll bet you can't stay on," she called back. "If you've got $100, we'll see."

"Can I help it," said the cowboy running the bull, "if the girls are better at riding on top than we are?"

Then Debbie Welburn, a nineteen-year-old waitress at the Piza Hut, rode the bucking bull so well it seemed she could have ridden and carried a pizza on a tray at the same time. She is something of a legend around the bullring because she rode last fall right after her feet were operated on. She came to the bullring on crutches with her feet encased in soft casts. Cowboys had to carry her out to the bull and set her on its back. If she had been thrown, she would have ripped out all her stitches or worse. She might have been crippled. No male rider ever did anything that brave or that crazy. The honky-tonk cowgirls keep putting more and more pressure on the honky-tonk cowboys.

After Debbie's impressive ride, two cowgirls got on the bull and rode it together. They faced one another, bending, swaying, bouncing, moving together in a rhythm that was almost sexual. They were the queens of the mountain.

Then a woman mounted the bull who had never ridden it before. With the speed turned down, she rode the bucking machine easily.

"Throw her," begged her boyfriend, "or I'll never hear the last of it."

But she wasn't thrown.

Several cowboys responded to the cowgirls' challenges. They paid their two dollars and took their chances playing Gilley's roulette with their sex lives. One by one, they were thrown. And one by one, they crawled off the mattresses with their hands between their legs.

"I just busted two nuts," Steve bragged after throwing one cowboy. "He won't get none tonight."

The lot of the urban cowboy becomes harder and harder. He tries to escape from the overwhelming complexities of his petrochemical days into the simplicity of his honky-tonk nights. But then Gilley's turns out to be a complicated world too. Once the bullring was the simplest of the simple entertainments at Gilley's. Either you rode the bull or you got bucked off. You beat the bull or it beat you. It was perfect for an urban cowboy who never beat anything beyond the walls of the saloon. But then Eve entered the bullring. The cowboys were no longer simply measured against the bull, they were measured against the cowgirls.

And yet the values represented by the cowboy hat prevailed. The cowboys did not try to exclude the cowgirls from the bullring, for that would have violated the code of egalitarianism. The cowboys didn't tell the cowgirls that a woman's place wasn't on the back of a bull. No, the cowboys just tried to keep up with the cowgirls as well as they could. I could tell, though, that they weren't happy with the way things were turning out.

"My favorite thing," said Betty, who had come up to talk to me, "is to watch all the guys fall off. Then I get up and ride it."

Dew decided to ride again. He got back on the bull a little stiffly. He braced himself, leaned back, and raised his right working hand. He was ready. The bullring master put the bull into a dead spin. It turned about half a dozen circles in a row. Dew did not sit the bull very prettily, but he sat it.

"I think," Betty said, "I can ride it better than he can."

Betty and Eddie's marriage turned out to be a rough ride. They quarreled about the bull and many other things too. He didn't want her to ride the bull, so she rode it. He told her not to do other things, so she did them. Soon Eddie was going to Gilley's without Betty, *twang-twang.*

One Friday night, Dew met Jan. He felt her watching him on the bull. Actually, he had sensed her studying him for two months. But now he decided to do something about it. When Dew got down off the bull, he walked over to chat with the bullring master. The woman came closer. They continued to circle each other warily for a while, like beginners approaching the bull.

Then Dew spoke his first words to Jan: "When are you going to take me home and rape me?"

Reminiscing about his opening line later on, Dew explained that he was a "direct" person. He said meeting someone was like driving a car. He didn't want to "piddle around." He wanted to get where he was going. Directness is one of the cardinal cowboy virtues. Dew had his cowboy hat on so he could say what was on his mind.

Jan answered: "Whenever you get ready."

Sometime after they had agreed to sleep together, they got around to introducing themselves. But these introductions were not really necessary. After all, they both had their names clearly tooled on their belts. Everyone at Gilley's does. It is part of the Cowboy Code of openness. The belt goes with the hat.

Dew and Jan stayed until closing time. He showed off by riding the bull again for her. And then Jan took Dew home and raped him.

They stayed together all night Friday and all day Saturday. Then they went back to Gilley's Saturday night. Sunday night they went back to Gilley's again. Monday night they went bowling.

On Tuesday, Dew started work insulating an offshore drilling rig. That meant working a twelve-hour shift from noon until midnight. Jan would drive down to the dock, pick him up, and whisk him back to Gilley's. They would get there just before closing time, but they would get there.

Betty obviously must have known something was going on, but she didn't know just what or with whom until she came home and found Eddie ironing his blue jeans. She asked him why he was ironing. He said he was going riding with Jan. Which was bad enough. What made it worse was that Eddie was going riding with Jan on Betty's horse. As the band at Gilley's sings:

> *Honky-tonk, the same old song,*
> *Honky-tonk, all night long,*
> *Honky-tonk, my money is all gone,*
> *Honky-tonk, he done me wrong.*

Betty went home to live with her parents in a little house on Peach Street with a herd of cars out front. But Betty, who still loved Eddie, was so unhappy that she wanted to get out of town completely for a while. She decided to visit her sister in San Antonio for a couple of weeks.

Betty was happy to get away to San Antonio, perhaps the most beautiful city in Texas. But when the sun went down, she missed Gilley's. The later it got, the more she pined for her saloon. She missed the music and the dancing and the friends. And perhaps most of all she missed the bull. The next morning, Betty called Les Walker, one of the bull masters, and asked him to come get her. Les drove to San Antonio and picked her up. Betty lasted exactly one night away from Gilley's.

But Betty still did not know herself. A short while later, she decided she had to get away again. She went to visit a girl friend who lived in Huntsville, the home of the prison rodeo. This time she didn't even last the night. At 11:00 P.M., Betty told her girl friend that she had to get back to Gilley's. They drove to Houston together. Without even stopping by Betty's home, they went straight to the saloon. The two cowgirls arrived at Gilley's at 1:30 A.M., a half hour before closing time. The night was saved. Betty could ride the bull before she went to sleep.

Meanwhile, two months after they met, Jan agreed to move in with Dew on one condition: She wanted him to give up riding the bull at Gilley's. She didn't want the man she slept with to get hurt. They had a big fight. He would ride the bull if he damned well wanted to. Not if he wanted to sleep with her, he wouldn't. He was threatened with a kind of sexual strike unless he gave up his violent ways. It was *Lysistrata* in cowboy clothes. Dew chose loving over bull riding. And Jan moved in.

Dew kept his promise. He didn't ride the bull again until I came into his life. And I brought a photographer with me. The old bull rider could not resist riding for the camera, but his bull riding days are really behind him now. At least, they are behind him as long as he stays with Jan. When a real cowboy rides a bucking animal, he is trying to break it, to tame it. But Dew could never break the mechanical bull. A motor doesn't get tired. But an urban cowboy can be broken. Jan has broken Dew.

After Eddie's ride, Betty walked up to him and said hello. But Jan was there, so Eddie did not return the greeting. This scene has been repeated at Gilley's ever since Betty and Eddie broke up. It usually ends with Betty going to the far side of the bullring and crying. The worst night was back in May, when Betty saw Eddie at Gilley's and tried to tell him that their divorce had come through that day. But Jan wouldn't let him talk to her. Betty went in the cowgirls' room and cried for a long time, *twang-twang*.

But Betty didn't cry this Saturday night. She decided to try to make Eddie jealous instead. Walking up to Steve, the head bull master, she asked him to put his hands up in the air. He looked like a badman caught by the sheriff in a western movie. With her victim now properly positioned, Betty reached out, grabbed the front of his cowboy shirt, and popped open all his mother-of-pearl snaps with one motion. Steve just stood there for a moment, more or less topless, with his shirt gaping open from his navel to his throat.

Then he counterattacked. Steve grabbed Betty and started trying to pull her knit halter off. The honky-tonk cowboy bulldogged the cowgirl to the floor and kept trying to do to her what she had done to him. They rolled together on the bottom of the saloon with the cigarette butts and the expectorated chewing tobacco. Steve got Betty's top partway off, but then she pulled away from him.

Dew and Jan tried to ignore this whole scene. They moved off toward the dance floor. If Betty had expected her ex-husband to come to her rescue, she was disappointed.

Steve got up and resnapped his cowboy shirt, but by then the urge to unsnap had become infectious. Another cowgirl came up and popped open his shirt. This time Steve's counterattack was more fruitful. Since his new assailant wore a cowboy shirt, Steve reached out and unsnapped her from top to bottom. She had nothing on underneath.

Betty stood by calmly combing her hair. When she finished, she returned to her favorite toy. Jan had gotten Dew, but Betty had gotten the bull. She crawled up on its bucking back and played. She stood up, moved from one end to the other, sat down, turned around, and rode backward.

Dew had to get up at six-thirty Monday morning to go to work. After getting dressed hurriedly, he drove his pickup thirty-eight miles to Texas City Refining. That is a long commute for someone who lives in a mobile home. He could move his trailer closer to the refinery, but then he would be farther from Gilley's. He would rather commute to his hard-hat days than to his cowboy-hat nights.

Pulling into the refinery's dusty parking lot, Dew got out of his truck with his tape measure strapped to his hip like a six-gun. He walked into the plant a little stiffly. He was still feeling the aftereffects of his bull ride.

Inside the refinery, Dew found himself swallowed up by one of the most denatured landscapes on the face of the earth. The petrochemical cowboy works on a giant spread crowded with metal trees (oil derricks and cracking towers), with metal underbrush (valves and pipelines), and with metal lakes (giant oil tanks). This is petrochemical pastoral.

Taking hold of his saw, Dew cut into the foam glass, which in turn dug its teeth into him. And as he worked, he remembered the band at Gilley's singing: "Take this job and shove it!"

It is one of Dew's favorite songs. After a day spent working inside the refinery, no wonder Gilley's seems like the great good place. When Dew talks about his saloon, he sounds idealistic. But when he talks about his job, he sounds sullen, complaining about Mexicans who, he says, will work so cheap they are taking away union jobs. At work, the urban cowboy is a small, threatened creature, but at the honky-tonk, he rides tall in the saddle.

A mechanized refinery can actually be a lot more dangerous to ride than a mechanized bull. An explosion recently killed seven workers at Texas City Refining. Luckily, Dew was home asleep at the time. Back in 1947, almost all of Texas City blew up. Close to 550 people were killed.

One workday at the killer refinery, a valve near Dew caught on fire. He dropped everything and ran as fast as he could in his track shoes. He doesn't wear boots on the job. He wouldn't be able to run fast enough. This time someone put the fire out before the killer refinery went up again.

Dew has had much worse falls on the job than he ever had in the bullring. He once fell off a scaffold 200 feet in the air, but he landed half on and half off a grating ten feet below. Somehow he hung on.

Right now, Dew works in the shop sawing and sawing. When all the foam glass is cut in just the right curving shapes, like pieces of a giant girdle, Dew will help fit these pieces around towers soaring hundreds of feet in the air. Some days, he will work on scaffolds high over the dead earth. Other days, he will labor suspended at the end of a rope, like a spider.

Dew makes $9.60 an hour and time and a half on Saturday—a forty-eight-hour week. But he pays 25 cents an hour to his union. Theoretically, he earns $460 a week, but he only takes home $250. He wants to save up to move to Longview, but so far he has not been able to save anything. He says he hopes his little brother stays out of the refineries.

Quitting time is 4:00 P.M. After work, the refinery parking lot is full of men in pickups taking off hard hats and putting on cowboy hats. Some of the pickups have bucking broncos painted on them.

When Dew reached his mobile home Monday evening at five o'clock, he found an unexpected note waiting for him. It had not come in the mail. It had been hand delivered and tucked under the windshield wiper of his second pickup. It was a request for money to pay for a vacuum cleaner. Eddie had given Betty the vacuum cleaner as a Christmas present, but he had never made any payments on it after the marriage broke up. Now Betty was convinced she was going to jail. So she carried the bill over to the trailer park. It was more than a bill, it was also a love letter. On the back, Betty had written in huge block letters: "I LOVE YOU."

A love letter on the back of a bill . . . it sounded like a honky-tonk song.

Dew looked up from the love bill and said, "Bein' a cowboy ain't easy."

He didn't go to Gilley's that night. He stayed home and saved his money.

◆

At 6:00 P.M. Monday evening, Betty started getting ready, as she does almost every day of her life. She took her time. She washed her hair, and she dried it while she watched some television. In all, she spent almost four hours getting ready. At 10:00 P.M., right on time, according to her rigid internalized schedule, she walked through the door at Gilley's.

As always, Betty headed right for the bullring. On the way, she looked for Eddie, but she didn't see him. She hoped he would come later, but even if he did, he wouldn't come back to the bull. The bull was all hers now.

Entering the ring she vaulted onto the back of the beast. She stood, she sat, she jumped back and forth over the rigging. From on high, Betty surveyed the saloon again, looking for Eddie. But he still wasn't there. Oh, well. She clung to the bull, which pounded her harder than any man had ever been able to.

Wrung out, she slid off the bull and came to the sidelines. She would take a break and then ride again. She would ride over and over all night long.

"I've got people to tell me," Betty said, "that I care more about this bull than anything else."

◆　　◆　　◆

I had just come in from riding a bucking sailboat when I got the first call. A Hollywood producer—who had managed to locate me on Nantucket where I was on vacation—said he wanted to buy the movie rights to my saloon story. I told him I would be home in Washington the next day and would call him back. When I got home, I had messages from other producers and studios and the phone was ringing.

I eventually sold the movie rights to Paramount Pictures. And then I began working with some of the best and some of the worst people in the world.

Among my least favorite was a Paramount Executive. On my first day at the studio, the casting director handed me two stacks of pictures of actresses. She explained that one stack was made up of actresses who could act—and the other stack were girls for the executive. On the very last day of shooting—a day spent mostly planning the wrap party—a young woman approached me on the lot and asked directions to the executive's office. She explained that she was on her way to audition for *Urban Cowboy*.

One of my favorite people turned out to be James Bridges, who was hired to direct the movie. Like many good friendships, this one got off to an uncertain beginning. I showed him fifty pages of screenplay that I had written. He didn't like them. So he went off and wrote some sixty pages of screenplay and showed them to me. I didn't like his any more than he liked mine. So we decided to get together in one room and write the screenplay together. The room was an office at Paramount. We were screenwriters typing out our movie right on the lot, just the way they used to do it in the old days. And we were trying to write the kind of movie they wrote in the old days, a B-western, but ours would be set in a honky-tonk. We only had one desk, so he put his electric typewriter on one side, and I put my old Royal on the other side, and we sat there day after day, facing each other, like gunmen in a main-street gunfight, both of us firing away with typewriter keys.

Some nights when we went home we still had some energy left, so we would keep on writing, he in his Frank Lloyd Wright house, me at the Sunset Marquis Hotel. And then the next morning we would come in and compare notes, and invariably we would have both written the same scene in the same way with the same dialogue.

PERFECT!

• • •

If John De Lorean had not been arrested and charged with conspiracy to distribute cocaine, I would never have written *Perfect*. After his collision with the law, I wanted to do a story on him and started calling everyone who had ever known him. And a lot of his friends in turn called him and told him that a reporter from *Rolling Stone* was asking a lot of questions about him.

Soon John De Lorean's public relations man called me where I was staying in New York. He said he had heard about the story I was doing and suggested we get together at a place called the Atrium Club on Fifty-seventh Street between Madison and Park avenues. I walked over.

John De Lorean's P. R. man and I had drinks in the Atrium Club's lounge. While we were sipping our scotches, he kept studying me, trying to decide if he could trust me.

And I kept studying the strange new environment in which I found myself. Some of the people in the lounge wore pin-striped suits and striped ties, while others were dressed in nothing but revealing leotards. I felt as if I had inadvertently stumbled into Edouard Manet's *Le déjeuner sur l'herbe*, where a nude girl picnics with fully clothed men. And a lot of the business suits seemed to be getting acquainted with the leotards.

"What kind of place is this?" I asked.

24

"It's a health club," explained the P. R. man.

I had never been inside one before.

"It looks like a singles bar," I said.

After my talk with the public relations man, I dropped by *Rolling Stone*, my new journalistic home. A refugee in the magazine wars, I had fled from *New York* when it was sold and sought sanctuary at *Esquire*, until it was sold, too, and I fled to the *Stone*. I went to lunch with my new editor and told him I had stumbled onto a new story I wanted to write. It was about how health clubs were turning into the new singles bars. He liked the idea.

Much later, I got involved in making a movie about a reporter writing a piece about health clubs turning into singles bars. And the reporter in the movie got the idea the same way I had gotten it. We even filmed the scene at the Atrium Club.

◆　　◆　　◆

Rolling Stone, June 1983

The jumps and kicks and sensuous contortions performed are the new dances.

The exercise instructors—who play records to keep these dances throbbing—are the new disc jockeys. Coed health clubs, the new singles bars of the eighties, have usurped the sounds and the energy of the discothèques.

They have also usurped the discothèques' raison d'être. They have become part of the mating ritual. They are the new places where couples meet for one night or for many nights. They are spawning everything from lustful matinees to matrimony.

They have become the place to exercise every muscle in the body, including the most important, the heart.

"There's something kind of sexy about doing all that sweating and grunting," says a black leotard.

"Sweat," says a gray body stocking, "is sensuous."

One of the most successful of the new breed of health clubs has an intriguing name. The Sports Connection. It is a place where members connect not only with sports, but also with one another. They connect with their own bodies and with other bodies. They connect with a solution to the loneliness that characterizes, for many, life in the big city. The Sports Connection has four branches located in and around Los Angeles, which is one of the capitals of the lonely.

The building that houses the Sports Connection in Santa Monica—on Ocean Park Boulevard, not far from the beach—is the size of a Hollywood sound stage. It is crammed with racquetball courts, big exercise classrooms, an indoor pool, saunas, Jacuzzis, a women-only gym, and a huge coed gym with all sorts of body-building hardware. Weights, Nautilus equipment, computerized cardiovascular bikes known as "Life Cycles." And a cast of a thousand leotards.

In the lobby-lounge of the Connection, you would be likely to meet such regulars as Leslie Borkin and Lori Segal. Leslie and Lori. The Laverne and Shirley of the Sports Connection. They are both tall. Leslie is the blonde, Lori the brunette. They might well be sitting at one of the round wooden tables watching a racquetball game being played on the other side of a transparent wall. Lori would probably be concentrating on the game, while Leslie would be paying more attention to the passing parade of men in various stages of gym undress.

Leslie and Lori joined the Sports Connection together several years ago. They both found themselves looking for a health-club Prince Charming who would carry them off on a Life Cycle bike. Lori actually found her prince, right there in the gym, although he was not at all what she had imagined. He was such an unlikely prince . . . an exotic male dancer prince . . . a stripper prince . . . but, nonetheless, *her* prince.

Leslie was not so lucky. She has had one disappointing romance after another. But she has nonetheless managed to become a health-club legend, thanks to a workout at a bachelor party that will be talked about for years.

"At the bars, you look like you're just waiting to meet somebody," Leslie Borkin says. "At a health club, at least you have an excuse to be there. You don't look so obvious."

"One reason it's a good place to meet people," says Lori Segal, "is because of the way everybody dresses. What you see is what you get."

Several of their girl friends, who are scattered about the health-club lounge, come over to join in the conversation.

"It's an alternative to the disco era," says a blue leotard with matching blue leg warmers. "Now it's not fashionable to go to a disco, but it is fashionable to go to a health club. It's a socially acceptable way of meeting someone. You could tell your mother."

"You know they're healthy if you meet them here," says a pink leotard with matching leg warmers and headband. "Physically healthy and mentally healthy. They're not out drinking."

"It's safer than looking for Mr. Goodbar," says a red leotard with red leg warmers, a read headband and a red-and-white bandanna tied around her throat.

Listening to the women of the Sports Connection, I was reminded of a conversation I had a few days earlier with Dr. Bernard Mullin, professor of sports marketing and management at the University of Massachusetts. The New England academic and the California "health-club honeys"—as they are often called—had more or less reached the same conclusions.

"Fitness and health centers have become the socially acceptable way for young, white-collar workers to meet members of the opposite sex," Dr. Mullin told me. "They are fed up with singles bars and the singles-bar routine. Health clubs provide a place where people with similar life-styles and interests can meet."

Dr. Mullin adds that health clubs that understand their role as the new meeting place are doing very well, while many clubs that don't are going broke. Industry figures bear him out. The operations that are having the most trouble—that have gone bankrupt or are approaching bankruptcy—are often the small, storefront, ladies-only reducing parlors. Clubs that rely primarily on racquetball are doing well, but they're not growing. Clubs that rely on indoor tennis are growing modestly. But multipurpose clubs—with weight rooms and exercise classes and racquetball courts and, especially, lots of men and women thrown together—are in the midst of a boom.

A fitness-industry survey shows that in 1982, multipurpose clubs took in an average of $719,000 (up almost 20 percent over the previous two years), while indoor tennis clubs averaged only $467,000 in revenues and racquetball clubs brought in $388,000.

The Sports Connection, which one industry expert has described as a "vanguard multidimensional club," took in almost $10 million last year. It is very social and very successful. While single-sex reducing clubs grow thinner and thinner, the coed Connection, financially speaking, keeps getting fatter and fatter.

Who is that over there pedaling the Life Cycle? The old guy? The one Leslie is trying to pick up? Why, he looks like Emerson. But Leslie seems to have got to know him well enough to call him Ralph Waldo.

What is old Mr. Self-Reliance doing in the Sports Connection? Well, his presence is felt symbolically in health clubs across the land because they represent a return to his values.

"People are taking responsibility," observed Dr. Mullin, "for controlling and dictating their own lives. There is the general notion of personal responsibility rather than looking to institutions. It's the so-called new federalism. But it also involves taking care of your own body and your own health."

John Naisbitt, author of the best seller *Megatrends*, agrees. "In a sense," he writes, "we have come full circle. We are reclaiming America's traditional sense of self-reliance after four decades of trusting in institutional help." He goes on: "At around the same time we admitted to having lost the war on poverty, as well as the war in Vietnam, we began to mistrust medicine as well." The result was a "shift to self-help." And, specifically, medical self-help. The foundation of medical self-help is all the exercise that Americans are now doing: "At least 100 million Americans, almost half the population, are now exercising in some way—up from only about one-quarter of the population in 1960. That is a 100 percent increase in regular exercisers."

Viewed in this light, what could be more American, more all-American, more old-fashioned American, than institutions like the Sports Connection? Health clubs turn out to be little capitals of Emersonian America scattered from sea to shining sea.

"Do that which is assigned thee," Emerson wrote in "Self-Reliance," "and thou canst not hope too much or dare too much."

Leslie Borkin believes this. She is very much in the great American Emersonian tradition—in her own way, of course. Like the old essayist, she believes in the perfectability of man. Or, rather, the perfectability of woman. Or, perhaps, the perfectability of both man *and* woman. That is why she works out so hard. And that is why she is planning to have surgery. Plastic surgery. She already considers herself pretty, but she wants to be, well, perfect.

"The health club and the surgery," Leslie says, "are all part of the same thing. I want to be the best I can be. I want to be prettier. I want to be as pretty as I can be."

When she talks this way, Leslie somehow sounds quintessentially American. After all, isn't it absolutely American to believe that perfection is hard work? You have to pedal the Life Cycle for hours. You have to take exercise classes without end. You have to strain on the Nautilus equipment. And you have to be willing to suffer, not just in the gym, but also on the operating table.

Leslie has a doctor friend who will do the actual cutting. And the doctor knows a Hollywood makeup artist—he used to work on "The Dukes of Hazzard"—who has volunteered to redesign Leslie's face. She wants a shorter, squarer chin and a different nose. It will be painful and scary, but . . .

If you work and suffer enough, Leslie believes, you can make yourself perfect. Or at least as perfect as you can be.

And if you perfect yourself, then you will be loved. That is the important point. The reward for perfection is love. Perfect.

"I'm nervous," Leslie says, "but I'm more excited than anything else. Lori thinks I'm mentally unstable."

Leslie Borkin and Lori Segal were best friends at Southwest Miami Senior High School. But they lost touch with each other after graduation. Years later, they accidentally rediscovered each other in Los Angeles. Leslie moved in with Lori. They both got jobs at the Apparel Mart, in downtown L.A., which was crammed with all the new fitness fashions. And they both joined the Sports Connection right after it opened. The health club became their home away from home.

Lori and Leslie are children of the baby boom, the great tidal wave of births that began in America in 1946 and crested in 1957. The two best friends were both born in 1952—Lori on January 3, Leslie on February 29. Their fathers fought in World War II; Lori's dad was even awarded a Purple Heart. Both started working out at the Sports Connection when they were twenty-eight. They suddenly felt the need, along with many other members of their generation—the largest generation in American history—to get in shape. It is probably no coincidence that the baby-boom generation approached thirty at the same time as the exercise boom exploded in American culture. The great American baby-boom generation felt its collective body aging and decided to do something about it. The group that caused the big bulge in the demographic graph was beginning to bulge physically—and it was ready for health-club self-help.

These baby boomers are leading a physical Great Awakening comparable to the spiritual Great Awakenings that have gripped America about every hundred years.

Around the same time Lori and Leslie joined the Sports Connection, so did a young man named Roger Menache. When Roger saw Lori, he was attracted to her well-developed chest. For weeks, he simply admired her chest across a crowded gym or a crowded exercise class. Although she had no idea that he was watching her, he found out her schedule and made a point of working out when she worked out, to lift weights when she lifted, to take the same exercise classes she took. In these classes, they would bounce together—which was almost like

dancing together—to the beat of songs like "Boy Meets Girl," by Haircut One Hundred:

> *Boy meets girl,*
> *And love, love is on its way,*
> *Boy meets girl,*
> *Boy meets girl, unnnh!*

That became one of Roger's favorites. Perhaps that *unnnh* sounded
like exercise class. Or maybe something else. At any rate, he loved to
grunt and sweat along with the music.

And while he was grunting, Roger loved to watch Lori's chest work
out. With all that exercise, that chest kept getting better and better,
more and more magnetic. Roger asked his exercise-class teacher about
Lori. (These teachers often end up acting as health-club matchmakers;
some have been offered money for phone numbers from the club files.)

Roger started saying hi to Lori at the club. And, occasionally, he
would volunteer tips about handling the weights in the gym.

"It's easier," Dr. Mullin said, "to tell someone she's got a nice
backhand than to ask her if she comes here often."

When Roger saw Lori doing bench presses to firm up her chest, he
joked that she did not need more work in that area.

Thanks to the Sports Connection, Roger and Lori got to know each
other before they started going out together. A lot of health-club couples
say that meeting someone in the gym is like meeting someone in high
school: You see a person day after day before you begin seeing them at
night.

At last, Roger asked Lori to come out after dark. He invited her to
spend an evening at Chippendales—a nightclub featuring male strippers
(or "exotic dancers," in their preferred parlance). Lori was surprised
and somewhat taken aback. Chippendales? Yes, Chippendales. Why?
Because he worked there. Was he a dancer? Yes. Oh.

Although she had never been to a nightclub where men take off
their clothes, Lori agreed to go. But she didn't want to go alone, so she
invited Leslie and some others to come along as bodyguards of a kind.

It was a Sunday night. The crowd was not as large as on other
nights. Roger was the third dancer. He came out dressed in a robe, boxing gloves, and a jump rope. He was supposed to be Rocky, the fighter
with the almost impossible dream. And now Roger/Rocky had a dream,
too: Lori.

He started taking off his clothes. In a sense, his act seemed an extension of the health-club ethic. After all, the health club, like the strip

club, accentuated physical beauty, the kind of body one might well want to show off.

"Knowing she was in the audience," Roger remembers, "I hammed it up. I paid attention to her. She tipped me, and I kissed her and rubbed my body against her."

And Lori?

"I had a great time at Chippendales," she remembers.

The music in the strip club was much the same as the music in the health club, including Roger's favorite, which Lori was beginning to like, too:

Boy meets girl, unnnh!

After the show, Roger met Lori for a drink at the bar. Actually, they had several drinks. And then Roger tried to take Lori home. She said no.

But Roger did not abandon all hope, because he knew he would see her the next day at the Sports Connection.

Meanwhile, Leslie's love life was running far from smoothly. She met a young man at the health club who invited her to dinner. She accepted but said she would first have to finish her workout. While he waited impatiently, she lifted and strained and pulled and pushed and pedaled. He was in such a hurry that she didn't even have time to take a shower after she finished her exercises.

They went to a Mexican restaurant for margaritas and then home to her apartment to talk. Leslie reclined on her couch and kicked off her sneakers.

Then, suddenly, her guest attacked her toes. She tried to pretend not to notice, but all she could think of was the unwashed condition of her feet.

When one of her girl friends dropped by, the young man with the unusual tastes simply got up and walked out of the apartment without even saying good-bye.

Leslie saw him several days later at the Sports Connection with a woman who turned out to be his wife.

Of course, Roger did see Lori shortly after their first inconclusive date. He saw her at the Sports Connection, as he knew he would, because the club is a kind of small town where you see everybody you know over and over again.

"It's a Peyton Place," Leslie says.

And a small town, a little Peyton Place, is just what a lot of people need in a big city. It's a place to belong. It's a place to know and be known. It's everything that the big, impersonal city isn't.

A visit to the club is like a stroll down Main Street. Everybody knows everybody else. And everybody knows everybody else's business. It is a soap opera.

In fact, Roger's friend Steve Bond actually works on a soap—the number-two-rated soap in the country, "General Hospital." He plays Jimmy Lee Holt, the bastard son of the show's patriarch, Edward Quartermaine.

"The Sports Connection is absolutely a soap," says Steve, who knows one when he sees one. "It's a lot of lives connecting."

Steve met his wife, Cindy—they were married just last fall—at the Sports Connection. Steve is famous at the club because he appears on everyone's favorite soap. Cindy is famous because she is a professional golfer, and because she once got in a fistfight with another woman at the club. When a totally naked woman pushed her away from her place in front of the mirror at one of the dressing tables in the women's locker room, Cindy delivered a right to the chin that knocked the woman upside down over a chair.

When the others heard about the fight, which didn't take long in this Peyton Place, they weren't surprised, because they know all about the competition for space around the dressing tables.

"In the locker room," Leslie says, "all the girls are primping and fixing their makeup to go out and exercise."

And there's Leslie's friend, the one in the white leotard, riding a Life Cycle—who recently moved from New York to Los Angeles.

"The very first night I got in," she says, "I went out and joined the Sports Connection. I looked it up in the Yellow Pages. I joined because I didn't know anyone in Los Angeles."

She knew that health clubs were a good place to meet people. She particularly wants to meet doctors and lawyers. A psychic told her she would find her second husband in California.

She now believes that most of the doctors and lawyers belong to the Century West Health Club. So she plans to join it, too.

And there's Julie McNew, working out on the Nautilus equipment. She believes not only in "muscle tone," but in "mental tone." So she gets up every day and memorizes a 150-digit number, a task her current boyfriend helps her with. It is mental weight lifting. Then she goes to the health club.

Julie is a body builder. She used to lift weights with her ex-boyfriend, whom she met in the gym. And they used to enter body-building competitions together. But then she started winning a lot more of those competitions than he did—and they broke up.

The toe man, who was outwardly normal, turned out to be weird. But Roger Menache, whose job was weird, turned out to be a normal, persistent, all-American suitor.

After a decent interval, Roger invited Lori once again to watch him take off his clothes at Chippendales. And Lori accepted on the condition that she could once again bring Leslie.

Realizing he was involved in a kind of chess game, Roger had anticipated Lori's defensive move—her use of the Leslie pawn. So he had his own offensive countermove ready. He told Lori to bring her girl friend but not her car. Why? Well, they would be going to a party after the show. Since she might have trouble finding the party, he would drive her in his car.

"We went to the party," Roger reminisces. "That's when we made some sparks. I took her home to my place. It was lovely. It was wonderful. It was worth the wait. She spent the night. We went to the beach for breakfast. I tried to make it romantic. Not just kick her out. We spent the day together. We went to the movies."

And Roger talked.

The stripper told his new girl friend all about himself. He told her about how his early years had been dominated by glasses. He had been a weak, frightened kid who wore thick glasses—who actually seemed to be hiding behind those glasses. Glasses meant so much to him that he went as far as to study for, and earn, his optician's certificate at Los Angeles City College. He was a glasses man.

But while he was learning to fit lenses, he was also learning to lift weights. He had discovered the college gym. The boy with weak eyes was developing a strong body.

"This was a great transition," Roger told her. "Body building remade my personality. My high school friends don't believe it. They remember me as a shy, scrawny bookworm who wore glasses. Now I wear contacts and strip to a G-string."

Leslie Borkin started dating a man with a van. They got to know each other during a celebrity racquetball tournament at the Sports Connection. One night, the man with a van asked her out for dinner at the Chicago Pizza Works. A few nights later, they dined again at Carlos & Pepe's.

"Then we went to the beach in the van," Leslie recalls. "Opened the doors and made love in the moonlight."

A few months later, Leslie's love life somehow got entangled with another man and another motor vehicle. It happened at a Christmas party. Several dozen friends gathered in Encino to celebrate the holiday. Leslie was perched on the trunk of a black Mustang, as if it were a sleigh, passing out her own kind of presents.

At first, she shared the trunk with her man with a van. But soon another young man came out and joined Leslie. This young man didn't like the man with a van, who had gone inside.

Soon, Leslie and the other man started "making out," as she puts it. The man with a van returned, and he wasn't the only one watching. Everyone arriving or departing the party had to walk right past them. Word spread, and their audience grew.

Leslie and the other man lay down and rolled around the trunk of the black car. Unable to stand it any longer, the man with a van went back inside the house.

Finally, Leslie and the other man got inside the car.

While the man with a van was failing in his attempts to hold Leslie, Roger was also having some difficulty with Lori. He asked her out several times, but she'd always tell him she had plans with other men.

"She turned me down," Roger recalls. "I thought it was in the bag, but it wasn't."

Roger's response was to work on Lori as patiently and as persistently as he worked on his own physique. He kept seeing her in the gym, and he kept asking her out. Eventually, he succeeded in transforming her attitude toward him—just as he had once transformed his own attitude toward himself. By sheer dint of effort, Roger made Lori like him.

The health-club crew knew that Roger and Lori were beginning to get along better when they started having wrestling matches in the corridors. Their friends would gather around and watch. Roger loved to perform in front of an audience.

Soon, Roger was at Leslie and Lori's apartment almost every night. Lori would rush home from her job at the Apparel Mart and take a nap. When she woke up, she would fix dinner for him to eat when he got off "work" at ten-thirty. Then they would stay up late. The only problem was that Lori had to get up early, at seven, to be at work on time. She worked days and he worked nights, but the twain did somehow manage to meet.

Eventually, they got their own place.

"Now we live together," says Lori, "and work out together."

Leslie fell in love with the man who won her on the trunk of a black Mustang. He was a fixture at the Sports Connection, too. She would follow her Mustang man all around the health club.

"For a while, I was crazy about him," Leslie remembers. "But he kept me hanging for over a year. He kept making all kinds of excuses. And everybody in the club knew."

At the health club, the most important muscle in Leslie's body was getting quite sore.

Lori Segal found herself going to Chippendales almost as often as she was going to the Sports Connection. In many ways, the strip club almost seemed an extension of the health club, and vice versa. The master of ceremonies always began the shows by asking how many of the women in the audience did aerobic exercises. Three-fourths of the women would raise their hands. And then the emcee would run a videotape of Roger and the other Chippendales males, dressed in shorts and tank tops, doing aerobic exercises.

A videotape of an exercise class, entitled "Muscle Motion," was actually being used to "warm up" the women for the exotic evening of stripping ahead of them. Now the undertones of sexuality in these exercises became overtones. Now the exercise movements were being presented as dance movements—as exotic movements in an erotic dance.

After the exercise tape, Roger would come onstage wearing a mask, a cape, and a sword and carrying a whip. He was no longer Rocky. He was Zorro.

The women would yell, "Take it off!"

And Roger would. The mask. The cape. The sword. The black shirt. The black pants. The black briefs. And then the red briefs beneath the black ones.

Lori managed to watch Roger "take it off" at least twice a week. She would be in the audience every Saturday night and at least one other night during the week. She was one of the most regular of the Chippendales regulars.

While Lori watched, Roger, clad only in a G-string the size of a slingshot, would accept tips from one woman after another. Every tip bought a kiss and often a hug and sometimes a pat on the ass.

And then Lori herself would always come down the aisle in a short dress. She would stop, kneel, and place a dollar bill between her legs, very near her crotch. Then Roger would approach, bend over backward, and remove the dollar with his teeth. The audience would always go crazy.

Boy meets girl, unnnh!

But Lori's little part of the show had one unforeseen result. Soon, other women in the audience, who had no idea she was the dancer's girl friend, started copying her, putting dollar bills between their own legs or between their breasts. Of course, Roger had to remove their dollars with his teeth, too.

At ten-thirty, after the strip show is over, the doors of the club are thrown open and men are allowed in. The club is transformed from a ladies-only burlesque house into a coed discothèque.

The videotape of the exercise class is played all over again: The disco dancers dance on the dance floor while Roger and his buddies do aerobics on the screens. The dancers themselves often come dressed as if they are at a health club rather than a discothèque. Wearing leotards covered with nice sweat shirts or simply wearing leotards all by themselves. Leopard leotards. Black leotards. Pink leotards. Striped leotards. Between the exercise video and all the health-club fashions, the dance floor actually looks like an exercise class.

So, not only is the health club the new discothèque, but in a strange way, the discothèque itself has been transformed into a new kind of ersatz health club.

The bachelor party, the one that made Leslie famous, a kind of star, was for her boss. He was a fixture at the Sports Connection, too. He had dated many of the best-looking women at the club, as well as many exercise-class "instructresses," as they call themselves.

And then he committed a kind of health-club treason. He got engaged to a woman who was not from the health club. She was someone he'd been living with while seeing health-club women on the sly. She was an outsider who was not a member of the leotard sorority. He seemed to have turned against all the insiders who had ridden the Life Cycle and strained on the Nautilus equipment (even doing leg-spreading exercises on a special machine) and huffed and puffed through aerobics classes all for nothing. They had worked and suffered and should have been loved. But they weren't. Or at least he didn't love them.

As it unexpectedly turned out, Leslie would show him love.

Leslie had worked out a plan. She recruited a helper, another young woman as tall and pretty as herself, and they crashed her boss's bachelor party.

The party was given by the men of the Sports Connection—the groom's "body buddies" (as some weight-lifting friends call themselves). Unlike the club's women, the men were not particularly saddened to see him removed from the social competition at the Sports Connection. The party was a single-sex affair, the way gyms used to be before the women's movement came along and integrated most of them. Leslie's plan was to make the bachelor party coed.

"I showed up with the other girl," Leslie remembers. "We got a little high and ended up in the bedroom with the groom. We gave him a nice present."

Leslie and her girl friend pretended the groom was a Life Cycle. They pretended he was a rowing machine. They pretended he was that Nautilus apparatus over against the west wall of the Sports Connection: the leg-spreading machine. They practiced what some health-club addicts call "aero*bed*ics"—defined as putting exercise into the bedroom and turning sex into a workout. They huffed and puffed and sweated and glistened.

But occasionally, the acrobatics and aerobedics were disturbed by a voice yelling through the bedroom door. The voice belonged to Leslie's accomplice's boyfriend. He had been invited to the bachelor party and had been quite surprised when his girl friend appeared uninvited. And now he was appalled by what his girl friend was doing on the other side of the bedroom door.

"I'm going to call your bride," he threatened the groom, "and tell her what you're doing!"

After the bachelor party, the bachelor and his fiancée went ahead and got married, in spite of everything. When the newlyweds got back from their honeymoon, the groom fired Leslie. She had given him a present at his party, and in return, he gave Leslie her walking papers. She still has not found a new job.

Sometimes free love just doesn't pay.

Roger asked Lori to drop by Chippendales for a drink after the show. She arrived at about 11:00 P.M. and found all of her friends waiting for her. Roger had arranged a good, wholesome, traditional surprise birthday party in this den of exotic dancers.

One of the guests, of course, was Lori's best friend, Leslie. She was a kind of star now, especially at a party.

When it was time to open presents, Roger gave Lori one in a small box. She tore off the ribbon and found a ring inside.

An engagement ring.

This was Roger's way of proposing to Lori. They had come to the strip club on their first date. And now they were betrothed at the strip club, surrounded by friends in all stages of dress and undress.

And once more, Leslie was present to grace a party thrown to celebrate someone else's engagement.

Perhaps Roger and Lori should consider holding the ceremony at the Sports Connection. One hopes they do. You can imagine all the guests, dressed in their fanciest leotards, gathered in the body-building gym. And picture all the ushers dressed like the waiters at Chippendales: black pants, white cuffs with cuff links and white collars with formal, black-tuxedo bow ties, but with no shirts connecting the collars to the cuffs. Visions of bridesmaids in pink leotards, bare-chested ushers and wedding barbells. For this wedding is not only the union between Roger and Lori, but also between the health club and the discothèque.

Of course, Leslie, in pink leg warmers and a hot-pink Chippendales sweat shirt, would be the maid of honor. She would naturally tip the groom before she kissed him. Perhaps she would also think about how strangely lives turn out. Leslie looks like a conventional blond California girl, but all her relationships with conventional California boys somehow turn out weird.

Lori, on the other hand, appears to be an unconventional brunette who is in love with a dark-haired, dark-side-of-life stripper, but she seems to be headed for a traditional happy ending.

"Roger and Lori, do you take each other for better, for worse, for richer, for poorer, in sickness and in health, in shape, but never out of shape, till death do you part?"

◆

After the article appeared, I sent a copy of the story to James Bridges, who had directed *Urban Cowboy*. We had always talked about wanting to work together again, and I hoped this new piece might provide the opportunity. After reading the story, Bridges agreed to help bring *Perfect* to the screen. He would produce and direct—and we would work on the screenplay together.

We wrote the script in Bungalow R at the Laird Studio—a proud old movie lot where such classics as *Gone with the Wind* and *Citizen Kane* and the Superman television series were shot. This time we used only one typewriter, an IBM Selectric. We took turns at the keyboard. First I would type and he would pace as we talked and wrote our way through the scenes. Then we would switch places and he would type and I would pace.

Jim persuaded me that the movie should be about a reporter who is writing a story much like the one that I had actually written. Of course, the reporter would need a boss, so we wrote in an editor who was similar to Jann Wenner, the actual editor and publisher of *Rolling Stone*.

When the script was finished and we started casting the movie, we decided to ask Jann if he would like to audition for the part. He said no, but we finally changed his mind.

So we flew Jann from New York to Hollywood for a screen test. He came in a day early in order to rehearse for the big moment. In the rehearsals, I played the reporter, Jann played the editor, and Jim directed. At first, Jann overacted, rolling his eyes all over the place as he delivered his lines. But Jim eventually calmed him down. By the time we finished rehearsing, I was beginning to feel optimistic.

That night, instead of getting plenty of rest, Jann went out on the town. Sometime during his dark Odyssey, Jann ran into Michael Douglas and Warren Beatty. He told them why he was in town and they wanted to help. They rehearsed with him, coached him, directed him, generally polished his performance.

When Jann came in the next morning—thanks to the help of his famous friends—he was the worst actor in America.

"If he keeps rolling his eyes like that," I asked Jim, "what are we going to do?"

"Put in gunshots," Jim said.

We were both ready to despair, but we had to go through with the screen test. So I worked with Jann for a while. Then Jim took over and worked with him longer. Jann's eyes rolled slower and slower and finally stopped altogether.

When the cameras rolled, Jann did a good screen test and got the part.

Jann did even better when we were filming the movie. We didn't have to put in any gunshots.

FALLING IN LOVE
WITH FOUR-WHEEL
DRIVE

• • •

I was supposed to write an article on the romance of four-wheel drive, but I kept putting it off because I was too busy working on *Urban Cowboy*. Jim Bridges and I were trying to write the movie and cast it at the same time, which didn't leave much time for anything else. Feeling guilty, I came to dread the almost daily calls form Clay Felker, then editor of *Esquire*, who kept pressuring me to finish my 4x4 story and turn it in.

I finally decided it was time to get to work on four-wheeling in the wake of an incident I have come to think of as High Noon at Paramount. The countdown to High Noon began when the studio refused to fly John Travolta to Houston. At that point, Travolta thought he wanted to do *Urban Cowboy*, but he said he couldn't be sure until he actually saw Gilley's. Paramount said it wouldn't pay for his plane ticket unless he committed to do the movie. Since Travolta had made *Saturday Night Fever* and *Grease* for the studio, which earned hundreds of millions of dollars, he was surprised and hurt to learn that they would not spend a few hundred for an airplane seat.

So Travolta issued an ultimatum: If Paramount did not agree to purchase a ticket to Houston by five o'clock that afternoon, he was going to pass on the picture.

The star and the studio both thought they were in a western movie.

They wanted to shoot it out on main street. Not at high noon but at high five o'clock.

Five o'clock came and went. The studio still refused to pay for the plane ticket. And John Travolta passed on *Urban Cowboy.*

Disgusted by the whole business, I decided it was time to get out of town. I jumped angrily into my rented car and headed into the desert. I knew a 4x4 "desert safari" was supposed to snake its way through the wasteland that weekend. Suddenly I wanted to go. Compared to Hollywood, the desert now seemed a kind and hospitable place.

◆　　◆　　◆

Esquire, June 1979

Dave Armstrong is in love with a Ford Bronco with four-wheel (4x4) drive. The Bronco is a sort of feminine version of the Jeep— slightly softer and prettier but just as tough. Dave loves his 4x4's shiny blue body. He likes the way it moves under him. It knows how to do so much more than other vehicles do. The Bronco always makes him feel like a real man. A man foursquare. A man 4x4 square.

Dave's wife, Debbie, also loves the Bronco in particular and machines in general. Machines actually brought Debbie and Dave together. Seated side by side in their 4x4, they make a handsome couple. Twenty-five-year-old Dave has the impish good looks of a blond Tom Sawyer; twenty-two-year-old Debbie has the freckled face of a female Huckleberry Finn. Their beloved Bronco is their raft.

Debbie and Dave have another loved one: their two-month-old daughter. Her name is Melissa. They love her enough to share their Bronco with her; when they go four-wheeling across some of the baddest badlands in the American West, they take their baby girl with them.

One weekend, Dave and Debbie took Melissa on a rough two-day outing called the Four-Wheel-Drive Desert Safari, which is annually sponsored by a California 4x4 club. Over 800 four-wheel-drive machines rendezvoused in the Borrego Badlands, south of Indio. The terrain was so treacherous that it took some four-wheelers twelve hours to go just twenty-four miles the first day. Melissa went up and down the horrific hills in an infant seat that was tied behind the parents' seats with yellow twine. The egg-fragile baby appeared to be about as safe as if she had gone four-wheeling in an eggcup.

Like the baby, I rode in the back. I was strapped to the spare tire. As we were climbing a mountain that went up as steeply as my pulse rate, Debbie took Melissa in her arms and started breast-feeding.

•

When Dave is not driving his Bronco over desert hills, he drives it to work at the telephone company. Actually, the Bronco has made a lot more trips to the phone company than it has to the badlands. Dave drives his 4x4 to the grocery store, to fast-food restaurants, to the bowling alley. He has driven it to a christening and a funeral. When the baby was coming, Dave jokingly tried to persuade Debbie to let him drive her to the hospital in the Bronco. But she said no. They drove to the delivery room in her Thunderbird.

In a sense, Dave's Bronco represents to him what the West represented to much younger America. When he gets to feeling trapped, when he feels hemmed in, when his ego needs more elbow room, Dave climbs into his Bronco. Four-wheeling is not just a way of going somewhere. It is a destination in itself. It is an escape.

When the gasoline runs out, it will be like the frontier running out. But four-wheelers go right on guzzling it. They burn up gas the way their forefathers massacred the buffalo—with no thought of what comes next. When Dave gets into his four-wheeler, he puts on all its attributes. He is rough. He is tough. He is even bigger than almost anyone else. And he can theoretically go anywhere. As people lose their hopes of social and economic mobility, they seem to turn more and more to wheeled mobility.

Especially four-wheel-drive mobility. These 4x4s are easily the fastest growing part of the automotive industry. In 1974, four-wheel-drive vehicles represented only about 3 percent of the car-and-truck business in this country. By last year, that figure had practically doubled to almost 6 percent, with sales amounting to over a million vehicles. So far this year, sales are running even higher.

Dave's belief in his 4x4 and what it can do for him is extraordinary. "I like the idea of being able to go anywhere I want to," Dave said as we were out riding one day. "If there was a nuclear attack, I could get away." His 4x4 in his Superman suit. In the immense web of our society, some people escape into discos, others escape into cowboy bars, but a growing number escape into 4x4 machines.

Dave and Debbie used to be married to other people, but their former mates did not love machines. Dave's first wife, Gretchen, was his sweetheart at Hoover-Crawford Adult School, in San Diego, California. Gretchen loved Dave but hated his motorcycle because she had once been in a terrible cyling accident. He understood her fears, but he still got tired of her complaining about his riding all the time.

Gretchen had had her accident a couple of years before she met Dave. It happened one day when she told her father that she was going to visit a girl friend. Instead, she went motorcycle riding with her boyfriend. Of course, she knew her father would disapprove. She was holding on to her boyfriend on the back of his bike when his machine skidded on a turn. The motorcycle slammed head on into a car driven by . . . Gretchen's father.

She was thrown a great distance, landing far from the road. Her father, who thought she was with her girl friend, did not even see her. He gave all his help to the badly injured boy, putting him in his car, rushing him to the hospital. Meanwhile, Gretchen lay broken far from the road, unattended for hours.

When the shattered boyfriend finally came to, he asked: "Where's Gretchen?"

Her father said: "With her girl friend."

"No, she's not."

When they found her, she was suffering from a concussion. Her face was badly torn, and her shoulder was crushed. Skin had to be grafted onto her cheek; an artificial socket was placed in her shoulder.

Her boyfriend lost a leg.

After Gretchen got well, she had the misfortune to fall in love with another motorcycle rider, Dave Armstrong. And then she compounded this misfortune by marrying him. The marriage became in some ways a love triangle: the wife, the husband, and the machine.

It was a Bultaco 250. One day, a drunk friend knocked over the bike, breaking the throttle. Then the embarrassed friend set the machine back up on its wheels, so Dave had no idea anything had happened. When he started it up, the bike suddenly took off with the gas open full bore. Dave, who was dressed in shorts and without any shoes, was completely open to injury. If he couldn't stop the bike, it would soon be going more than 75 miles per hour. He stepped down hard on the brake and snapped the cable.

Dave's bare foot slipped off the brake and dragged along the pavement. The skin and flesh of his toes and foot were rubbed away right down to the bone. And he lost part of the bone too. Then his knee hit the road. He lost more skin and flesh. When he finally came to a stop, he looked down and saw black lines that the gravel had worn in his kneecap.

"If you hadn't ridden the bike," his wife told him when he got home, "you wouldn't have gotten hurt."

In the end, they got divorced. Dave was still riding motorcycles.

And now he was married a second time, this time to a Madonna of the Machine, a woman who thought nothing of mixing breast-feeding with daredevil driving. As he watched her nursing Melissa, Dave talked to the baby, explaining everything to her as he drove along. He even tried to explain breast-feeding in terms that a modern American kid would understand: "This one's McDonald's," he told his child. "And the other one's Jack in the Box."

At that moment, all of us but Melissa were about as far from fast food as we could get. The Desert Safari was carrying us deeper and deeper into the badlands. It was the biggest safari ever. Last year, in bad weather, 565 four-wheelers participated. This year, 250 more showed up.

There were more Jeeps than anything else at the safari. In 1970, American Motors, which builds the Jeep, sold just 31,000 of these tough little machines. This year, AMC expects to sell in the neighborhood of 175,000 Jeeps. If this projection turns out to be correct, then sales will have grown more than 560 percent in less than a decade.

The 4x4 fundamentalists drive Jeeps. They consider theirs the original, pure four-wheel faith. And so they naturally look down on Broncos and vans and *especially* pickups. Rivalries among owners of different vehicles seem almost to take on the scale of feuds. They are so intense because four-wheeling is actually more about identity than it is about transportation. Four-wheelers are generally people who think their jobs are boring and mundane and so identify not with their work but with their vehicles.

What do you do?

I drive a Jeep.

Broncos, like Dave's, made up a sizable contingent at the safari. This vehicle, Ford's upscale answer to the Jeep, is catching on especially fast. In 1977, Ford sold 28,400 of these four-wheelers. In 1978, that figure jumped to 82,400—an increase of 190 percent in just one year. Bronco owners tend to consider their machines classier than Jeeps. But if war ever broke out between the Jeeps and the pickups, the Broncos would definitely fight on the Jeeps' side.

At the Desert Safari, 4x4 pickups were also numerous. Their sales are big and have been growing, too, but not quite as fast as their rivals'. Ford says that last year its four-wheel-drive pickup sales were up 27 percent over the previous year.

On one especially steep hill, a pickup got stuck and almost rolled. It clung precariously to the side of the slope, leaning dangerously sideways, blocking the path of the hundreds of vehicles behind it. What made this traffic jam all the more galling to the Jeeps stuck in it was this: The pickup was one of the new ones manufactured by—of all people—

Jeep! It was a kind of convert. It had been born into the Jeep family, but it had gone over to dreaded pickupism.

Dave stopped to help. A friend of his named John Beck, a Jeep driver, stopped to lend a hand too. They climbed up the hill toward the teetering pickup. The first person they met was the driver's girl friend, who had abandoned ship. She was furious at her boyfriend for getting stuck. She seemed ready to forsake the pickup ranks to defect to the Jeeps. After surveying the situation, Dave and John decided to try to winch the pickup back up onto the road. John drove his Jeep, which was equipped with a winch, into position. Dave's Bronco, which didn't have a winch, was left behind in the custody of Debbie and Melissa.

Dave and John worked together attaching a cable to the front of the pickup. Then they turned on the winch and began reeling in the pickup like a beached whale. The pickup almost tipped over sideways and rolled down the mountain, but John and Dave got it back on the road. And the 4x4 caravan could move on at last.

As John was getting back into his Jeep, Dave called to him: "You're the hero of the day."

Being a hero is, of course, what four-wheeling is all about. In real life, John is a welder, but in his Jeep he can be a hero. And he was. If his plan had not worked, the stranded driver would almost certainly have been injured or even killed. Still John had some reservations: "Yeah, I'm a hero, even if it was a pickup."

Jeep drivers versus pickup drivers is as serious as Harvard versus Yale . . . as IBM versus Honeywell . . . as *Time* versus *Newsweek* . . . as Merrill Lynch versus Paine, Webber.

Of course, there are wider gulfs than the one between Jeeps and Broncos, on the one hand, and pickups, on the other. Like the gulf between Debbie and her first husband.

Debbie and her first husband went together all four years that they attended Granite Hills High School, in El Cajon, breaking up three times but always getting back together. A year after they graduated, they got married. But he had a street motorcycle while she had a dirt bike. There was the conflict.

To make matters worse, the groom got a job in a clothing store, which meant that he had to start wearing a suit to work. The problem was that he came to like suits. As he fell in love with clothing, he fell out of love with machines, which only got his clothes dirty, after all.

The new husband wanted to ride on pavement; the new wife wanted to ride on earth. He wanted to stay in town; she wanted to go to the desert. He wanted to go to parties; she wanted to go camping. He wanted to get dressed up in coat and tie; she wanted to wear blue jeans. Yes, the marriage was in trouble.

Clothes and machines are both emblematic of value systems. The poor newlyweds could agree on neither what to wear nor what to ride. So they broke up.

On the safari trail, Debbie and Dave were in danger of breaking down. They had scraped bottom a couple of times, had got hung up more than once. But if they had got into trouble, they would have had plenty of help, for Debbie's father had come along, driving his own 4x4 Bronco. This Bronco family kept in touch during the safari by citizens band radio.

"Melissa's having her lunch," the mother informed the grandfather by CB.

"Nothing like having a good supply of baby food along all the time," the grandfather radioed back.

"That's a big roger."

"On this road it may turn to butter."

"Maybe that's why she's not eating too well."

Dave turned back to me and said: "There are three generations of fools out here today—Debbie's dad, Debbie, and Melissa."

Debbie's father was a little perplexed by the day's activities. He had spent almost his whole life working for road-construction companies. It had been his life's goal to help put pavement under every wheel in the country. And now here was his daughter trying to get as far away from pavement as possible. Still, he gamely followed her, wondering all the while what would become of this new generation that did not have the proper reverence for asphalt.

Suddenly we were at the foot of the steepest, tallest hill we had come to yet. While we waited our turn to test ourselves against the incline, Debbie got out and climbed to the top with a camera. She wanted to take a picture of the Bronco conquering the mountain.

Dave was left with Melissa in his lap. He held her up to the steering wheel. And she actually grasped it with her doll's hands.

"Hit it!" the father ordered.

And then we were racing up the hill. Somehow Dave held the steering wheel with one hand and the baby with the other. We bounced and jolted and skidded up into the sky. Sky was all you could see. To the left of you. To the right of you. Up in front of you. The edge of the world seemed to be on the other side of that hill.

And then, miraculously, we were over it. The ground came back up to meet us.

"I like to come out here and roll with the punches," Dave said. "And forget about the job."

Debbie and Dave met through a mutual friend named Jim, who was Dave's roommate. Debbie was Jim's ex-girl friend, but they were still good friends. So Dave and Debbie naturally saw something of each other. But they did not really get well acquainted until the weekend of the three's-company camping trip.

Both Jim *and* Dave asked Debbie if she would go camping with them in the Imperial Valley. She said no. She did not like the asymmetry of the sexes. When it came to relationships or wheels, two and four were better than three as far as she was concerned. Three wheels meant a tricycle, which was kid stuff, but three on a camping trip meant, well, adult stuff. Real adult. Or so she feared. And she was not sure she was that adult yet. No, she wouldn't go.

In spite of her refusal, Debbie went anyway. After all, she loved to camp. Dave drove his Datsun pickup with a camper on the back. Inside the camper, in lieu of a bed, was a Yamaha 250 motorcycle. All day Saturday, the bike remained in the pickup while Dave and Jim and Debbie climbed a mountain. That night, they slept in sleeping bags around a campfire. It was freezing.

When they got up Sunday morning, Dave finally got around to delivering his bike from the truck. It looked like one machine giving birth to another. Then he got on it and rode off, leaving his two friends in his dust. He was gone a long time and was exhausted when he got back. He collapsed behind a rock and went to sleep.

He was awakened by the sound of his motorcycle starting up and driving away. *Goddamn Jim! Who told him he could ride that bike! Bring it back right now! Damn you!*

With such thoughts raging in his tired brain, Dave came running furiously around the rock and saw . . .

. . . a petite, fragile-looking girl doing wheelies on his big bike.

Dave was in love.

We stopped in the middle of the desert at the base of Broken-Axle Hill to change the baby's diaper. Dave let down the Bronco's tailgate, which became a changing table. He taped on a clean, dry Pamper.

Meanwhile, one 4x4 after another assaulted Broken-Axle Hill as if it were Pork Chop Hill, as if the course of the war depended upon the taking of this peak. There were many casualties.

A Chevy 4x4 pickup took a running start, waded through the sand trap halfway up, and then made a dash at the almost vertical wall of clay. It seemed that a pickup would need a pickax and rope to climb such a cliff, but somehow the truck fought its way halfway up the impossible wall before there was a loud *crack!* The front wheels turned uselessly sideways. And the pickup slid back down the hill, a helpless paraplegic. Sometimes you have to destroy your vehicle to prove how good it is.

"Some hills are a body man's delight," explained John Beck, who had joined us for lunch. "This one is a mechanic's delight. Look at them—they're all standing around cheering."

A Jeep took a run at the hill. Jeep chauvinist Beck really wanted him to make it. A pickup busting up was no better than it deserved, but a Jeep deserved to conquer the hill. It foundered through the sand trap and then began groping its way up the face of the cliff.

Crack! The Jeep broke a drive shaft. The crippled machine rolled back down the hill dragging its drive shaft like a broken leg.

A Jeep with two children in the back launched itself at the car killer. At first, the Jeep went right up the hill like Audie Murphy. And all the Jeepers at the bottom of the hill were jubilant. But then it, too, ran into trouble on the cliff: Without warning, the Jeep's front wheels suddenly left the ground and it was in serious danger of toppling backward down the hill. The child-filled machine stood on its rear bumper, teetering backward, then forward, then backward again. Old "Audie Murphy" seemed to have taken one in the gut.

"There's a dog in there too," said Debbie.

Everyone in the car—father, mother, children, and dog—seemed to be leaning forward to try to keep the Jeep from tipping backward. The Jeep was like a rearing horse standing on its hind legs. At the bottom of the hill, even most of the pickupers hoped it would avert total disaster. After an impossibly long balancing act, the machine finally tipped forward onto all fours.

Then another Jeep tried the hill and it almost tipped over backward too. A pickup broke its drive shaft. A Scout kept flinging itself at the hill until it caught on fire. Finally a Bronco took a run at the cliff.

"Go, Bronco!" yelled Dave, the lover of Broncos.

And it did. The Bronco was just enough longer than a Jeep to keep from being in danger of flipping over backward. And it was enough shorter and lighter than a pickup to make it agile. The Bronco huffed and puffed but made it up the hill. Everyone cheered. The Jeep owners cheered. The pickup owners cheered. The van owners cheered. But the Bronco owners cheered loudest of all. Especially Dave.

"I'm going up it," Dave announced.

"Honey, do you have to go on every mountain?" complained Debbie.

For the first time, the second wife sounded the slightest bit like the first wife. She was interfering with his love affair with his machine.

Dave and Debbie's love was conceived in an atmosphere of wheels. After he saw the way she could ride a motorcycle, he asked her out to dinner. They went to a restaurant called the Springfield Wagon Works. The place was decorated with wagon wheels and other old wagon parts. If you wanted to, you could even eat inside an old stagecoach—the extinct ancestor of today's Jeeps and Broncos.

A short while later, Dave and Debbie went camping again. This time no third party was invited to join them. And they left the motorcycle behind so they would have room for a bed. At this point in their relationship, Dave was more interested in Debbie than in his beloved machine. For the moment, she had replaced it in his heart.

They camped out by Hurkey Creek up in the San Jacinto Mountains. They took walks and saw lots of deer. And at night they slept in the back of the truck.

After the camping trip, they felt they were in love with each other. But they had both been so badly hurt by the failures of their first marriages that they did not want to expose themselves to such pain again. So they just moved in together. After they had lived together for a year and a half, Debbie and Dave finally proposed to each other in the Mission Valley Center shopping mall. Then they went shopping for rings and a 4x4.

The newlyweds bought an old Blazer. They paid for it with the trade-in from Dave's Datsun pickup, plus $300. Dave had always wanted to own a four-wheeler, and he sensed that now was the time to make his move. He wanted his new marriage to roll on a new kind of wheels.

That was in 1977. A lot of Americans shifted into 4x4 that year. Dave and Debbie bought a secondhand four-wheeler, but a lot of people bought brand-new ones. Some 807,000 new four-wheel-drive vehicles were sold in 1977, an increase of 26 percent over the previous year. Unfortunately, the old 4x4 did not serve the newlyweds well. It had been driven in a couple of Baja races, which are probably the roughest races in the world. It was worn out.

So the couple began dreaming of a 4x4 as bright and new as their low-mileage marriage. Finally last fall, Debbie's parents surprised them with a new baby-blue Bronco. That year, 1,044,715 four-wheelers were sold, up more than 29 percent from the year before.

The sticker price on the young couple's Bronco was $12,000. With their trade-in, they got it for $9,000. Dave said: "A guy at work told me he paid $9,000 for his first house." That's right. Cars now cost what houses used to. And houses cost what mansions once did. People like Dave have largely been priced out of the housing market—but not yet out of the recreational vehicle market. They can no longer afford their dream house, but they can still afford their dream car. So their biggest investment becomes not their home but their vehicle.

And Dave and Debbie live in yet another vehicle: their mobile home. Their whole life happens on wheels: They identify not with where they live but with what they drive. Their romance started on motorcycles. Their marriage got rolling in four-wheel-drive. And even their daughter was conceived in a trailer.

After the newlyweds got their new Bronco, they took it out in the desert to see what it could do. It did pretty well—even proving to be a good desert bedroom. But Dave decided to make one improvement: He dressed his wheels in Armstrong Tru-Trac tires. Why? Because he is convinced they are good tires. And because the tires have the same name he has. Dave Armstrong, who rolls on Armstrongs, has much of his identity riding on his 4x4.

Dave grew to love his Bronco so much that he would spend hours cleaning and polishing it. This off-road machine was usually so waxed and shiny that you would never suspect it had ever been off the road.

When a friend told Dave about the Desert Safari, he decided to put his Bronco to its first big test, even if it meant getting it dirty. In the end, the safari put considerable stress on not only the family's automotive but also its emotional machinery.

As we rolled and bumped our way through the desert, Melissa began to cry. So Dave took us for a ride over some especially rough terrain. All the bouncing around scared the mother, but it calmed the baby.

"The rougher the better," Dave explained. "If it's real rough, Melissa enjoys that."

But Debbie enjoyed the rough stuff less and less. Especially after her dad reported an accident over the CB.

"A truck rolled between checkpoints two and three," he radioed. "The driver was going up a hill and couldn't see over his hood. He turned the wrong way at the top—went over a cliff. A girl got hurt."

We were climbing a hill. We couldn't see over our hood, and we were afraid we would turn the wrong way. But we crested the hill and started down the other side. The Bronco went faster . . . and *faster* . . . and FASTER . . . and *FASTER*.

"No brakes!" screamed Dave.

The Bronco hurtled down like a plane that had lost power. And all the passengers inside were terrified.

Then the machine stopped. We were all alive. The brakes were fine. Good old Dave had just been kidding.

"I almost lost her!" snapped Debbie. "Don't screw around when she's in my lap."

So we took it a little easier to make the mother happier. But the baby started crying again.

"She's saying, 'It's not bumpy enough, Dad,' " Dave cooed. " 'I like it bumpy.' "

So we took it a little rougher to quiet the baby.

"Another truck just rolled," radioed Debbie's father.

"My nerves are really on edge," Debbie said.

The Bronco slowed down, but then it sped up again.

"Dave, you're impossible!" snapped Debbie.

"A Jeep rolled over," her father radioed. "They're just calling the ambulance."

We arrived at the bottom of an incline only slightly less frightening than Broken-Axle Hill.

"I really don't want to go up that," Debbie said.

So we went around it, but in doing so we got lost. Dave became so furious that he threw a glass of water out the window—in spite of our being in the desert and low on water.

"Don't get frustrated," Debbie warned.

Melissa started crying louder than ever.

Eventually we found our way back to the foot of the hill that Debbie had not wanted to go up. Now we had to go up it. There was no other way. We struggled up the cliff, bouncing and bruising, but by now not even a rough ride would quiet the screaming baby.

With all this strain on the emotional gears, the Armstrongs did not quite complete the Saturday course. Melissa kept crying. And Debbie's nerves kept deteriorating. So they decided to take a shortcut back to camp along a paved road. In the end, they had turned back into asphalt four-wheelers.

"Melissa may be too little to take her through all this," Debbie said. "I'm not sure I'm going tomorrow."

Dave, Debbie, and Melissa spent the night on the desert floor along with 3,000 other four-wheelers. The Desert Safari had caused an instant city—a city built in a day—to spring up, composed of motor homes, campers, mobile homes, and tents. The weary Armstrongs slept in an Executive motor home lent to them by Debbie's parents.

Sunday morning they got up early, for there was another safari course to run that day. The whole family sat down to a hearty 4x4 breakfast. But then Dave kissed his wife and daughter good-bye as if he were going off to work at the phone company. Debbie and Melissa were staying home.

Dave got into his Bronco and drove off into the desert by himself, alone with his love at last.

◆　　◆　　◆

When I got back from the desert, everything had changed. John Travolta, who had walked away from *Urban Cowboy*, came striding back to it. And no one walks quite like he does. The studio backed down and agreed to buy him an airline ticket to Houston. First class.

THE NEW SPEAKEASIES

• • •

While we were shooting *Perfect*, I kept asking all the extras, "What is the New Saturday Night?" And they started telling me about a network of underground clubs—many of them illegal because they serve alcohol after hours. The New Speakeasies. Soon I started going to these clubs almost every night.

My daily schedule worked something like this: I would report to the set where we were filming *Perfect* around eight or nine in the morning. I would meet with James Bridges—my collaborator on the script and the director of the movie—and we would talk through the scenes to be shot that day. Then we would roll colored paper into an IBM Selectric and type through the day's dialogue, usually making small changes, sometimes large ones. Then we would assemble the actors and rehearse the scenes. These rehearsals almost always suggested additional rewriting, so we would roll more colored paper into the electric typewriter. Finally we would start shooting.

At the end of the day, I would rush home to my hotel, the Chateau Marmont, where I lived because Tom Wolfe once told me, "When in Los Angeles always stay at that hotel that sounds like a bottle of wine." In my comfortably seedy hotel room, I would take a nap. When I woke up, say around midnight, I would go to the clubs. I wouldn't get back to the hotel until five or six in the morning.

One night in the Fetish Club, a black waitress with orange hair, whose name was Tequila Mockingbird, came up to me and asked, "How did you get in here?"

I did look a little out of place, dressed in my blue blazer and khaki slacks, while everyone else wore black and skull earrings and bones.

"I'm doing a story for *Rolling Stone*," I said.

"That's my favorite magazine," she said.

And she became a good and helpful friend.

During the day, I was busy working on a movie about a reporter much like me. And at night I was busy being that reporter. I was never more self-conscious about how I did my job. It was as though a camera were following me through the night.

One day, I invited two of the nighttime people I planned to write about—Mad Mark and Iris—to visit the set of *Perfect*. Life seemed to be imitating a movie, which in turn was imitating life. On a sound stage, I sat down with Mark and Iris and interviewed them—while a few feet away the reporter in the movie was also interviewing somebody while the camera turned.

◆　◆　◆

Rolling Stone, June 1985

Alice was beginning to get very tired of sitting by her sister on the bank. Once or twice she had peeped into the book her sister was reading, but it had no pictures or conversation in it. And what is the use of a book, thought Alice, without pictures or conversations? So she was considering whether the pleasure of making a daisy-chain would be worth the trouble of picking the daisies, when suddenly a black rabbit wearing a skull earring ran close by her.

Alice started to her feet, for it flashed across her mind that she had never before seen a rabbit with such a grinning earring, and burning with curiosity, she ran across the field after it, and was just in time to see it pop into a doorway on Sunset Boulevard in Hollywood.

In another moment in went Alice after it, never once considering how in the world she was to get out again. She found herself in a foyer where everyone was dressed more or less like the funereal rabbit. Black clothes. Skull earrings. Miniature skeleton earrings. Living faces made up to look as if they were dead—death being the latest fad.

Seeing a smug, fat, smiling feline—with coal-black hair and ghoulish white makeup—taking money at the door, Alice advanced toward her. The grinning cat demanded $5 and then used a rubber stamp to make an imprint on Alice's inner wrist, right over the veins. Looking down at her wrist, Alice saw a word spelled out in blue that looked like an inky brand: FETISH.

Welcome to the Fetish Club. Passing through the door, Alice saw more creatures dressed in black and gloom. And she heard the club's sound system moaning a subspecies of rock 'n' roll known as doomsrock or gloomsrock. A music inspired by a love of death and bats and horror movies. The great classic being a tune called "Bella Lagosi Is Dead," to which the living dead love to dance.

"What you see is a modern-day Dance of Death," explains a doomsphilosopher named Dave Grave who wears crucifix earrings. "Back in the Middle Ages they were afraid of the plague. Now we are afraid of everything—especially the H-*boooommmmmbbbb!*"

A mushroom-shaped cloud billowed up on the club's giant video screen. Welcome to Ground Zero.

Moving on, Alice began to notice shadowy couples who seemed to have risen from the grave in pairs. Pairs like Mad Marc Rude and Iris Berry . . . Merrill Ward and Modi Frank . . . Club Couples who love bones and black and midnight and death and each other.

That is Iris, twenty-six, over there in the fishnet stockings and stiletto heels with a complexion as white and hair as black as the Queen of Clubs. And that is Marc, thirty, with the earring made of human bone and the black leather chaps and the black leather bondage bracelets, which seem to symbolize his emotional tie to the girl at his side. Before they met, Iris's bed was like another club where anyone and everyone felt free to drop in. Mark is trying to close that club—or at least make it a lot more exclusive.

And that is Merrill, twenty-two, wearing his omnipresent hat, this time a bowler, along with a black trench coat and black boots and black cane, looking, as he says, "like a New Wave detective," a New Sam Spade of the New Speakeasies. And that is Modi, twenty-three, in her omnipresent chapeau, also a bowler, along with a green Kermit watch and an earring made of wooden skulls. This happy chapeaux couple, who love hats almost as much as clubs and each other, were nearly broken up by feuding record companies. They are the vinyl Romeo and Juliet of West Hollywood.

And then over there, perched on a table, is what appears to be some sort of mythic creature, half woman and half animal. A girl with black-and-white stripes. A zebra with human breasts. Above the waist, this beautiful beast is wearing nothing but her swirling painted stripes which extend from the tip of her nose to the tips of her breasts. She almost seems a kind of missing link, not Darwin's but perhaps Freud's, that elusive link where human and animal sexuality are joined.

Other inmates wear spiders on their ears with black webs painted on their faces. One ghoul is even dressed in a shirt that seems to have been knitted by a spider.

These spider webs are appropriate since the Fetish is one of a web of clubs that has spread out all across Los Angeles and is beginning to spread across the entire country. They are in San Francisco, where the Batican (rhymes with the pope's home) is one of the best known. And in Chicago, where the Oz keeps dying and then coming back to life as Oz Again and then Oz Again Again. And there are many in New York, too, of course. These are the new underground nightclubs. The New Speakeasies.

Some are outlaw clubs—with no liquor licenses and no closing times—that deliberately flaunt the liquor laws. Others used to be outlaw clubs but are now trying to climb up to quasi-legality. Almost all have been harassed by the police at one time or another. Many have actually experienced classic raids like the Old Speakeasies of the twenties and thirties.

These New Speakeasies are usually open only one night a week. They divide up the week between them, each having its own night when it comes to life. So, for instance, in Los Angeles, The C-Beat Club is open Wednesdays. The Bar Delux, Thursdays. The Fetish Club, Fridays. Club Soda, Saturdays.

The new underground clubs differ from traditional nightclubs in another way also, for they don't own or lease a piece of property with their names on signs out front. Instead they simply rent space one night a week from a restaurant or warehouse or art gallery. Sometimes from 10:00 P.M. until 2:00 A.M., sometimes from midnight until morning, at any rate during hours when the space would not normally be used. Since there are no signs, you simply have to know where the club is and walk in. Or maybe knock.

The C-Beat Club happens at the Imperial Gardens Japanese restaurant on Sunset. The Bar DeLux is also at the Imperial Gardens but on another night. Club Soda takes place in the elegant ballroom of the Park Plaza Hotel on Parkview across the street from McArthur Park. The Fetish Club, which has had many homes, now spreads its black wings in the bar of the old Hollywood Athletic Club.

At least, these clubs were taking place at these locations last week. Next week may be another matter. For they all tend to change addresses fairly often, being by nature movable parties.

Some are more movable than others. Those deepest underground are so secretive that they float from place to place and night to night. If you are a member of the web, or the network, you receive a call late at night telling you when and where a club will be happening. You get in your car and follow the directions and drive, for instance, into some godforsaken, dying downtown factory district. You pass bums and derelicts and muggers and then enter a deserted warehouse and everyone is there. And the music is playing. And the beer is flowing. And the police are very likely on the way.

All of these underground nightclubs—all the New Speakeasies— are descended from a venerable establishment known as the Zero Club. Its history includes several openings and closings, multiple homes, and legendary raids with police on the roof. It is closed now but plans to reopen soon. The Zero is the great Once and Future Speakeasy of the new underground. All the other clubs are really its children. All of them are Little Zeros. All populated by the Zero Generation.

Allied with the underground nightclubs are a few aboveground clubs such as the Lingerie, which is next door to the Fetish. The Music Machine on Pico. And Al's Bar downtown.

Mad Marc met Iris at Al's Bar. They were brought together by a New Wave fairy godmother named Janet Cunningham, who used to live next door to the original Zero, where she befriended a few hundred Zero members of the Zero Generation. Now she makes her living getting her Zero friends jobs in movies as extras. Two of the Zeros cast by Janet were Marc and Iris. She placed them in a movie called *Trancers*, which was shooting in Al's Bar.

During a break in the filming, Marc found himself studying a beautiful girl with fishnet stockings and stiletto heels and elbow-length black gloves and blood-red lipstick and a complexion like the Queen of Clubs. An apt emblem for this princess of the underground nightclubs.

Someone walked up to her and asked, "How's life at Disgraceland?"

Referring to the house where Iris lives, a kind of Zero Generation dormitory, which has a sign on the front door proclaiming: WELCOME TO DISGRACELAND. The place was conceived as a white-trash version of Elvis Presley's Memphis mansion, Graceland. It is stuffed with pictures of Elvis and has a clothesline on the front porch. Iris sleeps in a single bed in a corner of the living room, where she enjoys very little privacy. All kinds of people, invited and uninvited, are always dropping into Disgraceland at all hours of the day and especially the night. And many of these visitors end up dropping into her bed . . . because it is there . . . and because she is there.

"It's terrible," Iris told her friend. "I keep waking up and finding someone in my bed trying to take my clothes off. I'm public property."

Just the other night she had gone to bed in a T-shirt and panties and had been awakened around 4:00 A.M. with her panties down around her knees. And some stranger was busy trying to pull them the rest of the way off. He was just some guy who had arrived in a van and was making himself very much at home. Iris was not even surprised. It had become a common occurrence.

Mad Marc decided it was time to intrude himself into the conversation.

"Well," he told the pretty girl, "you ought to put someone in your bed permanently to keep the others out."

"I wouldn't know where to begin to look," Iris said.

"You wouldn't have to look too far," said Marc.

Iris didn't say anything. She didn't want to get involved with anyone who looked the way Marc looked, someone with tattoos. But Marc already felt obsessed by this girl from Disgraceland.

During almost every break, he talked to her. And they began to learn something about each other. He was the son of a cop. She was the daughter of a nurse. He was an artist specializing in macabre posters and fliers and T-shirts. She was a cocktail waitress specializing in New Wave bars.

When they finished work around midnight, Marc told Iris he was going over to the Anti-Club to listen to a band named the Cult perform. He asked if she would like to come along with him. She said no, but she might show up there later.

After trading phone numbers, they said good-bye and parted. Then Iris saw Marc get in a car and drive off with a girl named Moussa, who was one of her bitterest enemies. Iris was upset. She felt sure that Moussa would be slandering her all night and that Marc would never call.

That night, Marc waited for Iris for hours at the Anti-Club, but she never showed up.

Merrill, the son of a city civil servant, met Modi, the daughter of a veteran television actor, at a Misfits concert. She was working at a T-shirt booth. He walked up to the booth, noticed her eyes were two different colors, and wanted to know her better. So he asked her if they hadn't met before. She thought he was "corny."

Then some big thug stole one of her T-shirts and ran away with it. Merrill ran after him. The New Wave detective was on the case. Detective Zero to the rescue. He came back with her T-shirt and she liked him better.

"Where do you work?" Merrill asked the now friendlier T-shirt saleswoman.

"For the enemy," Modi said.

"What do you mean?" he asked.

"Unicorn," she said.

Although Modi didn't know Merrill, she did know who he was and for whom he worked. Namely, SST. Modi's Unicorn and Merrill's SST were record labels that hated each other.

The trouble was over a band called Black Flag, whose motto is: "If anything lasts too long, it must be knocked down." Which could serve as a manifesto for the Zero Generation. Knock it all down to zero and start over again. Living by its motto, Black Flag changed its style every so often just for the sake of starting over.

And Black Flag tried to change record companies the same way. If a recording contract lasted too long, then knock that down, too, and move on. The band had a contract with Modi's label (Unicorn), but it wanted to move to Merrill's (SST). Which led to a blood lawsuit. Unicorn had actually managed to have some Black Flaggers put in jail.

Now Black Flag's Romeo was attracted to Unicorn's Juliet. He asked her for her phone number. But the Unicorn was a little shy or at least coy. She would only give the Black Flag boy part of her phone number.

"She put a fucking question mark in place of the last digit," Merrill remembers.

"I wanted him to work for it," Modi explains.

"She wanted me to spent more than a dollar looking for her. But I was broke. I was living in a boys dorm in art school. I tried a couple of numbers, but they were the wrong ones."

Then Merrill gave up and started making the rounds of concerts and clubs again. He was bound to meet some girls who would at least be willing to part with their whole phone numbers. He knew that one of the best places to look was the Zero, which was just about everybody's favortie club.

"The Zero was the best," remembers Merrill.

The Story of the Zero begins on August 1, 1980, at 1955 Cahuenga Boulevard in the shadow of the Hollywood Freeway. The club was actually christened the Zero Zero, but most people just called it the Zero. It was named after "the Zero Zero Club"—an old-fashioned speakeasy—in Mickey Spillane's *My Gun Is Quick*. The man who named the club is named John Pochna.

"The name caught on because everyone looked like a bunch of zeros," Pochna says wryly. Then adds, "Besides, zero encompasses everything."

But perhaps Zero had another meaning, too. As in starting from zero. Or starting from scratch. If there isn't a club you like, then make one of your own. And if this isn't a world you like, then make your own world within the alien world. Begin over at zero. Zero is the new beginning.

John Pochna got to be known around town as Mr. Zero, but he did not found the Zero alone. He had a partner named Wayzata Camerone. More or less in the spirit of "Let's find a barn and put on a show," Pochna and Camerone started the Zero Zero Club on the ground floor of a run-down hotel that was so bad hotel guests kept throwing things out of the windows. Trash. TV sets. Once even a body.

During the day, the Zero was an art gallery, but at night it transformed itself into an after-hours club. Its excuse for bending the liquor laws was that it wasn't a bar but just an art gallery having an all-night party. Money was collected at the door—from $5 to $500, depending on how rich you looked and how much the doorman liked you—and then the beer inside was free. So the Zero could claim that it was not actually selling drinks.

Our friend Iris, the Queen of Clubs, worked at the Zero Zero. She was present at the club's creation and so in a sense was one of the mothers of the Zero Generation.

During the day, Iris often watched the putative art gallery. Sometimes she watched alone. Sometimes she watched along with a young black woman with a wonderful name: Tequila Mockingbird. Iris and Tequila guarded artwork produced by Zero artists with names like Tomato du Plenty (formerly of the Screamers).

Sometimes at night, after hours, Iris helped out at the Zero bar. In the beginning, there hadn't been any bar, just a refrigerator stocked with beer, and everyone helped themselves. But then a would-be rock star named Top Jimmy—the lead singer of Top Jimmy and the Rhythm Pigs—started coming to the Zero. And he decided that the club needed not only a bar but a bartender. Top Jimmy volunteered, since he figured he could make more on bartender tips than he could on his rock 'n' roll royalties. The more you tipped, the more quickly and more often you got served.

"We used to throw cans of beer and people would jump for them," Iris recalls. "I was once tipped $20."

Most nights El Duce—of a band called El Duce and the Mentors—would drop in and sing duets with Top Jimmy, who would keep right on serving drinks. Top Jimmy would sing something like, "Shake it up, baby," and El Duce would chime in with, "Jack me off, baby." And then there would almost always be requests for El Duce to sing his greatest hit, "Going Through Your Purse," a romantic ballad with a verse that went:

> *While I'm giving her*
> *A real good ball,*
> *I take her purse and throw it*
> *To the band in the hall ...*
> *We're going through your purse,*
> *We're going through your purse.*

Everyone seemed to get along well at the Zero except John Pochna and Wayzata Camerone, the founding partners. The better the club did, the worse their relations became. They both turned out to have tempers as quick as Mickey Spillane's gun. A professional divorce and custody fight seemed inevitable.

The Queen of Clubs was worried.

While John and Wayzata seemed on their way to a permanent breach, Modi and Merrill were finally about to get together. After losing 40 cents in telephone roulette, Merrill had given up on Modi, but she hadn't given up on him. Since the Unicorn girl was afraid to call SST directly, she enlisted an intermediary, a kind of vinyl Miles Standish, who called and got Merrill's number.

"I phoned Merrill," Modi recalls, "and said, 'You didn't guess the missing number and it was so easy. It was a two.'"

They agreed to meet at the Cat and Fiddle at 11:00 P.M., but he was a few minutes late and she left in a rage.

Merrill called Modi late that night and apologized for not being on time. Modi forgave him and agreed to meet him the next night.

They went to the Cathay de Grande, one of the oldest of the undergound clubs, to see the Circle Jerks. In one corner of the club was a thrift shop, which was perfect for Modi, who loved putting together her own version of thrift fashion. Starting from zero. Starting from scratch.

Then they went over to the Zero, where they made out on a couch.

Afterward, Modi let Merrill come home with her. She even let him into her bedroom and her bed.

"But I wouldn't let him consummate," remembers Modi. "I made him just go to sleep. I did it because I liked him. If I had thought this was a one-night stand, I would have fucked him and said good-bye. But I wanted him to work for it. Like the phone number."

The second night, Modi and Merrill went to the Music Machine to hear the Red Cross play. They went home and made love. And then they got up and went to the Zero.

"Then we started going to all the clubs together," Modi recalls. "We like going to every single club there is."

But love was not easy in a dangerous world of warring record companies. Modi hoped that she could somehow be a mediator between the two feuding labels. Wasn't that how all those stories about feuds ended, with a girl from one side falling in love with a boy from the other side, with peace shortly to follow? But it didn't work in this case. They were both "given shit." The Black Flag band was rude to Modi and stopped speaking to Merrill. Modi decided she had to choose between her boyfriend and her label. So she quit her job at Unicorn.

Now Modi needed a job. She would eventually find one at the Zero, but by then it would be in a different place and have a different name.

In 1982, the Zero Zero divided in half. John Pochna stayed at the 1955 Cahuenga address, while Wayzata Camerone moved to Gardner and Sunset. What do you get when you divide Zero Zero by two? You get two Zero Zeros. The Double Zero had split like an amoeba into two Double Zeros. Both Pochna and Camerone claimed the name.

Needing a new partner, Wayzata teamed up with a young man named Jake Gehnan—who was Iris's roommate in those days. Iris naturally transferred her loyalties from the Cahuenga Boulevard Zero to the Gardner Street Zero. She transferred her services, too, becoming the new club's bartender. So Iris was present not only at the creation of the first Zero but at the birth of the Zero's first offspring. Ensconced behind her bar, quenching the thirst of her "children," the Queen of Clubs looked more than ever like the Young Mother of the Young Zero Generation.

This new Zero on Gardner was literally an underground nightclub. It was located in a basement.

"It was really like a speakeasy," says Iris, "with lots of creatures wandering in to get drinks after 2:00 A.M. There was a back room—you had to know a secret knock to get in—where they had all the drugs."

Soon Iris needed help behind the bar. So a second bartender was added, a would-be rock star named Pleasant Gehman, the lead singer of the Screaming Sirens, who found a beer bar more profitable than musical bars. Pleasant and Iris became fast friends. And Iris started pouring out her heart to Pleasant, one bartender to another, telling her about breaking up with Jake and moving in with someone else. But this someone else was driving her crazy.

"Move in with me," Pleasant said.

So, hoping to find a kind of refuge, Iris moved in with Pleasant, who lived in a crowded house named Disgraceland. But instead of peace she found strange bedfellows undressing her in the middle of the night.

Meanwhile, the new underground basement Zero on Gardner was becoming as crowded as Iris's bed. More and more people were doing what she had been one of the first to do, transferring their loyalties.

"My theory of life is that there are moths and there are flames," Iris says. "Me and my friends are the flames."

The crowd followed the flames to Gardner Street. The new Zero was beginning to eclipse the old Zero.

One night at the new Zero, a moth in the form of a Big Movie Star's Grandson was attracted to Iris. He handed her a blond fur coat and told her to go in the ladies room and take off all her clothes and come out wearing nothing but the coat. She went in the ladies room and took off everything but her trademarks—her garterbelt and fishnet stockings and stiletto heels—and put on the coat.

Then Iris and the Big Movie Star's Grandson rode around in a taxi for hours drinking bottles of champagne. They drove all over—even up to Sharon Tate's house.

Just before dawn, Iris got tired of the fur coat, took it off, and threw it out of the window of the cab. The taxi driver slammed on the brakes and ran back to pick it up. So Iris and the Big Movie Star's Grandson stole the cab's keys.

As the sun was coming up, they gave the driver his keys and $200 and a bottle of champagne.

Another night, a crowd from the Cahuenga Zero got bored and went over to the Gardner Zero to pay a visit. Wayzata wouldn't let them in. Which exacerbated the feud.

John Pochna and the original Zero were in trouble. Not only was Pochna losing business to the upstart Zero, but he was also having trouble with his landlord, the hotel, and that constant enemy of good times, the cops. His landlord went so far as to flood the room above the club, which also flooded the club, as a way of sending him a message. Then the landlord got tired of being subtle and moved Pochna's furniture and jukebox into the street—and locked the door.

Wayzata Camerone seemed to have won the Great Zero War.

But Pochna counterattacked by moving to a building at the corner of Wilcox and Hollywood Boulevard. It was actually a better location than the one he had been driven out of. He reopened under a new name. Zero One. Or 0l.

"I chose Zero One," Pochna explains, "because that is the entire binary alphabet of the computer age."

Then Wayzata's Zero Zero on Gardner got closed by the police, who got tired of listening to neighborhood complaints. So Pochna and the Zero One got all the business.

The Zero One seemed to have won the Zero War.

But then Wayzata reopened the Zero Zero downtown at Seventh and Alverado. He called it the Real Zero. But it had trouble because Zero customers did not fall in love with the winos-and-warehouses atmosphere of the neighborhood.

This Zero kept getting closer and closer to living up to its name because it was almost empty. The Real Zero failed and went out of business. And then there was only one. One Zero.

The Zero One.

Soon even the Queen of Clubs was knocking on John Pochna's speakeasy door.

Returning to the fold, Iris got a part-time job working as a hostess whenever the Zero One got organized enough to mount an actual art opening. One of the most memorable was for a show called "TV Dinners," featuring paintings of Swanson's frozen meals. Iris came dressed as a TV dinner with a dress of garbage bags and tin foil, bracelets of frozen vegetables, and an actual TV dinner worn as a belt buckle. All of which she found especially amusing since she had grown up on TV dinners.

But Iris made something of an art-world faux pas that evening. She got drunk and tried to watch TV on a set that had been painted as a work of art. When she started scraping the paint off so she could see better, the artist got upset. The human TV dinner was thrown out of the TV Dinner show.

Merrill and Modi moved in together. They shared an apartment in a Hollywood neighborhood where all but streetwalkers feared to tread. Since they both collected hats, they decorated their new home with chapeaux hung on pegs on the wall. A cowboy hat. His and hers bowlers. A Bogart hat. A Katharine Hepburn hat. A Spanish army hat. A

Marlon Brando *Wild Ones* cap. A white fur hat. A baret. A bondage
hood. And a gray top hat that Merrill wore as a part of his Mad Hatter's
costume on Halloween.

Modi's miniature coffin collection was also on display.

Not only did Merrill and Modi live together, they also worked together, at the Zero One. Where else? He was one of the doormen, but
the "hat" she wore at the club was a little harder to sum up in one word.

"I was like this little spy," Modi explains. "If I saw a fight, I would
run downstairs and get Merrill. Or if girls would get harassed—some
would freak out, because guys would be pulling their pants down, literally jumping on them—I would go for Merrill."

So Modi and Merrill helped keep the peace at the Zero One. They
were Mr. and Ms. New Wave detective. Mr. and Ms. Detective Zero.
New Speakeasy versions of Nick and Nora Charles, who loved to haunt
the old speakeasies.

One of the potential troublemakers whom Merrill and Modi kept an
eye on was Mad Marc Rude.

Marc was brand new in town and new at the Zero One. The club
made a good first impression on him.

"I got laid the first night I went there," Marc reminisces. "We went
to her place because I didn't have too much of a place at the time. I was
sleeping under a table at a friend's house."

After such an auspicious beginning, Marc quickly adopted the Zero
One. And it adopted him.

"I got invited into the back rooms, the party rooms, the 'who sent
you' rooms."

The club became a kind of home for the homeless artist.

"The Zero One was heaven. Heaven translates into no admission
charge—because I knew everyone at the door—and free beer at two
o'clock in the morning."

Of course, this heaven sometimes had its rough side.

"I got in a few good brawls. One night I crawled out crying. I
couldn't find my way home. A friend pointed me the wrong way."

But the only real problem with the Zero One, the only thing really
missing, was something Marc didn't even know about, not yet. Namely
Iris. She had departed the club shortly after the TV Dinner show fiasco.
When she was thrown out, like the TV dinner she appeared to be, she
stayed out.

There seemed to be room in the world for only one Zero, but there
was plenty of room for its children, all those clubs that copied the Zero
concept. Like a club called Radio that floated from warehouse to ware-

house. And a club called Odyssey. And one called At Sunset. And one called Mirage, whose name implied how hard it was to find. And one called the Fake Club, which took place on Fridays in the Trailways bus depot. And then one called the Crush Club, which succeeded the Fake Club at the bus station.

And even a club called the Garage. It took place at a big, multilevel parking structure downtown. This club was like a layered party with different entertainments assigned to each floor. One floor was for dancing. One floor for drugs. One floor for sex.

Iris was the coat check girl at the Garage. Since there was no coat room, she made a coat rack out of a light stand loaned to her by a photographer named Jules Bates. He had once done a Motels album cover, and he was one of her boyfriends. Jules would sometimes come down and sit with Iris while she collected coats. Then they would go up to the sex floor and see the pale bodies moving in the dark shadows, looking like sharks swimming through murky water.

Then suddenly the Garage was closed, not for lack of interest, but because the owner of the garage felt the club was getting out of hand. Jules was killed about the same time in a motorcycle accident.

And then there was a club called the Veil, which is of more than passing interest since it was in a sense the father of the Fetish. It started out at the Cathay de Grande and later moved to the Lingerie.

"I went to the Veil," says Iris, who went to them all. "It was a New Romantic place. Dandyism. Asexuality. Boy George. That kind of thing. Tuxedo shirts. White-face makeup. Hair slicked back. And, 'Where did you get your shoes?' I used to call it the Veal because it was such a meat market. A guy with a French accent came up to me and said, 'Do you want to come home with me? I want to know you better.' And his makeup was better than mine."

The Veil was the dream of Henry Peck and Joseph Brooks, who run a record store on Melrose Avenue's New Wave strip during the day. Eventually these men behind the Veil decided it was time for a change. They wanted darker colors and a darker note. They wanted Gothic Horror and Creep Chic. They were ready to move from the New Romanticism to the New Death. They were ready to found the Fetish.

When they first started it, back in the summer of 1982, it was a nomadic club.

"We used to float," remembers Joseph. "We used to move weekly."

The Fetish came to rest for a while in a restaurant called the Zoo on Melrose Avenue. Joseph and Henry rented the Zoo on Friday nights and put out a flyer saying: THE FETISH IS A SOCIAL CLUB FOR FALLEN ANGELS. They stayed open until 4:00 A.M.

"From the very beginning," Joseph says, "the look was home-made. Put together. Make your own everything. Like bone necklaces. People saying, 'I ate a chicken last night and I'm wearing it tonight.' "

Jewelry made from scratch, from zero.

After a few weeks, the Fetish moved from the Zoo to the old Stardust Studio, a vast warren of glass booths, where Fanny Brice used to make her recordings. But the place has come down in the world since. During working hours, it now houses a costume shop. The superannuated owner of the shop used to wander through the Fetish collecting a dozen girls at a time whom he would spirit away and bring back dressed as glamorous twenties silent movie queens. These living ghosts of dead stars would rub shoulders with the Fetish's living skeletons.

After eight months, the Fetish Club moved on to a deserted art-deco bank building, complete with vault, on Wilshire Boulevard. But the quiet neighborhood never really embraced the Fetish.

"They didn't like kids fucking on the lawn," Joseph recalls. "The police came down on us. If they want to close you down, they'll close you down."

It was time to move on.

There were getting to be so many underground nightclubs—and they moved so often—that it was hard to keep them all straight, no matter how hip you were. So several service magazines sprang up to help all the zeros sort out which Zero-style club they wanted to go to on a given night.

The Queen of Clubs helped mother one of these into existence. A group was sitting around trying to decide what to call this as yet unborn publication.

"How about *The Chosen Few?*" someone said.

"Don't you dare!" said Iris.

"Let's call it *Scratch*," said Ruben Blue, who was going to be the editor.

So that is what they called it.

"I looked up *scratch*," Iris remembers. "It means to make do with menial amounts, to get by on a hand-to-mouth basis, to scratch for a living, to survive. And to make things from scratch. It fit every aspect."

Because the Zero Generation does make do with menial amounts, living in places like Disgraceland. And it does make up much of its lifestyle from scratch, in part out of economic necessity, searching the thrift stores for the raw materials of new fashions, seeking out cheap rental space where new clubs can be invented, scratching out brand-new magazines. Like *Scratch*.

"I used to write for Ruben," Iris reminisces. "He would pick me up from work at 4:00 P.M. Fridays. He would have a typewriter, paper, white-out, pictures, everything we needed in a junk box. We would usually go to an apartment house where Violet lived. She was a good friend of mine. People would say, 'Iris and Violet, the two flowers of Hollywood.' Once we got there, we would have only a few hours to write the issue. We would write until 1:00 A.M. or later. Ruben would go to the market and buy sweets for us."

Ruben gave them cookies in lieu of any pay.

Iris did stories on bands like the Talking Heads. And Tupolo Chain Sex, whose leader, Limey Dave, is another of her ex-boyfriends.

"I even interviewed Pleasant Gehman—it was one of my best interviews and I never had to leave the house. And we had this column called 'Scratch Personals,' like: 'Selling used underwear owned by El Duce. Best offer.' "

Then Iris got caught up in some internecine *Scratch* literary battle. No pond is too small for a feud between the frogs. So Iris quit this pond—just as Mad Marc Rude was swimming toward it.

Mad Marc Rude was the new artist in town. He had gotten to know *Scratch*'s Ruben Blue at the clubs, and he had decided he wanted to contribute to Blue's magazine as a way of introducing himself to underground Hollywood. Last February, Marc saw Ruben walking on the other side of the street and yelled across at him: "Hey, Ruben, I want to do the Valentine cover!"

"Sure," Ruben called back.

Marc says it was important to him to do that particular cover because he is "a hopeless romantic." The cover this hopeless romantic produced depicted a man who had just pulled his heart out of his chest and was holding it in his hands. Be my bloody valentine. The artist explains: "That's how I wanted to portray giving my heart to you."

He finished the picture in two days, signed it Mad Marc Rude, and called Ruben and told him to come pick it up. Soon Marc was doing covers fairly regularly for *Scratch*.

The magazine almost brought Marc and Iris together.

After they met at Al's Bar, Marc called Iris again and again at Disgraceland. She was never in. He always left a message: Marc called. But Iris never called Marc back because she had another boyfriend with the same name, one with whom she was trying to break up, and she thought the calls were coming from him.

While Marc was wondering why Iris never returned his calls, she was actually plotting a second meeting with him. She had heard that

Mad Marc Rude had been helping Ruben Blue put on *Scratch* fashion shows at the various clubs. The next was to be held at the Lingerie, which was just down the block from Disgraceland. On the afternoon before the show, Iris walked over to Lingerie because she thought Marc might be there making last-minute preparations.

"He wasn't," Iris remembers, "but they asked me to emcee the show. The only reason I said yes was because I thought he would be there. Only he didn't show up."

"I was sick of doing fashion shows," Marc explains. "I had done one a couple of days before. So that night I didn't happen to go."

The following week, there was an advance showing of an underground movie called *DuBeato* at the Lingerie. A girl asked Marc to go with her and he accepted. Iris and her roommate Pleasant also planned to go, but got a late start and missed the movie. They decided to walk over to Lingerie anyway.

As they were strolling down Sunset, Iris told Pleasant: "I really like that Marc Rude, but damn that Moussa, I'm sure she's been badmouthing me, and now he'll never call."

Then Iris swept into the Lingerie and saw Mad Marc Rude on the other side of the room.

"I told Pleasant I would be right back," Iris recalls. "I ran up to him. It was really exciting."

"Iris swooped down on me," Marc remembers. "I felt this burst of energy. I was really glad to see her. I was overtaken by incredible feelings and desires. There was no one else in the club as far as I was concerned."

Marc told his Queen of Clubs that he had been calling her all week.

Iris explained that she thought the calls were from the other Marc, who had been giving her trouble.

Marc said they should go to her place.

She said, no, she couldn't.

After such a warm welcome, Marc was surprised.

"I had brought other people to Disgraceland," Iris explains, "and didn't hear from them again."

Then she should come over to his place.

No, she couldn't do that either.

"I had cramps."

And so another meeting began well and ended inconclusively. Marc went home with the girl who had brought him.

"Two days later, I was lying in bed," Iris remembers. "A drunk transvestite jumped on me. 'Get off!' I told him and pushed him to the floor."

Then the phone rang. It was an underground regular named Donnie Popejoy calling from the Cathay de Grande.

"How you doing, partner?" Donnie asked. "Anyone there?"

"No," Iris said.

"Maybe I'll stop by on my way home from the Laugh-ay," he said, using his pet name for the Cathay. "See you."

On his way to the door, Donnie bumped into Mad Marc.

"There's a party at Disgraceland," Donnie said.

"Is Iris going to be there?" Marc asked.

"I just talked to her."

"Let's go."

Donnie and Marc conned Ruben Blue into driving them over to Disgraceland, telling him he was missing a really big party.

"I heard footsteps on the porch," Iris remembers. "I heard a knock. I thought, I don't have to open the door. Thought, Should I or shouldn't I? Thought, It might be somebody important.

"I opened the door and there was Marc. I couldn't belive it. I was so glad to see him. It was like my savior, my hero, was finally here. We hugged."

Welcome to Disgraceland, Mad Marc Rude. He liked a lot of what he saw. The pictures of Elvis taped up everywhere. The pictures of Marilyn. Of James Dean. Of Brando in *The Wild Ones*. Of John Lydon of the Sex Pistols.

Of Jayne Mansfield. Pleasant has a Jayne Mansfield fetish. She rented this particular house because it is owned by Jayne Mansfield's former husband. She liked knowing that her landlord had been to bed with her heroine.

Marc was even amused by a wall known as the "art gallery," which contained an explicit poster advertising "New Porn Stars Angel and Karen in a Hot Lesbian Movie," a poster for Tupolo Chain Sex featuring a picture of Ronald Reagan and Nancy Reagan and Vicky Morgan having an orgy, a Tampax box, and a photograph of breasts wearing glasses, among other artifacts.

But even Mad Marc was appalled by one sight. On one wall, "Mr. T" was spelled out in huge letters made out of Kotex pads. Pleasant has a Mr. T fetish, too. She and the Screaming Sirens sing a song that goes:

> *Mr. T. be hot, Mr. T be wild,*
> *I want to have Mr. T's child.*

Marc did not mind Mr. T, but he did mind all that Kotex stuck to the wall.

"That's got to go," he said.

Then he suggested that they do likewise.

"Please come home with me," Marc begged Iris. "I want to be alone with you."

Almost before he got the words out, Iris had her coat on. A happy Marc woke up Ruben and told him it was time to go. On the way, they bought a bottle of Gallo wine.

Marc lives in an elegant horseshoe-shaped apartment house on Western Avenue. Its interior courtyard is protected by an iron grating, which somehow gives it the look of a lady behind a black net veil. The place is like an artists' coop. Marc's next-door neighbor used to work with Andy Warhol. Another neighbor is a tattoo artist. Another is one of the Tupolo Chain Sex musicians. Another is in a band called the Hollywood Sympathy Orchestra, which plays on rooftops downtown. On the back door of the complex, someone has scrawled a sign: THE MAGIC BUILDING.

Iris was as unprepared for Marc's apartment as he had been for Disgraceland. A complete human skeleton hung from the living room wall. And this collection of bones was handcuffed so it wouldn't get away.

"I traded a bass amplifier for it," Marc explained. "Skeletons are a lot harder to get than amplifiers."

Marc and Iris drank the Gallo and played records and talked. He tried to tell her who he was and where he came from. He told her about moving up to Hollywood only a few months back from a city best known for its zoo.

Down in San Diego, Marc had been confused and casting about for an identity when he saw a photograph in *Rolling Stone* of a Sex Pistol wearing a skull earring.

"A picture of an earring set me free," Mark said. "It was the call of the wild."

Soon Marc was helping to put on what he calls "hall shows," which meant renting a hall, like, say, an Elks Club Lodge, and booking bands, and putting on a show. The Elks Club Lodge was the modern equivalent of the barn in all those old movies.

"The bands were your roommates. There was no rock-star elitism."

A natural extension of putting on a show seemed to be putting on a club. So Marc decided to try that, too. He helped start an underground nightclub in San Diego called the Reptile House. It was "like the Fetish."

And he helped start several magazines. So-called "fanzines" printed on Xerox machines. One was called *Rude Situations,* another *My Way,* another *Fist and Flesh.* None lasted for more than three numbers. For the one and only issue of *Rude Situations,* he interviewed a band called the Zeros.

Marc also managed a band originally called the Neutrons. Then called the Battalion of Saints—but nicknamed the Bats. He helped them press their own record at a cost of about $2,000. And he drew their album cover.

Marc showed the cover to Iris. It was a version of the injured fife and drummer of the Revolutinary War but transformed into marching skeletons. He put the record on the stereo and played her a strange serenade that went:

> *The Hillside Strangler . . .*
> *Drove the streets looking for girls*
> *That he and his cousin Bono*
> *Could rape and kill . . .*
> *I wanta make you scream!*

Another song on the album included the following chorus:

> *Killers now are heroes*
> *Killers now are heroes*
> *Modern-day heroes*
> *Killers now are heroes.*

Down in San Diego, Mad Marc Rude had come close to making his life and life-style from scratch, from zero, in the best tradition of the Zero Generation. A generation whose motto he states as follows: "Put on your own shows. Press your own records. Draw your own labels. Start your own magazine. Make your own fashion. Create your own visual look. Create your own everything. You don't have to be a rich entrepreneur to open a club; all you need is an idea. It's a do-it-yourself-scene."

"Would you like to go to bed now?" Marc asked the Queen of Clubs at four-thirty in the morning.

"Sure, let's go," Iris said. "I'm ready."

She was ready for bed but not for the bedroom. For it contained Marc's collection of horrors: a human skull, a human heart in formaldehyde, three cow skulls, a dog skull, a coyote skull, a goat skull, a tarantula, and other macabre exhibits, all arranged on a low table that looked like a makeshift altar. But Iris, who does not like bones, nevertheless got bravely into bed.

"We made love for the first time," Mark remembers. "I kept telling her I loved her."

But she didn't say anything.

"So he grabbed my throat," Iris remembers, "and said, 'Say you love me back.' So I did."

The next night, Marc and Iris went to Lingerie to see the Red Hot Chili Peppers. It was their first real date. Ruben Blue took a picture of them and put it in *Scratch*.

Unfortunately, Iris's ex-boyfriend, the other Marc, saw the picture.

All was not well in the underground. Marc and Iris were finally getting together, but Merrill and Modi were beginning to have problems.

"I couldn't really understand people who had one-night stands," Modi says. "Then I met Merrill . . ."

"The king of one-night stands in my heyday," Merrill finishes the thought for her. "But I was with Modi and no one else for about a year. Which was weird for me. There's a lot of promiscuity in this scene. People are always throwing it at your face. But what was funny was *you* slept with someone else first."

"Actually I *was* first," Modi admits.

"I was proud of myself that I could be with one girl for so long. Then she came home one night and said she had slept with another guy. I had always assumed it would be the other way around and it would be no big deal. But it was a big deal. I was bummed."

"When it happened, I was so excited. It was like I had just opened a Christmas present. I wanted to tell my best friend, Merrill, all about it. Then I thought, Uh-oh."

And yet Modi told Merrill anyway. Told him about meeting this other guy. Told him about making love to him. And told him about going over to the Zero One afterward, which had always been *their* place.

"I told Merrill to go out and get laid. 'I did, you can, too.' That night, he went out and found someone. So did I. We had this kind of contest."

Again Modi won the contest—striking first. She met her Second

Other Guy at a bar called the Frolic Room across the street from the Zero One. She had gone there to wait for the Zero One to open, but she found someone long before the speakeasy unlocked its doors. And off they went into the Hollywood night to turn a bedroom into a private after-hours club. His place.

Merrill did not even get into the game until after the Zero One opened for business. But when it did, he soon found someone, too, the Other Girl, and then they, too, rushed off into the night. Her place.

When Merrill and Modi met the next day, they both confessed.

Modi asked where the Other Girl lived.

Merrill said on Cherokee.

What address?

He reeled off a long number

What floor?

He said a short number.

"I was down the hall," Modi said.

In America's second largest city, Merrill and Modi had been unfaithful to one another on the same night on the same street in the same building on the same floor.

"It hurt," Modi says. "It hurt obviously. But it's the eighties and I'm not going to let it cause the downfall of the longest relationship in my life."

Mad Marc and his roommate Andy went to Mexico with three girls for the weekend. The trip had been planned before Marc and Iris had gotten together. Marc had intended to sleep with one of his three female traveling companions—but he ended up not doing so.

He got in trouble anyway.

On their way back home, the group stopped in Tijuana. While the girls went shopping, Marc and Andy decided to watch the topless dancers at the Bambi Club. Marc noticed a wallet under his chair. He thought it was his and picked it up. But it wasn't. It was empty except for a navy ID card. As he was leaving, Marc tossed the wallet to the bartender. Outside on the street, he saw the bartender and a policeman running after him.

Marc was soon sharing a cell, which measured six by eleven feet, with twenty other prisoners. They were given a gallon of water a day to share among them. Each inmate had to buy his own food. Marc lived on scraps of tacos.

"It was horrible," he remembers. "But I kept thinking about Iris. I realized how much I loved her."

But he was afraid he might not see her for a long, long time, since he seemed to be lost in the labyrinthine Mexican prison system.

After three days in jail, Marc was rescued by his roommate Andy, who had sold his car to raise the money to unlock the doors. As soon as he got home, the first thing Marc did was call Iris.

"Marc who?" asked the Queen of Clubs, who had no idea that he had been in jail. She was feeling seduced and abandoned. She had taken his picture off the wall. "What do you want?"

Merrill was in trouble, too. He had an argument with Modi and she decided to leave him. When he left for work at the Zero One, she wrote a note and put it on the bureau: "I am running away and you can't find me."

But Merrill didn't even find the note, because he got arrested. He was taking a break in front of the Zero One when he saw two men drive up in a Mustang, get out, and start beating up people who were coming out of the club. They grabbed a girl, threw her to the ground, and cursed her. Merrill ran over and picked her up. The bullies called him names.

Then one of them pulled a gun and pointed it at a kid. Merrill tried to come to the kid's aid by throwing a bottle, but his aim was poor and he ended up hitting the kid he was trying to rescue. Merrill did accomplish what he set out to though: The gun stopped pointing at the kid. It found a new and more inviting target: Merrill. The self-styled New Wave detective found himself looking down a scary barrel that ended in a cold metal zero.

Suddenly a black-and-white police cruiser pulled up. Merrill ran over to report that a couple of thugs were beating everyone up. But the thugs turned out to be undercover cops. Merrill soon found himself under arrest. He was charged with assault with a deadly weapon (the bottle) and intent to do bodily harm to a police officer (the thug).

Merrill called Modi from the police station, but she wasn't there because she had left him, although he didn't know it yet. He was furious. Why wasn't she home? Where could she be at this time of night? He needed her and she was out doing who knew what.

A few hours later, Modi woke up at a friend's house. Then she started trying to find Merrill—just as he had been trying to find her—and with the same success. And she began to ask the same questions he had been asking: Why wasn't he home? Where was he? What was he doing?

She called a friend and asked, "Where's Merrill?"

"He got arrested," the friend told her.

So Modi got busy and arranged to have Merrill bailed out of jail. She could afford to do so because she had a pretty good job now working as a production assistant for a small movie company. And Merrill had a pretty good job, too, serving as an assistant to a much sought after photographer. Modi and Merrill are young, upwardly mobile, New Wave, post-punk zeros. All of which did not keep Merrill from ending up behind bars, or keep Modi from winding up in a bail-bondsman's shabby office.

Unfortunately, Modi did not tell Merrill that she had bought his freedom for him. And he assumed that someone else, some real friend, had done it.

A few days later, Merrill was talking on the telephone to someone named Spot. Merrill told Spot how thankful he was to this real friend, who had bailed him out.

"Fuck no!" yelled Modi. "I got you out."

And she stormed out of their apartment. He followed her. Outside the wind was actually howling. Soon they were screaming at each other in the middle of the street.

"How could you be so insensitive!" she shouted.

"You weren't there when I needed you!" he yelled.

They both started crying. Then they fell into each other's arms and started laughing. They went back in the apartment and made up.

Marc explained that he had not called earlier because he had been in a Mexican jail. Iris felt "really bad for being mad." She wanted to make it up to him somehow.

"That was when it really started," Iris says. "It's been a roller-coaster ride ever since."

Unfortunately, they weren't alone on the roller coaster. Iris's ex-boyfriend, the Other Marc, was also along for the ride. Seeing Marc and Iris's photograph in *Scratch*, he rushed over to Disgraceland and tore the door off its hinges. He screamed at Iris, hit her in the face, bloodied her nose, and threw her to the floor. And then he ordered her to get her remaining belongings out of his place right away if she valued them at all.

Iris pushed a borrowed shopping cart over to the Other Marc's apartment, where she found many of her things thrown into the hall. She gathered up makeup, hats, records, shoes, vintage clothing, radios. Crying, she pushed her shopping cart along Hollywood Boulevard back to Disgraceland, feeling like "a modern bag lady."

When she arrived at Disgraceland, Iris found Her Marc waiting for her. He wanted to know what had happened to her. She told him but begged him not to do anything about it. They made love.

The Other Marc barged back into Disgraceland. Mad Marc Rude told him that Iris was out of his life now. Leave her alone. With all those tattoos, he looked like someone to be listened to. Then Mad Marc borrowed a truck and went and got the rest of Iris's possessions out of his rival's apartment.

A few days later, the Other Marc pushed a note under the crippled front door at Disgraceland:

> Dear Iris,
>   I love you, I love you, I love you, I like you, I hate you, I hate you. You're scum. Your friends are scum.

"When the Zero One got busted," says Merrill, "it was like the speakeasies of the thirties."

The first time the police raided the Zero One, they just marched in the front door and scrambled up the steps into the upstairs party rooms. They wore helmets and had their visors down. The spirit of Eliot Ness seemed to be leading them. The cops handcuffed the bartender and the bouncer. The charge was violating the liquor laws. Yes, the Untouchables seemed to be back in business. The men behind the ominous visors told everyone else to clear out, and suddenly dozens of little zeros came rolling out into Hollywood Boulevard.

About a fortnight later, just before the XXIII Olympiad got under way in Los Angeles, the spirit of Eliot Ness was once again on the move. Evidently the city fathers wanted the Zero One closed before the Games opened. The speakeasy only had a few minutes' warning.

Derf Scratch, who used to play with a band called Fear, came in and said eight police cars were lined up a block away on Sunset. Merrill, who was working the door that night, looked around and thought he spotted several undercover cops among the customers.

Then a girl named Dinosaur Woman yelled, "They're here!"

Two dozen policemen in riot gear pushed past Merrill and charged up the two flights of stairs.

Simultaneously, up on the roof, there arose such a clatter, it sounded like Santa Claus in storm-trooper boots. The cops had used firemen's extension ladders to climb up on top of the building. Soon the law was coming through the ceiling of the club.

It was raining cops.

"Drop that beer!" one trooper ordered.

When the customer did not obey fast enough, the cop smashed the beer bottle out of his hand with a billy club.

"I don't work here," the club bouncer lied to a policeman. "I work at the Lingerie."

"I'll bet you *wear* lingerie, you maggot," the cop told the bouncer.

In the confusion, Merrill somehow made his way out into Hollywood Boulevard. Lifting his eyes, he saw Zero One employees up on the roof with their hands over their heads. Then the New Wave detective dissolved into the night.

The Big Raid closed the Zero One. It will surely reopen again, and soon. But in the meantime, the king is dead—temporarily dead—long live the new king. Long live the Fetish, new King of the Clubs. The new Black Zero. The Bat-Black O.

As if to symbolize the transference of the Zero's mantle, that girl with the wonderful name, Tequila Mockingbird, of the original Zero Zero Club, has gone to work at the Fetish Club as a cocktail waitress.

One night about midnight, I drove toward the Fetish Club only to find my way barred by a police car parked diagonally across the street. I pulled over and got out to see what was wrong. Police were herding black-clad Zeros over the pavement, pushing some, hitting a few. One young man came up to me and showed me a bruise on his cheek. He said a cop had hit him in the face.

At first, I thought the police were busting the Fetish, but they weren't. They were busting the street. Busting the overflow crowd that regularly mills about the Fetish on Friday nights. Police sirens were wailing in the night like an extension of the doomsrock inside the club.

Inside the Fetish, in a dark corner, the zebra of the Zero Generation was kissing a black spider. If he was fortunate, and she generous, perhaps she would take him home to her bedroom, which is decorated with a coffin and a tombstone. Like so many in her generation, she seems to be in love with death, the ultimate zero.

Momentarily struggling free from the spider, the beautiful zebra, her painted breasts galloping, ran over and kissed a monk. The animal woman and the man of religion seemed to make a nice couple. He wore a black robe and was dripping silver crosses.

"I'm sorry about my paint coming off on you," apologized the zebra.

"That's all right," said Brother Joseph, founder of the Fetish, "I'm wearing black-and-white makeup anyway."

Then the zebra returned to the spider's web and the monk went back to his duties as disc jockey.

Brother Joseph spun his favorite gloomy classics. Records by the Cramps. And the Banchees. And Birthday Party. And T. Rex, which is short for Tyrannosaurus Rex. And the Christian Death Band, which is "one of the most requested at the Fetish." And of course Bauhaus doing "Bella Lagosi Is Dead"—the all-time most requested.

Of course, the evening wouldn't be complete without some knock-out nuclear numbers. Songs about reducing our living globe to a dead zero. Like Fishbone playing "Pink Vapor Stew," with its refrain that goes: "Let's party at ground zero." Which could be the motto of the Zero Generation.

"The bomb creates a desperation," says Iris. "Fuck my future. I want to have fun. I don't want to plan my future if I'm not going to live it."

"Going to clubs is like having bomb drills when we were kids in school," Marc says. "They were the best times. Hiding under desks. Or running out of class. A good excuse to be disruptive. We have fun to pretend it doesn't exist."

"The realization that nuclear war could really happen now," says Modi, "happened for me with the Diablo Canyon nuclear plant. I remember my father and I were driving past the Diablo Canyon. I ducked in the car, thinking it would help me stop getting nuclear radiation. When I got up, I realized it wasn't going to help."

"But you can't get a pessimistic view," says Merrill, who once played in a band called Overkill. "You have to say, Okay, we are going to be killed by a nuclear bomb. Ha! Ha! Ha!"

You bounce and gyrate and kick up your heels in the Modern-day Doomsrock Gloomsrock Dance of Nuclear Death.

"In the twelfth century, the cathedrals were all decorated with bones," says Dave Grave. "Now antinuke protestors paint themselves like skeletons. It's their chance to spit on death, spit in death's eye. These are the eighties and we were all raised in fear. When I was fourteen I prayed to thermonuclear warheads; you never see them but they're always there."

The Zero Generation feels that it is standing at gound zero counting down to zero.

Both Mad Marc Rude and the Queen of Clubs have already picked ou the clothes they plan to wear when the world blows up. Her "bomb dress," as she calls it, is a pink party dress with spangles and sparkles. (She used to have a black "bomb dress," but the cleaners lost it.) Marc plans to wear his favorite black chaps.

"I just hope I have enough time to dress up," says Marc, "and have my lady with me."

But Marc's chances of having Iris with him don't look good at the moment. Perhaps no Jack could hold the Queen of Clubs for long. Shortly after our talk about doomsday, the couple blew up even before the world did. Maybe *they* blew up in part because *she* feels she must live fast before the final explosion. She says the threat of nuclear destruction makes it hard to think about having long-term relationships, like a husband or children. So in a sense Marc and Iris may be casualties of the bomb.

Now the Queen of Clubs is putting her energy into looking for space to start her own club. And Marc feels as if his Valentine cover has come true, as if his heart has been ripped out and handed to him. Beware what you draw.

But Merrill and Modi continue to be a durable couple in this not very durable world, much to the delight and surprise of them both.

"That any relationship lasts is just amazing to me," says Merrill. "Because none do. They're here today and gone tomorrow, like the clubs."

"Off with her head!" the Queen of Clubs shouted at the top of her voice.

It was an order very much in the spirit of the Fetish.

"Who cares for you?" said Alice to the paper soldiers. "You're nothing but a pack of cards."

Actually only half a pack. The dark cards. The bright red hearts and diamonds never came here. They hung out at dressy places like Club Soda or the Crush. The spades and clubs loved the Fetish.

No sooner had Alice uttered her challenge than the black pack rose up into a great black mushroom-shaped cloud.

Alice kept expecting her sister to say, "Wake up, Alice dear," but the words never came.

◆   ◆   ◆

After this article appeared, Iris called me up. She liked the story. I ran into Mad Marc at one of the clubs. He said he liked it too. Then Modi and Merrill called and also liked it. I had never had such a positive reaction from the subjects of one of my stories. I was pleased but also a little disturbed. I wondered if my writing was losing its bite.

"I guess I've mellowed," I told friends. "I'm probably washed up as a journalist."

LIFE IS A HAMBURGER

．　◆　◆

When *Rolling Stone* asked me to write about junk food, I supposed there was no way to hitch this subject to a love story. I began calling places like McDonald's and Burger King and Wendy's to ask if there were any new developments in mass-market food. And I started hearing about couples getting married in their favorite fast-food restaurants.

◆　◆　◆

Rolling Stone, December 1983

The bride wore a white gown and a rose tattoo. She was fourteen. The groom wore a pink-trimmed shirt and a white tuxedo. He was eighteen. The wedding was held at Burger King.

While the guests were arriving, Debby Beard, the bride, passed the time with her bridesmaids in the crowded women's room. Two of her attendants were arrayed in pink, while the third wore lavender. Meanwhile, the groom stood by in the men's room with his groomsmen. The wedding party was stranded in the restrooms because there was no other place to wait in the tiny restaurant.

A groomsman named Roger tried to flush the toilet, but it wouldn't work. So he delivered a kick and broke a pipe. Suddenly, it seemed to be raining. Someone finally stopped the flood, but not before the groom and all his groomsmen got wet. Paper towels were used to wipe the water off all the white tuxedos and pink-and-lavender ruffles.

Finally, everyone filed out of the restrooms. The bride walked solemnly to her place in front of the counter. The minister could see Whopper and Whaler and french-fry prices over the bride's and groom's shoulders as they repeated their vows.

Debby and Rudy, junk-food bride and groom. Theirs is a story that tells us something about a new American generation that has grown up believing in Whoppers of all sorts.

Once upon a time, couples used to get married in churches. Then they started getting married in parks. But today, more and more people are getting married in junk-food saloons like Burger King and McDonald's. Gothic arches have been replaced by golden arches. And a whole new generation has grown up with a whole new iconography.

The Junk Generation.

Junk food was born in the suburbs. The rise of the Junk Generation represents the victory of the suburbs. The suburbs have conquered America. And like any conquering army, suburbia's minions have built outposts all over its conquered territories: Fort McDonalds, Fort Burger King, Fort Wendy's, Fort Roy Rogers, Fort Pizza Hut . . .

All the junk-food joints have reduced us to a national suburb. And in this Great American Suburb, the paramount value is mass-produced conformity—a conformity that is reflected not only in the sameness of the hamburgers we eat but also in the conventionality of the clothes we wear and even the mediocrity of our dreams.

The evidence is all over our newsstands. On the cover of its fall fashion issue, *Esquire* magazine celebrated "The Return to Elegant Dressing." Which, of course, means a return to a conventional dress code. A lot of this new "elegance" is being mass-produced in much the same way as Chicken McNuggets. *Ad Week* noted that the Halston III collection has recently gone on sale at a mass-market chain store and commented: "There is something disarming—perhaps eerie—about manufacturing enough puff-sleeve suits and polyester blouses to provide for an army of low-budget Nancy Reagans." The junk-journalism newspaper *USA Today* recently gave us the ultimate conformity-on-campus headline: *"Frats Are Back."* Pollster and visionary Daniel Yankelovich says we are in a period of "psychic devaluation," in which we no longer dream big dreams. Rather, we dream low-rise suburban dreams. Junk dreams.

The first McDonald's opened on April 15, 1955, in a suburb of Chicago named Des Plaines, now known as Burger Bethlehem. Hamburgers were 15 cents and shakes were 20. McDonald's has since grown into the world's largest restaurant chain, taking in $7.8 billion last year. And the fast-food industry it helped to start has more than tripled in size in the past ten years, having become a $31 billion phenomenon by 1982—a fat lady in the American economy.

"McDonald's is twenty-eight years old," says Stephanie Skurdy, a spokesperson for the hamburger giant. "A lot of us have grown up with McDonald's."

Indeed. The median age in the country is now thirty, which means that junk food and the average American are almost the same age. McDonald's is a baby-boom baby who grew up, like many other members of its generation, in the suburbs.

Of course, McDonald's and the other junk-food factories have left their imprint on the suburbs as they've grown. They reflect and reinforce suburban uniformity. Houses in suburban subdivisions tend to look similar, and what you find in them tends to be as alike as what you find inside the junk-food joints. Mom and Dad and Sister and Brother seem as mass-produced as Big Macs.

As the junk-food parlors spread, they tended to homogenize all suburbia. A southern suburb with a McDonald's and a Burger King and a Pizza Hut looked like a northern or western suburb with a McDonald's and a Burger King and a Pizza Hut. Soon, all the suburbs were as alike as Whoppers.

About ten years ago, the junk-food joints started spreading from the suburbs into the inner cities and small towns. Soon, downtown Chicago began to look like downtown Dallas, which began to look like downtown Los Angeles.

Even in the small towns, Route 1 began to look like Route 2 or Route 3. And they all began to look like the intersection of Routes 96 and 190, which is in the middle of Jasper, Texas. This particular crossroads would seem to set some small-town record for the most junk-food saloons in one location. It boasts a McDonald's, a Burger King, a Top Burger (with a statue of a bull), a Dairy Queen, a Kentucky Fried Chicken, a Farmer Brown's Fried Chicken, a Pizza Hut, a Pizza Inn, a Snow Cone stand, and a place called Sonic Happy Eating, which specializes in chili dogs.

Yet Jasper is a town of only 6,959 people. Among them are Rudy Lane and Debby Beard, our junk-food bride and groom.

◆

When the bride left the women's room for her short walk to the Burger King counter, she tripped and almost fell on top of her mother. Her mom happens to be the manager of the Pizza Hut down the street. The groom happens to work at the nearby Pizza Inn as a delivery boy, though he hopes to be promoted to cook soon. On her wedding day, the bride herself was a manager-trainee at Burger King. Truly a fast-food family.

The bride was born on December 27, 1967, in Port Arthur, Texas. Debby was one of six children—one boy, five girls.

When she was ten, Debby moved with her family to Charlotte, North Carolina, where her life started to fall apart, the way Whoppers often do after the first few bites. She was just eleven when her boy-friend, a nineteen-year-old drifter named Bubba, gave her a home-made tattoo, using dye and a needle wrapped with thread.

"It hurt," she remembers. "It hurt for two or three weeks."

Other things hurt, too. Debby was unhappy at home because of "family problems." She was unhappy at school, too, because the kids made fun of her tattoo.

While the tattoo was still sore, the eleven-year-old schoolgirl and her nineteen-year-old boyfriend hit the road. They hitchhiked to Flor-ida, stayed about a week, then headed west. In Houston, Debby and Bubba went to work in a Pizza Hut.

"I grew up faster than I should have," says the Burger King bride.

"That's what you call no childhood," says her short-order groom.

Such talk emphasizes other characteristics of the Junk Genera-tion—characteristics both reflected and shaped by America's junk-food obsession. Namely, a love of speed, coupled with a tendency to throw away anything that might slow us down. We eat fast food and throw away the disposable paper containers. We guzzle soft drinks and throw away the nonreturnable, disposable bottles. We hurriedly cook TV din-ners and throw away the disposable foil trays. And we grow up fast, turning childhood into something disposable, too.

Disposable childhood.

Disposable children.

Brooke Shields could be the poster child of this phenomenon.

The television series "St. Elsewhere" once tried medically to link junk food with the disposable-childhood syndrome. A doctor on the show lamented that all those burgers were just brimming with estrogen because they were made from cattle that had been given large doses of the hormone to make them grow quickly. When teen-age girls ate these burgers, so the argument went, they absorbed all this excess estrogen, which made *them* grow faster. They turned from little girls into women sooner than they should have.

Still, the primary fault is probably not in our burgers but in ourselves. We seem to want everything fast and disposable. Our lovers. Our marriages. Our families.

Debby's parents had separated shortly before she ran away from home.

Debby and Bubba's breakup was bizarre. When she threatened to leave him, he cut his wrists with a razor blade. He said he didn't want to live without her. He appeared to be throwing himself away—which many members of the Junk Generation seem compelled to do. The National Institute of Mental Health estimates that adolescent and young-adult suicides have tripled in the last twenty years.

"Kids today feel more pressure to grow up quickly," says Dr. Susan Blumenthal, a psychiatrist with the institute. "There is more nuclear-family disruption. Young people feel they can only be failures. When they commit suicide, they're saying: 'I'll show them!' "

She pauses.

"The secret to a generation is in their music. The music this generation listens to tells them there's no future, no hope."

Punk junk.

All sorts of hopeless lyrics come to mind. Like the band White Cross singing: "How much more can I take/Before I make my last mistake?"

Those who don't destroy themselves with guns (the most popular means) or razor blades often manage to achieve the same results with needles. They give an additional meaning to the words Junk Generation.

A survey of drug-related deaths in America's twenty-six largest metropolitan areas by the National Institute on Drug Abuse indicates a lethal trend. There were 3,519 drug deaths in 1978, 3,626 in 1979, 3,825 in 1980, and 3,961 in 1981. All of them suicides of a sort.

Disposable life.

Disposable self.

Debby stayed with Bubba and patched up his wounds. But she was still unhappy and soon began to think of leaving again. He cut himself again. Disposable lifeblood.

Again, she stayed. But eventually she couldn't take it any longer. "If you want to kill yourself," Debby said, "go ahead."

She walked out of his life—which he failed to throw away, when put to the test.

When she was thirteen, Debby flew home to North Carolina, where she was reunited with her mother and sisters and brother. Before long, she was on her way back to Texas—but with her family this time. They settled in Jasper, the little town with the big appetite for junk food, and moved into a mobile home.

Debby had only been in town a few weeks when she met Rudy. Her brother worked at the Pizza Hut. Debby's future husband liked to eat there. The two boys became friends. Almost every evening, Debby's brother and Rudy would arm wrestle to see who would pay for dinner—always a pizza. One evening, Debby's brother asked his buddy if he would like a date with his sister. Well, yes, maybe he would.

So Debby's brother arranged the blind date. Rudy took off the suit he was wearing (he had just come from singing at a high school dance) and put on red cords and a red shirt.

Rudy picked up Debby, and they went for a drive in his 1975 Oldsmobile Starfire.

The next day, Debby just happened to drop by the Pizza Hut where she found Rudy playing a junk videogame called Phoenix. This fast game, a kind of junk sport, seemed right at home in an atmosphere of fast food. After all, it was sport without exercise, just as junk food is calories without nutrition.

Rudy only scored about 30,000 points that afternoon because he had not discovered the secret that would later allow him to score 200,000 at will.

This second meeting between the future bride and groom did not go well. Rudy paid more attention to Phoenix then he did to Debby. She left the Pizza Hut in a bad mood.

Although still jealous of the machine, Debby decided to call Rudy that night. She hinted that she wanted to see him. He asked if she would come to a band practice. He was a member of a small band that performed rock 'n' roll versions of traditional gospel hymns. They were scheduled to give a concert at the local high school in a few days.

Debby went to the practice, which was held in a shed behind a minister's house. It had a couch and a woodburning stove and a cozy feeling. It was like the headquarters of a kids' club. Which is another symptom of this generation: clubbiness.

Tom Wolfe named the seventies the Me Decade. But now we are into the eighties: The Group Decade. The Club Decade. The Us Decade.

Chicken McNuggets could be seen as a metaphor for the era. When introduced in 1981—a new product for a new decade—they came in packs of six. But they proved so popular as a group food that packs of nine and twenty McNuggets were introduced. You can eat a Big Mac alone. But McNuggets run in packs and so do the people who eat them.

The problem with the Us Decade is that the people tend to be as alike as Chicken McNuggets.

Madison Avenue has recognized the Us Decade. During the Me

Decade, the McDonald's ads sang, "You deserve a break today." Be good to yourself. Give yourself a break. But in 1981, evidently sensing a change in the country, McDonald's switched advertising agencies and slogans. The ads started singing, "Together, McDonald's and you." Big Mac began advertising itself as the "leader of the pack."

Perhaps what we have here is a search for community in a transitory society. Since we are a nation on the move (the massive migration from the North to the Sun Belt, for example), we miss the feeling of community. So we stop at McDonald's and feel at home because the one here is just like the one where we grew up.

Rudy felt a sense of community when he was rehearsing with his buddies in the shed out behind the preacher's house. But Debby didn't feel at home or at ease. The gospel singers, who by and large believe in that old-time religion, didn't like her tattoo.

"They were snobbing me," Debby says.

After practice, Debby and Rudy went for another ride. She was nervous because she intended to make a confession. She knew it would be difficult. Finally Debby told Rudy that she had something to tell him—but she was afraid he would get mad.

He said he wouldn't.

She said he would.

He promised not to.

"I'm not nineteen like I said," she said. "I'm fourteen."

He got mad.

When Rudy's gospel-rock band gave its concert at the high school, Debby sat in the first row. Onstage, Rudy played bass guitar. The group performed a rock version of "Amazing Grace" and an even funkier "The Old Rugged Cross." Then they sang some original lyrics written by a member of the band: "If Jesus were a drug, I'd overdose on him . . ."

After the concert, the Jesus junkies and their friends retired to the Pizza Hut, where they overdosed on anchovies.

Soon, Debby and Rudy were also overdosing on junk TV in the afternoon. She introduced him to the soaps, and he quickly came to like them as much as she did.

"My favorite TV show is 'General Hospital,' " Rudy says.

"I like 'All My Children,' 'One Life to Live,' and 'General Hospital,' " Debby says. "We're soap-opera addicts."

Sometimes, the whole generation seems to be addicted. Of course, the soaps themselves are well aware of their new audience. All these addictive dramas have added young characters. One of the most unrealistic things about the kids on the soaps is that they never watch soaps.

All Jasper needs to be complete is a clubby place where you can eat junk while you watch your favorite daytime drama on a giant screen. There is only one such establishment in the country so far—in Mount Rainier, Maryland, a suburb of Washington, D.C.—but it has ambitions to spread. Its name is the Queenstown Soap Opera Restaurant, but people call it the Soap Saloon. The menu has headings like "Days of Our Soups" and "Guiding Lights" and "As the Pizza Turns." Debby and Rudy would love it.

Junk television and junk food are mass-produced in much the same way. Soap opera assembly lines turn out the equivalent of a full-length movie every two days. When the show is over, it is thrown away and forgotten like the debris of a fast-food meal. Soaps aren't rerun or syndicated. Junk drama is disposable.

Alongside the big screen, what the Soap Saloon needs, of course, is a paperback stand stocked with assembly-line Harlequin and Silhouette gothic romances. The junk-book business has grown almost as fast as the junk-food business. Harlequin used to be the only publisher of romances, but now there are a dozen competitors. Still, Harlequin has more than doubled its business over the past decade, skyrocketing from $90 million in sales in 1970 to $218 million in 1982.

The Soap Saloon could also use a newsstand so customers can read about their favorite soap stars in downscale junk journals like the *National Enquirer*, the *Star*, and the *New York Post*. Or upscale junk magazines like *People*. Or a junk newspaper like *USA Today*, which one reviewer described as "snappy, snazzy, and filled with short McNuggets of easily digested information."

The problem with junk drama, junk books, and junk journalism is that, intellectually, they are full of empty calories. They engage the mind the way junk food engages the body: without really nourishing.

When the Soap Saloon finally comes to Jasper, it's likely that a member of Debby's or Rudy's family will work there.

"The soaps are great," says Rudy. "They're like everyday life, more or less."

At least, they are something like Debby's and Rudy's lives. The couple could easily be written into a soap.

And then Rudy joined the navy. He seemed to be responding to jingo junk. It was as though he wanted to enlist in the cast of *An Officer and a Gentleman*—a movie that wouldn't have been a hit a few years ago, when a uniform meant not romance but Vietnam. Rudy was in tune with a new patriotism that has embraced the country. Many Americans are lining up at the local recruiting office. But many more are lining up in front of cash registers. They are consumer patriots.

A recent survey by an advertising agency found that "in product categories such as automobiles, televisions, wine, and clothing, a strong majority of people said they would be more likely to buy an American brand rather than a foreign brand."

Today, patriotism is as American as a Big Mac.

Leaving an upset Debby behind, Rudy headed for San Diego and basic training. But he lasted only a few weeks. He was in and out of the navy as if it were a fast-food stand. He developed back trouble and was given a medical discharge. When he knew he was coming home, Rudy called Debby.

"Wanna get married?" he asked, with a laugh.

He meant it as a kind of joke.

"Yes," she said.

By then, she was fourteen years old.

Like the proposal, the junk-food wedding began as a kind of joke. At work one day, Debby asked the owner of the Burger King to come to her wedding.

"I will," the boss said, "if you'll get married in your uniform."

"The next thing you know," said a co-worker, "you'll want to get married here."

The idea took hold. A few days later, Debby talked to Rudy on the phone.

"What would you think," she asked, "about getting married at Burger King?"

"Well, all right," he laughed.

"It's not a joke," she said.

When Rudy got home, he began to change his mind. He wanted to get married in church. After all, he was something of a Jesus junkie.

What finally won him over was hearing about another wedding on the radio. A couple up north someplace had gotten married in a K Mart.

Well, he thought to himself, if we got married in a Burger King, we would have something to tell our kids about.

A sign outside announced, in hand-drawn block letters: "Due to the exchange of wedding vows today at Burger King, we will be closed 2 to 4. Drive-thru is open!"

Inside, a waitress doubling as a bridesmaid rushed up and gave the groom a big hug. She got makeup on the shoulder of his white tuxedo and it wouldn't wipe off. Someone got some flour from behind the counter and sprinkled it on the stain. Then there was the flood in the men's room, and the flour got wet and turned to glue.

In her father's absence, the bride was given away by the owner of the Burger King.

Then the Reverend Sidney Jones, a southern Pentecostal minister, got down to business. Occasionally, he was interrupted by business of another sort being transacted at the drive-thru window.

"Rudy, do you take this woman, Debby . . ."

". . . I'll take a Whopper, please . . ."

". . . for better, for worse . . ."

". . . hold the pickles, hold the onions . . ."

". . . in sickness . . ."

". . . french fries . . ."

". . . and in health . . ."

". . . and I'll try one of them new pita salad things that's supposed to be good for you . . ."

". . . I now pronounce you . . ."

". . . a double-patty Whopper . . ."

The wedding was celebrated a little over a year ago. The birth of the couple's first child, a son, took place only a few weeks ago. This fast-food family believes in fast reproduction. The new father has just turned twenty-one. The new mother is sixteen.

The boss put up a sign that said: "The couple that got married at Burger King just had a little Whopper."

The other day, Debby and Rudy brought their son into Burger King to show him off. They set him down on the counter, and all the waiters and waitresses gathered around to have a look. Propped up next to the cash register, the baby looked like another order to go.

◆　　◆　　◆

As I was saying good-bye to Debbie and Rudy, I invited them to give me a call if they were ever in Washington. They said they probably wouldn't because they didn't like big cities. I asked what they disliked about them. They said people in big cities are in too much of a hurry. And they were married with a baby at the unhurried ages of twenty-one and sixteen. Life in small towns moves to such a slow beat.

After the article appeared, a San Francisco theater group wrote a play based on my story to be performed at a junk-food restaurant.

THE FANTASY
GENERATION GOES TO
THE MOVIES

. . .

I first saw *The Rocky Horror Picture Show* at the Tiffany Theater on Sunset Strip. I was working on the script of *Urban Cowboy* at the time and more or less living at the Sunset Marquis, which was half a block from the movie theater. At midnight on Friday and Saturday nights, I would walk up the hill and stand in line with all the transvestites, feeling a little underdressed without black fishnet stockings or stiletto heels.

When we went to Houston to film *Urban Cowboy*, I didn't see *Rocky Horror* for a while. Then I heard about the big birthday parties for the movie being planned around the country and decided to go to one in Miami. While *Urban Cowboy* took the weekend off, I flew to Florida to see *The Rocky Horror Picture Show*. When I got back to Houston, I did follow-up interviews from a phone in Gilley's saloon.

. . .

Unpublished, 1979

Micro Chip—as he shall be called—was sewing himself a new garter belt. Black. He needed it to hold up his fishnet stockings. Black, too. After a long, hard week doing computer programing for NASA, he was ready to kick up his high heels. After five days in sensible business clothes, he was anxious to array himself in glorious Transvestite Chic.

Not that he actually was a transvestite. Far from it. He was very much in heterosexual love with a college coed who shall be called Media Major because that is what she is. She was sewing, too, working on her own transvestite costume. She was making a black-and-red corset. Later on that evening, Micro Chip and Media Major would step out into the Miami night as a handsome Transvestite Chic couple.

While they worked on their costumes, their friends ran by in their underwear, boys in jockey shorts, girls in panties and bras. They were all getting ready to celebrate the third anniversary of a movie called *The Rocky Horror Picture Show*. There were celebrations going on in cities all over the country, including, of course, Miami. The Miami party—a birthday party for *Rocky*—would be held at a roller rink. With all the transvestites going around and around, the rink would be a giant blender in which male and female sexuality would be mixed up into some strange new brew.

As the boys and girls slipped into their transvestite drag, they looked like revelers getting ready for, say, Carnival in Rio de Janeiro. Down in Brazil, the sexual roles are so rigid, the men always expected to be so macho, that many love to escape from the burden of machismo by dressing up as women during Carnival. Farther north in America, we represent the other side of the cruzeiro, for our sex roles have lost much of their rigidity and are breaking down. Which can be a little confusing. So many of us are escaping from our modern sexual confusion into a sexual masquerade.

All cultures have always needed sexual escape hatches of one kind or another. But some cultures need them more than others. And ours seems to be in serious need right now. The feminists have told us that women should not be afraid to be more like men and men should not be afraid to be more like women. All of which sounds reasonable but disorienting. In the old days, little boys played with guns and little girls played with dolls to prepare themselves for old-fashioned gender roles. Now boys and girls play at being transvestites on Friday and Saturday nights to prepare themselves for today's new sex roles. For most, it's a game and it's fun.

Micro Chip and Media Major and their friends were getting dressed up at the home of a young *Rocky* convert who shall be called Business because that is her college major. It was actually Business's mother's house. And her mother sat right there watching the passing parade of fishnet and Fruit-of-the-loom. By now, Mom was used to it. She even seemed to be enjoying it. Finally, she started helping out, digging through closets, coming up with old stockings for the boys to wear.

Business herself was rummaging through the house, looking for something to make a corset out of. The problem of what to use was complicated by the size of her breasts. Most materials could not stand the strain.

At last, Business—perhaps she should be called Big Business—hit upon the idea of enclosing her breasts in a girdle. Black. She cut out the crotch and then wriggled into it as if it were a tube top. But even this stout garment had a disappointing tendency to give way and dump its burdens. So Big Business made shoulder straps out of transparent fishing leader to hold up her jerry-built corset. It looked as though this fishing line had hookéd a couple of Melvillian great white whales.

Yes, the fantasy generation was going to the movies. With no great cause to focus the Great American Imagination, this national asset has been defused into fantasies. An amazing myriad of fantasies. There was the disco fantasy that filled the discothèques. There was the Urban Cowboy fantasy that populated the honky-tonks. And there continues to be the *Rocky Horror* fantasy that crowds the movie theaters after midnight every weekend. In many ways, the *Rocky Horror* fantasy is the most fantastic of them all. It is the transvestite fantasy.

Big Business went to *The Rocky Horror Picture Show* for the first time a little over a year ago. She saw it the second weekend that it played in Gainesville, the home of the University of Florida, where she was a student. Her boyfriend, Pre Law, had seen it the first weekend it played in Gainesville. And then he had insisted that she come with him the next time it was shown. So there she was, a *Rocky* virgin, wondering what to expect.

Big Business and Pre Law were up late because the only time you can see *Rocky Horror* is at midnight on Friday and Saturday nights. If there is an overflow crowd, some theaters will reshow the film at 2:00 A.M.

As two huge, disembodied red lips began singing on the screen, Big Business had no suspicion that she would see this movie over and over—dozens and dozens of times—in the years to come. Then came the credits, which she hardly noticed. She had no way of knowing that she would later memorize those credits, and still later make friends with some of the people whose names flashed before her eyes. The screen said:

CREATED BY

RICHARD O'BRIEN

O'Brien originally created *Rocky Horror* for the London stage. When the play opened in 1973, he played Riff-Raff, the humpbacked butler, a role he had written for himself. Night after night, he welcomed a poor, lost, engaged couple—Brad and Janet—to his master's spooky old house haunted by transvestites.

STARRING

TIM CURRY

Curry played Riff-Raff's master, Dr. Frank N. Furter, a "sweet transvestite from transsexual Transylvania." He was a parody of Dr. Frankenstein, who was busy building not a monster, but a beautiful male sexual partner. This creature he named Rocky.

PRODUCED BY

LOU ADLER

Adler, a rock 'n' roll impresario, saw the show in London and decided to import it to America. He opened it in 1974 on the stage of the Roxy, a theater he owns on the Sunset Strip in Los Angeles. The play was a hit, packing the Roxy for nine months. So Adler decided to transform it into a rock 'n' roll movie musical.

He sold it to Twentieth Century Fox. Shooting started in England in October 1974. When filming was completed—but before the movie was released—Adler opened the play *Rocky Horror* on Broadway. This was backward, of course, making the movie of the play before the play ever played New York City. But no one was worried because *Rocky Horror* was bound to be a big hit in the big city.

The play was a big flop.

Suddenly Twentieth Century Fox lost faith in its *Rocky Horror Picture Show*. The studio was so discouraged that it made just seven prints of the film. It opened in only half a dozen cities and did poorly in all of them—all but Los Angeles. *The Rocky Horror Picture Show* seemed as dead as Boris Karloff.

But a Fox executive named Tim Degan had the idea of releasing it as a midnight movie. To see if it would work, Degan opened *The Rocky Horror Picture Show* at New York's Walter Reed Theater on Friday, April 2, 1976, at midnight. The entire cost of the premiere came to just $64. The money went to pay for a small ad in the *Village Voice* and a few handbills. The picture sold out the very first night. And it has been selling out ever since, spreading from city to city, like a Black Garter Belt Plague, until now it is shown in some 200 theaters nationwide. In the next three years, *The Rocky Horror Picture Show*, which cost a million dollars to make and $64 to premiere, grossed $12 million.

Big Business's first *Rocky* night was a Friday night. The next night, Saturday night, she went again, also with Pre Law. And up on the screen, Meatloaf sang: "Whatever happened to Saturday night? . . ."

And this time, Big Business started yelling comments at the movie along with everyone else. When Brad Majors appeared on the screen, they all screamed: "Asshole!" And when his bride made her entrance, they all hissed: "Janet Weissssssssss."

B.B. would have gone back the next night if the movie had been playing. Since it wasn't, she had to content herself with listening to a bootlegged tape of the soundtrack. She listened to it so many times that she almost drove her roommate, Media Major, crazy. B.B. especially hated the song that went: "I'm a sweet transvestite from transsexual Transylvania . . ."

When the next weekend came, B.B. tried to get M. M. to go with her to see *The Rocky Horror Picture Show,* but M. M. wouldn't go. She was already sick of *Rocky* and hadn't even seen it yet.

So M. M. stayed home, but Big Business and Pre Law went again. And again. And again. They began to meet new friends at the movie theater. The *Rocky Horror* audience was becoming a family. The people inside the theater were "us"—the people outside were "them." The Me Decade was giving way to the Us Decade . . . and a new "us" was forming. All over the country, this generation was looking for an "us" to join, and B.B. and P.L. had found theirs.

After about six weeks, Big Business and Pre Law decided to go to *The Rocky Horror Picture Show* in costume. The first time, they wore something easy. In one scene in the movie, Brad and Janet appear in blue and pink bathrobes, respectively, so Business and Law went to the movie in bathrobes. He borrowed a blue bathrobe from a fraternity brother. She borrowed a pink one from her sister. She wore a bra and panties under her robe the way Janet did in the movie. But he was not as accurate. In the picture, Brad wears jockey shorts under his robe. Pre Law insisted on wearing swimming trunks instead. In those days, he was modest. (He was the type whose shirt tail was always tucked in.)

That first time, Big Business was extremely self-conscious. She clung to Pre Law and kept her robe clamped tightly closed. At this point, she would not have believed you if you had told her how much she would eventually take off and how far she would eventually go.

In those days, Business was modest, but not nearly as modest as Law. She finally got so tired of his modesty and lack of accuracy that she stole his swim trunks. But he modestly replaced the trunks with cut-off blue jeans. It wasn't until much later that she got those cut-offs off.

"He finally saw the light," she says.

Big Business and Pre Law became celebrities on campus. As they would walk across the university lawns together, other students would

yell at them the way they yelled at Brad and Janet in the movie. They
hissed her. And they screamed "asshole" at him. Or they called him
"Bradhole." Sticks and stones were the stuff fame was made of.

And then Business and Law broke up. She even stopped going to
The Rocky Horror Picture Show for a while. But the movie would
eventually pull her back into the fantasy. And it would draw Business
and Law together again.

On the night of *Rocky Horror*'s third birthday party, Big Business
and all her weird friends drove over to the Kendall Skating Rink in full
costume. They trooped inside and put on roller skates over their black
fishnet stockings. And then they joined all the other transvestites on the
skating floor. They made roller derby look as innocent as a junior high
school skating party.

A thousand people in transvestite drag went around and around
and around in a maddening whirl. Black garters on wheels. Fishnet
stockings on wheels. Corsets on wheels. Gender in a giant blender. Ho-
mogenized. Transsexized. Swirled into a huge, frothy, unisexual milk-
shake.

One young woman skated by in a leopard skin with her wrists
handcuffed behind her back. A second young woman, armed with a
whip, skated along in the wake of the first, delivering lash after lash.
These costumes had nothing to do with the *Rocky Horror* movie. The
two women were acting out their own private fantasy movie that played
inside their heads. Lash, skate, lash, skate—pain on wheels.

Carnival on wheels.

A girl skated by in bra and panties. A boy rolled by in a cowboy
hat. Another young man glided past in bandages from head to foot. And
then here came the handcuffs and whip again.

"It's time for the costume contest," a disembodied voice said over a
loudspeaker. "If you want to enter, line up against the wall."

Almost everyone in the skating rink headed for the far wall to be
judged. Caught up in this transsexual stampede were Big Business and
all her friends.

The judge was to be Richard O'Brien, the great maker of madness
himself, the creator of *The Rocky Horror Picture Show*. His head was
shaved and he wore tight leather pants. Black.

"Thank you," O'Brien said, "for allowing me to come along and
enjoy your madness."

Business desperately wanted to win this costume contest. So did
Law. And so did all the other members of their Transvestite Chic
clique. They were like players on a transsexual football team who had

been pointing toward the big game for weeks. They were determined to emerge the queens of the long transvestite night. Beneath the fishnet stockings and black garter belts, they were American kids who wanted to win. Winning would validate the time and energy they gave to their fantasy. Surely it was all right to be a transvestite—if you were the best transvestite.

In a sense, Richard O'Brien brought Media Major and Micro Chip together. His movie caused them to meet. And then he entered their lives personally as a kind of bald, mad, kinky cupid.

M. M. was a reluctant *Rocky Horror* convert. Her roommate, B. B., finally managed to drag her to the film a couple of times, but she was not particularly impressed. Then she didn't see the movie for over half a year.

Finally, around Christmas time, Media Major went back a third time. And she fell hopelessly in love with *Rocky.*

She went back week after week, Fridays and Saturdays. And she dragged her then boyfriend with her. Soon they were both going in costume. The costume she selected for herself was relatively understated—funny sunglasses, that sort of thing. But the costume she chose for her boyfriend was much more dramatic—pink satin shorts!

"I dressed him in pink satin shorts because I wanted to see him in pink satin shorts," Media explains. "Boy, did he look like Rocky. He couldn't believe I was so into *Rocky.*"

Of course, the relationship was doomed. The boy in the pink satin shorts simply did not care enough about *The Rocky Horror Picture Show.* Soon Media was going to the show by herself.

Media became so involved with the movie that she began trying to live it. She would go up to college boys, sit in their laps, and ask, "Do you want to be seduced?"

And then she would sing a song from the show:

> *Toucha, toucha, touch me,*
> *I want to feel dirty . . .*

Media Major was still going through this phase when several of her friends started trying to put together a *Rocky Horror* cast. These friends dreamed of acting the movie out below the screen as the show was being shown above their heads.

Big Business would play Janet Weiss. And Pre Law would portray Brad Majors. Business and Law were no longer a couple in real life, but her Janet and his Brad would be a couple for a long time to come.

97

They say: "*Rocky* keeps us together."

It was as though the marriage were over, but they still had a child to bring up: *Rocky Horror*.

Media Major had to audition for a part in the *Rocky Horror* cast. Her audition came, of all times, during finals week. She stayed up all one night studying, took an important test, and then went to her tryout feeling about as bad as she had ever felt. Exhausted, she auditioned for the lead role, that of Dr. Frank N. Furter, the "sweet transvestite from transsexual Transylvania." She got the part. Media would play Frank.

But the Gainesville cast still did not have a Rocky. They searched everywhere for one, especially at the movie theater on Friday and Saturday nights after midnight.

One night, M. M. and B. B. went to their favorite movie together and got into a kind of competition with a young man they had never seen before. Whenever he would yell out a line, they would try to top it.

When Frank appeared on the screen arrayed in high heels, stockings, a garter belt, a corset, and a cape, the unfamiliar young man called out: "Ladies and gentlemen, Miss Judy Garland!"

M. M. and B. B. screamed out: "No, it's Anita Bryant in drag."

When the movie was over, M. M. asked the young man, "Where did you get all those great lines?"

"I've got a script," said the young man, holding up his treasure. "Where did you get all those lousy lines?"

A little later, Amy reported for a *Rocky Horror* cast rehearsal, and there was the young man with the script. But she didn't recognize him and he didn't recognize her.

He turned out to be Micro Chip. Pre Law had discovered him and cast him as Rocky. Since Frank N. Furter is in love with Rocky, that meant that Media/Frank and Chip/Rocky played a lot of scenes together. But they still did not realize that they had met before.

Not for weeks.

Finally, at one rehearsal, Rocky said to Frank: "Oh, you're the one with the lousy lines!"

It was not love at first recognition. Far from it. In the beginning, they simply tolerated one another. They worked hard on their parts, but they never considered living those parts, actually falling in love.

They were still just costars when opening night arrived, at last. Before their first public performance, the whole cast gathered in M. M. and B. B.'s apartment to get into their costumes.

"It was great," remembers Big Business. "It was so hectic. The apartment was not equipped to handle ten moving people. You know it's crazy when you find glitter in your cat."

Dressed in their costumes, the Gainesville cast looked like anything but the relatively solid students they actually were. The future Perry Mason. The future Barbara Walters. The future tycoon. The future NASA programmer. And the other members of the cast included a future chiropractor, an economics major, a political science major, and a future speech pathologist. These people, wriggling into their garter belts, were serious folks with serious ambitions.

And this is another way in which *Rocky* is like Rio during Carnival. In Rio, the more respectable you are in everyday life, the more disreputable your Carnival costume. Grande dames dress up as whores. So do bank presidents. So do American kids who love *Rocky Horror*. And the more serious the job for which they are preparing, the more dissolute their *Rocky* drag. Their subconscious attitude seems to be: Eat, drink, and be merry in a black garter belt, for tomorrow you may be an accountant.

On the way to the theater, Big Business was nervous for many reasons. One had to do with the "toucha toucha touch me" scene. Big/Janet and Micro/Rocky had never rehearsed this scene. They had been too shy. And now they were going to do it in front of hundreds of people.

At midnight, the Gainesville players took up their positions beneath the screen. When the projector rolled, the amateur actors aped all the actions of the movie actors, like visible echoes. Up on the screen, a gang of transsexuals stripped Brad and Janet to their underwear. Simultaneously, a flesh-and-blood gang started taking off Business and Law's clothes. Soon Business was undressed down to her half-slip, bra, and panties. And the formerly modest Law was standing in front of everyone in his jockey shorts and black shoes.

A reel later, up on the screen, Janet and Rocky found themselves alone together, prompting her to burst into song:

> *Toucha, toucha, touch me,*
> *I want to feel dirty . . .*

Then the screen Janet offered the screen Rocky her scantily clad breasts, and he touched them eagerly. At the same time, Micro touched Big Business's macro Moby-Dick breasts. Giggles and gropes piled on top of each other. The living girl was better built than the image on the screen. And the live performance was more X-rated than the movie. The audience loved it. The Gainesville cast was a hit.

A few days later, Media Major went to Orlando to visit a friend. While she was there, she naturally went to see *The Rocky Horror Pic-*

ture Show. After the movie, she was standing in the lobby when she noticed a strange man with a shaved head. Several others noticed him, too.

Finally someone asked him, "Are you Richard O'Brien?"

"Yes, I am," he confessed.

When she returned to Gainesville, Media Major told everyone that she had met the creator of *The Rocky Horror Picture Show.* They were all dying to meet him, too, but Media did not know how to find him again. She did remember, however, his saying something about going to Miami.

The Gainesville cast hooked up six phones in Media's apartment from which they called thirty-one Holiday Inns before they found their quarry. Richard O'Brien said he was in Florida simply playing tourist, visiting places like Disney World.

That's right, *Rocky Horror*'s father had been paying his respects to the earthly remains of Mickey Mouse's father. The King of Kink had been amusing himself in the world's most wholesome amusement park. But perhaps visions of a future O'Brienland or O'Brien World danced in his head. A transsexual Transylvania where Snow White would be a man dressed in a black garter belt and high heels.

On the phone, the Gainesville players asked Richard O'Brien if he would like to see their show. He said he would.

So the whole Gainesville cast piled into a caravan of cars and headed for Miami. They worked on their makeup in the cars on the way. And they changed into their costumes in gas station rest rooms. Media Major rode down in Micro Chip's car but felt no romantic tug in his direction.

When they reached Miami, the full cast in full costume invaded the wrong Holiday Inn. Then they looked until they found the right one. They collected Richard O'Brien and took him to see his movie at a theater in Coconut Grove.

The Gainesville cast acted out the movie while the movie itself was projected above their heads on a giant screen. O'Brien seemed to like their performance.

Afterward, O'Brien took them all for drinks to a waterfront bar called Monty's Village Inn. They all sat around in full costume, frightening the regular customers and asking questions. Most of all, they wanted O'Brien to explain the symbolism in *The Rocky Horror Picture Show.*

"There isn't any," he said.

Then it was his turn to interrogate them on a subject about which he was most curious.

"Do you have any dope?" he asked.

"No," they admitted, humiliated.

Sometime near dawn, the party broke up. It was too late to return to Gainesville that night, so Big Business invited everyone to sleep at her mother's Miami home. Eight people passed out on couches and floors. And they all woke up the next morning in costume.

"The trip really knit the cast together," Media Major remembers. "Suddenly, we were living together. We became one huge, happy family. Well, not always happy."

The next weekend, the cast went to Jacksonville, where they had been invited to put on their show by a theater manager. The show went well. And for the first time, Media/Frank actually felt something for Chip/Rocky.

"It was the weekend after we met Richard O'Brien that we fell in love," Media remembers. "Chip just opened my eyes. He jumped from friend and member of the cast to *wow!*"

It was as though they were responding to O'Brien's spell. Life was beginning to imitate *The Rocky Horror Picture Show.*

The next weekend was *Rocky Horror*'s second birthday. And Media and Chip went to a big birthday party in Gainesville—which turned out to be a milestone in more ways than one.

"Chip and I really got together," Media remembers.

One year later, at Rocky's *third* birthday party, Richard O'Brien paced up and down in front of all the Janet Weisses. Since Janet appears in several costumes in the movie, the various Janets in the costume contest appeared in various states of dress and undress. Some wore only bra and panties. One girl had even smeared dirt on her breasts in the spirit of the song about wanting "to feel dirty." But Big Business was costumed the way Janet Weiss was dressed at the beginning of *The Rocky Horror Picture Show.* She wore a lavender dress, a white hat, and carried a bouquet of white and lavender flowers.

O'Brien walked over to B. B. and took her by the hand. She had won the Janet Weiss costume contest. The score was:

Gainesville cast   1
Other casts   0

The Gainesville players were off to such a good start that they began dreaming of sweeping all the awards. It was important to do well in this contest, very well, for if they did, than no other cast would dare challenge them once the movie began. If they did poorly, however, other casts would surely attempt to supplant them in that coveted space at the foot of the screen.

The creator of *Rocky Horror* moved over to a long line of Brad Majors. Again there were different costumes because Brad wears various costumes in the movie. Some Brads wore high heels, stockings, and garters. But Pre Law wore a dark suit with too-short trousers, "asshole glasses" with black frames, a plaid bow tie, and white socks. Law won. The Gainesville cast was two for two.

O'Brien went on to judge the Riff-Raffs, the Magentas (she is the mad maid in the movie), and the Columbias (she wears a gold top hat and striped shorts). In *Rocky Horror*, this trio has a complicated relationship that seems to be bisexual. And in real life, the people who wear these costumes sometimes have similar links to each other. The Gainesville cast's Magenta and Riff-Raff and Columbia lived together in a ménage à trois. They said they might never have found each other—or bisexuality—without the movie. After all, none of them was bisexual before falling in love with *Rocky Horror*. Gainesville's Riff-Raff won his division of the costume contest, but their Magenta and Columbia lost.

Richard O'Brien turned to judging the Dr. Frank N. Furters. All the Franks were dressed in full transvestite drag, with black high heels, black fishnet stockings, and red-and-black Merry Widow corsets. Like Maria in *West Side Story*, they all seemed to feel pretty. Especially Media Major. And she *was* pretty, too. But she lost, perhaps because she was a woman. Passing up all the women pretending to be men dressed as women, O'Brien chose a man in a Merry Widow as the winner.

The Rockys were dressed in pink satin shorts and gold lamé shorts and other shocking shades. The colors were about as understated as the muscles. The Rocky contest looked like a Mr. Universe contest. O'Brien marched up and down in front of all those pectorals—and chose Gainesville's Micro Chip.

When the movie started, the Gainesville cast took up the position they had earned directly below the big screen. The other actors who wanted to take part sprawled around them like suburbs.

Big Business's "toucha toucha touch me" scene turned out to be the most popular part of the act. Captain Ahab would have loved it, or been driven crazy by it, or run for his harpoons.

After their performance, the Gainesville players were too keyed up to go to sleep. They found their way to a big house with a back porch the size of a beach. In the middle of this concrete beach stood a hot tub. They all put on bathing suits—being modest transvestites—and jumped into the warm water. They splashed and giggled like children.

And then Media Major grinned wickedly, put her hands under the water, and pulled off Micro Chip's swimming trunks.

◆　　◆　　◆

I turned in my story on *Rocky Horror* just as *Esquire* magazine was changing hands. Clay Felker, my friend and mentor, lost *Esquire*—which was sold to new owners—just as he had lost *New York* magazine. It was a difficult time for Clay and his friends.

And my story about *Rocky Horror* was never published.

THE GREAT AMERICAN
FAMILY

◆　　◆　　◆

While reading a history of the West, I stumbled upon a few paragraphs about a white woman who was taken prisoner by Indians. Her name was Cynthia Ann Parker. She eventually married a chief and gave birth to a chief. When she was finally "freed" by the Texas Rangers, she didn't want to go "home." That was the part I liked best.

I became obsessed with Cynthia Ann and her story. I looked her up in other books about the West. I went down to the Library of Congress and searched out privately printed journals that were almost 150 years old.

While pursuing my obsession, I learned that the Parker family holds a unique family reunion every summer. The reunion is special because it is half white and half red. The Indian Parkers are all descendants of Cynthia Ann. The white Parkers are descended from her brothers and sister and uncles and aunts. It seemed to me that the story of the mixed Parker blood was also a story of Texas blood and American blood.

Needing an excuse—or call it license—to find out more, I contacted an editor at *Life* magazine and asked if he would like an article on the Parker family reunion. He wanted the story.

I flew off to Texas to try to capture Cynthia Ann Parker once again.

◆　　◆　　◆

Unpublished, 1981

The white boy and the Indian maiden studied each other curiously from opposite sides of an old tree. It was an ancient oak, with many dividing branches, like a family tree. The white boy belonged to one branch of the family, the Indian maiden to another branch, but they both traced their descent back to a common trunk. When he leaned against the tree, she turned away, as if they were doing a kind of dance, these two gentle red and white cousins, who had been brought together by a bloody day of massacre and kidnap and rape many generations ago.

The oak, which sheltered and separated them, stood near the site of the original bloodletting, which had joined the bloods of their two families, making one family, one blood. Before the night was over, the white boy and the Indian maiden would kiss here on this bloody ground where their forefathers and foremothers had killed and been killed.

From his side of the tree, fair-haired Robert Cooke, sixteen, smiled through braces. And from her side, dark-haired Susan Bradley, fifteen, whose Indian name is Tui Nahzuni, or Little Mirror, smiled back. Little Mirror—a modern reflection of the myth of the beautiful Indian maiden, wearing violet eye shadow for war paint—seemed well named.

The white boy and the Indian maiden had just met. He thought she was one of the prettiest girls he had ever seen. She thought he looked like a boy with whom she had just broken up. They were about the same heartbreak age as Romeo and Juliet, with families that had even more reason to hate each other. But their families no longer hated because a bloody deed had forged a blood tie.

Bobby and Suzy were now glad that they had decided to attend this unique American family reunion, half white and half red. The white boy and the Indian maiden were both the great-great-great-great-great-grandchildren of Elder John and Sarah Parker, whose descendants—some 250 of them—were gathered together for the weekend. The Parker family reunion was held in the Fort Parker State Park, which is near Groesbeck, Texas, about a hundred miles south of Dallas. These latter-day Parkers were housed in appropriately primitive cabins in the shadow of Old Fort Parker itself, where Elder John and many members of his family lost their lives.

A full moon was rising over the white boy and the Comanche girl, the kind the pioneers called a Comanche moon, because Comanches were known to raid when the moon was full. This dangerous moon, which shed such a romantic light, was red. The Indians have a saying: "There is blood on the moon."

•

A Comanche moon shone on Fort Parker the night before the attack, illuminating a classic western fortress built of sharp-pointed logs set side by side, like a row of giant pencils. The fort was just large enough to shelter one large family of grandparents, parents, cousins, and in-laws: the Parkers.

On the morning of May 19, 1836, most of the men of the family left the fort to till the fields. The crops had too often been neglected during Texas's war of independence from Mexico, but the fighting was over now. Sam Houston had whipped Santa Anna at San Jacinto just one month earlier. Now the brand-new Texas Republic was celebrating, but a new violence was coming. A tragedy would haunt Texas from birth.

"Indians!"

Cynthia Ann Parker, nine, who was playing inside the fort, heard the cry at about 10:00 A.M. Through the fort's gaping front gate, carelessly left open, the little girl saw perhaps a hundred Comanche warriors on horseback. Their faces were painted black, the color of death, but they carried a confusing white flag.

The little girl watched her uncle, Benjamin Parker, walk out through the open gate. And she saw her father, Silas Parker, take up a position next to the gate, so he could close it if there was trouble.

When he finally returned, Uncle Ben said the Indians wanted a cow to eat, but he was afraid they really wanted a fight. In spite of his misgivings, he started back out to try to talk the Comanches out of killing and scalping. Silas tried to stop him but failed.

"I know they will kill Benjamin," Silas said.

Cynthia Ann saw her father's prediction come true. The Comanches surrounded her Uncle Ben and plunged lances and arrows into him, as if they wanted to kill him a hundred times.

The little girl saw her father struggling to close the gate before the Indians could burst through it, but a Comanche arrow struck him before he could complete his task. He fell in the open gate. The daughter watched the Indians come riding in over her father's body, dirtying it, trampling it, adding insult to death.

A few white men rushed forward to try to cover the flight of the white women and children. Cynthia Ann fled with what was left of her family—her mother, her two younger brothers, and her baby sister. They ran diagonally across the fort toward a back gate, which was so small that it seemed to belong in a doll house, almost giving an air of play to their flight. While the Comanches were busy killing the fort's few defenders, Cynthia Ann and several others managed to squeeze through the tiny door. And then they scattered.

Arthritic Elder John Parker—Bobby and Suzy's great-great-great-great-great-grandfather—led one group in their flight. But the Indians overtook the old man and his party before they had gone a mile. The Comanches descended upon Elder John Parker and stripped him nude. They also stripped an old woman named Mrs. Duty. And they stripped a young woman named Elizabeth Kellogg.

Then they drove their naked herd back toward the fort. When they neared the walls, the Indians paused to castrate, scalp, and kill Elder John Parker. They raped old Mrs. Duty, slashed her breasts, and left her for dead. And they threw a nude Elizabeth Kellogg onto a horse to be carried off into slavery.

A young woman named Rachel Plummer fled with her infant son, James Pratt, in her arms. She later wrote in a privately printed memoir: "Oh! how vain were my feeble efforts to try to run to save myself and little James Pratt. A large sulky Indian picked up a hoe and knocked me down. I well recollect of their taking my child out of my arms, but whether they hit me any more I do not know, for I swooned away. The first I recollect, they were dragging me along by the hair."

The Stone Age warriors dragged her naked to a horse and threw her across it—another slave, another handsome trophy.

Another band of Indians pursued Cynthia Ann Parker and her family as they ran toward the nearby Navasoat River. Soon the braves overtook and surrounded the family—the mother, Lucy, widow of Silas, Cynthia Ann, John, Silas, Jr., and Orlena, the baby. One of the Indians motioned for Lucy Parker to lift Cynthia Ann up onto the back of his horse. The mother hesitated but then raised her nine-year-old daughter up behind the warrior. Then the Indians wanted Lucy to lift up John. So the mother placed her six-year-old son behind another brave. Then several other Indians on foot took hold of Lucy and her other two children and started dragging them away.

The whole family seemed bound for captivity when David Faulkenberry, returning from the fields, came rushing up with a rifle. The startled Indians released Lucy Parker and her two youngest children—but rode away with John and Cynthia Ann.

Before leaving the fort, the Indians plundered it. They seemed to reserve their special fury for the books and beds, symbols of soft civilization. They tore the stuffing out of both so that the air was thick with pages and feathers. It was a great angry white storm. Pages and feathers snowed down upon the dead, dying, and suffering. The captives were led through a blizzard of pages and feathers toward an unknown world.

Cynthia Ann, who would remain "lost" the longest, was Suzy's great-great-great-grandmother.

The whites were once again pitted against the Indians on the same old battleground at Fort Parker. It was club against club around the card table. The war between the white man and the Comanche had come down to a gin game.

The game was played in a small cabin beneath a weak electric light. The Indians were Suzy and her twelve-year-old brother, Stevie. The whites were Bobby and his uncle, Dwight Shaw, who was only three months his senior. This time the white man, Bobby, won the war, the gin war.

Then they all decided to go for a walk in the wilderness. They found a trail through the woods, which did not seem to have changed much since the original tragedy. Little Mirror was especially struck by the Comanche moon that lighted the way. The unreal, late-night brightness seemed to gild the oaks and enchant the wilderness. She began to imagine a journey through this fantastic forest a long time ago.

Long after the sun set and the Comanche moon rose, the Indians and their captives rode on through the bright woods. The Comanches liked to raid during a full moon because it would light their escape. Cynthia Ann, John, and Rachel Plummer's baby, James, were exhausted. Rachel and Elizabeth Kellogg, who were making the long journey nude, were not only tired but badly sunburned.

"About midnight they stopped," Rachel later wrote. "They now tied a plaited thong around my arms, and drew my hands behind me. They tied them so tight that the scars can be easily seen to this day. They then tied a similar thong around my ankles, and drew my feet and hands together. They now turned me on my face and I was unable to turn over, when they commenced beating me . . . with their bows . . ."

The Comanches bound Elizabeth, John, and Cynthia Ann in the same way, helpless as beetles on their backs. They even tied up the baby, James. By the light of a victory fire, the Indians danced and screamed and kicked and beat and shook white scalps in white faces. They all saw hair that they could recognize and name—grandfather, uncle, father!

Eventually, the Comanches began to lose interest in the children as they concentrated more and more on the grown women. They untied the feet of their adult female captives. And then Elizabeth Kellogg and Rachel Plummer were raped by the entire band of warriors.

"I now ask you, my Christian reader, to pause," Rachel Plummer wrote. "You who are living secure from danger—you who have read the sacred scriptures of truth—who have been raised in a land boasting of Christian philanthropy—I say, I now ask you to form some idea of what my feelings were."

The raping of the women took place in full view of the children and lasted until the Comanche moon went down and the sun came up.

Shook me all night long . . . shook me all night long . . . These lyrics kept running through Little Mirror's head as she walked in the wilderness. The song was on the *Back in Black* album by a heavy-metal English band called AC/DC. It was on her mind because this was her ex-boyfriend's favorite song. Since Bobby reminded her of her old boyfriend, Suzy asked him what he thought of "Shook Me All Night Long."

Bobby said he liked it. He even owned the *Back in Black* album. He had *even* brought a tape of it with him to the family reunion. He could play it for her on a car tape deck if she liked. Suzy was shocked. Bobby was more like her old boyfriend than she had guessed. Somehow he was now easier to talk to.

Soon all four—Bobby, Suzy, Stevie, and Dwight—had piled into a small car with bucket seats and a tape deck. Bobby and Suzy shared the bucket seat on the passenger side. And AC/DC was blaring . . .

In the night all around them, the red and white descendants of the tragic family were going to bed in the park. To borrow the words of many an old peace treaty: The white man's camp and the Indian's camp were now one. But the peace was somewhat disturbed by rock 'n' roll:

The earth was quakin' . . .

And whites and Indians were thinking of their ancestors' ordeals (rape and torture and murder) and of their own modern worries (low farm prices and high taxes).

My mind was achin' . . .

Cynthia Ann Parker's great-great-great-granddaughter was thinking of the recent past rather then the distant past when she heard the chorus:

You shook me all night long . . .

After the song, the Indians and the white boys were hot, so they all went off to take showers.

Then they returned to the car to listen to more music. They played the rest of the *Back in Black* album. On the site of the original abduction, the white boy and the Indian maiden heard:

> *Don't you struggle*
> *Don't you fight*
> *'Cause it's your turn tonight . . .*

The Indians had a tradition: On the first night, all the captives belonged to all the warriors to enjoy. But the next morning, the private property imperative reasserted itself: The captives belonged to the first braves who touched them during the battle. The new slave owners now led their new slaves off in different directions as the raiding party scattered. Cynthia Ann was separated from her brother John. Rachel Plummer was separated from her baby, James. Elizabeth Kellogg was separated from the rest. They were all separated from each other.

Meanwhile, Rachel Plummer's father, James Parker, led the survivors of the attack toward the safety of Fort Houston, which was ninety miles away. They were suffering terribly from hunger when a curious savior came to their rescue. "Through the mercy of Providence," James Parker wrote in his memoir, "a skunk (or polecat) came in our way. . . . I succeeded in catching it as it jumped into the river; and the only way I could kill it, was by holding it under the water until it was drowned. . . . We soon had it cooked and equally divided among our company."

After delivering his band of survivors to Fort Houston, James Parker set out on a Wild West odyssey in search of his daughter. When he heard that Indians were holding a white woman near Nacogdoches, he immediately rushed there, hoping to find his Rachel. What he found instead must have left him feeling both happy and sad.

"I was rejoiced to meet with my sister-in-law, Mrs. Kellogg," he wrote, "who had been purchased by some Delaware Indians, and brought in. The consideration claimed by the Indians for their services was $150, which Gen. Houston generously paid, as I was penniless."

On the 140-mile journey home, James Parker and Elizabeth Kellogg had a bloody adventure. Their party came across an unfortunate Indian. "Mrs. Kellogg immediately recognized the Indian," James Parker wrote, "as not only being one of the band that had captured Fort Parker, but the very one that had shot and scalped my father. . . . What followed, it is unnecessary to relate—suffice it to say, that it was the unanimous verdict of the company that he would never kill and scalp another white man."

One suspects that these victims of the Fort Parker tragedy simply saw what they wanted to see. Their desire for vengeance made all Indians look alike. And so the innocent massacre victims were now ready to massacre an innocent.

Elizabeth Kellogg's homecoming did not turn out to be a happy ending. Her Christian friends and neighbors treated her as a fallen woman. Since she had been raped by Indians, she seemed to have been branded with a scarlet "R." She was not allowed to forget that she had been the plaything of heathens. Perhaps even her husband treated her differently. She could stand what the Indians did to her body, but she could not endure what the whites did to her soul.

Within a year of her homecoming, Elizabeth Kellogg died.

> *You're only young,*
> *But you're gonna die . . .*

Cynthia Ann Parker's great-great-great-granddaughter listened to AC/DC sing. When they finally finished playing music—at almost 1:00 A.M.—they all got out of the small car and leaned against it. Since it was so late, Little Mirror was afraid her Indian grandmother would come out to get her.

"Did you know," Dwight asked, "that Bobby's gonna be a rock star?"

Suzy didn't know, so Bobby explained that he played lead electric guitar in a teen-age rock 'n' roll band named Overlord. And he wrote songs and titles like "Good Enough for Rock 'n' Roll" and "Born to Be Bad." When he grows up, he doesn't want to be a fireman or a cowboy or an Indian chief. He wants to be a star.

The Indian princess decided not to tell the white boy her dream: to go to the Massachusetts Institute of Technology and learn all about computers. She would need a scholarship to go to MIT, which does not seem impossible, since she has gotten straight A's ever since fourth grade, except for one B way back in sixth grade. Keeping her space-age longings to herself, she listened to the white boy's dream of making primitive music with a Stone Age beat.

"When we make it big," Bobby told Suzy, "I'll come through Cache and give you some free tickets."

"I'm going to bed," Dwight said.

Suzy thought perhaps his departure was prearranged in order to give the future rock star a better chance with her. Still she had her little brother to look after her. But soon he, too, got sleepy and went off to his bed. The Indian princess was left all alone with the white man. She wondered if he would try to kiss her. Suzy glanced nervously around to see if her grandmother was coming for her.

Searching for his daughter, James Parker rode northwest into Red River country, where he almost starved to death. He had all but given up hope of ever finding Rachel—or even surviving—when an old savior once again came to his aid. "I saw a skunk near me," he wrote, "and at the same moment I saw it, I felt that the kind protecting care of Providence was yet around . . ."

Saved from starvation, James Parker continued searching for his daughter for over a year. Along the way, he kept finding Indians who had raided Fort Parker, for in his bloody eyes, all Indians seemed to be guilty of that crime. In one village, he saw an Indian who appeared to be wearing "one of my vests." Leveling his rifle, he fired and was pleased to see "that my vest *had got a new button hole!*"

While the father was killing Indians, his daughter was fighting her own battles not far away on the high plains. One morning, her mistress ordered her to fetch a digging tool, but she refused. "She then with savage screams ran at me," Rachel Plummer wrote. "I knocked, or, rather, pushed her down. . . . I got hold of a large buffalo bone. I beat her over the head with it, although expecting at every moment to feel a spear reach my heart . . ." But no one touched her. Afterward, her treatment improved.

Rachel Plummer had been in the hands of the Indians for nearly eighteen months when Mexican traders visited her village and sought out her master. "They asked if he would sell me," she wrote. "No music, no sounds that ever reached my anxious ear, was half so sweet as *'ce senure'* (yes, sir). The trader made an offer for me. My owner refused. He offered more, but my owner still refused. . . . I can only ask my reader, if he can, to fancy himself in my situation; for language will fail to describe the anxious thoughts that revolved in my throbbing breast when I heard the trader say he could give no more."

But in the end, the trader raised his bid and bought the white woman.

So Rachel Plummer, who had endured eighteen months of barbarity, was returned to civilized society, which, as it turned out, she could not endure at all. Civilization, which had already killed her Aunt Elizabeth, now went to work killing her. Rachel, too, was treated as a fallen woman. And she, too, died in less than a year.

•

The white boy leaned toward the Indian maiden with the words of an AC/DC song still fresh in his memory: *I'm gonna getcha.* The Indian maiden stood her ground. The white boy's braces, bright by the light of the Comanche moon, came closer: *I'm gonna getcha.* Then the white boy kissed the Indian maiden, pressing her back against the Japanese car.

When she opened her brown eyes, Little Mirror saw her Indian grandmother coming to get her. The grandmother was wrapped in a dressing gown and disapproval.

"It's one o'clock in the morning," said the grandmother. "We were worried about you."

If Cynthia Ann Parker's great-great-great-granddaughter caused so much worry by one late night, one can imagine how much concern Cynthia Ann herself caused when she did not come home for years. All the others came back—Elizabeth Kellogg, who died before her niece Rachel returned, Rachel Plummer, who died before her son, James, returned, and finally James and even Cynthia Ann's brother John. But Cynthia Ann Parker herself was still in the hands of the Indians.

All Texas was traumatized by the fate of the lone white girl held by the Comanches. Texans were learning in the mid-nineteenth century what Americans would learn in the mid-twentieth: how hostage taking can drive a whole society almost insane. All Texas was obsessed with freeing Cynthia Ann Parker, as a later America would be obsessed with freeing hostages in Iran and later in Lebanon. She was sighted from time to time by white traders, but they were told that *this* white woman was *not* for sale. These sightings only served to tantalize Texas and to keep alive the story—almost the myth—of Cynthia Ann Parker.

Cynthia Ann was not for sale because she was now a *nu-mu-nu,* or human being, as the Comanches called themselves. The humans had transformed her into a human being in a solemn adoption ceremony. They had even given her a human name: Nora. Naturally, the humans would not sell this new human being back to the inhumans: It would be a fate worse than death.

As she slowly forgot her mother tongue, Cynthia Ann was taught to talk like a human being. She learned that the whites were called *taibos.* And the black slaves owned by the *taibos* were called *tu-taibos* or black white men. And Mexicans were *yu-taibos* or common white men.

And Chinese were *ku-eckwusi-taibos* or white men with braids. And monkeys were *kwasi-taibos* or white men with tails.

In the summer of 1840, Cynthia Ann was taken along on an extraordinary raid. On this journey, she retraced the path she had taken in 1836, only now she was one of the attackers rather than one of the victims. When she passed near the site of the old fort in the heat of that summer, Cynthia Ann was thirteen years old.

On this same raid rode a young war chief named Peta Nocona. Perhaps Peta and Cynthia Ann met on this raid. Perhaps they courted as they rode past Fort Parker, past San Antonio, all the way to the town of Linnville on the Texas coast.

The Great Linnville Raid began with an attack on a small cabin on the outskirts of town. The Indians pulled a white woman from the cabin, stripped her, and carried her off. She was Daniel Boone's granddaughter.

When the human army swooped down on the town of Linnville itself, most of the *taibos* fled out to sea in boats. The Indians then began to sack what was now a kind of ghost town. They moved from house to house until they reached the great prize: the Linnville warehouse.

Inside the warehouse, the human beings made war on bolts of red cloth, ladies' dresses, ladies' undergarments, umbrellas, and stovepipe hats suitable for boxes at the opera. Perhaps Cynthia Ann, like many others, put on an opera hat and then unfurled a brightly colored parasol over her head. Perhaps Peta, like many others, slipped into a swallow-tailed coat. Perhaps it was as though they were children playing dress-up together, he dressing up for her, she dressing up for him. The wild Indians were children in the attic.

After plundering the warehouse, a spectacular Indian army headed north, armed with top hats and tomahawks, bows and arrows and bow ties, spears and parasols. Cynthia Ann and Peta must have been dressed as gaudily as the rest—with bright ribbons tied to their horses' tails.

As they approached Plum Creek, the Comanches found an impromptu *taibo* army waiting for them. The whites were dressed in faded jeans and flannel shirts as if they were going to work. The Indians were arrayed like a savage tribe on its way to the opera or for a ride in Hyde Park. Firing their Colt revolvers, the drab inhumans charged the festive human line. All the noise stampeded the Comanches' herd of stolen horses and pack animals. And this stampede turned the battle. The looters were in the end to be defeated by their loot. In the fight, Daniel Boone's granddaughter was killed.

Cynthia Ann and Peta escaped from Plum Creek with their lives, fled north to the high human plains, and were married. In 1847, the white woman and the chief had their first child, a son, whom they named Quanah. Some say his name means "fragrance." Others say it means "eagle." He would become the greatest chief in the history of the Comanches.

The next day, Quanah's great-great-granddaughter went swimming with the white boy she had met at the family reunion. Little Mirror was worried about her hair—not about getting it lifted, but about getting it wet. The Indian and the white man had a pitched battle—a water fight.

Then they went canoeing. The white boy had to teach the Indian maiden how to paddle. She did not know to put her hand on top of the oar.

Cynthia Ann taught her children the Indian ways. After Quanah came a second son, named Pecos, or Peanut, and then a daughter, named Topsannah, or Prairie Flower. She taught her offspring, who were half white and half red, that they were *nu-mu-nus* and the *taibos* were their enemies.

She had her children around her on that day in 1858 when the dreaded alarm—*taibos!*—spread through the camp. Soon a line of human warriors were drawn up opposite a line of *taibo* warriors.

While Cynthia Ann watched, the great chief Iron Jacket—named for the 300-year-old coat of Spanish mail that he wore—charged out to challenge the white chief to fight him in single combat. Colonel Rip Ford of the Texas Rangers later wrote that his mind "was vividly carried back to the days of chivalry . . . and tournaments of knights." Iron Jacket was the reverse of Mark Twain's Connecticut Yankee in King Arthur's Court—he was an Arthurian knight who had somehow been transported into Twain's own century. And he could find no one to joust with him. An inhuman Texas Ranger simply raised his rifle and shot the knightly Iron Jacket dead.

Then the Rangers charged the demoralized humans who ran before them. The *taibos* bore down upon Cynthia Ann and her children, *just as the Comanches had born down upon Lucy Parker and her brood.* They were almost in the hands of the inhumans when Peta suddenly came to their rescue, *just as David Faulkenberry had come to Lucy Parker's aid.* He led a counterattack that came between the inhumans and the human women and children. The Comanches lost the Battle of Antelope Hills, but they did not lose their families.

In retaliation for the killing of Iron Jacket and the attack on the village, Peta led a punitive raid deep into Texas. Cynthia Ann and her children went along. They burned and massacred and scalped and raped in Parker County.

Then the *taibos* demanded retribution. The Texas Rangers were dispatched in late 1860 to pursue Peta and Cynthia Ann—and to exact revenge.

The *taibo* Rangers would eventually catch up with the human beings on a morning eerily like another morning almost twenty-five years earlier. Shortly after dawn, Peta and his warriors left the human village to hunt buffalo, *just as the men of Fort Parker had left to till the fields.* Quanah and Pecos played in the human village now populated mostly by women and children, *just as Cynthia Ann and John had played in the defenseless fort.* Suddenly the morning peace was disturbed by the cry of alarm.

"*Taibos! Taibos! Taibos!*"

"Indians! Indians! Indians!"

The alarm sent Parker women fleeing for cover. A handful of Parker men rushed forward clutching old black-powder rifles. When the first black-powder shot was fired, the surprisingly loud *bang* made everyone in old Fort Parker jump.

Even Bobby jumped, although he loved Indians, or rather an Indian. He sat in an audience of several hundred who had come out to watch a reenactment of the Fort Parker massacre. This evening's entertainment was to be the centerpiece of the Parker family reunion. The whole town of Groesbeck had been invited. Many had brought lawn chairs, so they could watch the massacre in comfort, but Bobby sat cross-legged on the ground, Indian fashion.

Suddenly a band of Indians burst through the fort's gate, which was still left open after almost a century and a half. The wild savages were led by a war chief who wore a pair of glasses because, as he explained, "If I don't wear them, I'll be groping in the dark in the massacre . . ."

Cynthia Ann Parker, human being, ran with her baby, Prairie Flower, in her arms . . .

Lucy Parker, or rather the actress playing her, ran with her baby in her arms . . .

◆

While Cynthia Ann and her children fled, a male with bow and arrows began firing missiles to cover their retreat. He appeared to be a warrior, but he was actually a Mexican captive, a slave, named Pepe. And now this slave fought fiercely to save his master's family.

Pepe managed to hold off the Texas Rangers long enough for his master's family to mount horses. Cynthia Ann rode with her baby in her arms. It was a race against death. Or worse—captivity.

Then Pepe jumped on a horse, but he paused in his flight to pull a wounded squaw up behind him. This pause allowed Captain Sul Ross, who was in charge of this massacre, to come within firing range. As Captain Ross later wrote in his military report: "I fired my pistol, striking the girl . . . near the heart, killing her instantly. . . . When the girl fell from the horse she pulled him off also."

But Pepe, the captive, the slave, the warrior, was soon on his feet again, firing arrows. One arrow hit Ross's horse, not killing it, but making it buck. As Ross wrote: "Being in such a disadvantage he would have killed me in a few minutes but for a random shot from my pistol (while I was clinging with my left hand to the pommel of my saddle) which broke his right arm at the elbow, completely disabling him. My horse then became quiet, and I shot [him] twice through the body, whereupon he deliberately walked to a small tree, the only one in sight, and leaning against it began to sing a wild, weird song."

While Pepe was dying his strangely heroic death, a young Texas Ranger named Charles Goodnight bore down on Cynthia Ann Parker. His Colt was aimed at her back. He was going to make a good Indian of her . . .

In Fort Parker, the Indians pursued their victims through a fog of thick, pungent gunsmoke. Women screamed. Frightened children cried. Two young braves appeared out of the black-powder cloud and pursued "Cynthia Ann." The little girl was pretty, with long blond braids. A neat, old-fashioned calico dress covered her already budding body. One warrior grabbed her high, the other grabbed her low. As they carried her away, she shrieked loudly and kicked violenty.

"I kept thinking," she said later, "what if it were really real. I'd be a goner . . ."

The hammer of Goodnight's gun was already back when the Comanche woman suddenly turned and tore open the front of her dress to expose *white* breasts.

"Americano!" she cried.

"Don't shoot!" Goodnight yelled. "She's white!"

"Tonight we celebrate the family," Jack Seldon, the chief organizer of the family reunion, said after the mock attack. "This family and all families—the family of man. For at some place in the dim past, we are all related. But this weekend we have met as members of the Parker family. We can all trace our line back to the year 1780, when Sarah White and John Parker became man and wife. Their first child, Daniel, was born 200 years ago this year."

Seldon seemed to study his audience of white Parkers and red Parkers.

"If we wonder what sort of people John and Sarah Parker were, we have only to look around. And through the day today, I have looked into the faces of Parkers, and seen Daniel, James, Silas, Quanah, Peta Nocona. . . . They are all with us tonight. . . . We are *them* and they are *us* . . ."

Listening to this speech, Little Mirror—whose features reflected Quanah and Peta and Cynthia Ann—was scared to death. She was on next. She had never before stood up all alone in front of an audience, *never*. *All* those faces frightened her, but she was especially worried about a few faces in particular. Bobby's face and the faces of his friends. They were sitting right there in the second row. She had warned them not to make faces at her during the performance. She heard herself being introduced . . .

Little Mirror—standing before the crowd in a dress made from the skin of a deer shot by Quanah—recited the Lord's Prayer in Indian sign language. She began by pointing to the sky—*Our Father Who art in heaven*. She seemed to throw something away—*Forgive us our debts*. She threw it away again—*as we forgive our debtors*. Which seemed to be the point of the weekend.

As her hands prayed, Suzy could see the white boys staring at her . . .

The white men around the campfire stared at Cynthia Ann Parker. They wondered who she was. Even more, they wondered *what* she was. She seemed like a Comanche, but she looked like a white woman under her clothes. What was most confusing of all was her habit of trying to escape. So they watched her closely. As far as she was concerned, the captivity of Cynthia Ann Parker was just beginning.

Of course, the Texas Rangers remembered the legend of Cynthia Ann Parker and sent for a member of the Parker family. Isaac Parker, a member of the Texas legislature, journeyed out to the frontier. When Isaac Parker spoke her name, Cynthia Ann Parker recognized it, but she had forgotten all the other words she used to know.

An unpublished letter written by Isaac Parker's son describes the reunion between uncle and niece: "[She] asked him for his knife. She then went out in the yard and kindled up a fire. Tuckasanna, getting the chips, seemed to understand what she was going to do. When the fire was started, she knelt down by it and held up her hands and then bring them down saying some sort of a ceremony. Then rise up and lean over the fire and cut her breast and let the blood drop on the fire . . . ."

After this greeting, Isaac Parker brought his niece Cynthia Ann home with him, but she and her baby daughter found it difficult to adjust to inhuman ways. "They did not eat hearty," wrote Isaac Parker's son. "It seemed that our diet did not suit them till we would kill a beef. When the beef was down, she came with a butcher knife and went to skinning and Tuckasanna dancing round and whooping the Comanche war whoop in real Indian style. As soon as the beef was opened, she took out the kidneys and liver and then commenced eating and dancing and yelling in real savage style, the blood running down their faces and the smoke from the warm liver rising as they eat it . . . ."

It was just like a buffalo kill.

"She would see a crowd . . . and . . . crawl under the bed as she believed she would be killed . . . as the Indians teach their prisoners that the white people kill them when reclaimed."

And were not the Indians right? Where was Elizabeth Kellogg? Where was Rachel Plummer?

When she was not hiding under the bed, Cynthia Ann was trying to run away to rejoin "her people." She would steal a horse and ride toward the high plains. And the Parkers would track her, stalk her, capture her, and return her: a prisoner of civilization.

When Cynthia Ann Parker's baby daughter, Prairie Flower, died of some civilized fever, the mother grieved like a human being. She slashed her breasts.

And then she starved herself to death: It was her only escape.

After the program, Little Mirror changed clothes and then ran from the white boys. Bobby chased her. And so did his cousin, Collin Farmer, who had just arrived in camp. Taking refuge in a cabin, Suzy was out of breath and upset at the damage suffered by her pretty new blouse. A lavender ribbon had been torn off one sleeve. Such was the suffering that a modern descendant of Cynthia Ann Parker had to endure.

Bobby wanted the lavender ribbon, so she gave it to him. He wrapped it around his finger. But then Collin wanted the ribbon on her other sleeve. So she tore it off and gave it to him. Suddenly Bobby saw that he had a rival. Both white boys competed for the ribbon on her breast pocket.

Quanah loved Weckeah, but she already belonged to someone else. She was engaged to a brave named Tennap, who had paid a "bride price" of many ponies for her. Quanah was now a poor orphan completely alone in the world—his mother and sister carried off into fatal captivity, his father dead of an infected wound, his brother Pecos dead of disease. The orphan did not have enough horses to compete with Tennap. But still he loved Weckeah.

One night, Weckeah told her mother that she was going down to the stream to wash her hair. Tennap's promised bride eloped with Quanah.

Naturally, Tennap raised a war party and went after Quanah and Weckeah. But when he caught up with them, he did not know what to do with them. Quanah was so fierce that Tennap simply turned around and went home.

Bobby, who did not give up so easily, dealt the cards. The gin war was taken up again. Collin won the first hand. And he seemed to be winning with Suzy, too. Bobby, last night's big winner, looked on jealously.

Quanah led his people in the great Buffalo War of 1874, which attempted to kill the buffalo hunters before they could kill all the buffalo. To fight this war, Quanah raised the greatest Comanche army ever assembled. In the past, the Comanches had always fought in small raiding parties, like the one that attacked Fort Parker, never fighting together as a single people. But Quanah led a united Comanche army, made up of warriors from all the Comanche tribes, for the first and last time in Comanche history. Quanah was the first and last supreme chief of the Comanche people.

The largest battle took place when Quanah's Comanche army attacked a buffalo-hide boomtown known as Adobe Walls. During the fighting, Quanah's horse was shot from under him, and he took cover behind the rotting carcass of a skinned buffalo. The great battle ended in a stalemate—the Indians too many for the buffalo hunters, the buffalo hunters' guns too accurate over distances of up to a mile for the Indians.

Afterward, Quanah never again made war on a whole town. He killed buffalo hunters in their camps, he killed them in hide-heavy wagons, he hunted and killed them while they were hunting and killing the buffalo.

On the one hand, Quanah became the most feared man in Texas; but on the other hand, Texans were proud of him. After all, he was Cynthia Ann's boy, and he was making a name for himself. White Texans never called him anything but Quanah *Parker*.

The next hand was won by the Indian, Suzy. Bobby looked beaten.

Quanah was finally defeated by hunger. All the buffalo were killed. The United States Army pursued him everywhere. When the soldiers caught up with him in Palo Duro Canyon, Quanah's tribe lost only a few lives but almost all its horses. The U.S. Army shot 1,400 Indian ponies dead.

In the summer of 1875, Quanah led his hungry people to Fort Sill in what is now Oklahoma. He turned in his weapons. He surrendered.

A dejected Bobby did not want to play cards anymore. The battle around the gin table was over. The cards were put away.

Collin said he was going to bed. Bobby, for the first time in a long time, looked pleased. But Suzy begged Collin to stay. And he did. Bobby went back to looking as unhappy as ever.

They all decided to go for a walk in the woods. It would be just like last night—only this time Collin would be along.

They walked along the narrow path through the trees in single file, Indian fashion.

Quanah Parker led the Comanches on the "white man's road." He proved to be a greater chief in peace than in war. Since he was both red and white, he was trusted by both sides. He helped "his people" adjust to reservation life.

The Great Comanche Chief even met the Great White Father, Teddy Roosevelt, at a Rough Riders' reunion in Oklahoma City. Soon the two were not only friends but hunting buddies. They stalked wolves together. And in 1905, Quanah Parker, Cynthia Ann's boy, rode a white horse down Pennsylvania Avenue in Theodore Roosevelt's inaugural day procession.

On the reservation, Quanah built a great white house, which some people called the Western White House because of his friendship with the president. Others called it the Star House because stars were painted on its roof. He hung a picture of his friend Teddy Roosevelt in the dining room. And in the living room, Quanah Parker, the defeated chief, hung a big, colorful painting of George Custer's Last Stand.

The white boy, Bobby, was less graceful in his seeming defeat. While they were all filing through the woods, Collin tripped and put his hands on the Indian maiden's shoulders to support himself. And the Indian maiden covered the white boy's hands with her own. Bobby got so angry that he started punching an ancient oak that towered above them like a family tree.

Back in camp, the Indian grandmother sensed trouble. It was time to start looking for her granddaughter.

Quanah Parker went in search of his mother, as years earlier James Parker had gone in search of his daughter. The chief knew his mother was dead, but he wanted to find out as much about her and her fate as he could. And he wanted to return her body to the land of "her people."

On a trip to Fort Worth, Quanah walked into a photography studio and asked for a picture of his mother. He thought the photographer had pictures of everyone. When he learned his mistake, the chief advertised in a Fort Worth paper for a picture of his mother. And Sul Ross, the Texas Ranger who had "freed" her, sent him one. Quanah hung it in the master bedroom in the Star House.

Quanah even journeyed to Parker County. The great Indian chief met his white relatives. He slept in his mother's bed. And he eventually convinced these relatives to let him have his mother's bones.

When the body was uncovered, Cynthia Ann Parker was positively identified by the Comanche necklace her skeleton still wore. Prairie Flower's smaller bones lay beside her. Quanah loaded two coffins, one larger than the other, onto a wagon and headed north. Cynthia Ann Parker's captivity was over at last: She was escaping back to her people.

◆

The Indian grandmother found her granddaughter in the woods talking to the white boys. She fetched Little Mirror back to the family cabin. There would be no kissing that night.

Quanah buried his mother on Comanche land on a cold December day in 1910. A few weeks later, his work done, the chief caught pneumonia. He was attended in the Star House by a white doctor and an Indian medicine man, but neither could help him. On February 22, 1911, Quanah Parker, the greatest chief of the Comanches, died in a brass bed. He was buried beside his mother beneath these words:

> *Resting here until day breaks*
> *And darkness disappears*
> *Is Quanah Parker*
> *Last Chief of the Comanches . . .*

The stone was wrong. The rest was disturbed. In 1957, the U.S. Army dug up these Stone Age human beings, Quanah and Cynthia Ann, and turned their resting place into a missile firing range. They were reburied on an army base.

"See you next year," Suzy called the next morning as her family pulled out of camp. The Indian maiden waved good-bye to the white boys.

In the Indian family's Japanese car, it only took a little over four hours to drive from Fort Parker, where the family drama began, to Fort Sill, where it ended. After all these years, Suzy's family still lives just down the road from Fort Sill in the tiny town of Cache. Her frame house, crowded with dolls and school awards, is on Buffalo Drive.

Soon word spread through Cache that the prettiest girl in town was back in town. Her return was marked by a 21-telephone-call salute. But eventually the Indian maiden had a chance between calls to telephone her white cousins.

First she told Bobby: "I think about you, too. (Pause.) You thought I would forget all about you, huh? Heartbroken? (Pause.) You took both ribbons, huh? (Pause.) No, you can't have the one on the pocket."

Then she told Collin: "I don't know if you'll remember who this is.

(Pause.) Bob told me you wouldn't remember me. (Pause.) You mean you actually told someone about me? I told everyone about you. I said you were good-looking. (Pause.) I want to see you again. I think I'm just gonna pack up and come down there and live. (Pause.) Bob's gonna get mad again. Start a family feud."

When the next weekend came, the Indian maiden, with no family reunion to attend, went where she went every weekend: to an extraordinary amusement park. You go down a one-lane paved road, which dwindles into a dirt road, which leads deeper and deeper into oblivion. And then suddenly out of the wilderness appears a woebegone Wonderland, a broken-down Brigadoon, a faded Ferris wheel, a moldy merry-go-round, all sorts of rickety rides—and Quanah Parker's Star House! The huge old home, with its elaborate porches and balconies, is peeling—even the stars. The owner of the amusement park bought the Star House and moved it in among the rides in 1958. He is building a roller coaster beside the home of the last chief of the Comanches.

When Little Mirror entered the amusement park, a wave of energy seemed to move through this fabulous place. Quanah's house might be crumbling, but his genes are his real monument.

Little Mirror's friends crowded around. She told them about Texas over the electronic beeps of the new computerized pinball machines. The descendants of the great Comanche warriors were going on an electronic pinball warpath fighting pinball battles in pinball wars. She was attracted by these machines, with their complicated, "intelligent" electronic circuitry. After all, she hopes to see her family move from the Stone Age to the computer age in just a hundred years. At last, she, too, went over to the game machines.

Quanah Parker's great-great-granddaughter stood in the shadow of his Star House in the middle of an amusement park playing Space Invaders.

◆　◆　◆

I finished the story and turned it in and my editor got fired. The new editor wanted his own stories in the magazine. My story was never published.

I am now at work on a novel about Cynthia Ann Parker and her descendants.

THE RETURN OF THE
URBAN COWBOY

•   •   •

When I wrote "The Ballad of the Urban Cowboy" for *Esquire* magazine, I used plenty of irony to make my point. Every sentence seemed to
say in one way or another: The kids at Gilley's think they are real cowboys, but they really aren't. And the corollary seemed to be: They all
think they are in a western movie, but they aren't. I was viewing all
those urban cowboys from above and smiling to myself.

When we started working on the movie *Urban Cowboy*, I stopped
laughing. I stopped because a work of fiction—unlike a work of journalism—must embrace its characters. Of course, there are exceptions, but
generally speaking, journalism is critical of people, fiction is forgiving.
Journalism emphasizes negatives—news is bad news—while fiction emphasizes positives. Otherwise there would be no heroes. If a fiction
writer doesn't like—doesn't care about what happens to—his characters,
then no one else will.

So I started to identify with the cowboys and cowgirls in Gilley's
in part because I had moved from writing journalism to writing fiction.
But I also identified with them because I got to know them better. I
really did come to care what happened to them.

And, well, they were right about one thing: They *were* in a western
movie. We used hundreds of Gilley's regulars as extras in *Urban Cowboy*, and some even got speaking parts.

After the movie came out, I continued to go back to Gilley's whenever I got the chance. Each return was like a high school reunion. I promised myself that someday I would write about what had happened to them all.

And then *Texas Monthly* called and asked me to do just that.

◆　　◆　　◆

Texas Monthly, November 1985

Half a decade after *Urban Cowboy* bucked its way into America's consciousness, I made a sentimental trip back to Gilley's, the legendary saloon where the movie was set. In a way I felt like Sancho Panza going back to La Mancha for a rematch with the windmills, only my windmill was a spinning mechanical bull.

I jousted with my windmill of a bull again, and I got hurt again, naturally. If this story were a country song, the steel guitar would now go *twang, twang,* the way it always does whenever somebody gets hurt. And people get hurt in country songs even more often than they do on the mechanical bull, *twang, twang.*

Limping badly, I left the bull behind and moved on to Gilley's newest attraction, the Wild West, *High Noon,* shoot-out-on-Main-Street, fastest-gun-in-Gilley's gunfight. You strap on six-guns and step into what looks like a movie set of a western town. And you face the man or woman whom you are trying to "kill" and who is trying to "kill" you. You are Alan Ladd in *Shane.* You are Gary Cooper in *High Noon.* You are the hero of your own movie. Then you fire three shots and look for red "blood" on him—or on her—or on you. The bullets are paint pellets, but they hurt when they hit. Like the bull, this shoot-out is kind of a toy, but it will bruise you up pretty bad, because if you are a cowboy, it usually hurts to have fun, *twang, twang.*

I got painfully "killed" twice, but I "killed" the other guy twice too, so it was a dead heat, as they say. Bruised from the bull and from the bullets, I decided to try something a little less physical: listening to cowboys talk.

Soon I was hearing tales of shoot-outs with real bullets and real blood. Tales told by the real people whose real lives and real loves had been woven into the plot of *Urban Cowboy.* People I sought out after many years and one movie to see what had been happening in their private movies since I had seen them last. One was the real-life urban cowboy played on the screen by John Travolta, another was the real-life urban cowgirl played by Debra Winger, and then there was the real-life urban outlaw played by Scott Glenn.

I was especially eager to renew my acquaintance with the outlaw because he was the first friend I ever made at Gilley's, in many ways the best friend I made. Of course, when I met him I had no idea he was an escaped convict hiding out at Gilley's—a kind of vast indoor badlands.

All the boys in the saloon looked like cowboys, but they weren't, and all the girls looked like cowgirls, but they weren't, either. The outlaw didn't look like an outlaw, but he was. He didn't look like a hotshot who would fight it out with a gang of bikers and make them wish they had never met him, but he had. He didn't look like a lover who would get engaged and then—on the night of his fiancée's wedding shower—get arrested. But that is what happened. He looked like an innocent, white-hat, clean-cut, all-American cowboy, but he wasn't.

In a sense his story symbolizes the rise and fall and rise again of the cowboy. Which, in turn, seems to symbolize what has happened to Houston during the past five years. For Houston rose and fell, going from oil boomtown to oil bust town. But Houston will surely come back, the way the cowboy always comes back. The cowboy fades away from time to time—as if absent on some long trail drive—but the cowboy always returns when we need him.

In the summer of 1978 I flew from Washington D.C., to Houston to do a magazine story on Gilley's. I already had a title in mind, "The Ballad of the Urban Cowboy." I also had an approach—I wanted to write a nonfiction love story set in the huge honky-tonk's wide-open indoor spaces.

Since I had grown up in Texas, I expected my visit to Gilley's to feel something like a family reunion. But when I actually got there and walked into the huge saloon I felt more like Margaret Mead stepping ashore on Samoa for the first time.

Before me stretched several thousand ersatz cowboys and cowgirls who worked in refineries or waited tables or did other urban work during the day but who turned themselves into B-movie western heroes at night. They were dancing and swinging at a mechancial punching bag and riding a mechanical bull on about four and a half acres of concrete prairie under a tin roof.

I felt as if I were watching a performance of a shit-kicking, red-necked, low-rent, pickup-driving, Skoal-chewing, longneck-drinking, armadillo-loving, country-music-singing, two-stepping, Stetson-wearing, mechanical-bull-riding *Man of La Mancha* with a drawl, y'all. These urban cowboys were to real cowboys what Don Quixote was to a real knight.

But the cowboys of La Mancha looked scary; they almost all did physical labor, had mean muscles, and were tough. I was a little frightened until I met Les Walker. I liked and trusted him right away, and I spent most of my first night at Gilley's watching Les run the mechanical bull. I saw him make the bull throw and hurt cowboys, *twang, twang.* I even saw him throw and hurt cops—most of whom believe they are the real inheritors of the cowboy mantle. And when I say "hurt" I mean bull riders were getting their nuts busted—for the bull is a more effective nutcracker than any that Tchaikovsky ever dreamed of, *twang, twang.* But the man running the nutcracker seemed so much gentler than his job.

I trusted him and his gentle nature so much that I let him give me a ride on the bull. Naturally I got bucked off. Naturally I got hurt. But pain seemed to be a part of the cowboy's initiation. Les continued to be my best friend at Gilley's. I never suspected that he might not be what he appeared to be.

Around midnight on that night, one of Les's girl friends came in and rode the bull standing up. I couldn't believe it. I decided she was a girl I should talk to. Her name was Betty Helmer, but she would be named Sissy in the movie, and Debra Winger would play her. She told me that she had met her husband at Gilley's. His name was Dew Westbrook, but he would be named Bud in the movie, and John Travolta would play him.

After meeting at Gilley's, Betty Helmer and Dew Westbrook courted at Gilley's almost every night. Then they got married and had their wedding reception at Gilley's. They were happy at Gilley's until the mechanical bull arrived—like the snake coming to Eden. The problem was that the cowgirl wife could ride the bull better than her cowboy husband. The poor cowboy had married a cowgirl who was a better cowboy than he was. And he couldn't stand it. He ordered her to stop riding the bull, but she wouldn't. The bull broke up their marriage, *twang, twang.*

The story seemed to me to be a curious and modern love triangle. The Cowgirl, the Cowboy, and the Mechanical Bull. Or the girl, the boy, and the machine. Since she couldn't fall in love with a machine, the cowgirl transferred her affections from the bull to the bull master and fell in love with him.

Lots of girls did. Betty loved the bull master. So did her cousin Sheryl and many others. Girls would gather around Les the way cows gather around a bull. He had his indoor herd. In the movie he would be played by Scott Glenn and would be called Wes. He called himself Les Walker, but "Les" was as fictitious as "Wes."

Once I had met Betty and Dew and Les and the bull, I knew I had my love story. Written as a magazine article, it was published in September 1978, and Hollywood started calling right away.

Two months later, I was beginning a new adventure, my first screenplay—and Les was about to begin a new adventure, marriage. Sheryl was to be his bride. Or so he thought. But something happened that changed his plans. The rumor was that one of the girls who hung around the bull—who was in love with the bull and with Les as an extension of it—turned in the bull master to keep him from getting married. Gilley's hath no fury like a cowgirl scorned, *twang, twang*.

Shortly before the wedding Sheryl's girl friends gave her a bridal shower and rained presents on her. Sexy lingerie for the wedding night. Small appliances to fix breakfast on the first morning of their marriage. Funny presents to make her blush.

After the shower the cowgirl carried the loot home to her outlaw. They were already living together. She had the fun of showing everything to him and blushing again. They were putting the gifts away when they heard a knock at the door.

Since the outlaw was a wanted man, he retired to a bedroom to hide. And he picked up his shotgun and made sure it was fully loaded. He was always careful. The cowgirl answered the knock.

When she opened the door, she found a posse on her doorstep. She knew what they wanted. They wanted her bridegroom, *twang, twang*.

"I'm David Mullican," said one of the policemen. "I'm a friend of Sherwood's."

The cop meant Sherwood Cryer, the owner of Gilley's.

"Les ain't here," said Sheryl.

But it was too late. The outlaw knew Mullican. His caution seemed to evaporate like a gambler's luck. He stepped out of the bedroom to say hello. He had his shotgun, but he leaned it against the wall.

Mullican pulled his gun.

Suddenly the room was full of law. Two FBI agents stormed into the bride's living room. And another policeman came charging in. Guns were drawn. And handcuffs closed on the outlaw's wrists, *click, click, twang, twang*.

"I got hysterical when they put the handcuffs on him," Sheryl remembers. "That was nine days before we planned to get married. Everything was paid for. All we had to do was go to the church."

The bride got so hysterical that she decided to use force to keep the cops from taking the outlaw. She grabbed one handcuffed arm, the law grabbed the other, and they had a tug-of-war.

"No, you can't take him!" she cried. "You can't take him! You can't take him!"

But they took him. Took her robber bridegroom. On the night of her wedding shower. Nine days before the wedding. The law put the groom in a police car and drove him away while a police helicopter hovered overhead. The bride, who had been robbed of her wedding, ran inside, grabbed a .22 pistol, ran back outside, and aimed at the chopper. It flew away and left her alone.

After her bridegroom was stolen from her, Sheryl didn't sleep for three days and nights. Then she passed out.

A while later she received a letter from her imprisoned groom. In the envelope she found a photograph, the only picture he had to send her: a mug shot. Beneath his picture was a name: "Richard Hayes." "Les Walker" had just been an alias. And beneath the name were all the crimes he was charged with, *twang, twang.*

The trouble began in his Hometown, which he does not want identified, where he got in with the wrong crowd and was accused of holding up a convenience store. Before he could be arrested, he fled the small town of Hometown and headed for the Big City: Houston.

He was having a good time until he walked into a topless bar called the Classic Cat, where a biker gang used to hang out. He started talking to a girl, which make the bikers jealous. The leather jackets asked him to meet them in the parking lot. Then they slammed him up against a wall, and explained the error of his ways.

The outlaw pulled away from the bikers and ran for his truck. He heard bullets hitting the ground and his pickup. Reaching his goal, the outlaw pulled a shotgun from behind the seat. Soon bullets were going back the other way.

The outlaw saw a biker standing by the door of the topless bar. He shot him. The leather jacket went down. Other jackets dragged him inside.

When the outlaw saw two other bikers hiding behind a car, he shot out all the car windows trying to hit the bikers.

When the shotgun was empty, he ran back to his truck and pulled out a rifle. He walked back into the topless bar. Jackets and breasts dived for cover.

The outlaw just stood there brandishing his weapon until the cops came. Then he handed his rifle to a uniform. And he went to jail.

After an investigation, the cops decided that he had been acting in self-defense. They were about to let him go when they learned of the outstanding warrants from Hometown. So instead of turning him loose, they sent him home. Home to jail.

The outlaw was placed in a solitary cell. He had three friends in another cell. One night his friends sawed through the bars of their cell, got the jailer's keys, and unlocked the outlaw's cell. Then they put the jailer in one of the cells. Since the outlaw was the one who closed the door on the jailer, with whom he had once gone to school, he would eventually be charged with kidnapping.

With the law after him once again, the outlaw headed for Houston. He went back and got a job down the street from where he had had the shoot-out with the bikers. He went to work running the bull at Gilley's—where he met Sheryl and Betty and the bull-loving cowgirl who turned him in and put him back behind bars.

Sheryl went to the outlaw's Hometown to attend his trial.

"I stole a kiss in the county courthouse," remembers Sheryl. "I stole it in the hall when he was being escorted back to the jail."

Which made her something of an outlaw—a jailhouse-kiss-stealing bandit.

Meanwhile, back at the concrete ranch, back at Gilley's, the course of true love was running about as smoothly as a mechanical bull ride. In the movie Bud and Sissy break up but get back together at the end of the story as the sound track wails "Lookin' for Love." In real life there was no happy ending. The mechanical bull split up Betty and Dew, and they stayed split up, *twang, twang.*

Then Betty fell in love with Somebody New the same way David O. Selznick met Vivien Leigh—in the glow of a fabulous fire. While he was still looking for his Scarlett, Selznick decided to begin shooting *Gone with the Wind* by filming the burning of Atlanta on a studio back lot. Vivien Leigh was introduced to him as the cameras were turning and Atlanta was blazing. Betty fell in love with Carl Lee Jones while Gilley's was engulfed in flames.

One day in February 1979 Betty heard fire engines and followed them to see what was happening. She was amazed to see fire trucks pull up in front of Gilley's. She parked in the vast parking lot and got out to watch the world's largest nightclub burn. Also drawn by the great Gilley's fire was a wiry young man named Carl. They stood in the heat of the flames and watched the blaze together. Gilley's had destroyed Betty's marriage, and now Gilley's itself was being destroyed. It seemed the right time and the right place to begin something new.

A few days later they decided to go four-wheel-driving together in Carl's green Bronco. They came to a stream that Betty said looked like trouble. He decided to try to cross it anyway. "We'll get stuck," she warned. "No we won't," he said. They got stuck for twelve hours. From 2:00 P.M. to 2:00 A.M. They dug with their hands in the mud until they looked like Adam and Eve before God breathed life into their clay bodies.

When they finally got the Bronco unstuck, they drove it to an all-night car wash. They started putting in quarters and spraying the truck. They spent $6. By the time they got back to her apartment, it was three-thirty in the morning. He stayed the night.

Not too long afterward, Betty proposed to Carl, and they got married. The date was August 24, her first husband's birthday. The ceremony was performed in the office of a justice of the peace. The bride wore a flowered dress. The groom wouldn't wear a suit, just brown slacks and a silk shirt. After a one-night honeymoon at a Ramada Inn the newlyweds moved into a mobile home.

The new bride and groom started going back to Gilley's—which had suffered some damage from the fire, about half an acre destroyed, leaving only about four acres of concrete prairie on which to play. But Carl soon decided he didn't like going to Gilley's. He found it annoying that Betty could ride the bull better than he could and was better known than he was. He told her not to work in the movie *Urban Cowboy*, then being filmed on location in Gilley's, even though the movie was about her. Or perhaps especially because it was about her.

Carl and Betty had a daughter and a son.

Then, like a lot of people in Houston, Carl suddenly found himself without a paycheck. He got laid off from his job at U.S. Steel. The lay-off lasted eighteen months and was tough on everyone. The mobile home became such an unhappy place that Betty went home to her parents' house. She needed a break.

Around that time Dew, who had been out of town for months, came back into town and went to see his former wife. They sat around her mother's living room and talked just the way they had when they were courting. They talked about going back to Gilley's, but never got around to it, *twang, twang.*

A few days later Betty returned to her trailer-park home to talk to her husband, to try to straighten things out, but he wasn't there. She went in and waited for him. Hearing a truck pull up out front, Betty looked out the window. She saw her husband with a woman. While she hid, they entered the trailer. He went to the back bathroom. The woman went to the front bathroom.

Betty knocked on the door of the front bathroom. The woman opened the door and was horrified to see Carl's wife standing there.

"You can leave anytime," Betty said, *twang, twang.*

Which was a real-life scene almost identical to a scene in the movie that had been released more than a year before.

Betty and Carl's marriage was all over for good.

Then Betty's father, who had been sick for a long time, committed suicide.

And Betty seemed to come full circle. She moved back in with her mother more or less permanently, into the house on Peach where she had grown up, just down the street from Gilley's. Soon she started going to Gilley's again. She went back to riding the bull standing up. And now she is once again the best bull rider at Gilley's.

It is as though she cannot stay away from the bull. When she was younger, she once visited Huntsville, a trip that was supposed to last a week, but she stayed just a few hours because she realized that she could not miss even one night with the bull, so she rushed home to it. Her marriage to Carl lasted a little longer but ended the same way—with Betty coming home to the bull.

The bull may have a heart of steel, but its body never gets tired. It will buck forever if you want. And Betty wants.

The outlaw was convicted of kidnapping the guard whom he had locked up during his jailbreak, but Sheryl married him anyway. Les was sent to the penitentiary and she rented a place in a nearby town. That is how the newlyweds spent the first years of their marriage—with walls and bars and barbed wire between them, *twang, twang*.

"I thought so many nights I would break him out," remembers Sheryl. "I thought of coming in the visitors' section with a gun. I told him—"

"And I said nope, nope," he remembers, "we'll both get killed."

She was lonely and frustrated at night. He was lonely and frustrated and tense and scared.

"In prison you need to get around people doing life," he reminisces, "because they are going to be there a long time and don't want no trouble." Short-timers were more unpredictable. "I saw a guy get knifed over a comb."

One morning a guard came into Les's section and woke him up by shaking his shoulder. Reacting with convict instincts, Les turned and hit the guard, knocking him into the wall. He thought he was in big trouble, but the guard later apologized, saying that he was new at the job and didn't know how on edge prisoners were all the time.

Then Les got a pleasant surprise. He was called into an office and told he was going to be given work release. He was overjoyed—yet at the same time puzzled because he had not applied for work release. As soon as he could, he called his wife and told her the good news. She was ecstatic.

But then he was called back into the office and told that there had been a mistake. He wasn't going to be given work release; it was somebody else. Sorry. So he had to call Sheryl back and tell her the bad news, *twang, twang.*

And then *she* started making calls. She called the prison officials and accused them of cruel and unusual punishment, not to him but to her, telling her she could have her husband back, then snatching him away. The prison didn't seem to give a damn.

So she started calling everybody else she could think of. "When I get mad, my mouth will not stay shut." She kept calling until she had worked her way up to the governor's office. And she raised the same hell there that she had raised with everyone else. But the difference was that the governor's office called her back and said, okay, she had a point, it was cruel and unusual. And her husband was going to be given a work release after all.

After spending two years inside the walls, he was transferred to the prison farm, where he remained for a short while.

And then he was freed.

Thanks to his good wife, who had broken him out of the big house with her big mouth. She had not needed a gun, after all.

The ex-outlaw and his good wife went back to Houston and back to Gilley's. He got his old job running the mechanical bull. The ex-outlaw was once again the bull master.

And more.

The ex-outlaw was also drawn into the Great Saloon War then rocking Texas. Dividing Texas. Like the Civil War.

Gilley's had long claimed to be the biggest nightclub in the world. It had four and a half acres of concrete prairie under one roof to back up its claim. But then a saloon called Billy Bob's Texas opened up in the stockyards of Fort Worth, and it was even bigger. Instead of a mechanical bull, Billy Bob's had real bulls that bucked in a real rodeo arena right inside the honky-tonk. So Gilley's decided it needed a real rodeo arena with real bulls too.

The ex-outlaw was hired to build the new rodeo arena. Sheryl worked on it some too. And so did a lot of other cowboys. But the former bad guy was largely responsible for the building of the huge rodeo arena, which was much bigger than Billy Bob's. The arena doubled the size of Gilley's and made it once again the biggest nightclub in the world.

With the help of a desperado Gilley's won the Great Saloon Shoot-Out. Appropriately, the arena was finished on the Fourth of July.

The new rodeo arena turned out to be an especially happy place for Jesse La Rive, a Gilley's cowgirl who had played a small but memorable part as Sissy's best friend in *Urban Cowboy*.

When Gilley's started having rodeos Jessie naturally wanted to take part. She wasn't quite ready to ride a live bull, so she contented herself with carrying the Texas flag in the grand parade at the beginning of the rodeo. One night a sailor in the stands looked down at this pretty girl on horseback gracefully carrying the Lone Star flag, which streamed behind her. He told a friend who was with him, "I'm going to marry that girl."

The sailor made a point of meeting Jessie that night. Two weeks later he asked her to marry him. A justice of the peace performed the ceremony, and then the bride and groom went over to Gilley's to announce their wedding from the bandstand.

Other couples from all over the country who had seen the movie about Gilley's started coming to the old saloon to get married. Some got married on the bandstand. One couple got married on the dance floor. Some even got married on the mechanical bull.

Those were great, romantic days at Gilley's, with new brides and grooms and big crowds and singing cash registers. Gilley's was on top of the saloon business, and Houston was on top of the oil business. Gilley's was the boom saloon in the boomtown, where you couldn't walk down the street without dollar bills sticking to your boots.

And then when everything was going so well, one night a young boy, a teenager, was thrown by a bull inside Gilley's. He landed on the bull's horns and was gored in the chest. His aorta was severed and he was probably dead before he hit the arena floor. The boy's father watched it all from the bleachers.

Perhaps that tragedy was an omen.

The romance could not last forever. The cowboy romance. The boom saloon romance. The boomtown romance. They all would eventually end the way a movie ends, and the lights would come back on.

The problem was oil. When the price of oil went up in the seventies, it made Houston rich. When the price went down in the eighties, it made Houston poor—or at least poorer. A lot of bang went out of the boomtown.

"There's been a big recession in this Houston area," Sherwood Cryer, the boss at Gilley's, says. "We still get the people in here, but they don't have the money to spend they once had."

The cash registers at Gilley's are still singing, but a slower song, a country song, full of trouble and pain, *twang, twang.*

The ex-outlaw had his troubles too. At home in his own bed with his own wife, he was still as tense as he had been in prison.

Nor was life on Gilley's concrete range entirely peaceful. The ex-outlaw started drinking too much. And fighting too much. And his wife blamed Gilley's.

One night a drunk old man accused the bull master of bumping his wife. The bull master hit him in the face and knocked out teeth. Then a dozen guys jumped on top of the bull master. Sheryl started screaming and trying to pull them off.

When she finally pulled him from beneath the pile, the two of them fled out the side door because the cops were on the way. He had a bloody eye.

Another night, the bull master saw his wife dancing with a teenager. He came up and grabbed her by the ponytail.

"Having fun?" he asked.

"Yeah," she said, "and you?"

She thought someone was going to die, but her husband just walked away.

On another night someone almost did die. The husband and wife were sharing an evening at home—just the kind of evening they had dreamed of when he was locked up. Suddenly, he announced that he was going out. She started in the direction of the family's .357 Magnum.

He was already in the car when she emerged from the front door wearing her nightgown and wielding Dirty Harry's pistol. She thought she would shoot the tires out so her restless husband couldn't leave. She pulled the trigger. *Click.* The misfire made her mad. She pulled a second time. This time the gun fired, but she missed the tires, which made her even madder—so mad that she aimed the third shot at her husband's head. She had tried to be reasonable, to be moderate, to aim at the machine rather than at the person, but the gun had not cooperated, had made her mad, and so now she was just going to have to kill the husband for whom she had waited so long, *bang, bang, twang, twang.*

But the third shot was high.

Her husband drove off, and she ran into the house to look for more bullets because she knew he would be back. She knew very well that she was in a race. She simply had to reload her weapon before he came back with the only weapons he would need, his hands. But where were the bullets? Where were the bullets? She had worked so hard to get her husband out of jail, and now she was working even harder to find bullets to kill him with. But where were they? Where were they? She couldn't just go next door and explain that she was out of .357 shells and ask to borrow a cupful. But she had to find some somewhere, because he would be back any minute and he would be drunk and he would be mad.

The outlaw husband returned home before the wife could find bullets to kill him with. And he did what she had known he would do, what Wes kept doing in *Urban Cowboy*. He beat her up.

"My hair was all over the front yard," she remembers.

It was about then that she started lying awake nights dreaming up ways to kill the man for whom she had waited so long and fought so hard. Maybe poison. Maybe a knife. Maybe a shotgun because it was easier to hit somebody with a shotgun.

In the movie and in real life Dew Westbrook lived in Houston because it was *the* boomtown. The city itself was a kind of gusher, a job gusher, a money gusher. But when the gusher started to go dry, and money got scarcer, and jobs got fewer, a lot of workers started leaving town. Dew was one of them, *twang, twang.*

"I left Houston not long after the movie came out," Dew says. "I started traveling. I've been in every state west of the Mississippi except Wyoming and Utah. Plus some states east of the Mississippi—Ohio, Illinois. I drove sixty thousand miles last year."

In the old days cowboys went on long trail drives. Now urban cowboys like Dew go on job drives. They are every bit as rootless as their historical counterparts, driving all over the country following work.

Two of the things Dew left behind when he hit the road were a wife and a child. After his marriage to Betty had ended, he married another girl, named Jan, and they had a son. But that marriage was in trouble too, thanks in part to Dew's nomadic life-style, which had been imposed upon him by the economy.

Dew's first stop after he left Texas was California, where he took a job at the San Onofre nuclear power plant. Oil had let him down, so he was turning to atoms. He became an atomic cowboy.

Then Dew went to Beulah, North Dakota, where the weather was cold but the money was good. He joined a crew of five thousand who were building one of America's first coal gasification plants, which turn coal into gas. Oil and atoms had let him down, so he was turning to

America's most abundant resource, coal. He was a bituminous cowboy.

He was also lonely and cold and two thousand miles from his wife.

"That's when I met Kelly," he remembers. "I met her at a party the first weekend in Beulah. She couldn't stand me at first. She thought I was bold and arrogant. She was from the North and had never known anyone from the South."

At some point during the party Dew, three other guys, and Kelly decided to take a ride. A cop pulled them over and searched the car for drugs. He didn't find any, but he did find a gun. So the cop announced that he was going to arrest the driver.

But Dew said, hold on, no, you can't do that.

The cop wondered why not.

Dew said the gun was in plain sight. Which meant that it wasn't a concealed weapon. Which meant that it was covered by the bill of rights, specifically the right to bear arms.

The cop just stood there amazed. Kelly stood there amazed. What was she doing riding around with this guy?

Dew said the National Rifle Association would back him up on this. He was wearing a big belt buckle decorated with an American flag and a skeleton holding a rifle and the words "I will give up my gun when they pry it from my cold dead fingers."

The cop was beginning to wish that he had never met this cowboy with the mechanical mouth. And Kelly felt the same way.

But the cop eventually backed down.

And Kelly eventually changed her mind.

Some five thousand men had come to build the plant at Beulah, a tiny town that contained fewer than one hundred datable women, so there were not enough females to go around, to put it mildly. But Dew got one—blond, green-eyed, beautiful Kelly.

Soon she was living with him in the huge Man Camp, where no women were allowed. One night a guard saw Kelly and chased her through the snow, but she ducked into a building and got away and returned to Dew's narrow bed.

In Beulah the ex–urban cowboy and his new girl friend watched the northern lights together. They went skating in their boots by holding onto the back of a pickup as it drove across a frozen lake. And they partied in the bar of the Best Western motel and danced to a song on the jukebox that went like this:

> *I was lookin' for love in all the wrong places,*
> *Searchin' your eyes, lookin' for traces,*
> *Of what I'm dreaming of.*

Then the gasification plant was finished, and Kelly had a decision to make. Would she go with Dew to Seattle? Or would she return to her ex-husband in New York? The ex-husband, who was some sort of gangster, wanted her back, and he was used to getting what he wanted.

Kelly chose the cowboy over the godfather.

Kelly and Dew moved from Seattle to Baton Rouge, Lousiana, to Lima, Ohio, to Chicago and finally to Dallas, where they are now. The original urban cowboy lives in a trailer parked near the stadium where the Dallas Cowboys play.

He works for a roofing company, but he plans to borrow enough money to buy some laundromats, which he hopes will make him enough money to buy a little piece of dirt up in Montana. He already has a place picked out. When I first met Dew, he was twenty-one years old and already dreaming his dirt dream. He is twenty-eight now and dreaming it still.

While he is waiting for his dirt dream to come true, Dew spends his time practicing cowboy arts so he will be ready. He has six guns, but it is hard to do much practicing with them in a crowded trailer park. So he practices with a crossbow instead. A sixty-pounder.

"Very quiet and very deadly," he explains.

The original urban cowboy spends many an evening in his trailer firing his crossbow at a target on the wall. Firing a medieval weapon. A knight's weapon, for God's sake. A weapon of which Don Quixote would have approved. And he shoots it in the house.

Dew Westbrook has gone from being a quixotic indoor cowboy to being a quixotic indoor knight.

"Hello," Sheryl answered the phone.

"Somebody shot me with a crossbow," her husband said.

"What?"

"A crossbow. Some son of a bitch shot me with a crossbow."

"Where's the truck?"

"I don't know. Call it in stolen."

"What? Where are you?"

"Near some grain elevators. Some son of a bitch shot me with a crossbow. Come get me!"

Sheryl went out looking for grain elevators and the victim of a twentieth-century crossbow shooting. And she finally found them. Her husband was slumped beside a phone with a metal shaft sticking out of his chest.

She somehow got him into the car and headed for the hospital. The crossbow-shot cowboy kept complaining about all the bumps she was hitting.

When they reached the hospital, emergency room attendants carried him inside on a stretcher.

He looked up at her and asked, "Are you going to leave me?"

"Yes," she said, *twang, twang.*

Later on, the sheriff's department was able to piece together what had happened. The ex-outlaw had spent years restoring a classic 1961 pickup. When he finally got it finished, he got drunk and went for a drive to celebrate. Boxes of welding rods were rattling around in the back of the truck, but all else was well. Until he hit a railroad track going a hundred miles an hour. The truck was airborne for about a hundred feet. When it came down, it started rolling. The engine went one way. The truck went another. And a welding rod from the back of the truck came crashing into the cab and "shot" him between his heart and his lung.

Yes, she told him, she was going to leave him, but somebody had to take care of the cowboy who had been shot out of the saddle of his classic truck by a welding rod. So she didn't go.

But Sheryl had decided it was time to make a stand. The good-hearted woman told her good-timin' man—as the song goes—that he had to make a choice. Her or the booze. Her or Gilley's.

"If you love that place more than you love me," she said, "that's it."

So the bull master quit his job at Gilley's. He moved his family to the Hill Country and opened a mechanical general store and fix-it shop.

"He straightened up," says Sheryl. "Now our lives are dull."

"But I've got it about how I want it," says the ex-outlaw, ex-convict, ex–bull master, ex–hell raiser.

Of Betty, Dew, and "Les," the main characters I wrote about in my original story eight years ago, the outlaw has fared the best. He is the only one who has a steady job, a good marriage, and a stable family life. Betty's children live with her some of the time and with their father some of the time. Dew has not seen his son for two years. But the outlaw is raising his own children with no custody battles and no back talk—as a matter of fact. He turns out to have been the best all-around cowboy of them all.

"I hear," says Sheryl, "a whole bunch of the old people are going out to Gilley's again."

"I'd like to go in there," says the ex-outlaw, "if the old ones are there."

"No!!!" screams Sheryl.

Whether the ex-outlaw will ever return to Gilley's remains to be seen, but many of the regulars have started coming back. They come back to spend their money, which means that Gilley's is beginning to feel like a boom saloon again. They come back to dance the two-step and the cotton-eyed Joe. They come back to break their hands on the mechanical punching bag, *twang, twang.* They come back to break their balls on the mechanical bull, *twang, twang.* And they come back to play with Gilley's new cowboy toy, the Wild West, fast-draw game, *bang, bang,* you're dead, *twang, twang.*

Betty, who may be the best cowboy ever to walk into Gilley's, loves the new shoot-out. Of course. The first time she ever tried to "kill" anybody, it was Steve Strange, the cowboy with the wonderful name, who has worked at Gilley's longer than anybody. Even Steve left Gilley's a couple of years ago—got mad and quit—but he is back now. It was Steve who taught Betty to ride the bull way back in the beginning. And now he is teaching her to draw and shoot and "kill."

Betty and Steve strap on their six-guns and step into a huge box, about six feet wide by twenty feet long, with a clear plastic front so spectators can see the action. Which makes Betty and Steve look a little like cowboy mannequins about to shoot it out in a department store window. The back wall of the box is painted to look like the main street of a western town, with signs that read "J. Wilson Stagecoach Lines," "The Yellow Rose Hotel and Saloon," "The Long Horn Cafe," "Telegraph Office," "Barber Shop," "Livery Stable," "Saddle and Leather Goods," and just plain "Guns." Betty and Steve take up positions at opposite ends of the box (Main Street).

Steve draws and fires and hits the floor in front of him. He is fast but not always accurate. Betty takes her time and shoots him in the stomach, *twang, twang.*

They reload.

Steve draws and fires and misses again. Betty shoots him in the right eye. Luckily he is wearing a plastic visor like those worn by cops in riots. Steve isn't hurt, but he is "dead," *twang, twang.*

They reload.

Steve shoots Betty in the stomach. And Betty shoots Steve in the stomach. A dead heat.

Then Steve shoots Betty in the arm, and she shoots him in the shoulder.

Then he shoots her in the leg and she shoots him in the stomach.

Then they reload and take up their positions for the last shot. Betty stares at Steve, and Steve stares at Betty. It is the scene that always comes at the end of the movie. Who will live and who will die? Who is the fastest gun?

Steve draws and fires and hits Betty in the leg.

Betty draws and fires and hits Steve in the balls. Her bullet punishes the cowboy right where the bull always punishes cowboys. Steve is learning a lesson that Dew had learned a long time ago: Betty is too much cowboy for most cowboys to handle, *twang, twang.*

Yes, Betty is back. And Steve Strange is back. And lots of others are back at Gilley's. Back to the cowboy fantasy.

And America seems to be going back to dreaming its own cowboy dreams—dreams about shoot-outs on Main Street—once again. Clint Eastwood recently starred in *Pale Rider*, the first old-fashioned Hollywood western to be made in a long time. A short time later, *Silverado* shot its way into America's movie theaters. When it first opened, *Silverado* did not do very well, but the audiences began to get larger. Like romances in a western movie, America's romance with *Silverado* began slowly and shakily but grew into a passion. America was again in love with a western. A western starring, among others, Scott Glenn, who was the outlaw in *Urban Cowboy.*

So America's love affair with the cowboy continues. Sometimes the lovers fight and break up and never want to see each other again. But America always has and always will come back to the cowboy. The ghost of the cowboy fades away and reappears like the ghost of King Arthur, who, according to legend, comes back when his country needs him. Which is appropriate. Because the cowboy myth is an American reinvention of the European knight-errant myth. Both are warriors on horseback. The cowboy hat is the knight's visor; the six-shooter is his lance. And most important of all, the cowboy code is an American code of chivalry. The cowboy—the American knight—is the only truly mythical figure ever created by American culture.

No wonder we keep coming back to him.

Perhaps the country turns to the cowboy when it does not know where else to turn. During the economic depression of the thirties America watched a lot of westerns. All those brave, self-reliant, independent cowboys seemed momentarily to make us feel less helpless. And during the spiritual depression of Joe McCarthy's witch-hunting, paranoid fifties America again embraced the cowboy. All those forthright and honest cowboys made us seem less morally confused, at least until we came back out into the light. During the malaise—as Jimmy Carter called it—of the seventies America welcomed the urban cowboy, who did not even know what *malaise* meant.

When Ronald Reagan took office the country seemed to turn away from the cowboy at the movies. With a movie cowboy in the White House—one who seemed to know where he wanted to lead the country—the country no longer needed cowboy movies. But Reagan's second term seems much less focused than the first, like a trail drive that grows more ragged with every mile. America isn't so sure anymore.

And so more and more of us seem once again to be lookin' for love in honky-tonks, lookin' for reassurance at the movies, lookin' for cowboys.

Twang, twang.

PART TWO

◆ ◆ ◆

STARS

JESSIE

Do you always follow your subjects around?

ADAM

You're interviewing me again. I'm supposed to be interviewing you.

JESSIE

Any suggestions to improve my style?

ADAM

Always treat famous people as if they're not. And treat people who aren't famous as if they were. And always think of an interview as a seduction.

from the screenplay of *Perfect*

WARREN BEATTY
SERIOUSLY

• • •

This was an interesting exercise: How do you do a story on someone who won't talk to you?

Once I finally thought up a solution, I was afraid Beatty might change his mind and grant an interview, which would have ruined everything. He called me twice, and both times my heart stopped, but luckily he was just calling to say that he wouldn't talk to me.

• • •

Rolling Stone, April 1982

"It's been a long movie," Warren Beatty said in a voice that sounded as tired as the voice he had used to portray a dying John Reed at the end of Reds. *"Long to make it. Long to finish it."*

Beatty had called to tell me that he wouldn't talk to me. In 1967, Rex Reed wrote a piece about him called "Will the Real Warren Beatty Please Shut Up?" And ever since then, he has. We had a nice, long, rambling talk about how he wouldn't talk to me.

"I haven't been doing any talking to anybody," he said. *"It's not directed at any publication. I'm sure you can understand what the reasons for that would be. But ummmmm . . ."* He trailed off.

"All right," I said, *"I'm going to do my story about you the way you did your movie about John Reed. I'm going to pretend you're as dead as Reed and go around and interview the people who knew you during*

your lifetime. I'm going to do just what you did: find all the witnesses."
Warren Beatty laughed—proving he has a good sense of humor for
a dead man.

Imagine a giant close-up of George Plimpton on the screen, with
half-moon lighting—bright on one side, dark on the other, just like the
witnesses were displayed in *Reds*. He is wearing a tweed coat over a
pink sweater.

"Warren got absolutely possessed by the John Reed story," Plimpton says. "It possessed him for ten years. The way I got cast in the
movie is like a Schwab's drugstore story."

Plimpton was staying with Hugh Hefner at his Playboy Mansion
in Los Angeles. One night, he decided to go for a swim sometime between three and four in the morning. Returning dripping wet from the
pool, Plimpton found a body collapsed on the floor in the foyer of the
Playboy Mansion.

"Warren?" Plimpton said. "Is that you, Warren?"

A worried Plimpton bent over the prostrate movie star. "Warren,
Warren, are you all right?"

Suddenly, the famous eyes snapped open and stared at the wet man
dripping on him.

"Whigham," Warren Beatty said.

The movie star seemed to be raving.

"What?" Plimpton asked. "Warren, are you okay?"

Beatty eventually explained that he wanted Plimpton to play the
role of Whigham, a wealthy publisher, in a movie about John Reed, the
radical reporter. Upton Sinclair had called John Reed the Playboy of the
Revolution. And now Warren Beatty, the Playboy of the Movies, was
lying there in the Playboy Mansion casting his movie about the Playboy
of the Revolution.

Reed did not like being called a playboy because it meant that he
was not being taken seriously. And Beatty has often had much the same
problem.

To prove that he was *serious* about the Revolution, Reed had to go
to Russia, die for the cause, and be buried in the Kremlin. And to prove
he is *serious*, Beatty has had to make a three-and-a-half-hour movie
about the Russian Revolution, an undertaking that was not unlike fighting a revolutionary war.

In that movie, John Reed (Warren Beatty) has a conversation with
Louise Bryant (Diane Keaton) about being taken seriously. Beatty, who
did the screenplay, wrote the scene as a dialogue, but it sounds like a dialogue of one, like a talk he must have had with himself more than once.

LOUISE:
I'm not taken seriously. . . .

JOHN:
Maybe if you took yourself a little more seriously, other people
would, too! I told you what I thought about the Armory piece. . . .
I think it's very nice, but, no, I don't take it very seriously.

In his dialogues with himself on this subject, Beatty probably sub-
stitutes a movie like *Heaven Can Wait* for the Armory piece.

LOUISE:
Thank you.

JOHN:
Why do you expect to be taken seriously if you don't write about
serious things?

LOUISE:
Well, I don't really care!

JOHN:
You care!

The screen is filled with what looks like the head of a skinny lion,
mane flaring. He is novelist Jerzy Kosinski, an escapee from the Eastern
bloc half a lifetime ago, who plays the evil Zinoviev in *Reds*.

"Warren does see himself as John Reed," Kosinski says with a Polish accent. "In his movies so far, Warren has been as socially insignifi-
cant as John Reed before he began writing about the Revolution.
Beatty's *Bonnie and Clyde* was like Reed's book about Pancho Villa—
gangsters shooting at one another. And Beatty's *Shampoo* was about the
morality of the middle class, like John Reed's little articles about the
minor failings of America. Political fellatio. Warren knows that."

Kosinski gets up and starts pacing. He cannot sit patiently for his
close-up.

"In Hollywood, which is a company town, Warren has been a
nonthreatened, very successful achiever. And so was John Reed in the
company town of America until he committed himself to something that
could have brought him down. What could Warren possibly do in the
company town of Hollywood that would be revolutionary, truly quali-
tatively different from what Brando or Eastwood or Reynolds has done?

Warren looked for a big subject, just as John Reed also looked for something big to report for the *Masses*. And so one day, Warren came across the story of John Reed—and he saw himself as John Reed. The project of making a movie about John Reed became what going to Russia was for Reed. It would affect his life."

Pacing, pacing, pacing.

"Warren's predicament was: How do I sell to the American people the idea of John Reed? Just as John Reed's predicament was: How do I convey to the American people the idea of the Revolution? What faced Warren was the same thing that faced John Reed. He could have been killed by the company town, could have died an artistic death and been buried in the wall of Hollywood. Just as John Reed reclaimed for America a part of the future, Warren reclaimed for this country a part of its past. Beatty was writing his own *Ten Days that Shook the World*— only his is three hours long, with an intermission."

The screen is now filled by the half-lit face of Steve Roberts, a reporter for the *New York Times*, who spent several years as his paper's Los Angeles bureau chief. He wears a sport coat because he believes he can't write in a suit.

"In those days, I had a very attractive assistant," Roberts remembers. "Beatty pursued her relentlessly. He called her so often, he was driving her crazy. I told her, 'Think how many women would love to be in your position.' She said, 'Think of how many have been.'"

The Playboy of Hollywood and the Playboy of the Revolution both spawned legendary love lives. Reed used to sweep the women in his life into his wars (he took Mabel Dodge to World War I and Louise Bryant to the Russian Revolution) just as Beatty sweeps the women in his life into his movies.

In 1960, Warren Beatty was engaged to actress Joan Collins, who maintains: "He was insatiable. Three, four, five times a day, every day, was not unusual for him, and he was also able to accept phone calls at the same time."

And then, later that year, Warren Beatty and Natalie Wood made *Splendor in the Grass* together—and she left her husband for him. And then he met Leslie Caron, and another marriage was doomed.

A perfect porcelain face appears on the screen. The lipstick is bright red. The blouse is lacy white. She is Gigi and lots of other pretty girls.

"Warren has an interesting psychology," Leslie Caron says in her attractive French accent. "He has always fallen in love with girls who have just won or been nominated for an Academy Award."

She had just been nominated for her performance in *The L-Shaped Room* when she met Warren Beatty at a party given by Freddie Fields at the Bistro.

"It was quite strong wooing. We practically didn't leave each other after that party for the next couple of years."

One rare night when they were separated, Leslie Caron went to a party up on Mulholland Drive with an old friend. When she walked into the living room, she saw Natalie Wood seated on a sofa. Warren Beatty's former lover moved over and graciously made room beside her on the couch for his current lover. Leslie Caron sat down next to Natalie Wood, but she did not stay. She soon stood up and glided away in a becoming blue dress.

"Leslie is looking so beautiful," someone said.

"Warren," explained Natalie Wood.

When Leslie Caron went to Jamaica to make *Father Goose* with Cary Grant, Warren Beatty secretly came along. Since she was still married, he hid out in her house as if he were Clyde Barrow, a character still in his future. In those days, trapped in the house, he spent a lot of time talking about the trio of actors whom he took the most seriously: Marlon Brando, Montgomery Clift, and himself. He talked about them as if they were a kind of acting trinity, but no one took *him* seriously.

"He was considered just a playboy," recalls Leslie Caron. "He had spent too much time wooing women in the public eye. Of course it bothered him that he wasn't taken seriously. We used to talk about it. He was in despair about it."

Returning to Hollywood, Leslie Caron and Warren Beatty attended a party one evening where an artist-witch read his palm. She took his hand and told him that he was going to be a murderer. Caron screamed. The reader would later claim that she saw "Clyde" in Beatty's palm.

Moving on to Paris in search of a movie to star in together, Leslie Caron and Warren Beatty had lunch with Francois Truffaut. And he had a suggestion for them.

"If you two want to make a film together," Truffaut said, "you should do *Bonnie and Clyde.*"

The great French director went on to explain that he was talking about a script by a couple of *Esquire* magazine writers who had never made a movie. The men from *Esquire*—Robert Benton and David Newman—had tried to persuade Truffaut to direct the movie. He was impressed by the script but too busy to do *Bonnie and Clyde*.

A few days later, Benton's phone rang in New York City. When he answered, he found himself talking to Warren Beatty, who wanted to read his script. Beatty showed up at Benton's Lexington Avenue apartment half an hour later. Benton's wife answered the door. Her knees buckled.

Benton told Beatty that he wouldn't want to do *Bonnie and Clyde*. Beatty asked why not. Benton said the movie involved Bonnie and Clyde and C.W.'s participation in curious sexual practices. Benton did not think Beatty would want to have anything to do with homosexuality. Beatty said he still wanted to read the script.

That evening, Beatty called Benton and said he wanted to do the movie. Benton asked what page he was on. Beatty said page 38. Benton said, "Wait until you get to page 64. You won't want to do it."

A little later, Beatty called back. He had finished the script. He said he still wanted to do it. Benton couldn't talk him out of it.

Leslie Caron says that, at the last minute, Beatty had doubts about *Bonnie and Clyde*, not because of the baroque sexuality, but because westerns weren't making any money. But she told him by transatlantic telephone that *Bonnie and Clyde* wasn't really a western. And she persuaded him to buy the movie for the *two* of them.

So Beatty bought *Bonnie and Clyde*, bought it to star in—but also bought it to produce. Then in his new role as producer, he met Leslie Caron in Los Angeles and informed her that she was not right for the part of Bonnie.

Caron maintains, "The way he discarded me after I got him to buy *Bonnie and Clyde* was rather ruthless." She adds, "Anyone who has come close to Warren has shed quite a few feathers. He tends to maul you."

For the part of Bonnie, Beatty wanted an American actress. As a matter of fact, he wanted his old girl friend Natalie Wood, but she turned him down.

Bob Benton's large head fills the screen. His hair is gray now. He speaks with an earnest lisp, which you soon stop hearing.

"I remember him from the beginning of *Bonnie and Clyde*," he says. "Nobody took him seriously then. Especially not as a producer. He came along as a kind of young actor in California. They don't take actors seriously. He was one of the first actors to make that move out into producing. And now, well, if there is such a thing as an *auteur* producer, he is it."

Beatty persuaded Benton and Newman to hire Arthur Penn to direct the movie. And then Penn persuaded them to take the homosexuality out of the plot. He told them they didn't know anything about gay love and had written a heterosexual story in spite of themselves.

They had a script, a star, and a director, but they still needed a studio. Beatty got down on his knees and begged Jack Warner to let him make *Bonnie and Clyde*. And Warner kept saying, come on, kid, you're embarrassing me.

When Warner finally said yes, probably just out of embarrassment, Beatty went off to Texas to play an outlaw. And one way or another, he would keep on playing outlaws in his films—the sexual outlaw in *Shampoo*, the ideological outlaw in *Reds*.

"There is an aspect of Clyde Barrow in Warren," says Benton. "There is a part of him that is an outlaw. He's chosen to be aloof. I think he's always remained outside the movie business."

When Beatty finally finished *Bonnie and Clyde*, the studio did not take it seriously. A Warner Brothers executive called it "a piece of shit." And Warners booked the film in second-class theaters as if it were a B-western. When the movie began to get good reviews, Beatty forced the studio to shut the movie down and reopen it in the best theaters. *Bonnie and Clyde* is one of the few movies in history to have opened twice.

"He was a tiger," recalls Arthur Penn, who did direct the film. "He was not going to let that movie not have its day."

When the Russians saw *Bonnie and Clyde*, after it was released in 1967, they thought Clyde Barrow looked like John Reed. And so they tried to get Barrow-Beatty to play Reed in a big Russian epic movie. When the American star read the Russian screenplay, he did not like the approach, which was just so much propaganda, but he became fascinated with the character. So, in a sense, the screen version of John Reed was descended from the screen version of Clyde Barrow, which was as it should be, since both were great American outlaws.

Beatty visited Harvard, Reed's alma mater, and read his hero's letters, poetry, and stories. Then he started reading Louise Bryant's writings. He wrote a screen treatment by 1969, a step outline by 1971 and filmed his first witness interview by 1972.

The filming of witness interviews continued on and off for almost a decade, with Warren Beatty, who does not talk to reporters, acting as a reporter and interviewing the people who had known Reed. Once he asked an aged witness, "What was World War I all about?" And the witness said, "England owned the world, and Germany wanted it."

The face of a politician who looks like a movie star appears on the screen.

"Warren was attracted to politics by the Kennedys," says Senator Gary Hart, of Colorado. "He got involved in Bobby Kennedy's 1968 campaign, and then he was drawn to McGovern. I met him at a party for McGovern in early 1971, and he told me he was interested in John Reed. He said he was thinking of doing a movie about him. The subject plagued him."

Later that year, Warren Beatty and George McGovern appeared at a campaign rally at the University of Wisconsin. When Beatty addressed the crowd, some of the students booed. They had not come to hear what a movie star had to say about the world's problems. They didn't take him seriously.

Afterward, Warren Beatty told Gary Hart, then the manager of the McGovern campaign, that he did not want to make any more appearances. He said people weren't interested in listening to movie stars. He wanted to help but wasn't sure how. So he went to Hollywood and considered the problem.

And he came up with a solution.

"He invented the political concert," Gary Hart says.

Beatty organized a whole series of concerts all across the country to raise money for McGovern. The biggest was staged in Madison Square Garden, an interesting setting, because John Reed had put on a very similar show there in 1913. Reed's show was a huge pageant with a cast of hundreds, which he hoped would raise money for the International Workers of the World (IWW), the Wobblies, who were on strike. Almost literally following in Reed's footsteps, Beatty put on a show so big he had movie stars—Ryan O'Neal, Paul Newman, Racquel Welch, Goldie Hawn—working as ushers. The show's theme was the reunion of groups that had broken up: Peter, Paul, and Mary; Nichols and May; Simon and Garfunkel. While Reed lost money on the show, Beatty grossed over a quarter of a million dollars.

Reed's strike failed, and he went off in search of other causes. Beatty's candidate failed, and he went back to his own search—his search for John Reed.

The well-lined face of Dick Sylbert, the art director of *Reds*, fills the screen. His clothes are spattered with the murky paint that he uses to age a set. The combination of wrinkles and paint makes it look as though he has been aging himself.

"In March of 1979, we went to Russia to talk to the boys in Moscow," Sylbert remembers. "Beatty had been there several times before, once with Natalie Wood. He was very Russia-wise about the bureaucracy."

In 1917, John Reed had convinced Louise Bryant to go to Russia with him to see the Revolution. In 1979, Warren Beatty convinced Diane Keaton to go to Russia with him to see about filming the Revolution. He also took along Dick Sylbert and Vittorio Storaro, his cameraman. There were endless meetings and endless dinners with endless vodka toasts.

Over and over, Warren Beatty would lift his glass and say, "Let us drink to an end to bureaucracy."

One day, Beatty wanted to go to the revolutionary museum in Leningrad. When they arrived at the building, their guide told them it was closed. They decided to come back the next day. That night, they celebrated Beatty's forty-second birthday by going to the Kirov Circus, where they had a good time. The next day, they went back to the museum, which the guide said was still closed. Beatty told the guide he wanted to stretch his legs. Getting out of the car, he led his party to the front door of the museum, which was open. They went in. And then Beatty grilled the Russians about why there were no pictures in the museum of Trotsky.

In the end, the Russians said Beatty could not film in Russia unless he showed them the script. He refused. And they refused.

Returning to Hollywood, Beatty spent his first night back not at home but at the Playboy Mansion. The Playboy of Hollywood, who would play the Playboy of the Revolution, had rushed home from Red Russia to a house full of Playboy Bunnies. That was where George Plimpton found him, prostrate in the foyer, with visions of revolutions and Playmates dancing in his head.

Several months later, in midsummer, George Plimpton was busy writing in his office—which is a mélange of animal heads, animal skins, and photographs of Ernest Hemingway—when the phone rang. He answered it.

"Is this the man," a deep voice asked, "who has never eaten an olive?"

"Warren?" Plimpton said. "Is that you, Warren?"

Beatty said he was calling from his limousine. He said he had Diane Keaton with him.

"Can I come up and introduce her to you?" Beatty asked. "Because you're in her scene."

A few minutes later, Beatty and Keaton joined the animal heads and Papa pictures in Plimpton's office. The three of them chatted for half an hour, and then the two movie stars got up to go. Plimpton said he had expected to have to read for the part. After all, how did they know he could act? Beatty said, no, he would be fine.

A few minutes later, the phone rang again. Plimpton answered.

"Am I still speaking," a deep voice asked, "to the man who's never eaten an olive?"

"Warren? Is that you, Warren?"

Beatty said that he had been thinking, and, well, maybe Plimpton *should* read for the part. While he waited for his guests to arrive, Plimpton nervously had a drink. The reading did not go well. Plimpton thought he was out of the movie, but Beatty simply tossed the script to the floor and told him to ad-lib.

"You know the kind of person you are," Beatty, the director, directed. "Put the make on her."

So Plimpton made love to Keaton as they sat side by side on the green couch with their feet on the zebra-skin rug, facing a herd of antelope heads. At first, Plimpton was frightened, but he soon found it even more fun than Intellivision games. This seduction went on uninterrupted for ten minutes. Then the director jealously stepped in.

"That's enough," Beatty said. "Stop it."

Franklin D. Roosevelt's face fills the screen. Actually, it isn't FDR himself but Edward Herrmann, who played FDR in the television mini-series *Eleanor and Franklin*. In *Reds,* Herrmann plays Max Eastman, editor of the *Masses*.

"To be serious about his work," Herrmann says. "Clearly that was behind his madness. He conceived of the Russian Revolution as a need for power and change. That montage at the end of the first act sums up his political beliefs. One's sexual potency, one's drive into life, and that was all in that footage."

One afternoon, Herrmann went up to what he calls "Beatty's beautiful Bauhaus palace up on top of Mulholland Drive" to talk about playing Eastman in the movie. In the living room they discussed a picture about a rebel with a cause, while Margaux Hemingway was down below in the basement screening room watching *Rebel Without a Cause.*

After a while, Beatty took Herrmann into a room where a picture of Herrmann's wife, Leigh Curran, was tacked onto a bulletin board. The husband was taken aback. He wondered what his wife's picture was doing there.

"Do you know her?" asked Beatty.

"Yes," Herrmann said.

"Do you work well with her?"

"She's my wife."

"Yeah, I know she's your wife." Beatty burst out laughing. "But do you work well together?"

Herrmann explained that he and his wife had never worked together, but thought they would work well together if they ever got the chance. So Herrmann was cast as Max Eastman, and his wife was cast as Eastman's wife. Beatty was obviously interested in how couples in life would work as couples on the screen. Herrmann and Curran would, in a sense, be like Beatty and Keaton writ small. In this movie, which happened to be about a couple who worked together, Warren Beatty was going to see how loving couples got along as working couples.

Soon they would all be going to Europe together to shoot the movie. They would begin in England, where they would film the Portland scenes, the Provincetown scenes, the Croton scenes, the Greenwich Village scenes . . .

One member of the cast was already on the other side of the Atlantic, which meant saving one plane ticket. George Plimpton was in Monte Carlo to compete in the Fireworks Championship of the World. Which he won. While he was still celebrating, Plimpton, who was convinced Beatty had forgotten all about him, got a call from a wardrobe woman in London, who said they needed him for a costume fitting *immediately*.

Jack Nicholson's big-bad-boy smile appears on the screen. Like all else about him, his hair seems to want to behave but simply isn't able. His nickname for Beatty is "the Pro," because Nicholson believes he is one.

"*Reds* is about the conflict between the private man and the socially active man," says Nicholson, who plays Eugene O'Neill in the movie. "It is about giving up your private life to a tremendous degree." John Reed tried to resolve this conflict between his public work and his private life by recruiting his women into his work life. And of course, Warren Beatty has been known to attempt the same solution. "Just look at how many movies the Pro's made with his girl friends. Of course, there are classic pitfalls. Making a movie is psychologically brutal."

On the screen, Jack Nicholson's sturdy, working-class teeth dissolve out. And we dissolve in once again on the patrician teeth that have never touched an olive.

"Warren was very fastidious," Plimpton remembers. "He did thirty or forty takes all the time. Diane almost got broken. I thought he was trying to break her into what Louise Bryant had been like with John Reed."

In the movie, John Reed asks Louise Bryant to leave Portland and come to New York with him. She says, "What as?" He says, "It's nearly Thanksgiving, ah, why don't you come as a turkey?" And just as Louise

Bryant worried about her role vis-à-vis John Reed, Diane Keaton must have been concerned about her own role vis-à-vis Warren Beatty. When they flew to Europe together to make *Reds*, Beatty went as the star, the writer, the director, and the producer. And Diane Keaton went as an actress, or, as they say in Hollywood, as "the girl." In bad moments, she must have felt that she had indeed gone as a turkey.

Jerzy Kosinski (Zinoviev), whose hobby is photography, kept a photograph album of the making of the movie. And in those photographs, Diane Keaton is seen again and again, standing in front of the movie camera, her eyes flaring, as she argues with her director, a scowling Warren Beatty, who stands behind the camera. In one picture, she seems to be shaking her script at him.

"These were not moments of absence of tension," says Kosinski. "It was not easy directing Diane."

And all the fatiguing takes did not improve anyone's mood. The fights onscreen between John Reed and Louise Bryant, and the fights offscreen between the leading lady and her director, sometimes carried over into their evenings as a couple. Still, they worked well together in the sense that neither of them has ever done better work. But they ultimately did not work as a couple: They broke up before the movie was finished.

And what of Beatty's and Keaton's alter egos, Reed and Bryant? Would they have stayed together if Reed had lived?

"No way!" says Jack Nicholson.

Beatty had some problems with another of his actresses, one of the first ladies of the theater, Maureen Stapleton. First of all, she is afraid to fly, so she took a tiny Polish freighter, the *General Poplawski*, from Baltimore to Europe. When she saw the ship, she asked if it was too late to back out—and was told it was. Two days out of Baltimore, the engines quit, and the star and the ship bobbed for two days. And then when she finally arrived in London, Warren Beatty wanted to do all these takes.

"Do it again," Warren Beatty said one day.

"No," snapped Maureen Stapleton.

"Do it again."

"What do you want me to do? Take off my clothes?"

"I don't know. Do it again."

One night, Maureen Stapleton as Emma Goldman was addressing a group of workers in a cold, driving rainstorm. She made her speech to the workers—actually extras—and Beatty asked her to do it again. And again. And again. Then she did an especially good take.

"Great," Beatty said. There was a beat. And he said, "One more time."

Maureen Stapleton turned on him and shouted, "Are you out of your fucking mind?"

All the workers erupted into applause. At that moment, Maureen Stapleton could have run for public office. Or led a revolution.

But they did it again.

FDR comes back on the screen.

"Warren Beatty," says Edward Herrmann, "is *mysterium tremendum*. We never saw a script. It was like shooting *Casablanca.*"

The legend, which is not entirely correct, is that when *Casablanca* was being made, the actors did not have a script and more or less made up the movie as they went along. Making *Reds*, they had a script, but Beatty would not show it to anyone. Actually, Diane Keaton and Jack Nicholson had scripts, but none of the other actors did. They would be given their lines in the morning, before they worked in a scene. Or, if it was a long scene, they might be given their lines the night before. Once, Edward Herrmann complained to Diane Keaton about not having a script.

"It doesn't matter," she said. "It's all in Warren's head anyway. He keeps changing it all the time."

The screen is filled by a balding head with an ironical face. The face is grave but somehow seems to be laughing at its own gravity.

"Producing *Reds* was misunderstood by all of us," says Barry Diller, [then] chairman of the board of Paramount Pictures [who has since moved over to run Twentieth Century Fox]. "It was miscalculated. What happened was, no preproduction work was done on the film; we had to start immediately because of the availability of the actors. So it was always catch-up. It was originally budgeted at $20 million. It should have been budgeted in the high twenties or low thirties. I got very frustrated, because the film was clearly going to cost vastly more than contemplated. My knee-jerk reaction was to get angry with Warren. At the worst stage, I just refused to talk to him. I wanted to make him feel guilty. I thought that would have some effect. That was naive. Hurtful. Cruel. My behavior was unfortunate."

Barry Diller would not take Warren Beatty's transatlantic phone calls for six weeks. And then he decided that perhaps he was making a mistake. So on Thanksgiving 1979, he flew to London and "apologized, in a sense."

Diller was back again a month later, just before Christmas. And when he landed in London, he found what amounted to an unexpected present waiting for him. He saw five hours of film. He watched a lot of the Provincetown part of the story and a lot of Diane Keaton. He was surprised at how much he loved it.

Diller then flew to Manchester, where the cast and crew were filming at the time. He located Beatty and told him that the movie had potential for "real greatness." The fights between Beatty and Diller were not over, but they were conducted at a different level.

"We fought in our normal territory. You can't work in that process unless you fight. If you have a point, the only way to make it is with a certain level of viciousness, or the other person doesn't know you mean it. You have to show you care."

The wrinkled specialist on aging comes back onscreen.

"Warren was like a field marshal," says Dick Sylbert. "Every movie is like a war. A little war. A big war."

This movie was a world war, and after Christmas, they moved to the Finnish front. Since Russia would not let *Reds* into the Soviet Union, they filmed most of the Russian scenes in Finland.

Shortly after they arrived, Dick Sylbert took Beatty to see a railroad station that he had built a hundred miles north of the Arctic Circle. They flew to this frozen, desolate location in a helicopter. Beatty and Sylbert were walking along a lonely railroad track in the middle of arctic nowhere, moving through a vast snow-laden landscape like something out of *Dr. Zhivago*, when, to their surprise, they came upon two other human beings, a man and a woman, who appeared to be lost.

"Warren?" said the woman. "Is that you, Warren?"

Beatty had met her at the Cannes Film Festival. His women were scattered all over the face of the earth, even well above the Arctic Circle.

Zinoviev comes back on the screen.

"The more Warren got into the project," says Jerzy Kosinski, "the more he saw himself as John Reed. It's the same path. I was with him the last three months. He dressed like John Reed onstage and off. He was in worse shape than Reed. Exhausted. Coughing all the time. Sick. Emaciated. I was so astonished by all this."

Now they were fighting on the southern front, the Spanish front, fighting the last big battle of the movie war. The train ride through the Caucasus to Baku, where Reed addressed the Arab people, was actually shot in Spain. And while they were in Spain, Beatty did an extraordinarily Reed-like thing.

When he returned to Russia shortly before his death, Reed declined the government's offer of a comfortable apartment and moved into a cold-water shack, where he did all his cooking over a lamp. It was from this shack that Reed departed on the train ride that would eventually kill him. As if consciously, or subconsciously, aping Reed, Beatty moved into a very similar abandoned shack in Spain. Located near Guadix, thirty miles from Granada, this tiny house had no hot water, only a hot plate to cook on and a bathroom with a door that would not close. The house was surrounded by guards, insisted on by the owner, who coughed and tramped noisily through the rooms all night long.

Beatty shared the shack's three rooms with Jerzy Kosinski and Kosinski's girl friend, Kiki von Frauenhofer. She made tea and toast by leaning slices of bread against a kettle on the hot plate.

"Warren was living in this house with me," says Kosinski, "and I am really Zinoviev. For me, as a novelist, I am living in a revolution. But I am also living with this pathetic American. I'm back into my past, like Zinoviev—hot days, cold nights. I'm enjoying it. But I'm living with John Reed, who is doing this ridiculous thing, and I'm annoyed by it. I'm very cynical. To me, it's all a game. To him, it's an idea. And I laugh at him daily. I became just as impatient as Zinoviev. Why was Beatty there? What helped me to become Zinoviev was questioning why this crazy American was doing this crazy thing. I honestly didn't think this was going to work. I thought he was going to be buried in the Kremlin wall again. The analogy would run its course."

The final apotheosis came at Baku. Warren Beatty became Saint John Reed as he addressed a multitude of extras who were to work in the big speech scene. Since he believed in explaining the story to extras, Beatty told the crowd all about the course of Reed's life that had led him to this speaker's platform in Baku just before he died. Beatty's words had to be translated into Spanish so the extras could understand—just as Reed's words at Baku had to be translated into Arabic so his Arabian audience could understand him. Beatty proclaimed that Reed was against the exploitation of the working man by American capitalism, that he was for the right of the working man to rise up. It was a very moving speech, as good as, or even better than, Reed himself could have done.

Then they broke for lunch in the 105-degree heat.

At the end of the lunch hour, several representatives of the extras came to see Beatty. Over their midday meal, the extras had decided that Beatty/Reed was right. They should not allow themselves to be exploited by American capitalism. They should band together and rise up. The extras announced that they had formed an impromptu union and would strike unless their wages were raised. Warren Beatty rolled his eyes and smiled ironically. The workers' pay was raised from about seventy dollars to about ninety dollars a day. Actually, Warren Beatty was a better John Reed than Reed was, for the workers lost most of the strikes in which Reed got involved; Beatty had led a successful strike—against himself.

Fade out to suggest a passage of time.

Fade in on Zinoviev.

"John Reed talking to Zinoviev," says Jerzy Kosinski, "is no different from Warren Beatty talking to Charlie Bluhdorn."

Warren Beatty was worried about what Super Capitalist Charles Bluhdorn—[now deceased but then] the chairman of the board of Gulf & Western (which owns Paramount)—would think of *Reds*. When the movie was finished, a special screening was arranged in a small, posh, leather-upholstered projection room on the thirtieth floor of the Gulf & Western building in New York City. Only three people attended: Warren Beatty, Barry Diller, and Charles Bluhdorn.

During the screening, Beatty and Diller watched Bluhdorn as closely as the chairman of the board of Gulf & Western watched the screen. They knew that Bluhdorn—an immigrant who believed in the American dream because his own American dreams had come true a few billion times over—was passionately patriotic. So what would this American Dreamer make of a movie about a man who considered the American System an American Nightmare?

Beatty and Diller also knew that Bluhdorn had invested a lot of money in *Reds*. In fact, it is ironical that it cost so much Good Old American Capital to stage the Russian Revolution. Just how high the price was is hard to say with precision. Official Paramount spokesmen have repeatedly said that "the official figure is $33.5 million." Barry Diller says emphatically that *Reds* cost "$34 million and change." But other Paramount sources say the cost was around $50 million. Since Bluhdorn had spent a lot, Beatty and Diller hoped he would like the movie *a lot* as it flickered by at a price of something between $170,000 and a quarter of a million dollars per minute.

"It was a very emotional screening," remembers Diller. "We could have brought shame and degradation on the company. We badly, emotionally, wanted him to say that he approved."

When the movie was finally over, they talked and talked. They had dinner sent into the screening room and kept on talking. These three Great American Capitalists talked about *Reds* until one o'clock in the morning.

Bluhdorn loved Diane Keaton's performance. He loved Warren Beatty's performance. He approved.

"I am sorry to be the one to have to say it," Diller says, "but not one media person, no liberal writer, has pointed out that this big American corporation supported a film that deals with a story that had been buried, a story never told, the absolutely hidden story of the IWW, the American Socialist Party, the American Communist Party. Not one has said, Gulf & Western may be rat bastards but at least they did that."

Zinoviev again.

"When John Reed finished *Ten Days that Shook the World*," Kosinski says, "he took his book to Lenin and said, 'Please give me a good quote.' And one of the first people Warren showed his *Ten Days* to was Reagan. And he asked for a quote. Lenin gave a quote. And Reagan gave a quote."

After Beatty showed *Reds* to Ronald Reagan at the White House, the president said he liked the movie but wished it had a happy ending.

And then Reagan supposedly said something even more curious. He told a story about a B-17 that was hit by enemy fire in World War II. The pilot watched everyone bail out except his tail gunner, who was trapped in his glass bubble under the plane. The pilot tried to free the tail gunner but couldn't. And so the pilot took the gunner's hand and held it all the way to the ground until they crashed. Reagan said, "That's the American spirit—going down together." Or so Beatty tells the story to friends.

In the American spirit, a lot of people risked going down with *Reds*—a fact that added drama to its opening. The movie received generally favorable reviews, but some on the Left and some on the Right have objected to its politics. *Reds* made disappointingly little capital during its first three weeks in the theaters, but then it began to pick up. It even had a brief reign as the number-one picture in the country, which was all the more impressive since the film is so long it can only be shown once a night. But then *On Golden Pond* overtook it. And it began to lose theaters. *Reds* has grossed over $30 million, but a big chunk of this money goes to the theater owners, and another piece goes toward prints and advertising. So *Reds* is a long way from paying off what it cost to make. *Reds* may never get out of the red.

Gigi comes, smiling, back onto the screen.

"The story he used to be interested in is Howard Hughes," says

Leslie Caron. "He wanted to make a movie about him. He was very intrigued because Howard Hughes was so rich and powerful, because he wielded so much power, because of the paranoia and secrecy."

When Warren Beatty and Leslie Caron were together, they lived on top of the Beverly Wilshire Hotel; Howard Hughes had rooms there, too. They were never sure whether Hughes was there, but Beatty worked hard at finding out. While reporters and fans attempted to spy on world-famous lovers Warren Beatty and Leslie Caron, Beatty himself was attempting to spy on Howard Hughes. He was always trying to interview the billionaire's bodyguards.

And now, Warren Beatty plans to make a movie about Howard Hughes. Once again, he will be dealing with a long-standing obsession. Once again, he will be playing a hero in whom he sees a version of himself. Like Hughes, Beatty has lived much of his life in impersonal hotels—the Carlyle in New York, the Beverly Wilshire in Los Angeles—and until he bought his new house, even spent Christmases alone in a hotel room watching television. Like Hughes, Beatty is rich, although not as rich. Like Hughes, Beatty is powerful, although not as powerful. And like Hughes, Beatty seems to have a psychological need for extreme secrecy, to be the hero of a mystery.

Perhaps, in making the movie, Warren Beatty will purge the Howard Hughes in him. Or perhaps he will feed the Hughes in him so that the monster grows. Perhaps the movie will be as successful as the Hughes drill bit. Or perhaps it will prove to be a *Spruce Goose*.

And then Warren Beatty will need the ultimate Beatty role to play. Once again, he will probably look around him for a hero with whom he can identify. And again he will have to decide: Who does Warren Beatty want to be next?

"If you woke him up in the middle of the night," says Leslie Caron, "before his defenses were up, if that is ever possible, and asked him what he wanted to be, I think he would say, 'President.' I don't think he'll stop until he's president."

What if Warren Beatty/John Reed/Howard Hughes were to conclude his career by playing Ronald Reagan, not in the movie theaters but in the White House? After all, Warren Beatty has a lot in common with Ronald Reagan: They are both actors, both are interested in politics, and both have been underestimated for years.

I can imagine Warren Beatty calling George Plimpton to see if he wants to be in the cabinet.

"Hello, is this the man who has never eaten a jelly bean?"

"Mr. President? Is that you, Mr. President?"

•   •   •

When the piece appeared, Beatty was most upset by what Leslie Caron had said about him. He burst into the office of one of her close friends and angrily demanded that he read all her quotes out loud. News of how upset Beatty was quickly reached Leslie Caron in Paris, and then she was upset, too.

I saw her months later in Bungalow R at the Laird Studio, where we were preparing to shoot *Perfect.* On that particular afternoon, a number of actors had come to audition, but somehow the tryouts had turned into a party. In the room were John Travolta, Jamie Lee Curtis, Laraine Newman, Marilu Henner, Dudley Moore (who just dropped by to say hello), and a half dozen male strippers from Chippendale's. Into this group walked Leslie Caron, who stopped, stared at me, pointed her finger at me, and said: "Apologize!"

"For what?" I asked, embarrassed.

"You promised to put in the good things I said about Warren, too."

"I apologize," I said.

But I still don't remember making any promises.

SNOW WHITE IN
SOUTH AFRICA

•   •   •

When *Rolling Stone* asked me to cover Linda Ronstadt's concerts in racist South Africa, I needed a visa. I drove over to the South African embassy on Massachusetts Avenue in Washington. I was ushered into the press attaché's office.

"Have you ever written about South Africa?" a woman asked me.

"No," I said.

"Has your magazine ever written about South Africa?"

"Not that I know of."

"What about this?"

She opened a file and produced a copy of *Rolling Stone* that was folded open to a huge, black headline: APARTHEID ROCK. It was a story by another writer about rock stars who played South Africa. It took the position that such stars were traitors and criminals. That sounded about right to me.

The woman informed me that my request for a visa was being denied. She looked so mad I thought she might try to arrest me.

A few hours later, my phone rang. It was the South African embassy. They had inexplicably changed their minds. I could go.

•   •   •

Rolling Stone, August 1983

Linda Ronstadt is special. Her voice is special. Her choices have been special, too. Especially her choice to become the rock star who sings grand opera. She started with Gilbert and Sullivan's *Pirates of Penzance*. And now she is preparing to undertake the role of Mimi in Puccini's *La Bohème*. While other rock stars have been taking drug overdoses, she has been taking Italian.

Linda Ronstadt is special, and yet she went to South Africa. She is special, and yet she chose to perform in a reviled racist country. She is special, and yet she gave six concerts in the cradle of apartheid. She is special, and yet she lent her talents to an especially mean place. She is special, and yet she allowed her very specialness to be exploited by an outlaw nation in search of legitimacy. Her special price: $500,000.

All the time I was in South Africa, I kept wrestling with my image of Linda Ronstadt, the special rock star. And all the time she was there, she wrestled with her conscience.

She kept asking if she had made a mistake in coming. She kept interviewing people—black and white—and asking them if she should have come. She asked in the casinos of Sun City. She asked in the discothèques. She asked in the jungles.

Meanwhile, the boys in her band had a different question: Why couldn't they get laid? It was as though the fates were punishing them for having come to this forbidden land. A plague had been visited on them. Worse than locusts. Worse than frogs.

A plague of chastity.

They suffered day and, especially, night. The special rock star tried to reassure them that there was nothing physically wrong with them— at least not much. And they tried to reassure her that there was nothing really wrong with her decision to lead them into this jungle of apartheid.

The jungles of South Africa kept reminding me of the jungles of Vietnam. The war in the jungles of Southest Asia provoked a moral outcry in this country that helped to set the tone for a decade. And rock 'n' roll added its loud voice to those protests. The music and the musicians seemed to have a moral dimension. But no more. Now rock 'n' roll can be hired by apartheid. Now the music is amoral. Now Linda Ronstadt sings in Sun City.

The sixties—which began in the jungles of South Vietnam— seemed finally to be coming to a troubling close in the jungles of South Africa.

Since Joseph Conrad's day, the trip into the Heart of Darkness has been shortened by jet planes, but it is still something of an ordeal. I flew seven hours overnight to London, laid over for a few hours, then flew another thirteen hours to Johannesburg. Then I rented a car with the steering wheel and gearshift on the wrong side and drove two and a half hours to Sun City, which is the Las Vegas of South Africa.

Sun City is a collection of casinos and hotels built in an architectural style that might be described as outer-space pueblo. The buildings are brown and chunky and modern all at the same time. They form what amounts to an oasis of expensive pleasures surrounded by poverty and hovels and drought.

The Las Vegas of South Africa is not located in South Africa itself. It is nestled in the semiautonomous—and semifictitious—Bophuthatswana homeland. The homelands are slightly different from South Africa proper because integration is allowed. But they are also a lot like Indian reservations, with many blacks being forced to live there whether they want to or not.

Linda Ronstadt gave her concerts in a structure called the Sun City Super Bowl, which really isn't very super. It is just a big auditorium with a red curtain, orange seats, and fountains on either side of the stage. The uniformed guards and ushers are black. The crowd that came to see Linda Ronstadt was almost totally—99.44 percent pure—white.

It was also relatively small. There were 6,200 seats in the Super Bowl. About half of those were empty.

"It's nice to be down here in Southern Africa, as I've been instructed to call it," Linda Ronstadt told her audience. "It looks like Mexico. But the cacti are a little fatter. After twenty-four hours in a plane, you get out, and it looks like you've gone two hours from Los Angeles. And then the architecture here is sort of Aztec-Dorito-Bauhaus. It's not so bad if you look at it from far away."

She was dressed in a black-and-white striped blouse, like a zebra, and a short red leather skirt, unbuttoned halfway up the back. The effect was corrupt cute.

Her special voice filled the great room with "Get Closer" and "Willin' " and "Desperado" and "Prisoner in Disguise" and, especially, "Back in the USA."

"In case you're wondering why I keep studying the floor," she told the crowd, "well, I always check out what the ants are like in every country. Mexico has the cutest ants. My steady beau for the last eight years used to . . . well . . . he used to work for the government. I wanted to get him a present, so I bought him an ant farm. He didn't have much furniture in his office. I thought an ant farm would be this metaphor for government—everyone working together.

"He opened it up and asked: 'Why did you buy me an ant farm?' "

In her dressing room after the concert, Linda Ronstadt talked some more about her beau who used to work for the government, Jerry Brown, the former governor of California. The political beau had advised his rock-star girl friend not to perform in South Africa, where a minority of 4.5 million whites rules over a majority of 21 million blacks.

"I don't take his advice very much," she said. "He doesn't want me to do things that are controversial. He's political. I'm not. He tries not to say no to me because he knows it won't work. He just looks into his napkin and writhes."

The offer to sing in South Africa had come at the last minute, when another singer and a boxer had to cancel out. Boom Boom Mancini, who killed a man in the ring last year, was supposed to fight. And Frank Sinatra, whose eyes are apartheid blue, was supposed to sing and help announce the fight. It was all a cable-television package. But then Boom Boom broke his collarbone. Sun City, needing a fill-in, turned to Linda Ronstadt.

"I was getting ready to go to Italy," she remembered. "They wanted me to pinch-hit for Sinatra and boxing. I had two days to decide. I talked to everyone. I called friends of mine at Motown. Their story was: 'Black artists go, so we can't tell you not to go.' I called up John Rockwell at the *New York Times* and got him to send me clips on South Africa."

(Rockwell remembers that call this way: "Linda had pretty much made her decision to go. She had passed the time when she could bow out. It didn't strike me as a thrilling idea. I had personal reservations. I'm not a big fan of South Africa. I didn't seem enthusiastic, but she's a voluble person. She does what she wants to do. What can you do?")

"If I won't play a repressive government, a police state," Linda continued, "then I couldn't play the black countries or Alabama or Boston."

I asked her if she thought there was any difference between playing Bophuthatswana and playing South Africa.

"Clearly, there's no difference to me, Bophuthatswana or South Africa," she said. "The policy of the homelands is wrong. This isn't in any way an endorsement of the government."

She maintained that she did not learn of the United Nations' cultural and economic boycott of South Africa until after she arrived in Sun City. The UN resolution supporting the boycott was passed in 1968, but it has evidently not been popular reading material in the capitals of American music. A number of American musicians have defied the boycott and played South Africa: the Beach Boys, Glen Campbell, Cher, the Osmonds, Sha Na Na, Tina Turner, Frank Sinatra, and even a group called America. Linda Ronstadt is different only in that I thought she was special.

"It's very strange performing here," she said. "I seem like a mirage to them, they to me. It's scary, like the Twilight Zone. Things seem nice. Then people get drunk and talk about their fear of a knock in the night."

Still: "I'm glad I came."

She took a bite of chicken.

"The last place for a boycott is in the arts. I don't like being told I can't go somewhere. Like when they told Jane Fonda she couldn't go to North Vietnam. Of course she should have gone to North Vietnam."

But of course, Jane Fonda was not paid a half million dollars to visit Hanoi.

Linda Ronstadt joined the other members of her band in a hospitality suite set aside for their use. Black waiters in livery offered to fetch drinks. The boys, as usual, were discussing their sexual frustrations.

"I asked a girl in the audience what was wrong," said Andrew Gold, who plays guitar. "And do you know what she told me?"

"No," said Don Grolnick, who plays keyboards.

"She said: 'We don't like your bodies.' "

"You should have said: 'We don't much like them, either. See, we have something in common. Let's talk.' "

Actually, the band did seem a little out of shape. A few pounds overweight. Bodies formed sort of like guitars stood on end with the big end at the bottom.

Linda Ronstadt changed the subject to another kind of hunt, a big-game hunt. A safari was planned for their next-to-last day. But it meant getting up very early, 5:00 A.M. She wanted to know who was going. There was a show of hands. I asked if I could go. She said they would try to squeeze me in. I was already looking forward to it: pursuing wild animals through the jungle with a sometimes wild rock star. Rhinos. Giraffes. Wildebeests.

When the party broke up, the band went out to prowl through the casinos and bars and discothèques in search of that most elusive game— the South African woman in heat. The rare wildewoman.

"What did she mean?" they kept asking one another. "What's wrong with our bodies? Why don't they like our bodies?"

Linda Ronstadt went off to pet a German shepherd attack dog. And I went along. The dog belonged to one of Sun City's many plainclothes security men, all white, either Afrikaner or of English ancestry. This particular security man was an Afrikaner, but his wife was English, so his dog was bilingual, responding to commands in both languages. The rock star had asked to pet the German shepherd because she missed her own dogs, who were at home in Los Angeles.

The scene was not unlike what she had described earlier: Twilight Zone. It seemed nice. Almost too nice. Sentimental. And yet this dog with the wagging tail was trained to kill people in an obviously dangerous world. Bring up the "Twilight Zone" theme.

A report of trouble crackled over the security man's walkie-talkie! Fire! There was a fire at the country club. Arson was suspected. The security man and his attack dog had to hurry away.

While the security man searched for arsonists—and the band for women—the rock star and the reporter went for a walk down by the lake. We lay down on our backs on the beach and stared up at the stars that come out in the Southern Hemisphere. The moonlit sky was an incredible shade of dark violet.

"It's like a color in a Crayola box," she said. "It's a Crayola sky."

She studied the southern heavens a little longer.

"It's a Bethlehem sky."

Once she said it, I saw that it did have that deep purple of the skies of innumerable Nativity scenes.

"It's just my luck," she said, "to come to Africa under a full moon."

A stray cat with long, gray hair seemed to rise up out of the lake. She reached out to it just the way she had reached out to the attack dog. She befriended the stray, petted it, and soon had it purring loudly. Sitting up, she took it in her lap.

In the middle of the lake was a small island. The moon lit it so brightly with such a strange light that it looked unreal. It seemed to be a storybook island, perhaps inhabited by pirates, perhaps by the Pirates of Penzance.

"This place looks so normal and peaceful," she said, repeating a thought she had expressed earlier, a thought that keeps recurring in South Africa. "But there is obviously trouble lurking just out of sight. And sometimes it comes into sight. That report on the radio about arson at the country club."

"Yeah, the whole country seems a lot like that German shepherd," I said. "He looks beautiful, but he'll kill you."

"He probably would," she said.

Watching her stroke the stray cat, I could not help wondering if she herself could not be described in the words she had used to describe the country. She seemed normal and pleasant and more. She was a friend of animals. She was articulate. She was good company. She was charming.

She was special. But lurking just out of sight was something that had brought her to an evil land.

"I want to play Snow White," Linda Ronstadt said. "She's my favorite character in literature."

Studying her, I realized that she looked uncannily like Walt Disney's Snow White. Her skin so absolutely white. Her hair so black. Of course, ironically, Snow White happens to be South Africa's official favorite color. It occurred to me that the story of Snow White was yet another version of the pattern Linda had been talking about—a nice world, a peaceful world, a snug little Snow White world, but with trouble lurking just out of sight in the form of a poison apple.

Snow White had taken the witch's apple. And Linda Ronstadt had taken Sun City's money.

Turning our backs on the moon and the fantasy island and the trouble lurking just out of sight, we returned to the casino in search of the band. Unlucky at love, several of the musicians had taken to the gaming tables in the hope of seducing Lady Luck. So far, she hadn't given them a tumble, either.

"My social life has been going like this," Andrew Gold confessed. "I go up to a girl and ask if she wants a drink. She says, 'No.' I say, 'How about a dance?' She says 'No.' And I say, 'Then I suppose a fuck is out of the question.' "

I noticed a few blacks in the casino. One or two at the blackjack tables. More playing the slots. They represented the first integration I had seen in South Africa.

Linda Ronstadt and I made our way into a discothèque that adjoined the casino. We were surprised to see the black and white races in about equal numbers on the crowded floor. It was a boiling black-and-white mob.

"They aren't afraid to touch on the dance floor," she said. "The white people don't seem to mind rubbing up against the black people."

The place was so crowded that it was hard to find seats, but we finally managed to shoehorn ourselves in next to a twenty-six-year-old engineer who works in a gold mine.

"Hi, I'm Linda Ronstadt," she said. "And this is Aaron Latham. He's an American reporter. He's going to get me in trouble back home."

Then we just sat there and watched this extraordinary sight—a sight as remarkable as anything we were to discover in Africa, a sight as memorable and as moving as the herds of game we would see later—the sight of blacks and whites dancing together in a racist nation. Black couples danced next to white couples. And some blacks even danced with whites.

The gold-mining engineer explained that such a dance floor could not exist in South Africa proper. Everyone would be arrested. It could only exist in the homelands.

By 3:00 A.M., I was so tired that the blacks and whites on the dance floor began to seem like a dream. I had been traveling for two days and two nights without much, if any, sleep. And this was the third night with no sleep. I was so exhausted that the milling black and white bodies took on the quality of a Twilight Zone hallucination. Twisting. Turning. Boiling. A black-and-white cauldron. A white-and-black melting pot.

It seemed almost too good to be real—when suddenly, all the lights went out. In the dark, Linda grabbed my arm and held on tight. Was it a power failure? Was it the revolution? Was it the evil that lurks out of sight? When the lights came back on, everything seemed "normal and peaceful" once again, but an army of security men had somehow appeared from nowhere, as if generated by the dark. Or by dark forces.

When I woke up the next morning, I couldn't remember how I had gotten to my bed. I had been so tired that I had fallen asleep on the way to my hotel room. As I came reluctantly back to life, I remembered that I was supposed to have breakfast with Linda Ronstadt. She had suggested that I drop by around noon.

She was in her nightgown and a robe. She had invited several others to breakfast, too. Her hairdresser. Her scheduler. And her producer, Peter Asher. We all ate granola topped with fresh fruit.

Linda talked about caroling at the old actors' home in L.A. last Christmas.

"Those people made you never want to take drugs again," she said. "Or else take them all in one night so you won't grow old."

She looked in the mirror. She frowned. She scowled. She tried out several other expressions.

"I look like Nancy in the funny papers," she decided. "Maybe I should play Nancy someday."

Then she tried to tell the others about the black-and-white disco the night before. So I had not dreamed it, after all.

A few hours later, Linda Ronstadt was back onstage.

"It's strange to fly such a long way," she told the audience, "and have it look like where you grew up. The sky is a slightly different color at night."

Linda Ronstadt had grown up in Tucson, Arizona, not far from the Mexican border. I knew because I had spent a part of my growing-up there, too. We went to high school together. Catalina High School. The Catalina High School mascot was the Trojan—which we knew had another meaning besides the Homeric one. I was in the class of 1962. She would have been in the class of 1964, but she dropped out to become a rock star.

After the concert, we went up to her hotel room and talked about her beginnings.

"My grandfather had a ranch called Las Delicias, which means the Delights," she said. "He was a musician as well as a rancher. He did an arrangement of *Pirates of Penzance* in 1880."

Her father grew up on her grandfather's ranch.

"That was where he was when he met my mother."

Her mother, who traced her ancestry back to Holland, seemed a little like South Africa's Afrikaner women, who are also of Dutch origin.

"All the women in Holland are like my mother. Rigid. Straightforward. Earnest. Disarming. A cultural stubbornness."

When her father and mother married and settled down, they opened a hardware store in Tucson.

"I lived twenty miles out of town. I learned a lot about animals. I thought town kids were limited. They didn't have horses. They wanted to squish bugs."

In those days, Linda had a Shetland pony. Her mother used to transport the pony by putting it in the back seat of the family car. When the little horse would stick its head out the car window, other drivers were startled into near accidents.

"I went to Catholic school through the eighth grade. I hated it. They didn't let me wear Levis. These nuns were ignorant. Nuns are the worst fascists."

She thought a moment.

"South Africa is like a Catholic school. Like a prison. I went to jail once for about twenty hours for something I didn't do. It was the same feeling."

Her father is still alive, but her mother died of lung cancer while she was filming the movie version of *Pirates of Penzance*. Linda was able to spend a little time with her mother in Tucson just before filming started. But then she had to go off to England to make her movie. The picture, on which millions had already been spent, could not be delayed. But the shooting schedule was rearranged to allow her to make a brief trip home in the middle of the movie to see her mom one last time.

"She still knew me," Linda remembered, "but she was in a lot of pain."

Then Linda went back to work.

"One day my father called me and told me my mom was dead. I couldn't even cry because it would mess up my makeup."

Then a couple of days later, one of her costars rushed in with the latest news. Hey, had she heard? John Belushi was dead. The dead man had been a friend of hers.

"First my mother and then my friend in the same week. I felt as if somebody had put a bucket over my head and was hitting it with a hammer."

Linda Ronstadt took her band to dinner at a restaurant called Raffles. While the waiter was taking drink orders, we chatted about what had happened to mutual friends from high school. Then she stared at me, and I felt a little uncomfortable.

"It's like a nightmare," she said, "having to go back and justify yourself to someone you knew in high school."

At Catalina High School, Linda Ronstadt was already a larger-than-life figure with an even larger voice. She didn't surprise anyone by becoming a singer. Not that anyone expected her fame to grow to the dimensions of that voice. But the voice itself was no secret.

The surprise wasn't really Linda's career but her brother Peter's. He is now the police chief of Tucson and charged with the control of certain substances that have long fueled rock 'n' roll. A rock star whose brother is a cop and whose boyfriend wants to be the chief executive officer of the whole country. What is the world coming to?

Fortunately, the brother is not very likely to have to bust his sister these days, for she says she gave up rock 'n' roll drugs when she discovered opera. She says she had to. They are bad for your voice. You can't get high and still hit the high notes in *La Bohème*.

"I first got interested in *La Bohème*," Linda Ronstadt said, "when I saw the silent movie with Lillian Gish." That's right, *silent*. "Lillian Gish was the real Snow White. After I saw the movie, I got the record. And I thought, Hey, this is pretty good. I called up Beverly Sills and told her I had discovered this opera and wanted to play Mimi.

"And Beverly said: 'My dear, every soprano in the world wants to play Mimi.'

"I felt as if I were a teen-age kid who had just discovered Chuck Berry."

Two pretty girls came over to the table to ask for Linda Ronstadt's autograph. The band insisted on being introduced. But the girls seemed unimpressed. Rich Marotta, the drummer, invited them to come to Hollywood. But he got no reaction whatsoever. Silence. The band was caught between apartheid and prudery.

The woman hunt was called off early that night—about 2:00 A.M.—because we all had to be up at 5:00 A.M. to leave on our safari.

At a few minutes past five, we met in the lobby of the hotel. Only Linda Ronstadt was missing. Bets were taken on whether she would make it.

Then someone said, "Here comes the boss."

She came down in layers of clothes with still more clothes clutched in her arms. She looked as if she were going to the laundromat rather than going on safari. She had been warned to expect cold weather early in the morning, so she came prepared.

We all tumbled into a small bus for the ride to the airport. The band was right at home. They spent most of their lives on buses.

At the airport, we crowded into a small plane with seats for twelve. The drowsy rock star put her head on her hairdresser's lap and her feet on mine and went to sleep.

Andrew Gold reached over, stroked her pale cheek, and called her Snow White.

Lying there fast asleep, with her skin so white and her hair so black, she really did look like Snow White—after the bite of poison apple.

After an hour and a half in the air, we finally landed, much to the relief of Andrew Gold, who is terrified of flying. We bounced down onto a small landing strip surrounded on all sides by jungle. We were now in the Sabi Sabi Game Reserve, which flanks South Africa's famous Kruger National Park.

"Now, almost nothing can kill us," Andrew Gold said, "unless the plane catches on fire. Or we open the door and find a carpet of puff adders."

Braving the puff adders, we all got off the plane, all but the boss. She stood in the doorway putting on the extra layers of clothing she had brought along to keep warm.

"I've gotta pee," she called to us.

Which meant taking almost everything off again.

But eventually we all loaded into two open Land Rovers and headed into the jungle. The big lumbering rhino of a car was driven by a white hunter in a starched khaki uniform. He looked very military. On the hood of the car sat a black tracker in blue coveralls.

We were no longer in the homelands. We were in serious South Africa, where apartheid rules with no pretenses. All the hunters are white hunters. And all the trackers are black trackers. The white hunters sit behind the wheels of the Land Rovers. The black trackers sit on top of the radiators.

Before we had gone very far, we stopped at a checkpoint. A black gun bearer, stationed beside the road, handed our white hunter a rifle. The white hunter loaded it with big .375-caliber shells and put it in a gun rack in front of the steering wheel.

The wild country through which we drove was beautiful. This land was much greener than the land around Sun City. When South Africa created the homelands—as when America created its Indian reservations—it tended to carve them out of the driest and poorest acres available. Here, the jungle actually looked like jungle. Africa looked the way it was supposed to look, with rolling hills and dense groves of thorn trees and over there . . .

A warthog!

And then a herd of impala, with their delicate build and beautiful reddish-brown color and curving scimitar horns. And a family of kudus, with their larger bodies and gray color and corkscrew horns. And hordes of funny wildebeests.

All made more beautiful and more dramatic by a background composed of a handsome blue mountain rising far in the distance. Like Ernest Hemingway's Mount Kilimanjaro. Only it wasn't Kilimanjaro. It was Mozambique, which South Africa had recently bombed in retaliation for a terrorist bombing in Pretoria. The landscape was peaceful, but with trouble lurking above it in the shape of a great blue mountain.

Before we had gone far, we heard an explosion that shook the jungle. It sounded too loud to be a rifle. Was it a bomb? Was a war beginning? Had the blacks finally risen up against the whites? Or were the whites launching some preemptive strike against the blacks? We learned later that a mysterious plane, entering the country from the direction of Mozambique, had been shot down by South African forces.

Our concern about distant danger was soon replaced by our interest in evidence of danger much closer at hand. Our black tracker spotted lion spoor. The white hunter stopped the Land Rover, grabbed his rifle, and got out. The hunter and the tracker conferred in a language we did not understand and then disappeared into the bush, leaving us to ask ourselves questions. What were they going to do if they did manage to catch up with the lion or lions? Drive them back in our direction so we could see them? And why had they taken the only gun?

Abandoned, with no game in sight to photograph, we took pictures of one another. Especially of Linda taking off her clothes. Since the weather had turned out to be warmer than expected, she was shedding some of the extra layers of clothing.

The white hunter and the black tracker finally returned. Empty-handed. The lions had gotten away.

We rolled on and soon saw a rhino about twenty yards away.

"He looks real earnest," Linda said.

And then she proceeded to ask our white hunter a series of earnest questions. She wanted to know all about the vegetation. What was this? A kind of thorn tree. What was that? Another kind of thorn tree. Could you ride zebras? No. What were the native languages like? They tended to rely on the present tense. Wasn't that good because it forced one to live in the present moment? Maybe.

We saw a herd of zebras. We saw a huge giraffe standing right by the road as if he were expecting us. Then we saw something really amazing.

Breakfast.

We crested a hill and saw a fancy table—the kind one associates with formal dinners at embassies—waiting for us in the middle of the jungle. It was covered with a colorful tablecloth, cloth napkins, real china, real silver, steaming coffee, orange juice, mango juice, bottles of bubbling champagne, mountains of breads, as many varieties of cheese as there are species in Africa, and a whole Garden of Eden of fruits. A black cook in a white uniform and a great billowing white chef's hat knelt over a campfire, frying up eggs and sausages and bacon. A platoon of black waiters in livery conveyed the hot dishes to the table. And poured fresh coffee. And generally hovered.

I realized that Margaret Mitchell was wrong. The way of life she immortalized had not gone with the wind. It lives on in South Africa. And today, Linda Ronstadt, with blacks handing her food and pouring her drink, was cast as Scarlett.

After breakfast, Linda Ronstadt climbed up on the hood of the Land Rover next to our tracker. Now we had two trackers. A black tracker and a white tracker. A male tracker and a female tracker. An anonymous tracker and a famous tracker. Riding the hood of the Land Rover must have been a lot like riding the back of a rhino. As we bounced over rocks and ruts, Linda Ronstadt was in real danger of fall-ing off.

With two trackers to help us spot game, we saw buffalo. We saw mongooses that reminded me of Kipling stories. We saw troops of ba-boons. We saw more impala and kudus and giraffes. We saw storks. We saw jackals.

We saw a world-famous rock star lose her balance and begin to fall. I had a vision of her under the wheels. The wilde-Rover seemed to have bucked her off. But at the last instant, she somehow saved herself, as stars—at least the kind who survive as long as she has—usually do.

Without even slowing down, we drove on into the jungle, preceded by our two figureheads, one black and one white.

At lunchtime, we stopped at a jungle outpost known as River House. It had thick white walls and a cool thatched roof. Linda Ronstadt decided to take a nap, but she didn't want to be cooped up indoors, not while she was on safari. So I helped her carry a twin bed outdoors. We set it down on the grass beneath a cloudless African sky. In her jungle bedroom, Linda promptly fell asleep.

Once again, she was a sleeping Snow White, Snow White after the apple, Snow White after the fall, Snow White where the dwarfs had laid her out on a bed under the heavens, Snow White waiting for her prince to wake her—waiting, perhaps, for Jerry Brown?

When she woke up about an hour later, she lay in bed and talked dreamily.

"I don't believe in chastity," she said. "Sex is only corrupting if your attitude is that it's bad. I thought that, even when I was a little girl. I had a bad reputation even in junior high school because my skirts were too tight. In high school, I decided to change my reputation, but I failed. I had sex when I was seventeen."

She crooked an arm up over her head.

"I had a friend in high school who had a bad reputation, but she didn't deserve it. Her problem was that one day her water broke in study hall. She just picked up her books and walked out." And hurried to a hospital to have her baby.

I said I might someday write a short story and call it "Her Water Broke in Study Hall."

After the lunch and nap break, our white hunter led us on foot down to a river. We had to make our way through grass that was taller than our heads. When we reached the water, he pointed out three hippos. They were like great gray icebergs with just their tips—in this case, the tips of their noses and ears—visible above the waterline.

"They have a nice life," our white hunter said, "just lying in the water all day, with fish tickling their backs."

"I want to join them," Linda Ronstadt said, "and have the fish tickle my back."

Our hunter explained that hippos can be dangerous. Most people tend to think of them as cute, like the ones dancing in pink skirts in

Fantasia. So people aren't afraid and get too close. And then the hippos, who haven't seen the movie and don't know how they're supposed to act, come charging out of the water. As they bear down on you, they look about as cute and lovable as an onrushing Mack truck.

As we all took a step backward, I saw a pattern repeating itself. The hippos were like the German shepherd, the landscape, and the country itself. They looked adorable and peaceful, but trouble lurked beneath the surface of the calm water.

Retreating from the river and the danger of hippo attack, we headed back for our Land Rovers. Once again, Linda Ronstadt took up her position as white tracker next to our black tracker, both perched side by side over the radiator. Seeing her, a group of natives laughed and called out: "*Snatza! Snatza!*" Which means: "Crazy! Crazy!"

A little later, we saw a rhino with a bird perched on its back. We sat quietly in the Land Rover and listened to our white hunter explain the symbiotic relationship between the bird and the rhino. The bird cleans the rhino by eating bugs off its back, and the rhino feeds the bird.

"Isn't nature wonderful?" said Andrew Gold, who was riding in the front seat, next to the driver. "Isn't it lucky that the bird rides on the rhino's back. What if the rhino had to get on top of the bird?"

"Remember that girl who didn't like your body?" said the hairdresser. "That's what she was worried about."

"I don't want to die," Andrew Gold said as soon as we were airborne. "I don't know what I would do without this body that the girls down here hate."

"Wait till this gets in *Rolling Stone*," said Don Grolnick.

"Girls at our concerts will be holding up signs that say: WE HATE YOUR BODIES," said Andrew.

"The bodies America loves to hate," said the scheduler.

"Or the bodies America hates to love," I said.

"We're trying to make a statement," Don said. "We're trying to say that there is more to rock 'n' roll than sex."

"Oh, my God," said Linda Ronstadt, who was lying down with her head in my lap. "You can say we're fascists. You can say we're racists. But please don't say the band is fat."

The mention of the word *racists*, although used in a joke, changed the tone of the conversation. The humor stopped. Linda looked up with a serious expression on her face.

"Do you really think I shouldn't have come?" she asked.

"Well, the issues are more complex than I realized before I came," I said. "But I still think you shouldn't have come."

"Why?" she asked. "What bothers you about my coming down here?"

"The facts," Andrew interrupted.

"What about today?" she asked. "Didn't you have a good time today?"

"Sure, I had a good time," I said. "But some things bothered me. Like all the blacks being trackers and all the whites being drivers."

"Well, maybe the blacks are better trackers and the whites are better drivers."

"That wasn't too bad," Andrew Gold said after we landed. "Take it back up again. No, never mind."

As we were getting off the plane, the guitar player proved that he had yet another unsuspected talent.

"Want to hear my impression of Linda Ronstadt?" he asked.

"Sure," I said.

"I've gotta pee," he said in a falsetto voice. "Can I snuggle? I'm gonna marry Jerry Brown."

Since we were running a little late, Linda had to go directly from the plane to the auditorium.

"We went on safari today," she told her audience. "I can't believe we had to come back and play music." Then she caught herself. "Oh, my God, I can't believe I said that."

She tried to make it up to the crowd by telling them how much she was enjoying her visit.

In the discothèque after the show, Linda Ronstadt was still trying to justify her trip to South Africa, not just to me, but to herself as well. She sought out people to ask if she had made a mistake. When two young black men came over to our table to tell her how much they had enjoyed her show, she asked them to join us.

They turned out to be American dancers who were working in what they called a "tits and ass" show modeled on similar extravaganzas staged in Las Vegas. After auditioning in Hollywood, they had signed one-year contracts and gotten on planes.

Tomkins Anderson, who was just twenty-one, said that an actress friend had tried to persuade him not to come. But he had come anyway because it was his first job in his first show.

I couldn't help thinking that it wasn't Linda Ronstadt's first job or first show.

Narvelle McGee, who was twenty-three, said friends had also tried to convince him not to come, but he hadn't taken the advice. Now the producers of the show were trying to get him to extend his contract, but he wasn't going to do it. A year in South Africa had made him appreciate America as never before, and he was ready to go home.

Linda Ronstadt admitted that some of her friends had opposed her trip, too, but she had made up her own mind and gotten on the plane, as they had.

"When I first got on South African Airlines," Anderson remembered, "they put me in the back of the plane. But they finally moved me up to first class where I belonged. When I got to the Johannesburg airport, I was the only black who stepped off the plane. When I walked through the airport, it felt very eerie. When my suitcase came up, it had been opened. I called a security guard over and asked him why my luggage was a shambles. I told him I didn't mind them searching my luggage, but they should've folded my stuff up nicely when they'd finished. All my clothes were filthy dirty."

"You were brave to come here all alone," said the rock star who had come with an entourage.

"We were in Johannesburg for the first seven weeks of rehearsals," McGee said. "We were scared to death to go anywhere. Once, we went to a nightclub outside of Jo'burg. We danced with some English girls. Some Afrikaners followed us into the parking lot and chased us with chains."

Soon, Linda Ronstadt returned to what was becoming a familiar chorus.

"I still don't think I've done anything wrong," she said. "Do you punish people by withholding entertainment?"

"People at home say that if you come here, you're supporting apartheid," said McGee. "But not all the whites here agree with it, either."

"That's right," said Linda. "Some people seem to feel that because I'm here I support apartheid. I see that it's vastly more complex than I ever imagined."

"Music is one of the only things we have holding the world together," Anderson said.

The black dancers wanted to make Linda Ronstadt feel good about her decision because it made them feel better about their own. And Linda wanted to make them feel good about coming so she would feel better about being there.

A handsome white boy came over and asked the rock star if she would like to dance. She declined, but asked him to find a chair and join us. He was an English-speaking South African who had been given an old-fashioned upbringing on an old-fashioned farm. Which meant that he was taught never to treat blacks as equals under any circumstances.

"Five years ago, I sat down beside a black man at the blackjack table in a casino," he said. "I thought he didn't belong there. Now I dance with black girls at the casino discothèques."

Of course, a country that relies on gambling casinos to right its social injustices is in trouble. But still . . .

The rock star asked the farm boy, as she had asked everyone, if she had made a mistake in coming to South Africa. And he tried to reassure her.

"I've been to black Africa," she told him. "I wanted to see what this would be like. I'll be criticized a lot when I get home. But I don't think it's fair. You can't not go to a country because there are some evil people in it. I'd love to get the chance to come back, but who knows? One of the things I'm trying to figure out while I'm down here is if I'm supposed to be here. I'm playing devil's advocate with myself."

The farm boy hoped she would come back.

"I'm trying to decide if it isn't a good idea to get a dialogue going," Linda said. "Now I have a whole other idea about what 'Desperado' means. Everybody here is a desperado. Everybody is a 'prisoner in disguise,' because all the people feel so misunderstood by the outside world."

In describing the South Africans, Linda seemed to be describing herself, for she, too, was beginning to feel misunderstood. She knew that she was going to be criticized at home for singing for apartheid. And she was already beginning to feel like a desperado.

The band was just feeling desperate. Rick Marotta went up to a young woman at the bar and asked her if she was in the big Las Vegas–style review.

"Of course I am," she said. "Don't you recognize my tits?"

But she declined the opportunity to show them to him again in a more private place.

"I haven't talked to a woman for so long," Don Grolnick said, "I'm thinking of calling my mother."

At breakfast the next morning, Linda Ronstadt was still wrestling with herself.

"What we are trying to decide," she said over granola and fresh fruit, "is if we did right in coming down here. We're talking about morals."

Snow White wrinkled her brow and took a bite of apple.

◆   ◆   ◆

I do not plan to ask the South African embassy for another visa. I don't think I should ask Linda Ronstadt for any more favors either. I saw her in Los Angeles at the unveiling of a portrait of former Governor Jerry Brown, but she did not speak to me. She just ducked her head.

NATIONAL VELVEETA

•   •   •

For some reason, I thought Elizabeth Taylor was about the last person in the world I wanted to meet. I thought she represented all that was wrong with bloated celebrity. I thought she was overrated.

I was wrong.

Traveling with her for a month—back when she was Mrs. John Warner—I really came to like fabulous Elizabeth Taylor.

•   •   •

Esquire, November 1977

Elizabeth Taylor passed the salad. Once she had passed a salad with a diamond in it to astound onlookers, but she is trying to be more discreet these days, since her husband is running for the Senate from conservative Virginia. These are Cleopatra's plain, green garden-variety salad days.

Over the lunch at their Georgetown home, the candidate and the candidate's wife, unlike most campaigning couples, disagreed on several points. They calmly argued a number of political questions but reserved their most heated exchange for the burning issue of how late they stayed out on their first date.

"I was invited to a small dinner for Queen Elizabeth," the other

Elizabeth said, explaining how she met her sixth husband. "And I said, 'I can't walk in by myself. I really feel terribly sort of shy.' So they said, 'We'll get back to you.' "

The party for which Elizabeth Taylor needed a date was one the British embassy was putting together for Queen Elizabeth II and President Gerald Ford on the occasion of the American bicentennial. When the embassy called back, Miss Taylor learned she had been fixed up with John Warner, then the head of the Bicentennial Administration. She called her friend Ardeshir Zahedi, the Iranian ambassador [who would soon fall from power along with the shah], to check Warner out. The ambassador reminded the movie star that she had met Warner once at the Iranian embassy and again at a dinner dance, but Miss Taylor could not remember ever having seen him before. So far as she was concerned, it was a blind date.

"He called for me at the Madison hotel," Elizabeth Taylor said. "My secretary went downstairs to case him. And she came back and said, 'Hey, he's not bad-looking at all. He's pretty dishy.' I said, 'Really? That's good luck.' And I went down and there was this very distinguished back with tails and grayish hair. And I gathered this was my escort, since he was the only one in white tie in the lobby. He turned around. 'Ah, Miss Taylor.' And I thought, *wow!*"

Telling the story, Elizabeth Taylor gave her husband a look that seemed to say he still wowed her. He is a rugged, handsome fifty-year-old man who resembles Hugh Hefner but is more virile—better playboy material. And he is quite trim. At forty-five, Elizabeth Taylor, on the other hand, reminds one of the trademark for Mike Todd's *Around the World in Eighty Days:* the hot-air balloon. She claims to get a sexual pleasure from eating (and refers to herself as a "lump"). It is a tribute to her beauty that she remains striking in spite of the padding.

"We sat next to each other," John Warner said, "and we had such an enjoyable time. Bob Hope was at the table."

I asked, "Did you drop her off back at the Madison?"

"Yes, he did," Elizabeth Taylor said archly. "Are you impugning my honor?" She laughed.

"Just curious," I said.

"Mind your own business!" Elizabeth Taylor ordered.

John (the candidate) Warner said, "I brought you home in a very proper fashion at a proper hour."

"Well, five o'clock," Elizabeth Taylor said.

I laughed. Lesley Stahl, who is a CBS correspondent and also my wife, laughed. And the candidate's wife laughed. But the candidate himself did not laugh.

"We went to Pisces," Elizabeth Taylor recalled, "and we talked until five o'clock in the morning."

"No! No!" Warner protested.

"*John!* I remember! Come on, Senator. It's okay on our first date to sit up and talk until five in the morning."

"I don't recall that."

"Well, I do, stuffed shirt," Elizabeth Taylor said. "Good God."

"I'm opposed to cheesecake either in reality or in discussion," declared the candidate.

"Oh, cheesecake's when you show your legs."

"I don't show mine in public," the husband said sternly. "Nor will you."

"Oooohhh," the wife said.

"Yeah, that's true."

"Well," said Elizabeth Taylor, "I can document our holding hands and sitting up in Pisces until five o'clock in the morning."

"No, no, you're wrong."

I asked, "When did you see each other again?"

Warner said, "We went out to my farm in Middleburg, Virginia, the next weekend."

"How much later was that?" I asked.

Warner said, "The next day."

"See, I held out," Elizabeth Taylor said, and then laughed loudly and merrily. "Oh, I love to drive John mad. He gets so squirmy."

Cleopatra has turned her back on the movies to campaign full time for her current Antony, who not only ran the bicentennial but also served as secretary of the navy. Of course, the original Antony went into politics with *his* Cleopatra with tragic results, and John Warner, a history buff, may well have pondered the story: how Cleopatra's ship turned and ran during the sea battle at Actium, and all was lost.

Our nation's capital has also pondered how it will all work out. Nor is the town quite sure which ending to hope for. If Elizabeth Taylor goes Washington for keeps, does that mean Washington will go Hollywood past all redemption? Politicians are America's new stars, but will stars be America's new politicians? But apart from all that, the big question is: Will Elizabeth Taylor stay to the end of the fight?

One evening, Mrs. Warner did seem to turn and run. At least she disappeared long enough to make Mr. Warner fidget. It happened at the American Cancer Society Crusade Ball at Washington's Sheraton-Park Hotel. At the beginning of the evening, the Warners stood at the head of a majestic flight of stairs overlooking a table decorated with ice sculptures in the form of anchors. The movie star wore a low-cut orange gown with what appeared to be another ice sculpture on her shoulder. This piece of ice turned out to be diamonds and emeralds. A receiving line resembling a centipede with 925 hands filed past Elizabeth Taylor. She shook all 925. I counted.

Then the Warners walked arm in arm to a far corner of the ballroom, where only the rest rooms were able to separate them. John Warner emerged from the men's room moments later and began his vigil for his wife. I kept him company.

"I'm here," Warner said, "because right after I came home from the navy in 1946, my father died of cancer. Then my only brother got cancer, but he was cured. That's why I'm here. Period."

While we talked, I sensed that Warner was concerned about why his wife was taking so long. Had she fled out the back door of the ladies' room?

Meanwhile, Mrs. Warner stood at the center of a crowd in the ladies' room. A dozen women were simultaneously trying to help her fix the diamond-and-emerald pin, which had fallen apart.

The door opened. A woman in a wheelchair rolled into the pink and gray room and bore down on the crowd in front of the washbasin. Please, could she have an autograph? Mrs. Warner usually turns down such requests, but a woman in a wheelchair is hard to put off in a crowded ladies' room. She signed.

The door opened again. John Warner had sent a young woman into the ladies' room to check on his wife. She quickly discovered the problem and departed to tell the anxious husband.

"Your wife's pin is broken," she explained.

"I'm not interested in jewelry," Warner said. "Period."

A bystander said, "Even the best jewelry sometimes breaks."

"Yes," Warner said, "and I think she has some of the best."

Giggling and girlish, Elizabeth Taylor finally emerged from the ladies' room and handed her husband a king's ransom wrapped in a tattered Kleenex. John Warner explained that I was from *Esquire* and would be following them around for a few weeks. Elizabeth Taylor looked as if her husband had announced that Caesar's army had come to carry her off.

"I know you don't like that," Warner said, "but that's the way it is."

After looking me over, Elizabeth Taylor led her husband off to inspect a fabulous display of Cartier jewelry. The Cancer Society was to receive a commission on all items sold. Walking among the cases was like touring a pharaoh's tomb. Mr. Warner tried to show an interest. Period.

At the lunch in Georgetown, I asked whether he proposed to her or she proposed to him.

"*He* proposed," Elizabeth Taylor said. "We have a hill at the farm that we call Engagement Hill. We went up in the Jeep, and we had a bottle of wine and some caviar."

"Oh, we didn't have any caviar," John Warner protested. "We had a bottle of California wine."

"Too rich for the Republican stomach?" the candidate's wife asked. "The caviar was a gift from Ardeshir."

"Ahhhh, that's a terrible story. I have no recollection of any caviar on that hill. We had a bottle of Paul Masson wine."

"I'm talking about caviar."

"That's blasphemy."

"Okay," Elizabeth Taylor said, violet light dancing in her eyes, "we went up with some ground groundhog meat. A little moonshine. Oh, that's illegal. What do you call that really cheap wine? Gallo?"

Lesley, my wife, said, "Muscatel."

"Muscatel," Mrs. Warner said. "Oh, a bottle of muscatel. Virginia muscatel. Virginia ham. Anyway, they were all Virginia products."

Lesley and I laughed, but Warner didn't.

Then Elizabeth Taylor added even more mischievously, "Virginia caviar. It's wonderful."

One campaign stop was at a children's hospital in Norfolk.

"Do you know who this is, children?" a nurse asked.

"They know!" John Warner said. "Don't you worry."

"Hello," Elizabeth Taylor said to her awestruck audience.

Shaking hands with a little boy, John Warner explained, "I'm really nobody."

From the hospital, the Warners went to a Republican party reception at the Norfolk Sheraton. The world's greatest movie star filed into an ugly room with a low ceiling and lots of smoke. Here was the caviar queen facing a buffet of cheddar cheese squares on toothpicks, the duchess of diamonds in the junk-jewelry department, a bird of paradise in a chicken coop. Here was Elizabeth Taylor campaigning at the county-committee level. As she shook her way through 424 outstretched hands, her own right hand grew larger and larger.

After the last painful handshake, Mrs. Warner shook her finger at me and scolded, "What sort of sneaky, devious things are you writing down?"

John Warner asked if I would like to come up to the couple's honeymoon/campaign suite to chat. I said I would.

"How could you?" Elizabeth Taylor asked me. "You should have said you knew how tired we were and that we wanted to get to bed."

I followed the Warners into the elevator.

"Elizabeth, I promised him we'd chat tonight," John Warner lied.

Elizabeth Taylor gave me her *Virginia Woolf* stare, which made the elevator walls close in on me.

"A person with a name like 'Aaron' should have better judgment," she said.

"That depends on how he spells it," Warner said.

"You spell it A-A-R-O-N, don't you?" Mrs. Warner asked me.

"Yes."

"You should have better judgment."

I was beginning to sense the similarity and the difference between a movie star and a politician. A star and a pol are alike in their unquenchable need for mass love. But they are different in their reaction to the press. A politician is taught to run toward notebooks and microphones, while a movie star is taught to run the other way. A movie star can reach her public on celluloid, whereas a politician must reach his public through the press.

When the elevator door opened I hesitated, but Warner insisted I come along. I followed the newlyweds down the corridor to their rooms. Elizabeth Taylor stormed off to the bedroom. Her husband and I retired to a sitting room.

"I love to work and charge twenty-four hours a day," John Warner said. "I can understand Liz. She has put in a hard day. When I was in the Pentagon, I got there every morning at seven-thirty and stayed until eight-fifteen in the evening. That's how I lost my first wife."

John Warner's first wife was Catherine Mellon, daughter of fabulously wealthy Paul Mellon. She left him four years ago—and left him wealthy. He got the house in Washington and the farm in Virginia. When I first heard that John Warner planned to marry Elizabeth Taylor, I thought he didn't know what he was getting into, but as I got to know him better, I thought differently. In a sense, John Warner had been in training for his marriage to Elizabeth Taylor all his life. Catherine Mellon had been a rehearsal.

"Warner!" Elizabeth Taylor yelled and began banging on the door. "Warner!! *Warner!!!*"

The lock was stuck, but Warner yanked and twisted until the door finally came open. Elizabeth Taylor burst into the room wearing a shapeless dressing gown that emphasized her weight. There was another tug-of-war. On the one hand, Elizabeth Taylor disliked the press, but on the other hand, she had been brought up to be a good hostess.

"Would you like something to drink?" the reluctant hostess asked. "A glass of wine?"

I accepted. Elizabeth Taylor poured me a glass of white wine and then talked about her struggle to convince her husband to support the Equal Rights Amendment.

"Through Elizabeth I have been able to better understand the plight of working women," John Warner said. "She has described to me in vivid detail how Louis B. Mayer shouted at her when she was ten."

Over fried fish and fattening potato salad, we talked about how the Warners decided to run for the Senate.

"A number of the so-called pols talked to me when they heard I was falling in love with Elizabeth," John Warner said. "They said, 'You can forget a political career.' So if forced to make the choice, I was going to take Elizabeth. I was going to forget a political career."

I asked why the pols said Elizabeth Taylor would destroy him politically.

"Because of her numerous marriages, principally," Warner said. "And because religious heritage is very important in Virginia. It's a Southern Baptist, Methodist, and Episcopalian state."

Elizabeth Taylor was raised a Christian Scientist but converted to Judaism before marrying Eddie Fisher.

In light of the uncertainty about her acceptance by the voting public, I asked if the Warners had anticipated a political campaign when they got married last December 5.

"Huh-uh," said the movie star. "When we got married, I thought: Oh, how great, I can unpack. I don't have to travel in this suitcase anymore. Little did I know I would break four suitcases in two months' traveling."

When they began discussing a campaign around Christmas, Warner was reluctant to involve his wife in politics. He was the one who wanted to run, but she was the one who had to do the convincing.

"Candidly," John Warner said, "I was very cautious because my first marriage broke up over politics. I wanted to make sure it didn't happen again. When I was secretary of the navy, my wife had to be involved in all kinds of political functions, but she was very shy and couldn't stand it. Also, candidly, we disagreed on Vietnam. I was in the administration and thought we had to finish something we had started.

My wife was almost a student radical. The marriage couldn't survive those pressures. I wanted to take it slowly with Elizabeth. I had to be convinced she not only accepted but enjoyed politics."

She convinced him. They held their premiere as a campaign couple at the Virginia Military Institute, where Warner gave the Founders' Day speech on November 11 last year.

"Right in the middle of my speech," Warner said, "I decided to try it. I just said, 'And my fiancée is here to salute the corps of cadets.' And Elizabeth, without a moment's hesitation, stood up and saluted. These kids threw their hats in the air. I said to myself: Those old pols don't know anything."

Almost overcome by mock theatrical emotion, the actress said, "I was accepted."

"Now we have to determine if we can take campaigning four, five, six nights a week," Warner said. Turning, he added, "That's up to you."

Elizabeth Taylor said, "I'm hanging in, aren't I?"

In three days, I had seen Elizabeth Taylor shake over sixteen hundred hands. At a Republican fund raiser in the Sheraton hotel in Hampton, Virginia, she shook one too many. Suddenly, she was crying and she wasn't acting. The tears weren't glycerin. Some he-man had proven his manhood by crushing her hand. A blood vessel had broken. Her hand swelled up and turned black and blue.

A doctor who happened to be standing right there examined the movie star and then hustled her out of the ballroom. She refused to go to the hospital but did accept some pain-killer.

Meanwhile, John Warner kept shaking hands with the hundreds of people who had been standing in line for an hour to shake hands with Elizabeth Taylor. All the faces were sad.

An hour or so later, Warner said, "Look who's here out of the hospital ward."

A wounded Cleopatra had returned to the battle.

"Bless him, poor thing, Neville Chamberlain used to come down to have barbecues at my mother and father's house in Kent," Elizabeth Taylor said as second helpings were passed. "Oh, did he make a few boo-boos."

As a newcomer to politics, the movie star would like to play the role of an old-time pol, so she dwells on the politicians she had known over the years.

"Anthony Eden rode my horse when I was a kid," she told us. "And my horse threw him."

John Warner reminded her, "You felt Richard Burton would have made a great politician."

"Oh, I have no question that he would have," the former Mrs. Burton said, "and that he should have."

Warner said, "I had a long conversation with Richard over New Year's weekend. We talked about politics."

Mrs. Warner said, "My godmother, Thelma Cazalet, was one of the first lady MPs in Britain."

I asked, "Did *you* ever think of running for office?"

"I did before I met John," Elizabeth Taylor said.

If Mrs. Warner has rushed headlong into Mr. Warner's political world, then Mr. Taylor has at least timidly tiptoed into Ms. Taylor's show-business world. He actually played a role opposite his wife in the movie *Winter Kills.*

"I played President Kennedy," John Warner explained.

"Don't get braggy," his movie-star wife said.

"But it's just my hands and a bit of my shoulder. It was a presidential hand. They did study the hand carefully."

"Especially the blotches," his wife said.

To change the subject, John Warner picked up a heavy, scholarly volume. He said he wanted to read us Lord Chesterfield's definition of a politician. Essentially, the definition said a politician is a person who has to keep from telling the truth while avoiding telling lies.

"What *I*'ve always heard about Lord Chesterfield," Elizabeth Taylor announced, "was that he had this marvelous personal aroma. In fact, his aroma was so wonderful that women competed to get his discarded shirts, which they rolled up and put in with their lingerie."

I said, "You really have had a long-time interest in politicians."

"No," Elizabeth Taylor said, "just in underwear."

While campaigning at Randolph-Macon Woman's College in Lynchburg, Elizabeth Taylor told the drama students how she got the part for which she is best remembered.

"I was under contract to MGM," she explained, recalling a time when she was twelve years old. "The studio had owned *National Velvet* for a long time before they got around to making the movie. At first, they had considered Katharine Hepburn, but she outgrew it."

Mr. and Mrs. Warner sat side by side on the stage of the college theater. She wore an Ace bandage on her right hand.

"The director said I was too young and too short for the part.

" 'I'll grow,' I told him.

" 'That's very sweet, honey,' he said.

"I went to work. I had huge breakfasts. Steaks. I hung from bars trying to stretch myself. I grew three inches in three months. The director marked it on his door. And I got the part. That was the last time I was ambitious."

"Who's your favorite actress?" a drama student asked.

"Vivien Leigh was my heroine," said Elizabeth Taylor, who bears a striking resemblance to Miss Leigh. "She was innocence on the verge of decadency. Always there to be saved."

She went on to name several other actresses whom she admired, including, appropriately, Jane Fonda. In a real sense, Elizabeth Taylor is now trying out for the part Jane Fonda failed to get in 1976: senator's wife.

"Did you always want to be an actress?" a student asked.

"I wanted to be a ballerina," Elizabeth Taylor said. "A nurse, a veterinarian, the first female fire-engine driver. My father was very much against my being an actress. Mother and I ganged up on him."

Once Elizabeth Taylor became an actress, her life was bounded by the studio and her omnipresent mother. During those early days, the child star had a pet chipmunk named Nibbles, with which she had much in common. Wherever Elizabeth went, Nibbles went, tethered to his mistress by a string around his neck. Elizabeth's mother kept her child on a leash as short.

Mom was too much with her and Dad not enough. In a sense, acting cost her her father, and she has been searching for another one ever since. Her hunts have normally taken the form of marriages. She probably married Conrad "Nicky" Hilton when she was eighteen to escape her mother's custody, but at nineteen she married Michael Wilding, a man twice her age and a definite father substitute, as she readily admits. At twenty-four she married Mike Todd, perhaps the most macho of all her surrogate fathers, who had a son older than his new wife and a grandson as well. After Todd died in the crash of his plane, *The Lucky Liz*, his widow married his best friend, Eddie Fisher. But Fisher was no Todd. At thirty-one he was only four years older than his new wife, and he was flimsy father material. During the filming of *Cleopatra*, Mrs. Fisher, true to the character she was playing, deserted Mr. Fisher. Then the celluloid Cleopatra married the celluloid Antony. She was thirty-two; he was thirty-nine. The great actor at first appeared to be the perfect macho replacement for macho Mike Todd, but Burton proved to have a tragic flaw, a love of alcohol. Now John Warner has his chance to play the domineering father. So far he has succeeded where her real father failed: He has gotten Elizabeth out of show business.

"Of all your films," a student said, "the one that made the biggest impression on me was *Cleopatra.*"

"Gasp!" said Elizabeth Taylor.

The Warners' secretary entered the room to say that Simcha Dinitz, the Israeli ambassador, was on the phone. Mrs. Warner took the call. When she returned, she whispered some news to her husband.

Warner sputtered, "Simcha Dinitz wants to do something that no self-respecting politician would do. I veto that."

I doubted he would tell me what it was no self-respecting politician would do. But I thought his wife might if I waited until she and I were alone.

While I was biding my time, Warner suggested we adjourn to the living room for coffee. We settled down on couches in the company of Renoir, Monet, Degas, Roualt, Modigliani, Pissarro, Utrillo, and an Andy Warhol Elizabeth Taylor. At first I thought this must be the Mellon collection, but I learned that all the paintings belonged to the new Mrs. Warner.

Struck especially by her Van Gogh, I asked her how she had acquired it. She explained that she had been looking for just the right Van Gogh for years, with no success. Then one day sixteen years ago, her father, an art dealer, took her to Sotheby's in London. One canvas made her suddenly dig her nails into his hand.

Her father ordered, "Don't even change your expression."

Meanwhile, Elizabeth Taylor's violet eyes were growing as big and bright and round as a Van Gogh sun.

"I don't even want you in the country when I buy it," her father warned, "or you'll have to pay twice as much."

When Elizabeth was safely out of the way, her father bought her the Van Gogh.

Three of the other paintings were purchased for her by Mike Todd. While she was in the hospital recuperating from a fall down stairs, Todd decided her quarters were too dull. So he went out and bought a Monet, a Renoir, and a Pissarro to cheer up her hospital room.

When John Warner finally left the living room to take a call, I got the opening I had been waiting for. I immediately asked Elizabeth Taylor what it was no self-respecting politician would do.

"Oh, just go somewhere," she said enigmatically.

"Las Vegas," Lesley guessed.

Elizabeth Taylor's expression confirmed the guess. And when her husband returned she announced: "We're going to Las Vegas, John."

"If we do," Warner warned, "I'll just sit in the room and read my history books."

"Come on, we're going to have a good time."

"No self-respecting politician would be seen in public in Las Vegas."

"Simcha's an ambassador."

"That makes it worse."

"Come out of your stuffed shirt," Mrs. Warner told her husband, then turned to us and smiled. "I just love to stick it to him. He's so easy. He always rises to the bait."

When the Warners were grand marshals of the Charlottesville Dogwood Festival parade, signs along the parade route read WARNER FOR SENATOR AND LIZ, WHEN ARE YOU GOING TO GET MARRIED AGAIN? After the parade, the Warners, escorted by the police, hurried from one Dogwood festival event to another, scattering pieces of their story behind them like crumbs.

"Poor Howard." Elizabeth meant Howard Hughes. "He offered me a million dollars under the table to give him two weeks to court me. I said, 'I'm not in love with you. I'm going to England to marry Michael Wilding.' "

Warner summed up his theory of why the movie star was attracted to him: "When she saw the farm, I won her heart."

In a sense, Elizabeth Taylor had been homeless for many years. When she was married to Richard Burton, they had many homes but lived mostly in hotels. Her secretary, Chen Sam, put it this way: "The lady needed a home." Her friends say she married John Warner's roots.

When we stopped at the Boar's Head Inn for lunch, Elizabeth Taylor and I shared a pizza. The works. Hold the anchovies. Mrs. Warner offered Mr. Warner a slice. He ate the topping but left the crust; she ate crust and all. Warner was careful not to stain his red, white, and blue striped tie.

"I've worn the same bicentennial tie for over a year," said the former director of the Bicentennial Administration.

"I'm going to get a pair of scissors," Elizabeth Taylor said, "and cut it in little pieces."

"It's old and frayed," Warner said, "like your husband." Then he went to the rest room.

"Where's Big Daddy going?" Elizabeth Taylor drawled in her *Cat on a Hot Tin Roof* voice. "Tell Big Daddy it's time to go."

It was time to go because the Warners were due at yet another Republican fund raiser. We drove to a beautiful horse farm outside Charlottesville, where the wounded movie star ran the gauntlet of another reception line.

"Ouch, ouch, ouch, ouch," Elizabeth Taylor said over and over, as if shooting infinite retakes of the same scene. She showed me her good hand, which was badly swollen.

"This hand hurts more than the other," she said. "Since it doesn't have a bandage, people think it's all right to squeeze it. Two bandages would be too much."

As the party was breaking up, a straggler said, "I hope you're not going to be *too* damn conservative."

"Gasp!" said Elizabeth Taylor.

Warner said, "She'd kick me out of bed if I were."

After finishing her coffee, Elizabeth Taylor curled up in John Warner's arms on the living room couch.

"I envy you having a baby," Elizabeth Taylor told my pregnant wife.

"Stick to your hysterical pregnancy," John Warner said to his wife.

When I dropped by the Warners' Georgetown home one morning, I found the candidate working on a speech he would deliver to the University of Virginia Alumni Association. He was in his study and was wearing a navy flight suit. He had an American flag on his shoulder and these words stitched above his breast pocket: SECRETARY OF THE NAVY.

"Get out," he ordered Elizabeth, who had shown me into his lair. "This is my room, my bastion."

"You're a male chauvinist," Elizabeth Taylor complained.

"Don't forget the present for Aaron," he said.

"What?" asked the star, who had obviously forgotten.

"You know—the arrowhead."

The political candidate was teaching his wife to woo the press. Picking up a white flint arrowhead from her husband's desk, she hesitated, choosing her words carefully. "I had planned to wait until the article came out," she said at last, giving me my present. "And then, depending on *how* it turned out, I'd give it to you in your hand, or through your head."

Mr. Warner threw Mrs. Warner out of his room and then sat down behind his cluttered desk, crouching over his speech.

"I always wear the flight suit to write speeches," Warner said. "It doesn't grab your balls and it's so seedy a woman won't touch you. You can work."

We were nonetheless invaded by another female. Warner introduced me to Elizabeth Taylor's overweight cat, Cleo. Then the cat's mistress, who had been banned from the study, called on the telephone to ask her husband to take her to the doctor's office. Her hand had been perpetually swollen ever since the blood vessel broke, getting so bad one evening that she complained, "I was barely able to force a diamond on it." Warner agreed to drive the hand to the doctor.

When we walked outside, Warner pointed to the house next door and explained that it belonged to his first wife. A pool separated the two homes. He said his children ran back and forth between their father's house and their mother's.

The next time I saw Elizabeth Taylor—shortly before her husband's alumni association speech at the Washington Hilton—she wore what looked like a corset on her hand. An old-fashioned corset. The kind her heroine Vivien Leigh wore in *Gone with the Wind*. The kind her slave laced up so tight. The hand corset was meant to act as a cast.

"The doctor told me I'm benched," she said. "I can't shake with either hand. I have to be careful of this finger for three months," she said, holding up a finger the color of her eyes, "or I may be crippled."

"You can't regret not shaking hands," a University of Virginia alumnus said.

"Yes, I do," Elizabeth Taylor said. "I'm a person who likes to touch."

Once again there was a receiving line, and once again the wounded star took her position beside her husband. I was surprised at her doing so and at his seeming to expect her to do so. She kept her right hand in her pocket, but that did not keep people from squeezing her arm.

"Let's go," Mrs. Warner finally said. "My arm is just throbbing."

For the first time, she turned and ran. And he ran after her.

Two days later, Elizabeth Taylor descended from a car in front of the Fort Pickett NCO Club—and shook my hand. I flinched. She didn't. Once again Elizabeth Taylor took her place in the reception line and shook every hand in the joint.

Then the movie star came over to where I was standing and started beating me over the head with her injured hand. I was afraid she would hurt herself.

"Never mind, I'm just attacking him," she explained to the startled crowd. "He's a journalist."

The next stop was the VFW Loyalty Day Parade in Colonel Heights, Virginia. As a crowd gathered, Mrs. Warner refused to sign autographs, but Mr. Warner did sign. Although Elizabeth Taylor could not write her name, she did cooperate to this extent: She let her husband use her back as a desk.

"Don't move, chicken fat," Warner ordered. "I'm signing something." He wrote: *John & Elizabeth Warner.*

After riding in the parade, the campaigning couple set off for Norfolk to make another speech. Riding through the Virginia countryside, Elizabeth Taylor was in a good mood. She was joking and laughing with her secretary, Chen Sam.

"All right, everybody, be quiet," Big Daddy said. "I want to take a nap."

Suddenly the car was utterly silent. John Warner closed his eyes and slept for a few minutes. The women seemed afraid to speak. Then Warner opened his eyes and started working on a speech.

"Does that mean we can talk?" Elizabeth Taylor asked.

Big Daddy nodded.

Chen Sam says Warner is more dominant than was Burton. And yet not even the man in the secretary of the navy's flight suit always gets his way with Elizabeth Taylor.

One evening in a Richmond hotel, John Warner practiced a speech in one room while his wife watched Merv Griffin in another room. The two endeavors competed with each other. Elizabeth Taylor turned up Merv, but John Warner retaliated by turning up his own volume. So the star made her show even louder. So the politician made his speech even louder. They kept escalating and counterescalating, decibel for decibel. The entertainment world and the political world were blaring at each other.

"Turn it down," Big Daddy ordered.

This time Elizabeth Taylor did not obey. She got up and slammed the door.

Wrapped tightly in John Warner's arms, Elizabeth Taylor reclined contentedly upon the living room couch. She declined a second cup of coffee because she did not want to move an inch. She seemed to have come to rest at last.

I asked, "Have you, Elizabeth, grown more conservative living with your husband? And have you, John, grown more liberal living with your wife?"

"I don't believe in labels," Elizabeth Taylor said, sounding like every old pol. "I'm a people person."

"Well, you must believe in one label," I persisted. "You must be a Republican."

This observation transformed the contented Cleopatra into Martha of *Who's Afraid of Virginia Woolf?* She burst out of her husband's arms and glared at me.

"I'm *not* a Republican," Martha flared. (In fact, she is not. She will not be voting for either party for three years because it will take her that long to become an American. She is currently a British subject. Elizabeth Taylor will not even be able to vote for her husband.)

"Oh, my God, you are *too* a Republican," John Warner sputtered. "You may have blown the whole thing."

"I'll become a Republican," Elizabeth Taylor declared, "when you come out for ERA."

The candidate jumped up off the couch and rushed out of the room as if he were going to be sick. She did not run after him.

Then Elizabeth Taylor leaned forward and said, "If you print what I said, I'll get my tit caught in a wringer."

◆　◆　◆

I like Elizabeth Taylor, but I don't think she likes me. When the story was published, she let me know that she wished she had held onto that white arrowhead so she could stick it into me.

This modern-day Cleopatra—unlike her historical counterpart—stayed with her Antony long enough to see him win his battle. He was elected to the Senate. But eventually the new Cleo, like the old one, deserted her man. She fled back to Hollywood and went on a diet. And the new senator was left to nurse a heart wounded by something sharper than a pretty arrowhead.

PAUL NEWMAN TAKES
THE STAND

•   •   •

Butch Cassidy is shy. Cool Hand Luke is shy. Hud is shy. These heroes are all shy because they are all Paul Newman, and he is very shy.

I got to know how shy by spending a week on the set of *The Verdict*, in which he starred. Between scenes, we would go up to his dressing room intending to talk, but often neither of us said very much. Perhaps I should have jumped into the silences, but I didn't because I am just as shy as he is. It was though we were having an inadvertent shyness contest. These quiet times were not particularly uncomfortable—perhaps because shy people learn to live with silence. So we did not particularly mind it when we sat together in his dressing room with him saying nothing and me saying nothing—the only sound in the room provided by my tape recorder turning around and around recording nothing.

Later on, when I played back the tapes of my interviews with Newman, they sounded like Richard Nixon's White House tapes—riddled with unexplained silent gaps.

•   •   •

Rolling Stone, January 1983

Paul Newman sat in the courtroom—in an atmosphere of robes and three-piece suits—with his shoes off. One antiheroic foot was propped up on the defense table. Rebel toes wiggled free inside a black sock. The rest of his body was dressed like Perry Mason, but his feet were still outlaws on the loose, Butch Cassidy and the Sundance Kid wearing sock masks.

"Having a good time?" I asked.

"Yeah," Newman said laughing, "because he's such a fuckup."

He did not mean that the judge was a fuckup, or that the baliff was a fuckup, or that any of the jurors were fuckups. He meant that Sidney Lumet, the distinguished director, was a fuckup.

"Come on," Lumet, the fuckup, said, "just because you were good this morning doesn't mean you can relax now."

"When you were taller," said Alan King, the comedian, who was visiting the set, "you were nicer."

"I could've been tall," said the fuckup, "but I turned it down."

Lumet turned down not only tall but also lots of other projects before he agreed to do this movie *The Verdict*, a courtroom drama starring Paul Newman. One of the extras hired to fill up the courtroom passed the time reading a book entitled *The Verdict*, by Barry Reed, the novel on which the movie is based. The extra went right on reading the book while the camera was filming the movie.

The Verdict is something of a departure for Paul Newman, because in this movie, he does not play a typical "Paul Newman character." In fact, George Roy Hill, the director and Newman's friend, told him, "I wouldn't cast you in the part, kid." And why not?

"This character is a distance from a lot of characters I've played," Newman explained, "because he's weak, he's panicked, he fucks up. He's not particularly macho. He's not the strong, silent type. It's an absolute 180 from the guy in *Absence of Malice*. He's vulnerable. He's on the edge of it. He starts face down in the urinal."

There, but for the grace of God—and an ungodly Hollywood fight—would have been Robert Redford with his face in the urinal. For Redford, America's Eagle Scout, was originally cast to play this role of an American fuckup. But who could believe cute Robert Redford with his face in the toilet? Well, Redford certainly couldn't. He wanted the character cleaned up. Which started the fight. A director quit, a studio was in turmoil. And finally Robert Redford himself was fired.

The producers went out and hired themselves another famous face to go in the urinal. In this case, Butch Cassidy was willing to take a bigger chance with his image than was the Sundance Kid. I wondered: Had the Kid lost his nerve? Had Butch found his?

•

Sitting on the set of *The Verdict,* surrounded by all the paraphernalia of our judicial system, I also began to think about guilt and innocence. And I even began to wonder what Paul Newman might, or might not, feel guilty about. I think I surprised him with my question.

"Do you feel guilty about anything?"

He hesitated. "I was about to say the thing that you should feel most guilty about is what they pay you." He paused. "But I give almost all of it—I give a lot of it—away. Except if you print that, the letters start coming in."

Ah, guilt *geld.* Guilt giving.

The movie star went back to work, and I went back to daydreaming. Movie sets are great places for daydreaming, for a movie company's cameras turn even more slowly than the wheels of justice. So while I watched the slow progress of this imaginary trial, I had plenty of time to imagine an imaginary trial of my own—sort of a make-believe trial within a make-believe trial. My daydream also starred Paul Newman.

I was the prosecutor and Paul Newman was the defendant. When he took the stand, I cross-examined him mercilessly. After all, I have long believed that reporters and prosecutors have a lot in common.

I imagined myself asking, "Mr. Newman, you are charged with being an actor. How do you plead?"

And I imagined Paul Newman responding, "Guilty."

ME: And how does being an actor make you feel?

NEWMAN: Guilty.

ME: You are further charged with being a movie star. How do you plead?

NEWMAN: Guilty.

ME: And how does that make you feel?

NEWMAN: Guilty.

ME: You are also charged with being a superstar. How does that make you feel?

NEWMAN: Guilty.

ME: You are also charged with being too good-looking. How do you feel?

NEWMAN: Guilty.

ME: And you are charged with making too much money. How do you feel?

NEWMAN: Guilty.

ME: Does all of this superstar guilt have anything to do with your choosing to play a character who is not a super anything? Not a super lawyer. Not a super looker. Just a super fuckup. Is this expiation?

NEWMAN: Guilty.

ME: Mr. Newman, in this movie, you try to protect your clients' rights, but in real life, you seem to want to protect the whole world. You seem to want to save the world from nuclear destruction. How do you plead to this charge?

NEWMAN: Guilty as sin.

ME: And how does trying to save the world make you feel?

NEWMAN: A little less guilty.

"I need this wall inverted," shouted Sidney Lumet, bringing me out of my reverie. "Probably without the columns."

While they were rearranging the courtroom walls, Paul Newman slipped his outlaw feet into black wing-tip lawyer shoes but did not bother to lace them up or tie them. I followed him as he shuffled through the maze of sets and props that cluttered the cavernous Astoria Studio in Astoria, Queens. When Paul Newman was a down-and-out actor trying to break into show business thirty years ago, he knocked on the door of this studio, but they wouldn't even let him in. And now he has the largest dressing room in the joint. When we reached it, he kicked off his shoes.

We sat down, and I started cross-examining him about his dual careers, the one as a movie star (which makes him a lot of money) and the other as a world saver (which costs him a lot of money). These two roles seemed to come together in a curious way a few years ago, when he visited the White House.

"I spent about fifteen minutes with Carter in the Oval Office," Paul Newman said. "God, I was uncomfortable. But that's my problem, not his."

He had gone to the White House for a briefing because he had been named a citizen's delegate to a United Nations conference on nuclear disarmament. The actor had been speaking out against nuclear weapons for years. He had also joined the board of—and given lots of money to—the Center for Defense Information, which does its best to wage a sort of propaganda war against the Defense Department. But his appointment by the Carter administration as a delegate to the United Nations conference would be an escalation of his war against nuclear war. So he did all he could to prepare for it, reading, studying—and going to Washington, D.C., to meet in the basement of the White House with David Aaron, one of the president's national security advisers. After the briefing, Paul Newman was on his way out of the White House when he was recognized by someone.

"I was just walking down the hall, and Carter came out of a door. And we just bumped into each other.

"He said, 'What are you doing here?'

"I said, 'Nothing.'

"He said, 'Why don't you come on up?' "

The movie star told the president of the United States that he thought he could work him into his schedule. He was looking forward to a heart-to-heart with the commander in chief about saving the world from nuclear destruction, but the commander in chief had other ideas.

"I wanted to talk to him about SALT II, and he wanted to talk about how you made movies. What made me pick the roles I picked? How long did it take to make a movie? What was the time it took to put the movie together after you finish shooting?"

The movie star wanted to talk about first strikes; the president of the United States wanted to talk about first breaks. The movie star wanted to talk about the Pentagon budget; the president of the United States wanted to talk about movie budgets. The movie star wanted to talk about bombs; the president of the United States wanted to talk about blockbusters. The movie star wanted to talk about nuclear shells; the president of the United States wanted to talk about bombshells. It was as if they would have liked to trade places.

And perhaps they would have.

Listening to Paul Newman, I began to appreciate the uneasiness the star must have felt in the Oval Office. Only a part of his discomfort was the result of the president's fan-magazine curiosity. Another part was simply due to his innate shyness.

ME: Mr. Newman, you are charged with being a shy superstar. How do you plead?

NEWMAN: Well, um, uh. . . .

Paul Newman was called back to the set, where some bad news awaited him. He was informed that the child of a close friend had committed suicide. This tragedy was sad not only in and of itself, but because it must have opened up an old wound: Newman could not help but remember his own son's death of a drug overdose in the fall of 1978.

But he still had a scene to do.

The camera had been moved into the judge's chambers, which were just off the courtroom. In this scene, Newman, playing a lawyer who is perilously near a personal breakdown, was supposed to get into a shouting match with the judge. His honor was played by Milo O'Shea. Sidney Lumet arrived on the set looking as refreshed as Paul Newman looked subdued.

"Did you have a good sleep?" asked Alan King.

Lumet formed a circle with his thumb and forefinger.

"He can sleep anywhere," King said.

While the crew did some last-minute lighting, King went on to tell a story about the worst coast-to-coast trip he'd ever taken. He'd boarded a plane in Vancouver that was bound nonstop for New York. He was alone in the first-class cabin until just before the aircraft took off, and then in walked Henny Youngman.

"I was locked in a first-class cabin with Henny Youngman from Vancouver to New York," King said. "He started right away: 'Take my wife, please.' All the way to New York. It was just unbelievable torture. What a nightmare!"

I wondered if Paul Newman felt the same way about this scene. Did he feel trapped on the set with a comedian (who did not know about the tragedy) making jokes? Did he wish he could escape into some private place for private mourning? Had the scene become a torture and a nightmare? I could not see the answer to my questions in the actor's face. Some actors use their talent to showcase their emotions; others use the same talent to hide what they are feeling. Paul Newman is one of the latter group. A very Cool Hand Luke.

And yet he must have been thinking back almost four years to the time he received the tragic news about son, Scott, who died at the age of twenty-eight. Back then, he had had work to do, too—ironically, work with young people, for he had returned to his alma mater, Kenyon College, to direct a college play. When he learned what had happened, he assembled his student players and told them, "It would help me if you'd be as rowdy as possible." That night, several of his actors dressed up in funny costumes and rang his doorbell as if they were collegiate trick-or-treaters. When he opened the door, these mummers handed him a case of beer and a bottle of Jack Daniel's. Newman took a swallow from the bottle and said, "It's the first time I've touched hard stuff in eight years."

ME: Weren't you left feeling more guilty than ever?

NEWMAN: I'd rather not talk about it.

"Okay, my dears," said Sidney Lumet, "from the top, Burtt, give me fresh bells."

"Ring 'em," said Burtt Harris, the first assistant director on the movie. And what sounded like a loud telephone rang out three times in the hangar of a soundstage. "Turn 'em."

"Rolling," someone yelled.

"Speed," someone else yelled.

Soon, Paul Newman was ranting and raving, accusing the judge of being on the take.

"I'm gonna take the transcript of this trial," Newman almost shouted, "and um, uh . . ." He grabbed his throat to show that he had choked. He laughed. "I'm gonna take this speech and stuff it."

"Like it, Alan?" asked Lumet.

"I think you should tell him to talk louder," King said. "You gotta tell these actors to project."

They got ready to try again.

"Okay, loves."

"Ring 'em. Turn 'em over."

"Rolling."

"Speed."

Newman started yelling at the judge again.

"I'm gonna take a transcript of this trial to the Judicial Conduct Board . . . and I'm gonna impeach your . . . gonna impeach your ass, if I can ever say it. Get Alan King to play it."

"Here he is," said Lumet.

"I don't use profanity," said King.

They tried again.

"Turn 'em over."

"Rolling."

"Speed."

"I'm gonna. . . ," faltered Newman. "I'm gonna . . . your ass."

"Get out of here," said the judge, continuing the already crippled scene, "before I call the bailiff and have you thrown in jail."

"Throw him in jail," said Lumet, laughing. "Fuck him."

They did another take. The bells rang. The camera turned over. Speed. But this one did not work either.

"I'm sorry," Newman said, "I'm way off."

"One more," said Lumet.

"Arggghh."

Now Newman seemed upset, but I could not be sure whether he was acting or living; whether what disturbed him was the real-life tragedy or the make-believe scene, or some combination of both.

ME: Mr. Newman, isn't it true that you mask your emotions?

NEWMAN: Fifth Amendment.

The next take was imperfect too, but Sidney Lumet adjourned court for the day anyway.

The next morning, Paul Newman got up at his New York apartment at five-thirty. While he was doing his exercises, he watched the twenty-four-hour cable news service.

And then came one of his favorite parts of the day. He retired into the wet womb of his sauna with no company but the *New York Times.* Newman treasures this time because it is the only time in his day when he can count upon being absolutely alone and undisturbed. Spreading the *Times* across his lap, the superstar absorbed his morning paper in more ways than one. The columns of newsprint were imprinted not only on his mind but also on his body, for the wet words came off on his hands and his thighs and, well, everything else. Newman sat there literally soaking up the Great Gray Lady—all the news that was fit to print being printed in places not normally fit for news. Soon, he looked like a living version of the *Absence of Malice* advertisement, which is a photograph of the actor with newsprint superimposed on it. When he finally emerged from the sauna, Paul Newman looked like a combination of superstar and newspaper . . . which is what he really wants to be.

When he arrived at the studio, Newman installed a big bowl of fresh popcorn on the coffee table in his dressing room. The movie star repeatedly dipped his hand into the movie food. Next to the popcorn was a book on disarmament. The coffee table was a microcosm of Paul Newman's two worlds.

Munching popcorn, too, I continued to interrogate the witness: "What kind of political atmosphere did you grow up in?"

"My mother was not political at all," said the defendant. "My father was Rooseveltian. He was incredibly moral and ethical about everything he did. He and his brother ran a sporting goods store. During the Depression, 85 percent of the sporting goods stores failed, because it was obviously a luxury. In the worst time of the Depression, they went to Spalding and Wilson and got something like $200,000 worth of goods on consignment, which was unheard of simply because they had never reneged on a bill or sent back a piece of equipment unless it was obviously defective. They had an incredible reputation."

"Do you consider yourself your father's boy or your mother's boy?"

"I guess I'm my father's boy," Newman said after a long, shy pause. "That's one of my great sadnesses, actually. He died in 1950. I had just graduated, and I had just made up my mind to be involved in the theater, one way or the other. And I think he saw that as a dead end. It would have been nice for him at least to have been around for . . ."

"How old was your father when he died?"

"Fifty-seven years old."

ME: Mr. Newman, you are charged with being fifty-seven yourself. How do you plead?

NEWMAN: Guilty.

"What did your father want you to do?"

"Oh, I think he wanted me to stay in business. Actually, after he died, I went back and worked at the store for a while. But I couldn't figure out the romance of retailing."

ME: Mr. Newman, you are charged with still trying to win your late father's approval. How do you plead?

NEWMAN: Guilty.

ME: Your father didn't respect acting, so you have to do something else to impress him. Like save the world. How do you plead?

NEWMAN: I said I was guilty.

"Do you have any idea why you happened to do such a rash thing as go into acting?"

"Well, I don't know. I had never done anything well. My ambition had always been greater than my talent, whether it was athletics or academics, or whatever it was. But the best of whatever I did was in the theater, and that wasn't very good, but it was still the best that I had."

"Did you try some sports that didn't work?"

"I wanted to play football so bad. And I played in junior high school. But in high school, in the ninth grade, I still weighed ninety-eight pounds and was about five foot three. So I had to get a special dispensation so I wouldn't have to play with the lightweights, because the lightweights were all sixth-graders. And I was fucked if I was going to play with those guys. So I couldn't play at all in high school."

ME: The son of the sporting goods mogul didn't play football?

NEWMAN: Guilty.

"After high school, I had three months of college and then joined the navy on my eighteenth birthday."
"You volunteered?"
"Times change. I volunteered. I don't think I would volunteer for duty now."
The year was 1943.
"I didn't know what was going on. Hadn't the slightest idea. Just reckless and irresponsible. The first test I took was the color-chart test. I was out on my ass. Colorblind."

ME: Mr. Newman, is it true that the most beautifully colored male eyes in the world are colorblind?"

NEWMAN: Guilty.

"I got sent to Yale for officer's training because they didn't know what to do with me. The first time I got in my uniform, I was walking down to get a peanut-butter-and-jelly sandwich. A guy looked over at me, and I thought he was gay or something. I had my sailor outfit, my hat on.
"He looked at me and said, 'Aren't you a little old to be in the Sea Scouts?' "

ME: Mr. Newman, isn't it a fact that you sometimes feel the same way as an actor? That you are a little old to be dressing up in costumes and playing roles?

NEWMAN: Guilty.

"Then I wound up in boot camp. I was a pretty good radio man but a terrible gunner. The guy who taught me was Bob Stack."

ME: Isn't it a fact, Mr. Newman, that Eliot Ness taught Butch Cassidy how to shoot?

NEWMAN: Ugh! You got me.

"I think we took some potshots at submarines that we saw. And a couple of times, flying over Saipan, we saw some Japanese guys, and we strafed them. I had a .30-caliber machine gun in the tail, which, of course, was like a pea shooter. It was the same as pissing into a propeller."

"Where were you," I asked the actor who wants to save the world from nuclear destruction, "when you heard about Hiroshima?"

"I was about seventy-five miles off the coast of Japan in a fleet carrier. I didn't know what it meant. I was twenty years old, and I had no idea of the consequences of it. No one even discussed the morality of it or the alternatives."

"On board ship, was there a sense of celebration?"

"Oh, sure, it was just over. We shipped right back to Pearl Harbor and came right back to this country. I came out of the navy just as dumb as I went in."

But Paul Newman did not emerge from the navy completely unchanged.

"In the navy, I grew six inches in one year. When I went back to college, Kenyon College, the first thing I did was try out for football. I was fast. I weighed 152 pounds and was a defensive linebacker.

"My first year, I was an economics major. My second year, I switched to an English major. And then I got kicked off the football team because a bunch of us got rowdy in a bar and got thrown in the slammer overnight. And all the kids in the courtyard were coming by singing Kenyon songs. It was just gorgeous. Very touching.

"What happened was, all of these college guys were trying to pick up town girls, 'cause Kenyon wasn't coed then. We were always getting in fights with the town guys—a bloody nose, a black eye, a chipped tooth—but the next day, you'd see the guy in the street and say, 'Hi.' So, anyway, one night somebody called the cops. And two plainclothesmen came through the door. Our quarterback didn't have any idea who they were, and he decked one of them. The cops dragged him and another guy off. And he flipped me his keys and said, 'Bring my car into town if you can.' I said, 'Sure.'

"So I walked into the police station and said, 'I would like to give these keys to my friend.'

"He said, 'Let me take a look at your knuckles.'

"So the door slammed behind me, and they went out and got the other two guys in the car, and they threw them in the slammer, too. And the next day, on the front page of the *Cleveland Plain Dealer*, the first bottom two columns, the sentence was, 'Kenyon's traditional nontraining football team is in trouble again.'

"So they threw two of us out of school and put three of us on probation. I was damned if I was going to study, so I just tried out for a play. And I think the next two years I did something like ten plays. I did the lead in *The Front Page.* I wrote, directed, starred in, and produced the only musical at Kenyon in Christ knows how long."

ME: Mr. Newman, isn't it a fact that you only became an actor because you got thrown off the football team?

NEWMAN: Maybe.

ME: And aren't you still trying to make that team? Don't you still want to play with the big boys and impress your father? Dabbling in politics? Racing cars?

"Oh, I suppose there is a connection," Newman said. "I don't know what the connection is exactly, but I suppose there is."

Back on the set, Paul Newman sat down at the defense table and slipped off his shoes. And then, sitting there in his stocking feet, he made an effort to bring his political life and his acting life together in one place at one time. While the director blocked out the scene, the star sat writing out, in longhand, an antinuclear tract. He was enough of an entertainer to make his propaganda funny. He was working on a checklist of what to do in case of an evacuation before a nuclear attack: Don't forget your vitamin pills, pack your stocks and bonds and other securities, and take along clean underwear.

Paul Newman explained that the antinuclear speech he was writing was for a small film to be called *The Last Epidemic,* in which a group of doctors would describe what a nuclear blast would do to a population center.

"They want Joanne and me to introduce it," Newman said.

Joanne Woodward, his wife, had recently been in the hospital for a foot operation.

"I thought Joanne was under doctor's orders to take it easy," someone said.

"The only way she would ever lie down and be quiet," Newman said, "would be on a hand grenade."

Then he suddenly broke out into a soft-shoe dance. It was as though he were no longer in his fifties but in his twenties. He seemed once again to be a Kenyon College boy putting on the only Kenyon musical in Christ knows how long.

◆

Up in his dressing room, we reminisced more about the early days of a superstar. He talked about the first stirrings of his acting and activist careers.

After his graduation from Kenyon College in 1949, Newman spent a season doing summer stock. But then his father died, and guilt sent him back to work in his father's store.

"I was a pretty good salesman," he said.

The superstar was a supersalesman for a little over a year before he turned the business over to his older brother. For some reason, first children, like Paul's older brother, tend to run businesses, run for office, run the country. Younger children, who have to show off to get attention, are more likely to go into show business. Young Paul went east to take lessons in showing off.

"I took off to Yale with a wife and a child," Newman remembered, "and I think I had about $1,300."

After a year at the Yale Drama School, he headed for New York, only to have the Astoria Studio close its doors to him. But he was not the only one having trouble getting work. A lot of people were being turned out of jobs they had had for a long time. Those troubled times made a lasting impression.

"I wasn't politically active until the early fifties," Paul Newman said.

"What happened?"

"McCarthy. I heard about people losing their jobs. As a matter of fact, my cousin was involved. I think that's probably what brought it home. He was with Westinghouse. He was one of the guys who was intimately involved with the development of the proximity fuse, which was probably the second most important military development in the war. He was thrown out because he was no longer considered a good security risk."

This cousin was considered unstable on several counts. "One, he had been divorced. Two, he was married to a woman of Russian extraction, but she had been a citizen of this country for I don't know how many years. And, three, he was known to consort with homosexuals, because he was on the board of the Cleveland Playhouse. It was just incredible. That whole time.

"I was just starting, in 1952, making the rounds and not getting a lot of work."

The cousin fought back in court, where he eventually won back his job. Paul Newman attempted to fight back on a broader front by getting into politics.

"I campaigned for Adlai Stevenson. Stuffing envelopes."

Sidney Lumet sat in his folding canvas director's chair attacking the script with a red grease pencil. He slashed back and forth, back and forth, treating the screenplay the way Jack the Ripper used to treat prostitutes. The pages were drenched in red and looked bloody. Actually, Lumet was simply crossing out the scenes that he had already filmed.

The movie star crept up on his director and began to imitate him. Sidney Lumet sliced a page from ear to ear. And Paul Newman sliced, too. Lumet carved a bloody *X* in the flesh of the script. And Newman did the same. Newman was in mid-imitation when Lumet looked up— and grinned. It was as if he were smiling at himself.

"How much time did we pick up in just that last section?" asked Newman.

"Two days," said Lumet.

Since moviemaking is such a slow business, there is really no such thing as a fast moviemaker, but Sidney Lumet is faster than most. He appears to make movies in a sort of fast slow motion. Lumet's style of moviemaking seems to be summed up by a T-shirt worn by one of his assistant directors—a T-shirt that sports a picture of two turtles who are making love, with one of the turtles saying, "Faster! Faster!"

"I'm gonna start calling him Speedy Gonzales," Newman said of Lumet. "He's the only guy who could double-park in front of a whorehouse. He's that fast."

Young Paul finally got a job as an understudy to Ralph Meeker in the stage play *Picnic*. And he was accepted by the Actors Studio, where he studied under Lee Strasberg. Then, he went to work for his once-and-future director: Sidney Lumet.

"The first live television shows that I did were with him," Newman recalled in his dressing room between faster-faster scenes. "He was directing *You Were There*. I played Aristotle once; I played Caesar, Socrates, Nathan Hale." Television was where Lumet learned to be the fastest fucking turtle in the race. "Interesting times."

Finally, in 1954, Paul Newman's motion-picture career got off to a start when he was cast in *The Silver Chalice*. This movie has embarrassed him ever since. At least his father did not live to see it.

ME: Isn't it a fact that recently, when *The Silver Chalice* appeared on television, you took out an ad in *Variety* asking people not to watch?

NEWMAN: Guilty.

ME: And didn't that just hype the ratings?

NEWMAN: Okay, okay, I plead guilty to doing somethin' dumb.

In 1956, Paul Newman made his second movie, *Somebody Up There Likes Me*, and somebody up there—and lots of people out there—seemed to.

And then, all the famous roles started coming, one after the other. He has been nominated for an Oscar five times, although he has yet to win one. *The Verdict* is his forty-third starring role.

"If you were going to play yourself in *The Paul Newman Story*, how would you do it?"

His makeup man was busy combing and spraying his graying hair.

"I haven't the slightest idea. You know, sometimes you think you have a very great sense of definition of yourself. And you wake up the next morning and you look in the mirror, and you think you're nothing but a hangover of all the parts you've played—a little bit of *Hud* over here, a little of *The Hustler* there, and you don't find any definition of your own character at all.

"One morning, you wake up and say the work you're doing is very important and difficult and worthwhile and rewarding. And the next day, you wake up and you say, 'What is this kid stuff?' You're just being a child out there. And the next day, you wake up and think you're a shit, that you can't do anything right, and you're terrible."

"Has this feeling grown as you've gotten older?"

"Yeah. I think it's grown."

"Have you ever said to yourself that maybe your dad was right, after all?"

"Well, there's some part of me, obviously, that would like to be a gentleman farmer or a marine biologist. Yeah, I'd like to get out of some aspects of this rat race . . . the flashbulbs. I guess the only thing that would have any kind of lure would be politics. But I would be elected for the wrong reasons."

ME: You are charged with wanting more out of life than being a movie star.

NEWMAN: Innocent Monday, Wednesday, and Friday. Guilty Tuesday, Thursday, and Saturday.

"You're almost finished," Sidney Lumet told his star. "All the looping you'll have to do are the cuss words for TV." By *looping*, he meant rerecording bits of dialogue that could be spliced into the picture's soundtrack. "You can say *ass* now. I heard it on ABC."

"This ABC guy called me the other day," said Newman. "He said, 'I don't know what to do. We've bought *Slapshot*, but there are 176 *fucks*.' He'd counted them all." And then Newman turned to me. "I hope you'll edit some of my profanity out of your story. Ever since *Slapshot*, I've been swearing more. You get a hangover from a character like that, and you simply don't get rid of it. I knew I had a problem when I turned to my daughter one day and said, 'Please pass the fuckin' salt.' "

ME: Mr. Newman, isn't it a fact that at an advanced age, you took up not only swearing but also racing, in an attempt to recapture youth?

NEWMAN: I'll bet my body's younger than yours.

ME: Guilty. But how *did* you get interested in racing?

"I did a picture about racing in 1967, *Winning*," Newman told me while he sat in a makeup chair. "It took me four years to clear my schedule so that I could go and get my license and start driving. Like everything else, it took a long time. I really don't have any natural talent for any of that stuff, and I suspect the guys on the circuit were calling me a real balloon foot. I'm a very slow learner. The same with acting. But one thing is interesting to learn in acting: You cannot let it affect you when people laugh at you. If you don't take chances in rehearsals, you might just as well get out of the business. You've got to have enough courage to fall on your ass and not pay any attention to what the people are saying."

"And you were able to apply this to racing as well?"

"Oh, yeah."

"And to life in general?"

"I'm not so sure about that."

"Okay, let's make a movie," yelled Sidney Lumet. "Paul, are you winded? Let me know when you're on your third lap."

Paul Newman was doing laps, but not the kind he enjoyed. Not race-car laps on a racetrack. But hard-breathing jogging laps. The fifty-seven-year-old actor was running laps around the huge soundstage so that he would be out of breath when the camera rolled.

"Bells. Turn over. Speed."

Newman burst into the judge's chambers breathing hard and apologizing for being late.

"Let's do it again."

The aging superstar ran more studio laps.

"Turn. Speed."

Another breathless apology.

"One more time."

Newman slumped in imitation of an old man who had to be helped around the set.

"You were twenty-six when you began this job," said a grip. "Or was that one of your kids?"

Onto the coffee table, beside the bowl of popcorn and the book on disarmament, Paul Newman dropped a letter from Sally Field, his co-star in *Absence of Malice*. In her loopy, girlish handwriting, she congratulated him for his Academy Award nomination for his performance in that picture. The letter closed, "I love you always." But it added, "P.S. Give Joanne a big kiss."

"The movie was a direct attack on the *New York Post*," Newman said. "Well, put it this way: I was emotionally receptive to doing a piece about sloppy journalism. I wish I could sue the *Post*, but it's awfully hard to sue a garbage can."

Absence of Malice tells the story of a man who is libeled by a newspaper and strikes back. The paper prints a misleading story that embarrasses him, and he tricks it into running a misleading story that embarrasses the journalists.

Newman felt that the *Post* had done a somewhat comparable injustice to him in real life when he was filming *Fort Apache, the Bronx*. The paper wrote endlessly about demonstrators who were supposedly against the movie but who, for the most part, did not really exist. Newman was particularly upset by a picture caption that said he was trying to ward off demonstrators; he was really warding off photographers. He says he hates Rupert Murdoch, the owner of the *Post*, almost as much as he hates nuclear warheads. He would like to rid the world of both menaces. At the very least, he dreams of getting even, like the character he played, perhaps even in the same way.

"What someone might do is invent something," Newman said. "Something really insulting. Like Murdoch can't spell and has to carry a pocket dictionary. That he got picked up at a very early age for having sex with chickens."

◆

After the break, Paul Newman went back to running laps on the soundstage. *Huff, puff. Huff, puff.* He no longer sounded like Butch Cassidy on the run. He sounded like what he was, a man in his fifties, out of breath. Which was appropriate, since he was playing an almost-over-the-hill, out-of-shape, down-and-out ambulance chaser.

ME: And now, Your Honor, I would like to call an important surprise witness.

"In the last year, he has been reaching out in a more direct way," said Susan Newman, Paul's twenty-nine-year-old daughter. "Less guarded. More open. We've become closer. Daddy has really made an effort recently. Perhaps his priorities have changed. Scott's death had something to do with it."

She paused.

"Maybe he's going through some sort of midlife crisis. He's changing physically. He's changing mentally. He's a sex symbol, and he's getting older. He decided he wanted to do some different roles. With *The Verdict*, he decided to take some chances. He used to say the public wouldn't come to see him do something like that."

She paused again as she seemed to be thinking back.

"There has been a going back and rehashing of old problems. Going back and picking up some things. Scars carried with you for fifteen years."

Yes, scars. Her scars and his scars. The scars her father inadvertently left on her. And the scars his father inadvertently left on him.

Paul Newman, whose father did not want him to become an actor, always played the kind of he-men his father seemed to want him to be. He was always trying to please his father. Always trying to make the team. But in his new movie, he is not trying to make the team anymore. And he seems to be coming to terms with trying to win the approval of a father who has been dead for a generation.

As the filming of *The Verdict* was winding down, the cast and crew began to talk about what they were going to do next. Even Paul Newman and Sidney Lumet. They sat in the jury box one day—with juror-serious faces—passing judgment on a new script. The screenwriter, whose first screenplay was being dissected and criticized, was Paul Newman.

Actually, Newman cowrote the script—entitled *Harry and Son*—with his friend Ron Buck, a Los Angeles restaurateur.

The story is about a son who wants to be a writer and a father who wants his boy to do something more practical. It reads like a fictionalized version of Paul Newman's conflict with his own father. Writing is substituted for acting, but the quarrel between art and a steady job remains essentially the same.

In one scene, the father (Harry) comes in and finds his son busy at his portable typewriter.

FATHER:

Don't you get sick of all these rejection slips?

SON:

Hemingway was rejected ninety-seven times before he was published.

FATHER:

And now you're out to break his record.

The son gets up from his typewriter.

SON:

Can I get you something, Pa?

FATHER:

Yeah, a job.

SON:

What?

FATHER:

You can get a job . . . that's what you can get for me. I want you to look for a job tomorrow. A real job . . .

SON:

I don't want to work a whole lifetime at something that pisses me off.

It is as though, by casting their relationship as a story and writing it, Paul Newman is trying to expiate the guilt he feels about having gone against his father's wishes. And in a movie, he can give the story the ending he wished it had had in real life.

In the script, the father lives to see his son's success. A check for

$1,500 arrives as payment for a story the son has written about his father.

FATHER:

Maybe . . . maybe I'm not too old to learn.

It is classic wish fulfillment, which most people confine to their dreams but which writers put down on paper. Paul Newman was able to write the speech his father never said to him.

And Newman, in an early version of the script, even gave the story one more turn.

SON:

Hi, Pa. You writin' a letter?

FATHER:

Story.

SON:

A what!? How's it going?

FATHER:

Slowly. But it's going. I feel like a man who's lost his shoes.

Paul Newman, the barefoot superstar turned barefoot screenwriter, finally wrote the ultimate, longed-for, wish-fulfillment, too-good-for-this-world sign of perfect paternal approval. The story the father is writing is about his *son*. And Newman is able to kick off some of his guilt along with his shoes.

Paul Newman would do this father-and-son movie next. Besides cowriting the script, he would also direct and star in it. So, in a sense, he would be playing his own father and would be giving himself absolution.

Of course, this movie would have to be entered as evidence in the imaginary trial of Paul Newman that I have been conducting. Mark it "exhibit G."

The prosecution rests.

NEWMAN: Wait a minute. This trial isn't over yet. How about you? Don't you ever feel guilty about anything?

ME: Well, I sometimes feel a little guilty when I sense myself really beginning to like someone I'm writing about. I'm afraid I'm mellowing.

NEWMAN: How do you feel about this piece? How do you plead?

ME: Guilty.

◆　　◆　　◆

A couple of years after the story appeared, I met Paul Newman again and he told a story about his mother. One night some twenty or more years ago, his mom had gone to the movies with his wife, Joanne Woodward, and one of his best friends, Gore Vidal. Paul was busy and couldn't go. During the movie, Joanne and Gore cut up, cuddled, and generally had fun. The elder Mrs. Newman, who evidently knew little of Vidal's romantic preferences, was upset.

After the movie, Paul Newman was driving his mother somewhere when she told him she had some bad news.

"Your wife is having an affair with Gore Vidal."

Paul slammed on the brakes, threw his mother out of the car, and refused to speak to her for over a decade.

AN EVENING IN THE NUDE WITH GAY TALESE

• • •

"Why don't you do a story on 'The Writer as Hero'?" said Clay Felker, then the editor of *New York* magazine, making up a title on the spot. "You could pick Halberstam or Talese or Mailer or whomever."

I liked the idea. I was naturally interested in writers because I was trying to become one. I was at the very beginning of my magazine career, having written only two stories so far.

"Sure," I told Clay.

I never said very much.

I decided to do the story on Gay Talese because I admired his writing, especially his magazine pieces. When he did articles, he didn't just interview his subjects, he hung around with them for days or weeks. He captured them in motion, doing their jobs, living their lives. I thought I would like to do the kind of story about him that he did about other people. It would be a Gay Talese–style piece on Gay Talese. In that sense, it would be a kind of compliment.

Or so I thought at the time.

I asked Talese if I could follow him around for a while, the way he always did, and he agreed. And so, like a little brother, I started tagging along after Talese, who went to a massage parlor that he managed, and then to a nude health club—and we seemed always to be talking about sex. At that time, Talese was working on his Sex in America book, which he eventually entitled *Thy Neighbor's Wife*. He was doing research.

I did what he would have done if he were writing the story I was writing. I watched closely and took notes. Then I wrote about what I had seen and heard and it had an immediacy because I had actually been there—a trick I had learned from him.

But the compliment I had originally intended turned out to be something else because of the places he had taken me. New York City was shocked to see and hear what it saw and heard in my story. In the eyes of many readers, the Writer as Hero had somehow turned into the Writer as Villain.

◆   ◆   ◆

New York, July 1973

Gay Talese and his party crowded into an old Ford and headed across town. The car bounced and rattled like the one in which Gay had first discovered sex long ago in high school. But this car was different in one crucial respect. Its back seat was missing. No matter. Gay had long since outgrown back-seat grappling as well as many other small-town sexual practices. He now knew fancier places to undress in. We were on our way to one of them.

Love in this car would have been torture—just riding in back was bad enough. Three of us squatted side by side on the car floor, like the monkeys who were blind, deaf, and dumb to evil. I felt a high-school-dance nervousness. I wondered how I would look. I was not at all sure that I would know the right steps. When we reached the Fifth Season at 315 West Fifty-seventh Street, we all staggered out of the car. As we walked toward the nudist health spa, my knees, which had been cramped during the ride, felt weak.

We squeezed into an elevator and rode it down to the basement, where we filed down a long Freudian corridor. There were six of us in all: Gay was with a girl named Janet whom he had met at George Plimpton's *Paris Review* party four days earlier. I was with Sally Keil, who has been my girl friend for the past two years. Gay had also invited a massage parlor manager named Stephan Weisenberger and a masseuse named Amy. At the end of the hall, Gay used his membership key to open a door behind which lay a brave nude world.

We all marched into a coed locker room. Amy, whose profession was taking off her clothes, was the first one to get undressed. Talese was almost as fast. The son of a tailor, Gay loves clothes, but he also loves to take them off. He slipped out of his cut-in tweed jacket, his turtleneck, his tweed trousers, and his jockey shorts. His forty-one-year-old body was in good shape. The rest of us watched Gay and Amy closely, as if to learn how to disrobe; then we haltingly followed their example.

We all wrapped towels around our waists and Gay led the way to the swimming pool. Amy shed her towel almost immediately and—wearing only a cigarette—walked up to a huddle of toweled men and asked them for a light. They looked as startled as Humphrey Bogart did in *To Have and Have Not* when Lauren Bacall appeared in the doorway of his hotel room with a similar request. Bogie had called Bacall "Slim." None of the men staring at Amy's chest called her "Slim."

After glasses of wine, we all dropped our towels and dived into the heated pool. We played a beach-ball game while overhead a giant mirror ball rotated, reflecting the light in every direction, reminding me of my high school's senior prom. When we got out of the pool, we did not put our towels back on.

Gay led the way into the weight room, showing it off proudly to his visitors. I picked up a barbell and found that my knees still felt weak. Amy, not interested in weights, picked up a long phallic cue and joined a game of eightball. Stephan showed Janet, the girl who had come with Gay, how to stand on her head. She toppled over several times but eventually managed to stand erect, her breasts seemingly confused by the reversal of gravity's demands.

Gay surveyed his upside-down "date" and decided to teach her something more useful than a headstand. When she had removed her clothes, he had discovered that she was getting fat. Gay put her down on a mat and started her doing sit-ups. Hard work had made *him* famous and hard work could make *her* thin. Gay Talese still believes in that much of the American Dream. He could shed his clothes and many old practices, but he is no more likely to shed his habit of work and self-improvement than the nuns who had once taught him were likely to shed their habits.

Gay, who is genuinely generous, always wants to help people, wants them to better themselves, wants them to succeed. If he is not playing girls' gym teacher, then he is coaching less polished writers on their craft. His advice to other journalists is similar to the advice he gave Janet: Strain for leanness.

When Amy finished her pool game, I wanted to play her, but there was one problem. The game cost a quarter and I did not have any pockets.

Gay, pursuing a cheaper entertainment, took Amy in his arms and they started to two-steps, their dance floor bordered by barbells. The puffing fat girl paused in her sit-ups to watch them. Gay pulled Amy very close as the mirror ball spun on its axis.

Gay said, "This is the way we used to do it in high school."

Amy stopped dancing. She wanted to ask Gay something. The question went back to last summer, when he had managed the massage parlor in which she was employed.

"All the time you worked at the Middle Earth, you never came on to me. Why not?" Amy demanded.

Gay said, "It would have been bad for business."

Amy reached out and took hold of Gay's penis as calmly as if it had been a pool cue. She was ready to play a new game.

"I'm going to tear it off," she said.

"I love it. I love it," he said. "Do it. I have dreams about it. I have fantasies about it."

Amy continued to tug gently at Gay as if his appendage were the knob of some reluctant bureau drawer.

Gay kidded, "Next time I work there you can chain me and then whip me."

Amy said, "I'd hit you with a chair."

Gay said, "I love chairs, especially Chippendale."

Amy gave another pull and repeated her threat: "I'm going to tear it off."

A less specific tug had drawn Gay into the massage parlor culture a little over two years before. The initial discovery had come one night when he was walking home from P. J. Clarke's with his wife, Nan. She had been the first to see the second-floor sign that advertised LIVE NUDE MODELS, and she had known her husband well enough to know that he would see it too and want to go up. She already half suspected that he might someday write a book about the world he found at the top of the stairs.

Gay not only wanted to go up, he wanted his wife to accompany him. Nan demurred. Gay gave her the keys to their Sixty-first Street brownstone. While she walked home alone, he mounted the steps.

Talese came back time and again, and he began thinking more and more about massage parlors and other embodiments of sexual ferment in the country. The idea of a book about an American Sexual Revolution gripped him and would not let go. It would be an ambitious book, but all Gay Talese's writing life his ambitions had grown with each project. He had started out doing sports pieces and later features as a reporter for the *New York Times*. Then he had moved on to become a contributing editor at *Esquire,* where his profiles of people like Floyd Patterson ("The Loser"), George Plimpton ("Looking for Hemingway"), Alden Whitman ("Mr. Bad News"), Joe Louis ("The King as a Middle-Aged Man"), and Frank Sinatra ("Frank Sinatra Has a Cold") may have changed American journalism more than any other work done by any other writer in the past decade. Tom Wolfe and Norman Mailer were more brilliant, more dazzling, more !!!!!!, but for that very reason they could not really be copied. Their techniques without their intelligence became ludicrous. But Talese was different. Other writers could read his *Esquire* pieces and actually learn from them. He taught them to shadow their subjects for days or weeks (the way he did), so that they were present at dramatic scenes, and then to work hard at the writing (the way he did) so that in the end it read like a nonfiction short story rather than a newspaper story.

After writing a long series of nonfiction *Esquire* articles that read like fiction, Talese was ready, by the late sixties, to attempt a nonfiction "novel." He chose as his subject the *New York Times,* where he had worked for a decade. The result was *The Kingdom and the Power,* which sold 85,000 in hardcover and 250,000 in paperback. Then, searching for a topic even bigger than the *Times,* he settled on the Mafia. The result was *Honor Thy Father*—an ironic title since his father did not want him to write about Italians who broke the law. The book sold 200,000 in hardcover, 736,000 in Literary Guild and Bargain editions, and 2.2 million copies in paperback. Ever since Gay finished *Honor Thy Father,* he had been looking for a subject even bigger than organized crime. There could be only one: sex.

Talese discussed the idea with Doubleday. He eventually signed a two-book contract with the company. The first book was to be about sex in America, both in and out of massage parlors; the second was to be about Frank Sinatra. The total price agreed upon for two books was $1.2 million. Talese was paid $200,000 on signing. Doubleday then sold the paperback rights to the sex book to Dell for $700,000. Talese had not yet written one word.

To research his book on America's sex change, Gay went to work managing not one but two massage parlors. He served as the day manager at one and as the night manager at the other. Gay defends massage parlors by saying, "It is obviously better to be masturbated by massage girls than to masturbate yourself."

His day would start about noon, when he would walk over to the Middle Earth, at Fifty-first Street and Third Avenue, and open up. The Middle Earth stood around the corner from the Random House building where Nan Talese worked as an editor. While Nan sat at her desk on the eleventh floor of a glass-and-steel skyscraper, Gay would sit at his desk on the second floor of a brownstone. While up above Nan flipped through the pages of manuscripts, down below Gay would flip through the pages of a photograph album displaying pictures of the girls he had available. When the customer selected a photo he liked, Gay would call out the girl's name and then ask for $18. The girl chosen would appear and lead the customer into a massage room. Half an hour later, she would say good-bye to the customer, stuff the sheet in a garbage can that served as a laundry hamper, and go to the bathroom to wash her hands.

At 7:00 P.M., Gay would leave the Middle Earth and proceed to his second job at the Secret Life, at Twenty-sixth Street and Lexington Avenue, where he not only took the customers' money ($15), but frisked them before he let them have a girl. He twice removed guns from men who had come for massages (one was a policeman). Gay held the guns at the desk until the men were finished with the girls. He did not want his book to turn into an *In Cold Blood.*

Amy relaxed her grip on Gay. She had been only kidding about wanting to injure him. He had hurt her pride by not making a pass at her at the Middle Earth, but she still considered him a good manager.

Amy said, "I doubt I would have stayed there if it hadn't been for you."

Gay, flattered, told her, "I always said you were the star—an Everyman's Myrna Loy."

Stephan, the massage parlor manager, said, "Gay, of all the managers, you are the only one who was sincere."

Gay said, "There is nothing wrong with being a massage parlor manager if you do it well."

And he *had* tried to do it well, applying his belief in hard work to his job as massage parlor manager just as he had always applied it to his writing. He had wanted the Middle Earth to be a success the way he had wanted *The Kingdom and the Power* and *Honor Thy Father* to be best sellers. If a customer came in and found his favorite girl occupied, Gay would charm him into waiting. If a neophyte crept in but lost his nerve and was on the verge of bolting, Gay would try to put him at his ease. Since Gay had worked so hard at the business, he had expected the girls to work hard, too. He had once fired a girl who didn't, who sent customers away early.

Stephan said, "The girls were in competition with Gay. He dressed nice. They had to look nice, too."

Amy reminded Gay that he had told her to go to an orthodontist. He had reasoned that with better teeth she would make a better masseuse. Gay wanted to straighten Amy's teeth the way he wanted to straighten out his friend David Halberstam's prose. Halberstam listens to Talese and says he has learned a lot. Amy didn't listen. Gay could not understand people who did not make an effort to be better.

Gay, a fight fan, told Amy, "I wanted you to go for the record. The record was eight sessions. I wanted you to do nine. You coulda been a contender."

Talese and the people with whom he had once worked reminisced at poolside about the business.

Gay said, "Remember the minor tycoon from the garment district who would come in and give you girls panties as a tip? He brought them in a paper bag."

Amy said, "He always wore see-through red underwear. At the end of a session, he would show me pictures of his wife and children."

Gay said, "One guy we had at the Secret Life would have fit right into the Nixon administration. Gray suit, gray tie, white shirt, tall. He walked the way I have seen men walk at the UN. He came into the Secret Life, took me aside, and told me, 'I want your most lovely girl.' It so happened that that same day I had had a high-fashion model come in with her portfolio. She had done television commercials. I hired her. When this man asked for my best girl, I nodded with great pride at her. The man said, 'I want a massage but I need time to set up my equipment.' He opened a beautiful attaché case. He had a camera. He also had lovely, lovely handcuffs, like from Tiffany's. These were jewels. He had a small whip made by a fine saddle-maker. Also a dildo, but not a mail-order dildo, a lovely dildo, beautifully done. He wanted the fashion model and he offered a $75 tip. She said sure but she wanted the money first. He was her first customer. I put them in the room nearest the desk. But what would I have done if there had been trouble, big macho massage parlor manager? After half an hour, the man came out just as natty as ever. He came back many times."

Gay suggested that we adjourn to the steam room. Inside, the vapor in the air gave everything an unearthly quality like a movie vision of the afterlife: We might have been on a Hollywood set for *Don Juan in Hell.* Amy, who was given to excesses, turned the steam up higher and higher until it was so hot that we could not stand it anymore. We retired to the showers.

Gay shared a spigot with Sally and washed her back. He seemed to have practiced hands. He had been to Esalen and had studied their massage book. (Once a woman had come into one of the massage parlors where he worked and asked for a session. Gay had taken her into one of the massage rooms and given her a rubdown.) I wondered what I would do if Gay's hands moved beyond Sally's back. They didn't.

We left the showers and returned to poolside, where we were met by a girl named Carol. She wore a gold cross that swung to and fro between the Gothic arches of her bare breasts. Carol sat down beside Gay. He playfully pulled her over on top of him, her crucifix bouncing against his chest.

As a boy growing up in Ocean City, New Jersey, Gay had watched the gold crosses hung on the chests of nuns. Their breasts, like their ideas of right and wrong, never moved. Ocean City was a small town on a small island in the Atlantic Ocean. It was a Methodist town. The Catholic minority, most of whom were Irish, composed a small island within the larger island. The Italian Catholics formed an even smaller island within the Catholic community itself. Born in 1932, Gaetano Talese grew up an Italian Catholic in an Irish Catholic school in a Methodist town, an island within an island within an island. From the very beginning, Gay was an outsider with a vengeance.

Since Gay was the son of Joseph Talese, a flamboyant tailor, he was even more of an outsider than he need necessarily have been. Gay says: "My father dressed elegantly in a town that did not appreciate elegance. He wore white suits. He had a mustache in a town where there were no mustaches. For a long time, I was embarrassed by him. He was different and he demanded that I be different at a time when I didn't want to be different."

When Gay tried to fit in, however, he was usually disappointed. He became an altar boy in the church, but the Irish priests gave him the worst mass, 6:00 A.M., leaving him feeling betrayed. Gay says: "The Catholic church was foreign to me because it was Irish." Still, the son was embarrassed when his father would stalk out of mass because he did not like something an Irish priest said. It would also embarrass Gay when he would discover his father down on his knees in the hallway at home. Gay says, "Other children caught their parents screwing. I caught my father praying."

Joe Talese often made Gay uncomfortable, but the father was also his son's greatest strength and perhaps *the* single largest influence on his life. Gay did poorly in parochial school, but the father did not blame his son, he blamed the school. As the owner of a dry-cleaning business, Gay's father and the fathers of the church had an understanding: So long as Joe Talese's son was passed from grade to grade, there would be no charge for cleaning the priests' dirty linen. The church was willing to be bribed, but it was not willing to enjoy it. Six out of eight years, Gay was promoted to the next grade "on trial."

The message that came through to Gay as he was growing up in Ocean City was, as he says, "The rules weren't for me." The town's blue laws were made by the Methodists and therefore were not for him; the Catholic church's commandments were enforced by dictatorial Irish priests and nuns and so were not for him; later on, the rules of fidelity would not be for him, nor the New York laws that rapped the knuckles of massage parlor managers.

After he finished parochial school, Gay entered the public high school, where he continued to do poorly. The summer before his senior year, Gay met a girl from Penn State University who had come to Ocean City to spend her vacation working as a waitress in one of the resort town's restaurants. She was much like the girls he would later know who would come to New York to spend their college vacations working in massage parlors. The year was 1948. Gay borrowed a 1946 Ford and drove the Penn State girl to the beach. The decade was the fumbling forties and Gay did fumble, but by the time he got home he was no longer a virgin.

The high school principal tried to convince Joe Talese that his son was not college material, but the father would not listen. When Gay was turned down by Rutgers and many other nearby schools, the Talese family doctor, who had attended the University of Alabama, helped the uncertain student get into his alma mater. In the fall of 1949, Gay Talese entered Alabama, where he was once again an outsider—a northerner in a southern school.

Gay liked Alabama. He majored in journalism and his grades improved. He also fell in love for the first time. Gay had a Chrysler that was big enough for him and his girl to make love in the front seat. Later they registered under pseudonyms in motels.

In the spring of 1950, Gay made love for the first time to an absolute stranger. He was in St. Petersburg, where he had gone to watch the Yankees in spring training. A pretty girl came up to him on the street and said, "Jerry—Jerry Coleman—I saw you play yesterday." Gay decided to be the Yankee star for the girl. That night they slept together. (Years later, when Gay told Jerry Coleman the story, the player was furious.)

After blue-law Ocean City, Gay found the South both sensuous and liberating. In the Confederacy, he enjoyed the beginnings of a sexual emancipation. And he stopped going to mass forever.

When Gay graduated from the University of Alabama, he reluctantly left his girl friend and came to New York hoping to land a job on the *New York Herald Tribune*. He had to settle for a job as a copy boy at the *Times*. His girl friend in Alabama thought that he was a reporter. One night, when Gay came in carrying a stack of newspapers that he was supposed to distribute around the city room, he saw his Alabama girl friend sitting on a couch waiting for him. He dropped his papers. The love affair ended with a thud.

Gay Talese's interest in the girl whom he had brought to the Fifth Season seemed to end with the dropping of a towel. It was shed by a tall girl who had just appeared at poolside. She made a graceful nude dive. She was the only one in the water. I watched her solitary figure moving back and forth from one end of the pool to the other. I looked away and when I looked back there were two figures swimming side by side, the girl and Gay.

Sitting by the pool, I noticed a scene that looked like a version of *Le déjeuner sur l'herbe*. A fully clothed man stood chatting with a gaggle of nude men and women. I learned that his name was Craig Nolan and that he operated the Middle Earth and the Victorian massage parlors and produced pornographic movies. Fifth Season regulars said that he never took his clothes off when he came there. This shy pornographer stood in the tropical heat of the health spa—wearing his turtleneck, his gray trousers, and his matching gray shoes—sweating.

After a few laps, Gay and the girl climbed out of the pool together. She turned out to be taller than he was. The girl's name was Kathe.

Gay told the story of a girl from Bogotá, Colombia, who had worked at the Secret Life. One day a man came in, put down his money, and then looked at the girls available. Expressions of mutual horror passed over his face and the face of the girl from Bogotá. The man was her brother-in-law. He picked up his money and ran out. She cried hysterically. Still the girl from Bogotá continued to work at the Secret Life, although *her* secret had been found out.

Gay said, "She was breaking out of her Catholic upbringing."

Talese, who was breaking out of his, went on to boast that some of his massage parlor customers were priests.

While Gay Talese chatted with nude girls at poolside, Nan Talese was at home with the couple's daughters. She was reading manuscripts, paying bills, and helping the girls, Pamela, nine, and Catherine, six, with their homework. Gay says, "I revel in the fact that the children are not doing well in school." Nan does not revel in that fact. She insists that she prefers an evening at home with her children to an evening skinny dipping in a health spa.

Nan is always having to explain to people why she does not go where Gay goes, do what he does, and act the way he acts. One evening, Nan & Gay had dinner with Shirley MacLaine & Pete Hamill & Joni Mitchell & Warren Beatty, who all asked as many questions as children who had just heard about sex. What they wanted to know was how Nan was reacting to her husband's liberation.

Shirley MacLaine took an equal rights position: She seemed to imply that every infidelity on the part of the husband deserved an equivalent infidelity on the part of the wife.

Nan tried to explain that if she adopted Gay's life-style, that would not be liberation but a new kind of subjugation. It would amount to her trying to be him. She did not want to take a lover for every lover Gay had, because to her sex was "terribly private." The discussion went on until the restaurant closed.

That dinner has been reenacted countless times since with a different cast but with more or less the same dialogue.

One evening during a dinner in the Talese apartment, Gay said, "I wanted to get into my subject and I did. Getting head from an NYU student is not going to threaten a marriage of fourteen years."

Nan said softly, "It *was* disturbing."

The massage parlors disturbed Nan. The whole sex book has disturbed her. She has been especially disturbed by the threat it poses to her own privacy, for Gay's project has made people embarrassingly curious about *her*.

One evening at a dinner party that Nan gave for playwright Robert Anderson, the conversation was almost exclusively about Gay's book. Gay told of interviewing the New York Knicks' Walt Frazier; he had asked the player if he made love before games. Frazier had said yes, explaining that if he was tired at game time, he passed the ball more often. Gay went on to tell about asking Masters and Johnson how often they made love; they had refused to answer. Gay criticized the sex researchers for their lack of candor; Nan defended them. Gay said that he would have no objection to telling anyone how often he and Nan made love. Nan said that *she* would object to his telling or writing about *her* in bed. Gay argued for frankness, but Nan opposed it. He could not wear her down. Nan was a velvet tank.

She told her guests, "There's been a *lot* of talk about sex around here lately."

Growing up in Rye, New York, the daughter of a banker-broker, Nan had not often heard sex discussed. When she was in her early teens, she had entered the Convent of the Sacred Heart in Greenwich, hoping to become a nun. She says that what attracted her to a life in a nunnery was "the marvelous privacy, safety, and study." She felt the opposite of an outsider.

But at Manhattanville College, she began to see philosophical contradictions in the church. By the time Nan met Gay in 1957, she had given up on the nunnery and the safety of chastity.

Gay—who says, "Sure, I would have liked to screw my mother"—thought Nan looked like his mother and the resemblance helped draw him to her. They dated for two years before deciding to marry. Gay had gone to Rome for the *New York Times* to cover the making of Fellini's *La Dolce Vita*. He asked Nan to join him there. When she arrived, Gay told her that he did not want to marry in the church. It was the impulse of a defiant outsider. He was flaunting his position as a fallen Catholic in *the* Catholic city, marrying *outside* the church in Rome. Nan went along with the idea, but when her parents found out they were horrified, blamed Gay, and never completely forgave him.

Nan and Gay both had careers. Nan's Random House office, where she pursued her privacy and her study, took on something of the air of a cloister. Meanwhile, Gay had no office at all but simply a desk in the *Times* newsroom, where a bedroom, opening off one of the editor's offices, gave the shop something of the air of a brothel. Gay says that if drink were the vice of the *Herald Tribune*, then sex was the vice of the *New York Times*. When it came to bedrooms, Gay was no longer an outsider.

Gay's adventures even found their way into Lois Gould's novel *Such Good Friends*, which was published by Nan's own Random House. Gay says that the character Timmy Spector was loosely based on him. Gould wrote of Timmy that he had "been sleeping around for years" but that he did not want a divorce because "he likes things this way, where he can come home when he's through playing." Nan says that she accepted Gay as he is years ago. Gay says that he would not mind his wife's doing as he does, but his friends remember a near fight when someone made a pass at Nan.

In the past, Gay's books have tended to draw him and his wife closer together. She would come home from her editing job and read whatever he had written that day *aloud*; then she would make suggestions. But the new book, the sex book, has been different. It has kept them apart. Gay told Nan at the beginning that, if she forced him to choose between his sex book and her, he would give up the book. But Nan says that she knew that if she precipitated such a showdown it would have broken up their marriage.

"I tried to get Nan to come to the massage parlor where I worked to have lunch," Gay said one evening. "I thought she would enjoy the massage parlor, too."

"It seemed indelicate for me to be there," Nan said. "I don't think there is anything wrong with the massage parlors, but they go against my own sense of privacy. Public sexuality is in every way antipathetic to my idea of sexuality. I can never imagine being a part of that world."

In that world, the world of public sexuality, Gay, the outsider, is an insider, and Nan, the insider, is an outsider. She did, however, agree to accompany Gay to a nudist camp in New Jersey because she made a distinction between open sex and open nudity. Gay was proud of his wife, but he kept peering at her as if he expected her to dissolve.

"There was a point when you realized that this was not exactly my field," Nan told Gay. "I was out of place."

For Nan, the worst thing about the book is that it has taken Gay out of town so often. Last fall, he went to California to stay a few weeks and ended up staying almost half a year. Gay stayed on because he was seduced by a place called Sandstone, a nudist sex commune in Los Angeles's Topanga Canyon. Sandstone had taken what Esalen had begun and carried it to its logical conclusion. Sandstone had institutionalized the orgy so that it was always there when you needed it. Sandstone stood as a monument to prostate power. Many of the openly copulating residents practiced the reverse of fidelity: They were strict about not making love to anyone to whom they had made love before. It was like patterning your life on *Oh! Calcutta!* Gay moved in and stayed. Oh! Sandstone!

Gay told a reporter for *Coast* magazine: "I'm not that young anymore, and lately the most I've been doing is about once a day. But I've been engaged at least four times a day since I've been here. After a hundred times, it gets a little wearing." But Nan could hear a kind of exhilaration in his voice when she talked to him on the telephone. When Gay returned to New York, his friends say that he was more easygoing than they had ever seen him. He had grown up in a resort town but he had had to go to California to learn to relax.

Gay says that his research on the sex book has not changed his sex life with his wife either for the better or for the worse. Nan, who tries to evade such questions, says that she is not sure and will only know later, in retrospect.

"After fourteen years, I still find her very exciting," Gay says. "There is just no comparison."

Gay and Nan are still very close and their marriage seems a strong one. They are not only husband and wife, but friends. Still, Gay concedes that since he started working on his sex book, his life with Nan "has not been a honeymoon."

◆

Gay lounged beside the Fifth Season's pool like some decadent John the Baptist waiting for new believers to baptize. He welled with the fervor of someone new to the faith. He seemed to want everyone to dive head first into the wet, warm sexual revolution.

Gay was preaching the advantages of life in a massage parlor to Kathe and Carol. He had left the trade months before, but he was still trying to recruit new masseuses for the Middle Earth. The girls were interested.

"I'll take you up to the Middle Earth tomorrow," Gay promised them, "and I'll give you a massage."

For a year now, Gay has been inviting people to join this new world that he has discovered. Many have accepted his invitations, but among them have been none of his closest friends. David Halberstam did once consent to come up to the Middle Earth for a visit, but he was appalled.

"Halberstam wanted it to be like a dentist's office," Gay told his poolside flock. He added, "David takes himself *so* seriously. He sees himself as a part of history. His sense of self is second only to that of Charles de Gaulle—maybe."

Since Gay has not been able to bring his celebrity world and his massage parlor world together, he commutes back and forth between the two. He hangs out with the social fringe at the Middle Earth to feed his outsider's need to be among other outsiders, but he also hangs out at Elaine's to satisfy his outsider's need to bé an insider. Actually the two places are not as irreconcilable as they might at first seem. In many ways, Elaine's and the Middle Earth are similar, for both are characterized by middle-aged men and young girls, the one establishment massaging the body, the other massaging the ego. (Once Gay actually took a masseuse to Elaine's, where she blended in perfectly. Later, he took her home to the folding couch next to his writing desk under the pretext of giving her copies of his books.)

Someone at poolside proposed an orgy. After all, it was almost midnight, the Fifth Season would be closing soon, and everyone needed something to do. A songwriter generously offered his nearby apartment. Gay led the way to the locker room, where we were to suit up for yet another sexual outing.

I had been undressed long enough so that now putting on clothes was its own kick, but one of the orgy volunteers found getting dressed to be a trial. His name was Bernhardt Hurwood, the author of *The Girls, the Massage, and Everything.*

"Where is my underwear?" yelled Hurwood. "Who stole my underwear? Why should anyone want to take my wretched old under-pants?"

We filed out of the Fifth Season and streamed onto Fifty-seventh Street, Hurwood hurrying to catch up. Gay and two girls walked three abreast, one big, one middle-sized, and one small, like Papa Bear (in this case Kathe, since she was tallest), Mama Bear (Gay), and Baby Bear (Janet). I am one of those people who have never been invited to an orgy and I may have been looking forward to it. In front of Carnegie Hall, Gay took Sally and me aside. He said that the others felt that the presence of a reporter would inhibit them. Sally and I agreed to go home. While we waited for a taxi on the corner, we watched the others walk off arm in arm into the orgiastic night.

◆　　◆　　◆

I have always wondered why Gay Talese took me to the places he took me to. The only reason I can imagine is that he intended to use my story as a kind of trial balloon for his book. If people—especially his wife—got too upset, then perhaps he should rethink and tone down that book.

Which is exactly what he did.

WAKING UP WITH SALLY QUINN

. . .

I ghostwrote Sally Quinn's first piece in the *Washington Post*. At the time, I was a summer intern at the *Post*. She wrote a freelance piece for the paper on how to pursue the Washington bachelor. An editor handed me her story and told me to rewrite it. I tried to copy her style as I did so.

Years later, when *New York* magazine asked me to write a story on Sally, I tried to copy her style again. Just as I had tried to copy Gay Talese's style when writing about him. Once more, I wanted to do the kind of piece about a writer that the writer did about other people. And what she did was get people to say outrageous things and then quote them in the paper.

She had a well-tuned technique for getting you to say shocking things. She would come up to you at a party and tell you a sexy story. And then you would find yourself telling her a sexy story. And then she would tell another one. And then you would. And the next morning your sexy quotes would be in her story—but hers wouldn't be.

My technique was just the opposite. Rather than trading stories with someone, I simply wouldn't say anything. Since most people find silence hard to tolerate, they will talk and talk.

Sally talked quite a lot.

She hasn't talked to me since.

Sally later wrote a book in which she blamed me for her failure at CBS, but there may have been other reasons as well. Among them her basic lack of knowledge about television. For instance, in her book she says that she didn't know what the red light on TV cameras meant, which does seem a bit odd, since even the dumbest fan at a football game knows enough to wave, cheer, and say hi to his mom whenever he sees that light go on.

◆   ◆   ◆

New York, July 1973

SYLVIA: You know I go to Michael's for my hair. You ought to go, pet. I despise whoever does yours. Well, there's the most wonderful new manicurist there. (*Shows her scarlet nails.*) Isn't that devine? Jungle Red—

NANCY: Looks as if you'd been tearing at somebody's throat.
—Clare Boothe Luce, *The Women*

They insist that it is not going to be like that. It will *not* be a catfight. It is sexist even to imply such a thing. Sally Quinn and Barbara Walters would never demean themselves by stooping to such behavior. They profess not to understand what all of the fuss is about anyway. Ms. Quinn, thirty-two, is going to join "The CBS Morning News," which competes with NBC's extravagantly successful "Today" show starring Ms. Walters, forty-two, but why must people jump to the conclusion that they will be clawing at one another?

Ms. Walters, who has been before the "Today" cameras for over nine years, even wrote Ms. Quinn a generous note when she heard the news:

Dear Sally,
    CBS could not have made a better choice. I mean this in all sincerity and look forward to seeing you very often now that you'll be in New York. I won't be able to catch you on camera, but I hope we'll get together off camera. For God's sake, let's avoid all those people in and out of the media who may try to create a feud between us. We like each other too much. Much love and affection, Barbara.

Sally Quinn has been getting a lot of mail lately. Old friends have been writing gushing letters congratulating her on her new job. Old enemies have been writing even more gushing letters. All the letters tell her that they think she made the right decision in choosing to leave the *Washington Post*, where she was the star of the Style section, to accept the position as cohost (along with Hughes Rudd) of "The CBS Morning News." The show is being revamped completely.

Ms. Quinn even got a letter from another Sally and another generation's idea of a career girl—one Sally Rand. Ms. Rand, the legendary fan dancer, wrote with some suggestions about, of all things, clothes:

> Dear Sally,
>   Bonwit Teller notwithstanding, Barbara Walters's clothes, in my opinion, leave something to be desired. In fact, I think she frequently looks frumpy, tacky even. So, subconsciously, one feels. "Ha, with all that stuff to choose from, how come she looks so—ordinary?—un-smart?—not chic?"—if she's this fallible as concerns her own person, chic, etc., how then infallible as concerns other areas?

Quinn and Walters cannot escape it. While they are busy saying that they are not competing with each other—that they are even considering giving a sisterly party together—others are busy comparing them. And those making those odious comparisons are not just men. Women are making them, too. Especially women.

Barbara Walters said after she finished the "Today" show one morning: "If my success here has made CBS aware that they should hire more women, that pleases me."

Walters says Quinn is her friend. Quinn says that Walters is her friend. Occasionally, though, Sally finds herself saying, "Barbara Walters *used to be* my friend." It is a tense change of tense.

Despite their protests to the contrary, sisterhood may end on August 6 at 7:00 A.M. sharp. Barring some last-minute change of plans, that morning Sally Quinn will go on the air opposite Barbara Walters. For the next hour, Ms. Quinn and Ms. Walters will be competing for the attention of several million men. They will also, however, be competing for the attention of over twice as many women. Most men who know Sally Quinn seem to like her, but the women who know her are divided. One of them says, "She treats women like Kleenex." And yet her success or failure on television could well depend on whether she can charm large numbers of her own sex. Her future could hang on the way the women of America answer this question: Who likes Sally Quinn?

•

The sisters in the movement do not much like Sally Quinn, nor do they wish her well on television. She feels about the same way toward them.

"I am not a joiner or a belonger," she said recently over coffee in the *Washington Post* snack bar. "The Junior League was my last major foray as a joiner—never again. That includes movements. The problem with the women's movement is that they have lost their sense of humor—they are very tedious, very boring. Their losing their sense of humor wouldn't be so bad if they were as righteous as they pretend to be. They are such hypocrites."

She mentioned the recent issue of *Esquire* that was devoted to women and edited by women.

"In *Esquire* one group of women was taking out after another group of women. They called Gloria Steinem a 'royal pain in the ass.' It's a catfight. They say 'sister' out of one side of their mouth and try to wipe each other out out of the other side. 'Sister'—I can't stand that word; it sounds so phony, like 'comrade.' "

She sipped her coffee.

"One problem women face now is, if you are attractive and admit that it helped, you get accused of being a sellout by the other women, when they do the very same thing. I don't know a woman who is attractive who hasn't taken advantage of her looks. An editor once said of Gloria, 'With legs like that, that girl ought to be a writer.' That doesn't demean Gloria. I just wish my legs were as good as Gloria's. Maybe I would have gotten on the evening news."

Sally Quinn was wearing pants. She almost always wears pants. She is self-conscious about her legs.

"If you are a woman who is lucky enough to get into a position of some power, the most important thing you can do is to try to be the best you can rather than spending your time raising your fist or hissing and booing when people open the door for you."

Sally Quinn is sensitive about booing. She was booed by feminists at the [*More*] journalism convention in Washington last May. They seemed to be calling her a male chauvinist pig lover.

Speaking on a panel of women reporters, Sally Quinn began by saying: "I think I should start out first by telling you how I got my job. I don't think any man would have gotten a job this way. I was unemployed three and a half years ago when I got a telephone call from a man who called himself Ben Bradlee [executive editor of the *Washington Post*], and he said, 'I don't think you know me, but I'd like you to come down tomorrow and talk to me in my office.' So I went down there the

next day and talked for about forty-five minutes, and when we got finished he said, 'Sally, I'd like to hire you to be a reporter. Are you interested?' I said, 'Yes? He said, 'Well, could you show me something
you've written?' I said, 'Well, actually I've never written anything.' He
said, 'Well, nobody's perfect.' "

The crowd laughed, but it was not the kind of story to warm a feminist's heart.

Ms. Quinn continued along this perilous route: "Powerful people
say things to women they would never say to men, especially over a
martini. When somebody calls me 'sweetheart' at a party, I know I've
got it made. I mean, I know he's going to tell me a story. Being a blonde
does not hurt."

That did it. Brunettes booed. Redheads booed. Even a few blondes
booed.

Ms. Quinn said: "If a senator is putting his hand on my fanny and
telling me how he's going to vote on impeaching Richard Nixon, I'm
going to have a conscience crisis because I'm not so sure I'm going to
remove his hand no matter how demeaning it is."

The auditorium sounded like Madison Square Garden when a ref-
eree calls a foul on one of the Knicks.

"I anticipated that reaction," she said. "I have made a decision and
that is that I'm a reporter first and a feminist second. Much of the time I
deplore that situation, but I will take advantage of it until things
change."

Marlene Cimons of the *Los Angeles Times* blurted out: "If a senator did that to me, I'd hit him, senator or no senator, story or no story."

When the panel was over, Nora Ephron, who had helped edit the
Esquire women's issue, told *Washington Post* reporter Myra MacPherson: "I am very offended. The image [she] portrays of women journalists as manipulating women who use their sex is demeaning to both men
and women." Ms. MacPherson used the quote in her story. When Ms.
Quinn read the quote in her own newspaper, the *Washington Post*'s
Style section experienced what used to be called, before the enlighten-
ment, a catfight.

Katharine Graham likes Sally Quinn and thinks she will do well on
television. Mrs. Graham, the publisher of the *Washington Post*, has
been Ms. Quinn's ultimate boss for the past several years. The country's
most powerful newspaperwoman expressed her admiration for Sally as
she drove her Cadillac to the tennis courts. She was asked to comment
on Sally's comment on the senatorial hand on the fanny.

"I guess I deplore it," she said. "But I agree with Sally. That is, it is deplorable to do it if we want to be equal. We shouldn't have to resort to that, but we do. To some extent, I think that there are moments when looking helpless seems to help."

Mrs. Graham went on to say that Sally was a master at letting people talk until they hanged themselves. The publisher recalled a comparison Henry Kissinger had made between Sally Quinn and the *Post*'s gossip columnist, Maxine Cheshire: "Maxine Cheshire makes you want to commit murder. Sally Quinn makes you want to commit suicide."

Mrs. Graham stopped the car to let her passenger descend.

"I talked too much," she said. "Protect me." She paused and then added, "You great big strong man." She laughed long and loud.

Back in the *Washington Post*'s Style section, the columnist who makes people want to commit murder approached the desk of the reporter who makes people want to commit suicide. Sally Quinn was typing, trying to finish one last story before she left the newspaper business for the television business. Maxine Cheshire told Sally about seeing Mrs. John Dean, who looks like a voluptuous Tricia Nixon, in a Washington bar the night before.

"What interested me," Maxine Cheshire said, "was the $50 gold piece that Mrs. Dean was wearing in her cleavage like a price tag."

Soon everyone was talking about prices. They were most interested in Sally's—the one CBS had offered her.

Sally said, "My agent told me to say that I make in excess of $45,000."

Judith Martin, a Style writer, said, "Unfortunately that was after you had already told us that you were making $75,000."

Sally said, "I'll have to go to work at one o'clock in the morning to write the show before we go on at seven."

Ms. Martin said, "With your salary you could just hire a sun to come up whenever you want."

Sally said, "*Playgirl* wants to interview me."

Ms. Martin said, "Sally has a lot of redeeming social value."

Sally said, "I have little tits."

Ms. Quinn left the Style section and walked out onto the main newsroom floor. She sought out the Watergate twins, Robert Woodward and Carl Bernstein, to ask them to dinner.

Woodward said, "Remember telling us about that live sex show you went to in New York. You said you had to pretend that you had never seen one before."

Sally said, "I'm a good actor."

Bernstein said, "She once went through my closet to see where I bought my clothes."

Tom Zito, who writes about rock music, walked up wearing a gas-station shirt with his name above his heart.

"I'm a blue-collar lover," Zito told Ms. Quinn.

She started unbuttoning his shirt right there in the middle of the newsroom to see what kind of an undershirt he had on.

Bernstein said, "Zito, what else you got on?"

Executive editor Ben Bradlee walked out of his glass office onto the newsroom floor. Sally Quinn went to talk to him. When Bradlee had learned that Gordon Manning of CBS was coming to Washington to try to woo his star Style reporter away from him, he had managed to find out where they were having dinner. He called the restaurant, Cantina D'Italia, and asked them to tell Manning that his office was calling. When Manning came to the telephone, Bradlee said: "Screw you!"

Big Ruby likes Sally Quinn. Big Ruby is Ruby Folsom Ellis Austin. She is Cornelia Wallace's mother. George Wallace's wife took Sally to visit her mother in Montgomery a few weeks before Wallace was shot. They found Big Ruby, who is almost six feet tall, in her kitchen, wearing a black-and-white suit, white blouse, and white plastic go-go boots.

"Ah been lookin' for a husband for two years now," Big Ruby said, "ever since Dr. Austin died."

"Ah got the only bachelor in Montgomery," Cornelia Wallace said. "And Ah'm scared to death Mama's gonna go after George."

"Shoooooot, honey," Big Ruby said. "He ain't even titty high."

Sally Quinn wrote a story about Big Ruby, one of her best, but she usually writes about men. That allows her to make the most of being blonde. Men seem to like to talk to her, at least until they read what they have said in the paper. If men like to talk to her, she likes to talk *about* them. She seems the reversal of a sexual stereotype. It used to be men who boasted about their sexual adventures. Now it is Sally Quinn who boasts. She indulges in a kind of sexual Advertisements for Myself. If no one is gossiping about her, she will call up and tell people stories that begin: "Everyone is saying that I . . ." And pretty soon everyone *is* saying it.

She recently told an auditorium full of people about a senator who put his hand on her fanny but did not have any impeachment stories to tell her: "I'd covered a party and it was raining. A senator came out whose wife was not at the party and he said, 'May I give you a lift home?' I said, 'Oh, I'd love it.' And we got to my apartment house and I started to get out of the car and he grabbed me and started mauling me and I said, 'What do you think you're doing?' And he said, 'Well, you asked for a ride home, what do you think I'm running, a taxi service?' I'd written about him often and he said, 'I thought you girls always slept with the people you wrote about.' So I got out of the car."

She is always telling stories like that or writing them into her articles. Her fine piece about Billy Friedkin, the motion picture director, read on one level like the diary of a flirtation. She wrote that he "enters the door, grabs a reporter [Sally Quinn] in his arms, presses her close, and asks, 'Will you come up to my room at nine o'clock tonight?' " Moments later: "A small white urinal appears from the closet. Friedkin pretends to use it. He wraps himself in a scarf and gloves, does a semi-striptease . . ." On their way to a screening, Friedkin took her arm and said, "I only take a girl out for one reason; that's all I want."

Sally Quinn also wrote a story on Bernardo Bertolucci's trip to New York. Bertolucci had her to his suite at the Sherry-Netherland Hotel for an interview. In her article, she told of following Bertolucci into his bedroom where the director, like Jay Gatsby, "brings out silk shirts for approval, then takes them back and hangs them up." He said, "I'm so excited about this whole interview. It's like a Hollywood movie. Here we are in a magnificent hotel suite with flowers, sexy music, and room service. I play the role of a famous movie director being interviewed by a female journalist trying to get me, through her feminine wiles, to reveal my innermost secrets." At one point, Bertolucci picked up a magazine with a picture of Marlon Brando on it and kissed it, saying, "Oh, Marlon!" He lowered the magazine and said, "All the relationships I have with people are sexual. Aren't yours?" Sally Quinn did not record her response, but her overall demeanor suggests an affirmative answer. Or at least that is what she would like everyone to think.

Sally Quinn spent most of one afternoon and evening interviewing Billy Kilmer, the quarterback of the Washington Redskins and the nation's capital's ideal of virility. Kilmer told her, "Fifty degrees and cloudy, that's my idea of perfect football weather. Good lovemakin' weather too." Sally tripped on the steps of the Sans Souci restaurant; the quarterback grabbed her arm to steady her and lifted her halfway off the floor. Over lunch, he told the reporter that the theory about no sex before games was silly. He told her flatly, "I know a few very good examples to disprove that theory. It's guys who stay up all night before a game trying to get it who are in trouble." He went on to say, however, that he did not believe in one-night stands. "I don't like to pick up women at a bar," he said. "I like closer, longer-lasting relationships. I've lived with a lot of women. I did in San Francisco and New Orleans and here, too, last year." Kilmer took Sally Quinn to see the horses run at the Charles Town racetrack. Afterward, he took her to the Pall Mall in Georgetown, a Redskin hangout. She took out her notebook and laid it on the table. He seemed hurt. He had evidently come to think of her interview as a date. Sally says that often happens. Kilmer drove her home and told her that she was the only woman who understood him. Sally later led friends to believe that before the quarterback went home he seemed to mistake her for a tackling dummy.

After the article appeared, Sally Quinn told friends that Billy Kilmer was telling people, "I screwed her so she screwed me."

One evening at a Washington dinner party, Sally Quinn was the center of attention as she verbally measured many of the town's most prominent politicians. Her conversation was a Gallup Poll of penis sizes. Then she outlined her theory of how all the best men in Washington "screwed beneath themselves"; she also said that the women in the city like to make love above themselves. It makes a nice Washington compromise.

Since Sally talks so outrageously and so much about herself, other people talk about her, repeating her stories. The *Washingtonian* magazine recently wrote: "She has joined a select handful of writers who transcend their copy and become media personalities in their own right." Sally Quinn has achieved this eminence, in part, by making herself appear to be a female Joe Namath.

Sally Quinn's mother likes Sally best of all and wishes her well on her television show. That, of course, is not surprising. What is surprising is that Sally likes her mother best of all, calling her "my best friend." Sally recently had dinner with her mother, her father, and several of her parents' friends, including a United States senator, at the Georgetown Club. The event was not extraordinary, for Sally often dines with her parents. Familial closeness seems to be handed down from generation to generation in Sally's family. Sally was brought into the world by her grandfather, a surgeon. Her mother had wanted her own father to deliver her baby.

The table at the Georgetown Club seemed a paradigm of generational continuity: It included not only retired army general William ("Buffalo Bill") Quinn; his wife, Bette; and their daughter Sally; but also Senator Barry Goldwater; his wife; and their son Barry, Jr. They were all anxious to advise Sally.

Senator Goldwater said: "Be careful of all that electronic gear at CBS. It might have bugs in it."

Barry Goldwater, Jr., advised, "Get a copy of the *Guinness Book of World Records*. If you can't think of what to say on the air, read a few records."

General Quinn, who looks almost exactly like Senator Goldwater, was more practical in his concerns. He asked his daughter, "Sally, do you still have your snow tires on your car?"

When she admitted that she did, he pointed out that, since it was June, she should take them off and put on regular tires.

Born by her grandfather's hand in Savannah, Georgia, in 1941, Sally moved with her family of five, including a sister and brother, as her father was transferred from post to post. (In this sense, her itinerant childhood was similar to that of Barbara Walters, whose father was a vaudeville booking agent and night club promoter who also moved his family from theater to theater and club to club.) Sally Quinn lived in Japan, Greece, Germany, and all over the United States, including Washington.

She says that what she learned from all this moving was adaptability. Socks and shoes were one of the first characteristics of a new town that she would study. In Enterprise, Alabama, the "peanut capital of the world," which boasts a statue of a boll weevil, she learned to go barefoot; in the East she wore loafers and rib socks; in the West she wore streamlined saddle shoes and colored lamb's wool socks that matched her sweater. (The young Barbara Walters was less perceptive about feet. She once told Sally about her first day at a New York private school: "I wore bobby socks and Cuban heels. I didn't know.")

Sally Quinn changed her accent along with her shoes and socks. She had a southern accent, a western accent, an eastern accent, and finally a mongrel accent. (Barbara Walters calls her own accent "bastard Boston.") Sally says that most army brats are extroverted. (Barbara Walters confessed to Sally that she had been introverted when she was growing up.)

While her father was stationed in Europe, Sally Quinn attended boarding school in the Alps for a year. Extroverted Sally told a reporter for the *Washingtonian*, "I was expelled once from finishing school in Switzerland for chasing after the goatherd."

She went to Smith College, where she majored in drama. When the Smith placement office asked her to fill out a questionnaire, she wrote that she wanted to be a famous movie star. The placement officer said that this was a serious questionnaire. Sally said that she *was* serious. An M-G-M talent scout saw her in a college production of *The Skin of Our Teeth* and she was offered the female lead in the movie *Flipper*. Sally remembers: "I got propositioned. The producer said that there would be other duties besides acting. I said that I would have to ask my father. They never called back."

After graduation in 1963, Sally accompanied her parents to Germany, where her father with his three stars was the commanding general of the Seventh Army. Being the general's daughter was almost better than being a movie star. She says that it was like being a "princess." Her father, who probably had more power than any European monarch, had orderlies who clicked their heels, a car and driver, and his own train. Sally, who had given up a career putting Flipper through hoops, watched men jump through hoops for her father. And she learned.

"I have always had total comprehension of power," she says. "That is why the people I like to interview must have power. I am interested in how they got power, how they stay there, what happens to them. The best thing about understanding power is that you learn not to be intimidated by it. I have never been intimidated by anyone in my life. Dig it."

She says that watching the people around her father helped her later when she became a party reporter: "I saw so many people ass-kissing my father that I know ass-kissing when I see it. It is a way of life in Washington."

Her father had a tangible power, based on a chain of command and military arms; Sally herself had a less tangible power based on sex. She says that she had fifty proposals while she was in Germany. The lieutenants called her "the Cobra." She once said: "I thought I could get any penis I wanted."

Amanda Burden probably does not like Sally Quinn as much as she once did. Moreover, Ms. Burden, the stepdaughter of William Paley, board chairman of CBS, has little reason to wish Ms. Quinn well on her new CBS show. The point of friction is Warren Hoge, who has dated Sally for years but who has recently dated Amanda Burden.

Ms. Quinn and Ms. Burden have known each other for a long time. In the mid-sixties, Sally was engaged to Henry Timothy Mortimer of Tuxedo Park, Amanda Burden's first cousin. Once when Sally was having dinner with Carter and Amanda Burden, Amanda said, "I just can't believe you grew up in the military." She had always thought of soldiers as being like policemen.

After Sally's engagement to Mortimer fell through, she met Warren Hoge at a Washington party. She says that the first thing he said to her was, "I have never met anybody so full of shit in my life." She told the reporter for the *Washingtonian*, "I knew at that very moment that I loved him. Of course, it was love at first sight for him, too, but he refuses to admit it."

They got engaged. It was terrible. Hoge was then a Washington correspondent for the *New York Post*. Quinn was unemployed. She says, "I thought that since I couldn't do anything else I would be a wife and mother. I pressured him about the marriage. I was crying all day and he was getting drunk at night. On George Washington's birthday, three weeks before the wedding, I gathered up all the stuffed animals that we had given each other. I got on the bus in Georgetown and rode down to the National Press Building. I threw the animals on the couch in his office. Then we both just cried and didn't say a word." Sally told Warren that she was going to the Circle Theater and he could come and get her if he wanted her. She sat through *King of Hearts* and *The African Queen* twice. Warren never came.

She went to California. He called her three months later and asked her to come back to Washington. She did, but they did not get engaged. They did not want to go through that again. They simply lived together until Hoge was called back to New York to be city editor of the *New York Post*. Warren and Sally became a couple united by the Metroliner, a weekend couple. They seemed to thrive on separation. Each had his own town and his own *Post*. Each dated other people during the week. Sally dated Phil Carter, a *Washington Post* reporter, until he moved to New Orleans.

Warren and Sally seem to enjoy nurturing a certain amount of jealousy. They both went to Miami to cover the Democratic Convention for their respective *Post*s. Sally ran into Warren Beatty and took him down to the basement of the convention hall to meet Warren Hoge. Her own Warren told her, "Just remember which Warren you're sleeping with tonight."

Within the last year, Warren began seeing Amanda Burden. Sally did not think that Warren and Amanda were discreet about their relationship. She heard too much gossip about them and read too much about them in *Women's Wear Daily*. Sally ordered Warren to stop seeing Amanda. In television language, she was canceling their show.

When Sally got the CBS offer, she and Warren had a long talk about whether he wanted her to live with him. He said that he did. They hoped that it would not be as bad as being engaged.

Asked if it disturbed him that Sally makes much more money than he does, Warren Hoge said, "It should be quite nice to live with someone who makes that kind of money." Asked if he minded her being more famous than he is, Warren said, "She was better known as a writer than I am, but this is much more enormous. I don't know."

Sally and Warren went to a party given by Ann and Walter Pincus recently in Washington. Douglas Kiker walked up to Warren Hoge and asked: "How does it feel to be Mr. Sally Quinn?"

Warren, who has spent much of his life being asked what it is like to
be the younger brother of James Hoge, editor of the *Chicago Sun-
Times,* did not answer.

Sally said, "Shut up!"

Barbara Walters likes Sally Quinn. She says that she wishes her
well on her new television show. The obvious fact remains, however,
that if Ms. Quinn's ratings go up, then Ms. Walters's ratings must come
down, because the number of television sets on at that hour will probably remain constant. There may be no catfight, but there will be competition. There can be only one queen of the morning.

Sally Quinn did a story on Barbara Walters a year and a half ago.

"I'm not beautiful, slick, glamorous," Barbara Walters said in the
article. "I may be one of the most envied women in America. And only
because anybody can be like me. They can't be Carol Burnett if they
can't sing, they can't be a great dancer if they can't dance, they can't be a
great actress if they can't act. They can be like me."

In the story, Sally Quinn wrote: "Oh, no, they can't." And yet,
ironically, she has now been hired to try to be like Barbara Walters,
more or less. The problem is that Sally *is* beautiful, slick, and glamorous. The women in the television audience may not identify with her
the way they seem to with Barbara Walters. Moreover, a wife in curlers
may not want to invite a stunning woman like Sally into her home at
breakfast time. It could hurt to be blond.

Sally Quinn spent the day with Barbara Walters, getting a preview,
although she did not know it, of what her life would one day be like. In
the evening, the blond reporter went home with the auburn-haired TV
star. Lee Guber—Mr. Barbara Walters—welcomed them. The couple
had not yet split up.

"We're both very independent," Barbara Walters said. "The first
six months of our marriage we kept both apartments. The hardest part
was moving in together."

Now Sally and Warren faced that adjustment.

"I want to be with Lee as much as I can," Mrs. Guber said. "I don't
want him to get used to being without me. Couples can grow apart easily, and it's hard with us because of my hours."

The hours problem would now face Sally and Warren. He would
work from 8:00 A.M. to 8:00 P.M. as city editor of the *New York Post.*
When he got home, she would already be asleep in order to be ready for
work at 1:00 A.M.

Lee Guber said, "I must have known what kind of woman I wanted to be married to. She's not the kind of woman not to be committed or involved. My involvement with her career is slight. I've helped guide her to the right managers, and I watch her most mornings unless she's got four women showing crewel work."

Mrs. Guber said, "I knew right away this was a man I could marry."

Mr. Guber said, "I knew right away that the trap was being set for me."

Mrs. Guber said, "We sound like Ozzie and Harriet."

They also sounded like Sally and Warren. Walters and Guber have already lived through many of the problems that Quinn and Hoge would shortly be experiencing for the first time. The Gubers made their marriage work for over eight years and then separated, not long after Sally wrote her article.

Barbara Walters predicts that Sally Quinn's biggest problem will involve not her change from newspapers to televison but the "change in her personal life." The professional competition between Quinn and Walters could turn out to be easier to deal with than the personal competition that could develop between Sally and Warren. Sally says that she fell in love with Warren because he is the most secure man she ever met. She would now get a chance to see how secure.

Sally Quinn brings as much television experience to her new job at CBS as she brought newspaper experience to her job at the *Post,* and there is some resentment at CBS just as there was at the *Post.* She is only being asked to do a job that a long string of veterans has failed to do. Taking a job opposite the "Today" show would now seem to qualify as hazardous duty. Ironically, Barbara Walters was once a writer for some of CBS's failed shows, including one starring the unlikely combination of Walter Cronkite and Dick Van Dyke. CBS even tried puppets in that time slot, but they too lost their jobs. "The CBS Morning News," took on the "Today" show in 1965, and it has featured an ever-changing cast that has included at one time or another: Mike Wallace, Joseph Benti, John Hart, Bernard Kalb, Nelson Benton. The "Today" show bullies continued to maul all comers.

Sally Rand wrote Sally Quinn to warn her what a tough life show business was. Her letter said, "I've been layed, relayed, parlayed, and beat over the ass with a broom! Harassed, blinded, robbed, wounded, left bleeding, unsuccored, without recourse or resources. Tough old broads stagger up, fight teeth and toenail, but God, at what cost! If you can save another from having to suffer it—"

Barbara Walters called Sally Quinn recently to give her what Sally took to be good news: Ms. Walters said she would be going on vacation shortly after Sally starts at CBS. Sally said, "You don't have to lean over backward to help me."

When it was first announced that Sally Quinn would leave the *Washington Post* to join CBS, she told a *Post* reporter that she and Barbara Walters "covered the shah's celebration in the desert of Iran together last year and stayed in the same dormitory. That's like being in combat together. I imagine this will be a similar situation."

Sally Quinn, the general's daughter, understands combat. She is not intimidated by Barbara Walters. Her fingernails are painted red. Sort of Jungle Red.

◆   ◆   ◆

The Sally Quinn piece coming on top of the Gay Talese piece upset a lot of *New York* magazine readers. Some subscriptions were canceled. The *New York Times* did a story. Someone told me I was infamous. Being young and new to magazines, I was as shocked at the reaction as some readers were shocked by the stories.

I couldn't write for several months.

DR. J'S MAGIC
BASKETBALL

•   •   •

We used to have spirited coed basketball games at *New York* magazine.
These games were played in Clay Felker's tiny office on the top floor of
an elegant old brownstone on East Thirty-second Street. A toy basketball goal was nailed up on his office wall. We used a toy basketball that
was about half regulation size. The ball was small enough for me to grip
in one hand and the goal was low enough for me to be able to dunk for
the first time in my life. Our games were really hard-fought contests, the
girls just as scrappy as the boys. We played tackle basketball in the
boss's office.

These games were good practice for the Big Game I was about to
play . . .

•   •   •

New York, September 1973

I asked Julius (Dr. J.) Erving if he would like to play a little one-
on-one. Since I had played high school basketball and occasionally daz-
zled very small children on city playgrounds with my jump shot, I did
not feel entirely foolish in making such a modest proposal. We were in a
New York photographer's studio that happened to be equipped with a
basket. Erving smiled and agreed to the game. He picked up the basketball and with surgical precision began cutting me to pieces.

The Doctor drove to the basket and made a twisting lay-up from the right side. He drove again and made a pirouetting shot from the left. He came straight down the center and leaped so high that his toes were even with my chest. He hung in the air and did what looked like a half gainer. His right hand was so huge that in his grip the ball looked like a small orange pill. He soared above the rim and stuffed this pill down the throat of the basket.

I could see that this Doctor was going to be bad medicine.

Actually, Dr. J., the newly acquired star of the New York Nets, is just the medicine that that sluggish team has needed. In fact, he is just the medicine all pro basketball has needed. Before he turned professional, basketball seemed to be getting as predictable as a missionary's sex life. The pro players always fired the same shots the same way with the same predictable results, but Dr. J. has as many moves with a basketball as Jimi Hendrix used to have with a guitar. "I dunk the ball a lot of different ways," says Julius Erving. "There is something about dunking the ball that excites people." He attacks the hoop from behind, from the side, from the front. He knows that doing it the same way every time is a bore. Dr. J., who is twenty-three and stands six feet seven inches tall, may be the best forward in professional basketball. He is almost certainly the most exciting.

Like most doctors, he does not come cheap. The Nets, the New York franchise of the American Basketball Association, paid close to $4 million to get him.

In joining the Nets, Julius Erving is coming home. He grew up on Long Island, first in Hempstead and then in Roosevelt, where his mother did domestic work, worked as a beautician, and collected welfare at different times. He got his nickname playing in Long Island playgrounds. Julius started calling one of his friends "the Professor" because he was always lecturing people on the court. In retaliation, the friend called Julius "the Doctor."

When Erving was ten years old, he started playing ball for a Salvation Army team. Erving says, "With that team, I began to travel all over New York and Pennsylvania. I had a chance to see how people lived on the other side of the fence—big houses, two cars, color TV. I wondered what you had to do to get them." Lately, he has been finding out. In addition to his Nets wages, endorsement money is beginning to come along. One of the first is a soft drink—Dr. J. drinks Dr Pepper.

In early August, Julius Erving happened to be in Los Angeles and went out on the town with Bill Russell and Jim Brown. Russell talked about basketball. Jim Brown talked about his women.

Dr. J.'s diagnosis of the running back turned movie star: "Jim Brown's love life dominates his thinking." Erving respects Brown but he does not want his own personal life to resemble the runner's. Dr. J. says he hopes that the razzle-dazzle of his court life will not carry over into his off-court hours. Until he can find a condominium by the ocean, he is living with his mother and stepfather in the Roosevelt, Long Island, house where he grew up.

Off court, Erving does not want to play games. He says, "As a ball-player, you meet a lot of girls. When this has happened to me, I have sensed the underestimating of me as a person—underestimating my ability to see through their game. After a while you get tired of it."

Dr. J. prefers to talk about basketball. When asked who would be on his dream team, he said: Kareem Abdul-Jabbar, Spencer Haywood, John Havlicek, Walt Frazier, and Jerry West. He did not include himself. Julius Erving is not exactly modest, but on the other hand, he does not talk like Muhammad Ali. Instead, he plays the way Ali talks. Dazzling.

Dr. J. completely anesthesized my game. I had not expected to win. I *had* expected to score. He refused to take my fakes. I would shoot but he would leap as if he were on the moon held by only one-sixth gravity and then slap the ball away before it had traveled two feet. He can jump as high as the big men and yet can control the ball as well as the little men.

In our entire game, I got off only three shots. Dr. J. blocked all of the others. I never scored. My best moment came when I was lucky enough to steal the ball from Dr. J. once. I wished for an instant replay.

When the doctor had finished operating on me, performing a partial removal of the ego, he went upstairs to shower. I stayed behind and played a game against the photographer's son and one of his friends. They stood about four feet tall.

The photographer's son told me, "Now you can be Dr. J." I relished the idea. The boys did much better against me than I did against the Doctor. Still I did not let this rattle me and I showed them no mercy. I needed this one.

Dr. A. won the game.

PART THREE

◆ ◆ ◆

SCANDALS

MARK
Get close to her while you're doing the research, but when you sit down to write—

ADAM
Forget she has a mother. Don't I always?

—from the screenplay of *Perfect*

ORCHIDS FOR MOTHER

. . .

This is how I met my Mother.

In early 1976, the Central Intelligence Agency was accused of conducting illegal spying operations in this country. The man at the center of the controversy was James Jesus Angleton—the head of the Counterintelligence Department—whom the CIA made a scapegoat and fired.

I decided to try calling Angleton. I knew he wouldn't talk to me, but I felt I should try anyway. Somehow I got his number in Arlington, Virginia, and dialed it.

Angleton himself answered.

I told him that I was a reporter for *New York* magazine doing a story on the CIA.

He didn't hang up as I had been afraid he might. But I heard a lot of clinking and clunking on the other end of the line. I assumed he was attaching his tape recorder to the phone. I already had mine hooked up.

I asked Angleton if he could tell me anything about why he had left the agency.

He said he couldn't talk about the agency.

There was an awkward pause. I felt I was about to lose him.

"Well, if you can't talk about the CIA," I said, "what about poetry?"

I knew from reading about him that Angleton was an avid reader of modern poetry. This passion began at Yale, where he edited a literary magazine and had continued ever since.

The spy and I talked about poetry for at least twenty minutes. One of the themes of our conversation was: Had Ezra Pound and T. S. Eliot been good or bad for poetry in the long run? We both agreed that they had been great poets, but we wondered if they had started poetry down a rather barren path. I felt as if I were a sophomore in college again.

When I ran out of anything else to say about modern poetry, there was another awkward pause. It finally occurred to me to ask him about his orchids, which I had read about in news reports.

So we talked about orchids for at least ten minutes. I asked him how one goes about growing orchids. I had not realized how many steps were involved or that an orchid can take fifteen years to bloom. The answer to my question was longer than I had anticipated and my ear was starting to hurt.

I decided it was time to end the conversation. I told Angleton it had been nice talking to him and I would call him back in a few months to see if he could talk about the agency then.

"Well, maybe we can talk a little about the agency now," he said.

And we did. We talked on and on and on. I was delighted, but at the same time my ear hurt worse and worse, and I was supposed to meet my future wife, Lesley, for dinner, and I was late.

"Thank you very much," I said. "This has been very helpful."

But Angleton did not take the hint. He kept on talking and talking. Then the tape in my tape recorder ran out.

"Well, I guess that's about it," Angleton said. "Good-bye."

I am sure that the tape had just run out in his tape recorder, too. He had not been able to stop talking while there was still a little tape on the spool because that would have been wasteful and sloppy. He is that meticulous.

A few days later, I received a large manila envelope in the mail. Opening it, I found an eight-by-ten photograph of e. e. cummings standing in front of a fireplace. I was puzzled. Turning to the enclosed letter, I found that it was from Angleton, signed in his tiny microdot handwriting. The letter informed me that Angleton himself had taken the picture. It went on to describe and give the history of every object in the photo—all the knickknacks on the mantelpiece, the painting on the wall, on and on. At the very end of the letter, Angleton wrote that I had "been seen" in Washington recently. He suggested that we have lunch the next time I came to the capital.

I called him and made a lunch date.

We met at his favorite restaurant, La Niçoise, where all the waiters wear roller skates. Sitting beside me, Angleton, who is literally as well as figuratively twisted, seemed a fabulous character who had come in, not from the cold, but from the world of fiction.

When I sat down to write, I decided to do a fictional short story, not a straight journalistic piece. I reasoned that the CIA was itself in the fiction business since it was always making up cover stories to cloak its true intentions—and one way to fight fiction is with fiction. At the center of my short story would be a veteran spy who grew orchids and worried about the modern poets. I made up some things but not his code name: Mother.

•　　•　　•

New York, August 1975

"Mother" wore black shoes, black socks, a black suit, a black tie, and a white shirt. He was not a man who had much affinity for the gray areas of life. When the bell chimed, he put down his book, unfolded his tall, thin body from his favorite chair, and walked slowly toward the door. He was stooped and his body was slightly twisted. Mother, slouching toward another conspiracy, looked like a crooked Abe Lincoln.

The man he met at the door wore a blue suit and brown leather gloves, which he did not remove upon entering the house. He was a tidy man, in his way. He might set a drink on a coffee table and leave a ring, but he would never leave a thumbprint. His regular employer was a Detroit Mafioso, but he occasionally did some moonlighting for the Central Intelligence Agency.

When the two men were seated in the Arlington living room, John J. Saxonton, whose code name was "Mother," picked up his book once again. It was a volume of poetry by one of Mother's late friends, Ezra Pound.

"They thought Ezra was crazy, too," Mother said, his voice low but firm.

"Did they?" the visitor said.

"Yes," Mother said, regretting once again that the spy business was no longer a gentlemen's preserve. "You remember, they locked him up in St. Elizabeth's."

"Why?"

"Because he hated the Communists more than the Fascists. Would you like to hear one of his poems?"

The visitor nodded unenthusiastically.

The old man turned the pages and then started reading in a voice that barely betrayed the self-pity: "For three years, out of key with his time,/He strove to resuscitate the dead art . . ./Wrong from the start—"

"That's nice," the uncomprehending visitor said.

"It's from a poem called 'Hugh Selwyn Mauberley,' " Mother went on. "I have a theory about that title that might interest you. You see, I believe Pound was indulging in a pun. I believe he was saying: *Où se loigne Mauberley?* You understand?"

"No, I'm afraid I don't."

"That's French for 'Where is Mauberley going?' Pound knew that his country and his age would ostracize him, but he did not know where he could go. You see?"

The visitor did not need an expensive liberal arts education to know that Mother was talking about himself.

"Well, you didn't come for a lecture on literature," Mother said. "You came for your assignment. I've got a score I want you to help me settle. Here are your instructions."

Mother picked up a sealed envelope from an end table and handed it to the gloved man. Mother had carefully typed out all that the visitor would need to know about the operation: the time, the location, the weapon, the target to be liquidated.

"Memorize the instructions, then destroy them," Mother said. "I wish I could discuss its finer points with you, but I consider it likely that our conversation is being monitored. If I were in their position, it certainly would be."

Mother had recently been fired from his position as the head of the CIA's Counterintelligence Department. It had been his job to spy on spies. Occasionally, an enemy agent or a double agent would be picked up and taken to the "human library" in the Allegheny Mountains, where he would be "read" by some persuasive interrogators. Afterward, more often than not, the unraveled agent "died of the measles" or had a fatal accident or killed himself. Mother took special pride in the suicides—the sleeping-pill overdoses, the engines left running in closed garages, the nooses tied to basement water pipes, the bullets through temples. They appealed to Mother's perverse appreciation of misleading appearances: to him it seemed appropriate that men who lived by deception should deceive even in death, passing for suicide victims when they were really murder victims.

"May I show you my orchids?" Mother asked.

"I would love to see them again," the visitor said. He preferred nature's beauties to poetry's.

Mother put on a long black coat and a black homburg. Looking like a crooked stovepipe, he led the way out into the backyard. The two men crossed thirty feet of lawn and entered one of the two greenhouses, where flowers hung from the ceiling like New Year's Eve decorations.

A voluptuous white orchid nuzzled Mother's black hat.

One morning almost a year earlier, in the spring of 1974, Scott Bannister had sat reading a story in the *Washington Post* that he knew his boss would not like. The article said that President Richard M. Nixon had reaffirmed his plans to visit Russia that summer in spite of his Watergate problems. Bannister served as an assistant to Mother in the Counterintelligence Department. He looked up as Mother entered.

"Good morning," Bannister said.

"No, it isn't," Mother replied grumpily.

"You saw the story," Bannister said lamely.

"Of course," Mother said. "The problem with this administration is that détente is all it has going for it. Nixon obviously prefers Moscow to Washington these days."

When Mother disappeared into his inner office, Bannister scanned the story about a quarrel between Special Prosecutor Leon Jaworski and the White House over presidential tapes. Then he turned inside the paper. He was staring at a picture of a pretty female streaker when the director's office telephoned. He covered the photograph with his hand as he listened to the director's secretary ask him to come up to the director's suite.

On his way, Bannister, who was the kind of aide who never took off his jacket or rolled up his sleeves, stopped in a men's room to check his grooming. He dressed the way Harvard men had once dressed. His suit was seersucker—he had had trouble finding a store that still carried this material, but it had been worth it because of the admiration his attire evoked from the agency's old guard. Running a comb carefully through his hair, he had no idea that he was staring into the eyes of a security officer stationed on the other side of a one-way mirror.

Bannister proceeded to the director's seventh-floor suite, passing, en route, the glass room that contained security aides armed with snub-nosed .38 revolvers under their conservative business suits. He stopped at the desk of the director's secretary. It occurred to him that the company was becoming much less colorful at almost every level, including the woman who sat behind that desk. Back when Richard Helms had been the director, his secretary had been an eccentric old woman who fed the birds on the agency's roof and kept a houseful of parakeets at home. The new secretary and her new boss were, outwardly at least, much drabber fare.

Bannister entered the director's office, which was fifty feet long with a desk at one end and living room furniture at the other. A long row of windows overlooked the Potomac River. The office had a thick carpet into which visitors sank—it was supposed to provide a sense of luxury, but to Bannister it felt like quicksand.

Director Robert Colgate, code-named "Sparrow," looked like a bad Xerox copy of a man. Or perhaps a Xerox of a Xerox. The original may have contained some black and white, but copying had reduced those to gray on gray.

Gray was a key to Colgate. He had spent much of his career operating in the "gray area" where patriotism shades off into criminality. He looked like an accountant, but his record indicated that he balanced his books with bodies: In Vietnam, he'd headed the Phoenix program, which attempted to dismantle the Vietcong infrastructure through systematic assassinations. This program, according to figures that Colgate himself had supplied Congress, was responsible for putting 20,587 people in the dead column. During the years when he was attempting to "pacify" Vietnam, his wife, who stayed behind in a Washington suburb, regularly attended peace demonstrations. Many parents in Vietnam lost children to Phoenix, but, as if to balance the account, Colgate had lost a child, too. While his men were killing in Southeast Asia, his daughter was dying of a mysterious disease in Springfield, Maryland. Some saw a link between her death and her opposition to her father's role in the war: They said she had lost her will to live. Colgate was no Ian Fleming spy who could forever hurt others without being hurt.

Director Colgate did not inhabit a black-and-white moral universe. He worried about the implications of operating a secret organization in an open society. And these concerns were always getting mixed up with thoughts about his dead child. He was a religious man and he asked himself questions that were almost biblical: Had he so loved his job that he had given his only begotten daughter that the agency should not perish, but have everlasting life? In the end, however, he would decide that his course was the right one. And then he would attack his duties with a Jesuit's zeal.

Sitting across from Colgate, Bannister was struck all over again by how different Mother was from the director. Mother was tall, with big bones and bold features; the director was short, with delicate features and bones as fragile as a bird's. Mother, the son of rich, aristocratic parents, had attended an exclusive British public school, summered in Italy, played soccer and written poetry at Yale; the director, an army brat, had attended parochial schools, joined the Boy Scouts, and was a poor boy at Princeton, where he was never really a member of the club. They were both Catholics, but one of them had learned his Catholicism from Italian aristocrats, while the other was an Irish Catholic, which made them as similar as fettuccine Alfredo and a boiled potato.

Director Colgate's meeting with Bannister began with a ruse. The director pretended to be interested in a certain budgetary matter. Bannister was immediately at a disadvantage. He did not know the proper figures. The deputy was being set up. Now, when the director changed the subject, Bannister would welcome the change.

"By the way, how is Mother?" the director asked, his voice betraying none of the animosity he felt.

Bannister said that Mother was well.

"I would like your advice," the director said. His deep blue eyes, the one exception to his grayness, shone with a counterfeit openness. "You know Mother better than I do. Some of my people say he's too old to go back on the front lines, but I'm not so sure. What do you think?"

The director went on at some length, always in that please-help-me-out tone that was meant to deceive and to flatter. The director reminded Bannister that Mother's intelligence career began in Italy, where he was an OSS officer during the war. After helping to save that country from the Fascists, Mother had stayed on to help save postwar Italy from the Communists.

"As you know, Italy is once again in danger," the director said. "In fact, the danger now may be even greater than it was in the forties. Once again, Italy needs the help of the kind of friends who helped her before. The problem is that those old friends may be *too* old. That's my question. Do you think Mother could still handle a job like, say, chief of station in Rome?"

Bannister sprang to Mother's defense. He assured the director that Mother was not too old to fight in the trenches. He mentioned that he knew that Mother was gravely concerned about the future of Italy. He even praised Mother's Italian, which he spoke without accent.

"Thank you very much," the director said at last. "You've been a great help."

As Bannister left the director's office, the carpet did not seem to suck at his feet as it had on the way in. He felt that he had really helped the director and at the same time helped Mother. It did not occur to Bannister that he was simply being used to deliver a message. He would have been less naive if he had been privy to the struggle between Mother and the director that had been going on for months.

The director had already made several attempts to persuade Mother to accept various transfers that would really have been demotions. Mother had always refused. The problem with Mother was that his "old-fashioned" distrust of the Russians was out of sync with his country's new foreign policy. Mother still considered the Russians to be an unreconstructed menace—which made Mother himself a menace in the eyes of the director. Mother was a cold warrior; the director was not. What had begun as a political disagreement between the two men had ripened into personal animosity.

Bannister hurried back to Mother's office to tell him about his talk with the director, but Mother wasn't there. He was in the "miscellaneous projects" office and could not be disturbed.

On the seventh floor, the director sat doodling. He wrote "Mother" on a pad and then crossed it out again and again until he tore a hole in the paper.

Spies are burrowing animals. The CIA once dug a tunnel under East Berlin to tap the opposition's telephone lines. The agency even dug a quarter-mile tunnel under its own property in Langley to provide a secret entrance to the complex. At the agency, "going underground" was more than just a metaphor.

One summer morning, an Israeli agent, who had an appointment with a high agency official, entered the compound "black," meaning through the tunnel. When he emerged, he found himself in a carpeted foyer facing mahogany elevator doors. A squad of gray-flannel guards looked the agent over. Then two of them escorted him into the elevator, which rose to an unnumbered floor.

The building led a double life. On the outside, it was just another office building—that was its cover story. Once the agent entered the "miscellaneous projects" office, however, he found himself inside a Swiss hunting lodge with exposed-beam rafters and a slanting ceiling twenty feet high at one end. Flanked by two greyhounds, Mother sat waiting for the agent in a huge leather armchair. Mother was so thin that he made the chair look fat.

"Would you like a drink?" Mother asked.

"Why, yes!" the agent said, unable to hide his surprise.

"I should explain," Mother said on his way to the bar. "This room and the director's private dining room are the only places we allow hard liquor. What will it be?"

Drinks in hand, the two men, the short Israeli and the tall Catholic, sat down to discuss a Middle Eastern operation. Mother had first befriended members of the Jewish underground in Italy after the war when they were helping European Jews escape to Palestine. In the spy business, making a Jewish connection back when Israel was still Palestine was like buying Xerox when it was still Haloid. For a generation, Mother had owned the "Israeli account" at the agency. Intelligence operations in all other countries were run out of Clandestine Services, but Israeli operations were run out of Mother's Counterintelligence shop. Fearing that others in the agency would try to take the account away from him, Mother had always kept his dealings with the Israelis ultrasecret. For years, the Israeli desk had remained hidden under Mother's skirts.

Mother and the Israeli agent had worked together on many operations, including one that become legend in the company: They had stolen King Farouk's urine. The agency's doctors had asked Mother to obtain a specimen so that they could check up on the fat king's health. Mother in turn had contacted the Israeli agent and given him the assignment. The Israeli and his men descended upon Monte Carlo, where they tapped into the plumbing of the men's room in one of the casinos. An agent was stationed on one of the toilet seats with a view of the urinals. When Farouk came in, the agent coughed in code so that another agent on the other side of the wall would know which urinal the king was using. Farouk flushed his urine all the way to Langley, Virginia.

Mother wanted to show the Israeli agent some pictures. He pressed several buttons on the arm of his chair and the hunting lodge darkened as a photograph of a man carrying a briefcase was projected onto the wall.

"So that's 'Octopus,' " the agent said. He was not referring to the man. He meant the system. Octopus is a huge computerized file with arms reaching out from Langley to link up with the computer files of other Western intelligence organizations like Britain's SIS and France's SDECE. Octopus specializes in storing information on terrorist groups, but it contains all kinds of other names as well. In a sense, Octopus is one of the most democratic aspects of that exclusive gentlemen's club known as the CIA: A computer is undiscriminating—it accepts anyone.

"Do you recognize the subject in the picture?" Mother asked.

"No," the agent said, "but I recognize the location. That's Foggy Bottom, isn't it?"

"That's right."

Mother punched up three more pictures. The agent did not recognize any of the men, but he guessed from the backgrounds that they were all associated with the State Department.

"Who are they?" the agent asked.

"The secretary of state's four closest aides," Mother said matter-of-factly.

"Don't tell me one of them is a KGB penetration," the agent said.

"No," Mother said. "I have no evidence that the Russians have placed agents inside the secretary of state's office, but they don't really need to. The secretary does just what they want him to anyway. He thinks the Russians are our friends. He's been taken in by détente."

"I think you may be right," the agent said.

"People forget about the days of Lenin and Dzerzhinsky," Mother said, a frown forming as he pronounced without accent the tongue-twisting name of the founding director of Cheka, which became successively the GPU, the OGPU, the GUGB/NKVD, the NKGB, the MGB, and finally the KGB. "When Dzerzhinsky had so many agents in Western countries, he went to Lenin and asked, 'What shall I tell them?' Lenin said, 'Tell the West what it wants to believe.' And, you know, Dzerzhinsky did just that. We were given the false impression that Russia was falling apart and moving toward capitalism. The Revolution was saved through disinformation."

"And now the same thing is happening all over again," the agent said.

"That's right," Mother said. "You see, de-Stalinization meant a return to Leninism. One aspect of that process has been turning the KGB from an instrument of personal terror back to what it was under Lenin when it had political objectives. They have reestablished a Department of Disinformation. That's how they sold us détente, but there hasn't really been any change in their central philosophy that the United States is the main enemy. They still want to destroy us."

"Of course, Lenin didn't have to worry about China," the agent said.

"No, no," Mother said. "That's just more disinformation. The alleged Sino-Soviet split is just another trick. They are as close as ever, but by pretending to quarrel they make us let down our guard. If the West thought China and the Soviet Union were still united, there would still be a cold war."

When Mother finished his lecture—one he had given countless times before, but rarely to such a receptive listener—they got down to a discussion of the upcoming operation.

"The secretary will visit the Middle East next month," Mother said. "Those aides I showed you will be going with him. He will be surrounded by a security blanket, but they won't be. They are your target. I want to know what they do, I want to know what they say. This time I want to know what my government is giving away."

Prying open the director's office door generally requires a certain amount of bureaucratic foreplay. The director's aides, who guard the outer office, must be fondled with memos and phone calls. When these aides have been properly wooed, they arrange an appointment.

Only one man in the company dispensed with even perfunctory courtship of the outer office. One morning this man brushed past the director's aides as if they were panhandlers and presented himself, without appointment, at the director's door.

Inside the director's office, Mother said, "I got your message and the answer is no."

"What message?" the director asked ingenuously.

"The one you gave Bannister," Mother said.

The director just smiled.

"Tell me," Mother went on, "is the secretary of state behind this?"

"You've been in the business too long," the director said. "You see conspiracies everywhere."

"So you still want to put me out to pasture," Mother said. "What makes you think I'll go this time? And don't tell me that Italy needs me. Is that what they told Cord Meyer? That Britain needed him? You seem to want to turn our stations into retirement homes."

In 1973, Meyer, another cold warrior, had been toppled from his position as the number-two man in Clandestine Services and the agency had packed him off to London as station chief.

"I want to install my own team," the director said, trying not to lose his temper. "You understand."

"And what if I don't understand?" Mother asked.

He was one of the few men in the agency who dared to speak to the director that way. He drew his courage from the same well that had so long sustained J. Edgar Hoover: his files. Mother, like Hoover, enjoyed the considerable leverage that devolves upon a man who is empowered to follow, to peek, and to tap. It was his job to make sure that the company was not penetrated by the other side. In performing his duties, Mother tried to think like a KGB officer: Whom in the CIA would he most like to recruit? His answer to this question was a list of fifty people in the agency whom he kept under surveillance. He also ran spot checks on the other 17,500 company employees. His files were bloated with other people's secrets. Mother, like Hoover, simply had too much on agency personnel to be an easy man to "retire."

"If you won't accept a transfer," the director said, "I may have to ask for your resignation."

"And what if I refuse to resign?" Mother asked. "What would you do to me then? Would you do to me what you did to that Vietnamese girl? I hope not, because the recordings of her screams make her sound extremely uncomfortable. Especially when you, oh, well, you must remember."

◆

"I saw a picture of you and some actress in the *Post* this morning," the director, a suburban Boy Scout leader, told the secretary of state.

"They are giving me quite a reputation as a swinger," the secretary said. "But I don't mind. Now when I go to a dinner party and I'm boring, the others at the table think it's their fault."

The line had become one of the secretary's favorites.

The secretary of state and the director of the Central Intelligence Agency were lunching in the secretary's private dining room in the State Department. The conversation, like the meal, began with light openers but inevitably progressed toward the meat of the matter, as the director had known it would.

"Have you taken care of that personnel problem we discussed?" the secretary asked.

"I talked to him," the director said, "but he's being difficult."

"He is a difficult man," the secretary said, "and that makes my job difficult. Sometimes I think he's a bigger barrier to peace in the Middle East than the terrorists."

The secretary enjoyed being secretive too much to explain such a statement. Therefore, he left unstated his suspicion that Mother, through his agents, had allied himself with right-wing forces in Israel, especially within the military. Time after time, the secretary had been on the verge of persuading the Israeli political leaders to give up territory in return for promises of peace; then the political leaders would confer with the military leaders and the agreement would come apart. The secretary felt that the generals were parroting Mother's line. The secretary was attempting to achieve a peace that would be guaranteed by the Americans and the Russians, but Mother had persuaded the Israeli intelligence community that the Russians could not be trusted. Such interference made the secretary furious. If Mother had been a city, the secretary would have bombed him.

"Perhaps we should simply fire him," the director said, "but if we do he may raise a lot of dust."

"Ah, yes," the secretary said. "I understand that he is a greatly feared man. A friend of mine who used to work for the agency told me a story about the way Saxonton works. It seems that back when Allen Dulles was the director, he called my friend in to his office and asked: 'Why did you say Bedell Smith [a former director] doesn't like my brother [John Foster Dulles]?' My friend remembered where it was that he had had that conversation. It was while he was in bed with his wife. Saxonton had bugged his bedroom."

"Yes, that's how he works," the director said. "If you complain, he tells you, 'If you don't want to give up your right to smoke cigarettes, you shouldn't have taken a job in an explosives factory.' "

"Of course," the secretary smiled, "I understand why Saxonton is so greatly feared. But now you must make a decision. Whom do you fear more, him or me?"

When lunch was over, the director went to his car and the secretary went into the State Department's press room to hold a news conference. His eye was caught by Washington's only female television sound technician. She looked like the women with whom the secretary was always having his picture taken.

The secretary walked over to the sound woman and said, "Tell me, what do you really do with that microphone?"

Richard Hill, a young intelligence officer, was rolling up his sleeves when his telephone rang. It was Director Colgate's secretary. Was he free that evening? He was. Did he have his car with him? He did. Would it be inconvenient for him to drive the director somewhere that evening? It would not. About 6:00 P.M.? Very good. Hill bolted from his office. He wanted to clean the McDonald's bags and Coke cups out of the back seat of his car.

After work, as the aide and his director walked through the parking lot, Hill launched into an apology for his car. It was too small, needed a tune-up, could use a wash.

"If I had wanted a limousine," the director said, "I could have arranged for one."

The two men crammed themselves into a small, canary-yellow Datsun 240-Z. Hill took a deep breath and turned the key. The car wouldn't start at first. It never would. He choked it and kept on trying. Finally he resuscitated the engine. Hill apologized again.

The director wanted Hill to drive him out to "the farm," which is to the company what boot camp is to the army. As they drove through the Virginia woods, Hill found himself recalling his own training at the enclave. He remembered the courses where he had received instruction on "agent handling," "agent recruiting," "flaps and seals," and "locks and picks." But his most vivid memory was of the night of the border crossing.

His class set off in teams of two in the middle of the night to cross a Communist border—complete with barbed wire, watchtowers, searchlights, and roving Commie guards—that stretches for two miles through the Virginia woodlands. Hill and his partner, their faces blackened, came upon a deep ditch that was filled with oil and other repugnant slime. Slipping down into this muck was easy enough, but climbing up the other side was almost impossible. Every time they tried to crawl out, they slid back into the mire. They felt like bugs trying to crawl out of a toilet bowl. They finally realized that they would have to work as a team. Hill cupped his hands and boosted his buddy up out of the hole. Then his buddy tried to pull him up, but instead Hill dragged his partner back into the slime. When they finally scrambled out, slippery from head to foot, they still had to scale a ten-foot wall. Hill tried to climb on his partner's shoulders, which was like climbing a greasy pole. After repeated failures, Hill made it to the top of the wall and then started pulling his buddy up, just like the last scene in *The Spy Who Came in from the Cold.* Once over the wall, they started rolling toward cover. Hill hit a tripwire. A flare went off overhead and Hill's crotch suddenly felt warm and wet. The "East German security officers" who interrogated Hill scared him to death.

Hill felt more or less the same way as he chauffeured the director deeper into the forest. Every time he started to say something, he suddenly had the feeling that he was about to set off another tripwire. So he sat silently and waited for the director to initiate some kind of conversation.

Hill's experiences at the farm had helped persuade him that he did not belong on the dark side of the agency, so he had made his career on the light side. The dark side penetrated the "enemy" with spies and played "dirty tricks," such as rigging elections, mounting coups, and just plain murder. The light side, his side, monitored radio transmissions, studied satellite photographs, and read the enemy's scientific journals. Advancement was faster on the light side, which appealed to Hill, but he knew he almost certainly had no chance of becoming the top man. Directors always came from the dark side—a monopoly that the light side deeply resented.

That was the principal schism within the company: the light side against the dark. But there were other divisions, too. The dark side was split into spies and political operators. The spies just wanted to find out what other governments were up to; the operators wanted to control other governments or else overthrow them. Richard Helms, who had run the agency in the sixties, had come out of the clean side of the dark side: What he loved best were classic spying operations like the tunnel under East Berlin. Colgate, who ran the agency in the seventies, had come out of the dirty side: He was a specialist at coups and assassinations. Now the dirty dark side (as embodied by Colgate) was about to ally itself with the light side (as embodied by Hill) to run an operation against the clean side of the dark side (as embodied by Mother).

"I have a job for you," the director said at last.

The job involved material to be added to a report on which Hill, a member of a special task force, had been working for months. Since Hill was not a bad writer for a bureaucrat, he had been asked to draft the report. When it was completed and approved, it would go to the chairmen of the congressional oversight committees.

The report had originally been ordered by James Schlesinger when he was the director. In February of 1973, Schlesinger, the former head of the Atomic Energy Commission, had been brought in to replace Helms as the head of the CIA. When Watergate broke, Schlesinger evidently followed a bureaucratic precedent of long standing: "Cover your ass." Since he was a newcomer at the agency, he knew that he could not possibly be implicated in the company's past misdeeds, but he could be criticized if those misdeeds continued. Therefore, he ordered an investigation of any CIA wrongdoing. He wanted to make sure that he did not get hanged for someone else's operations.

Before the report was completed, however, Schlesinger's tenure at the agency was cut short as the Nixon administration began to capsize. On April 30, 1973, Richard Kleindienst resigned as attorney general, to be replaced by Elliot Richardson, who had been secretary of defense; Richardson in turn was replaced by Schlesinger; and Robert Colgate, then the CIA's deputy director of operations, inherited not only Schlesinger's job but his report on wrongdoing as well.

Unlike Schlesinger, Colgate *had* worked his way up in the company, and so he had more of a vested interest in covering up the company's past mistakes. However, since he had spent most of his career out of the country, he saw to it that the report focused on domestic transgressions. Still, the new director tended to regard the report with the affection usually reserved for a bad cold. Until now. Now he thought he saw a way to make that report his lever.

"It has come to my attention," the director told Hill, "that John Saxonton was behind many of the questionable activities performed by our agency in this country. It has also come to my attention that several of these activities may have overstepped our charter. I realize that it is difficult to assign blame to one of our own, but in this case, in the climate in which we now operate, I do not believe we can afford to put the agency in jeopardy in order to protect one man. What I mean is that I do not believe the agency can afford to whitewash Saxonton."

The director and the young intelligence officer rode in silence for a mile or more. Something was troubling Hill, but he was not sure whether he should bring it up.

"Sir," he said at last, "I'm not sure that Saxonton is the only one at fault. He only has a staff of about thirty. He helps map out strategy, but most of the work is done by our security people or our domestic-operations people. They—"

"We are not discussing security or domestic operations," the director interrupted. "We are talking about John Saxonton. I have seen information that persuades me that he was behind the questionable activities. And that is how I expect the report to read."

"Of course," Hill said.

"We'll talk again in a couple of weeks. I'll want to know how things are going."

When they arrived at the farm, they parked the car and walked over to a large building known as the Club. They entered the main room just as an inebriated parachute-landing-fall (PLF) instructor jumped up on the bar and shouted: "The only way you guys are gonna learn PLF is to practice."

He pointed to a recruit and ordered: "Get up here!"

The trainee climbed drunkenly up onto the bar.

The instructor counted: "One . . . Two . . . Three!"

They both jumped off the bar. The instructor rolled over and bounced to his feet. The student was too drunk to remember how to roll. The fall knocked him out cold.

The director was such an inconspicuous little man that no one had noticed his arrival.

Several weeks later, Director Colgate decided that he should have another talk with Hill. The director wanted to be sure that the task-force report would be ready for submission to the congressional oversight committees by the end of the month. Once the committee chairmen read it, they would do their duty and demand retribution from Mother. The director hoped that Mother would realize it would be futile to put up a fight and would go gracefully without holding any tapes concerts.

The director's secretary called Hill, but the young intelligence officer was not in his office. He was over in one of the scientific shops, where a computer had been programed to replay and analyze the latest Washington Redskins game. Most of the men in the company were fanatical Redskins fans, perhaps in part because of their jobs; the spying business was supposed to be a very virile profession and yet they were desk-bound warriors, so they compensated by playing computer football and spiking their jargon with masculine metaphors like "penetration." The agency had better estimates of Sonny Jurgensen's potential strike force than it did of the Russians'.

When Hill returned to his office, he found a message to call the director's secretary. She asked: Could he come up to the director's suite? He could. Right away? Right away. On his way to the elevator, Hill felt the way he had as a trainee when he was heading for that wall. Just to be absolutely certain that the denouement was not the same, he stopped in a men's room on the way and relieved himself.

When Hill reached the director's office, Colgate told him that he would rather not talk there. Hill followed the director into his private elevator, rode down with him to a lower floor, followed him down a corridor and into a small room with one window. This window did not look out onto the heavily wooded Virginia hills. It looked instead into another room. The director and Hill were standing behind a one-way mirror. In the other room, a lie-detector test was being administered to a young man who was being considered for a job in the company.

"I wanted to talk to you," the director said, "but I didn't want to miss this interrogation. That young man used to be in my Boy Scout troop."

The director flipped a switch so that they could hear what was being said on the other side of the looking glass. The questions began innocently, but did not remain so.

The interrogator asked, "Did you masturbate when you were a teen-ager?"

There was a pause. The emotional seismograph into which the young man was strapped registered an internal earthquake.

"Why . . . er . . . ah . . . yes," the former Boy Scout said.

The interrogator asked immediately, "Do you still masturbate?"

The applicant shot back, "That's none of your business."

The interrogator said, "I'm afraid it is our business."

While the applicant thought over his answer, the needle on the machine acted like the tail of a happy dog.

Finally the young man answered meekly, "Yes."

The interrogator asked, "Did you ever experience fellatio?"

"Yes."

"Did you ever perform cunnilingus?"

"Yes."

Hill and the director listened for about fifteen minutes and then the director switched off the sound.

"The statistics that we get out of that machine are interesting," the director said. "It turns out that here in the agency, 10 percent of the single men habitually masturbate. Among married men the figure goes up to 15 percent."

"I had no idea," Hill said stiffly.

"They now give these tests all over the government," the director said. "It turns out that scientists masturbate even more than we do. They also write more poison-pen letters—you can't trust them. At the State Department, the only sin the machine ferrets out with any frequency is a college flirtation with leftist philosophy."

Hill did not know what to say. He was still thinking of his own interrogation as an applicant. He had left Langley that day feeling like a pervert, and he had been very surprised when he later learned that the agency was still interested in him.

"Well, how is the report coming?" the director asked, while the lie-detector test continued on the other side of the mirror like a silent movie.

"It's coming along," Hill said. "I hope to be able to show you a draft by the end of the week."

"What will it say about the head of our Counterintelligence Department?" the director asked.

Hill gave his boss a verbal review of what would be in the draft report: that John Saxonton had conducted extensive domestic operations against the antiwar movement; that Saxonton had ordered illegal break-ins, wire-tappings, and mail covers; that Saxonton had taken a particular interest in spying on Jane Fonda and Bella Abzug; and that Saxonton's department had intelligence files on 10,000 Americans.

"Probably more," the director said, "but let's leave it at 10,000."

"I've also come up with something else," Hill said, a touch of nervous pride entering his voice. "I have reason to believe that Saxonton penetrated the White House."

"Good God, who?" the director asked.

"Well, I'm told," Hill said, "that his man in the White House was Allen Butterworth."

"Perfect," said the director. In spite of himself, Colgate could not help admiring Mother's audacity in using as a spy the very man who was in charge of the whole White House taping operation. No one would have been in a better position to eavesdrop on the president of the United States. "Brilliant in fact. How did Saxonton recruit him?"

"I don't think he had to," Hill said. "I'm told he was recruited years ago. Evidently he was a young officer in the air force when the agency picked him up, trained him, and then played him back to the air force. But he stayed on the agency's payroll. For years the air force would pay him but he would just send those checks over here and we would cancel them. The agency helped him get ahead in the air force and then one day he ended up in the White House."

"Well, I suppose I shouldn't be surprised," the director said. "After all, Saxonton always said that if you couldn't find out what your own government is up to then you have no business trying to find out what other governments are doing. Because, you know, it's your own government that can really hurt you—cut your budget, even fire you. Still, I used to laugh when Saxonton would say: 'Penetration begins at home.' "

The two men stood quietly for a moment.

Then Hill said, "I know you said not to spare Saxonton, but I was wondering, do you think that connection with Butterworth should go in a report to Congress?"

"No," said the director. "We'll save that one for ourselves. Still, it's good to know. You've done good work."

He did not tell the young intelligence officer that it was always a good idea to have a few secrets with which to blackmail a blackmailer.

"I think some people in the company were more afraid of Nixon than of Brezhnev or Mao," Richard Hill said.

He was having lunch with one of his closest friends in a booth in the Yenching Palace on Connecticut Avenue. The friend worked in the agency's China shop. Other Far East experts were clumped about the restaurant, but there were no Soviet specialists in view. They had their own restaurant. Mother might be right about the Sino-Soviet split being a trick, but not even he could deny the reality of the schism between Chinese and Russian experts inside the agency.

"They had good reason to be," the friend said, "the way Nixon was trying to shake the place up."

When Richard Nixon put James Schlesinger in charge of the agency, he had given him a mandate: Reorganize the CIA so that it would be more responsive to the White House. That meant a house-cleaning. Schlesinger terminated 1,000 of the company's 17,500 employees. Many people at Langley began to regard Schlesinger as a greater menace than the KGB. After all, the other side had never rolled up that many of the agency's people.

"I heard Schlesinger had to hire extra bodyguards," Hill said.

This line of discussion had been precipitated by Hill's disclosure to his friend that Butterworth had been reporting to the agency. The friend's reaction had started out as shock and then worked its way over to amusement. Now they were trying to sort out the implications.

"If some of our boys wanted to get Schlesinger," the friend said, "how much more do you think they would have wanted to get Nixon? I wonder . . ."

"I've been wondering the same thing," Hill said. "Did our people send Butterworth up to testify before the Watergate committee?"

"If they did," the friend said, "that could mean that the agency has just pulled off its first domestic coup. Is that possible?"

"Well, not the agency itself," Hill said, "but some faction within the agency that thought Nixon was not only a threat to the company but a threat to the country."

"I don't believe it," the friend said.

"I don't believe it either," said Hill.

The alarm awakened Director Colgate in the middle of a dream about his daughter. He was always dreaming that she was alive and waking up to find that she wasn't. The dreams scratched at the scar tissue.

While he was still upset, he remembered what he would have to do that morning. It did not make him feel any better. As he was getting dressed, his dead child stared at him from her photograph on top of the bureau. He had to redo his tie several times.

At breakfast, Colgate was joined by his wife and two of his children. Two others had already moved away from home. His effervescent wife, who did not seem to go with such a colorless man, did most of the talking at the table. The director was even quieter than usual. He stared out the window at the residential street, which was quiet also.

Colgate's Springfield, Maryland, address was not nearly so fashionable as the Chevy Chase address where Richard Helms had lived when he was director. Helms's life had revolved around the Chevy Chase Club; Colgate's revolved around a church named Little Flower.

The director could not help associating Mother with Helms. They were both of the same class, the class that had always ruled the agency. They were part of the same gentlemen's club. But now Colgate was president of the club and he was going to get rid of some of the old overstuffed leather chairs.

On his way to work, the director made a brief detour. He stopped, as he often did, to attend an early-morning mass. Kneeling near the back of the church, he carefully rehearsed a scene in his mind: the man from Little Flower having it out with the orchid man.

The drive to Langley took about twenty minutes. The director rode his private elevator up to his suite, sat down behind his desk in the long room, and read through the overnight cable traffic. Later, during his morning staff meeting in the conference room, he lashed out at the deputy director of operations. Then he retired to his office and sent for Mother.

While he waited, the director found himself thinking about the Diem coup. Back then, he had been the company's Far East "dirty tricks" chief, but he had been stationed in Washington, so his victim had been halfway around the world. This time, however, he would have to meet the enemy face to face.

In the elevator, Mother was worried. He felt he did not have enough air, which was partially the result of his smoking so fast in a confined area. Mother had not felt so out of control since the October war when the Egyptians had done what he had been sure they would not do: attack. Perhaps his hatred of the Arabs had caused him to underestimate them. Perhaps his hatred of the director had caused him to make the same mistake all over again. He had wondered if that might not be the case ever since he had gotten an extremely disturbing telephone call the day before. He had slept poorly.

When the elevator door opened, Mother walked down the hall blowing smoke like a car that was about to break down. A long ash fell on his black lapel. He brushed at the gray smudge disgustedly.

It was a brief meeting.

"Have you heard what the *Times* is up to?" the director asked. He had his thumb tucked under his chin as if he were feeling his own pulse to make sure he was alive.

"Yes, a *Times* reporter called me yesterday," Mother said, and then sucked deeply at his cigarette.

"What did he ask you?"

"He accused me of all kinds of things, but I denied it all."

"I'm not sure that's good enough."

Matters had not gone exactly as the director had planned. The *New York Times* had somehow gotten hold of some of the information contained in the director's report. The director had known that that might happen, since congressmen were not famous for keeping secrets. He had hoped that there would not be any leaks, but he had resolved that if there were any, he would use them.

"What do you mean by that?" Mother asked.

"I mean that I must ask for your resignation," the director said. "We will hold up the announcement until after the story comes out."

"But that would be like confirming the story," Mother protested.

"It's for the good of the agency," the director said. "We don't want a prolonged investigation, and this will put an end to it. This is what Nixon should have done after the Watergate break-in. We have to learn from the past."

"But—"

"There's no telling what a prolonged investigation might uncover. They might even find out about Butterworth, and we wouldn't want that, would we? Believe me, it's for the good of the agency."

Sunday night, Mother could not sleep. The story that had appeared in the *New York Times* that day kept pounding in his head. The story had named him as the man responsible for a massive illegal domestic spying operation. Mother, whose successes had all been accomplished in secret, could not bear the thought of his disgrace being acted out in public.

Mother went over and over what he might have said to the reporter to cause the story to come out differently. Should he have cajoled? Should he have threatened? Should he have appealed to the reporter's patriotism? Since Mother had worked all his life hidden from publicity, he had known almost nothing about dealing with the press. He had simply thrown up weak denials, which were as ineffectual as hands raised to ward off an armed attacker.

Mother had plenty of time that night to think back over his long career. It cheered him some to remember the way he had tracked down the KGB's Colonel Rudolf Abel working in an obscure artist's studio in Brooklyn. It cheered him until he reminded himself that he would never again enjoy such a success. Recalling how he had uncovered Georges Pâques, the spy for Russia, who ran the Topaz network in France, also buoyed him up, but then let him down.

He remembered Kim Philby. For years, Philby had fooled him. When the British double agent had been stationed in Washington, the two men had lunched regularly. It briefly amused Mother to recall how he had told Philby, "I'm onto you and your KGB friends." Philby must have been terrified until he learned that Mother said the same thing to almost everyone with whom he lunched. Years later, Mother had partially redeemed himself by providing the British with some of the information they needed to unravel Philby's deceit. As a result, Philby had been forced to flee to Moscow, where he was reportedly despondent. But Mother wondered which of them, the hunter or the hunted, was more unhappy now.

Mother thought a drink might help him sleep. He got up and made himself one. When the sun rose, he was still wide awake but drunk.

At 7:30 A.M., the television cameras showed up on his front lawn. He staggered out to meet them. The TV people gathered around him like coyotes around a dying deer. When the microphones were thrust at him, he was incoherent: "I've sheen no change in the Shoviets . . . police shtate . . . Shoviet bloc . . . fragmentation . . . I had a son in the infantry in Vietnam . . . went from private to corporal."

A reporter asked if his son had been wounded.

"No, I think he'sh okay," Mother said.

Mother's black-rimmed glasses were stumbling down his nose.

For the next several weeks, Mother sank deeper and deeper into depression and even thought of suicide. He felt brittle, like a plant that needed water. He tried to read poetry, but his mind kept wandering. For the first time, he realized how deeply ran the vein of defeat and hopelessness in all his favorite poems. He kept butting his head against lines like T. S. Eliot's:

> *Here I am, an old man in a dry month . . . waiting*
> *for rain.*

After the first few days of almost total numbness, Mother began spending more and more time in his two greenhouses. Since he was retilling the past so much these days, remembering all kinds of things, he remembered the first plants he had raised. The time had been shortly after the war and the flora had been tomatoes. Over the next several years, there had been a slow progression from tomatoes to carnations to roses until, at last, he was overcome by an ambition to grow the perfect flower: an orchid.

And now, a generation after he had planted his first orchid, Mother was developing another ambition: perfect revenge. As he moved about his greenhouses, tending his orchids, a plot took root in his imagination and began to grow. His plan took further shape as he made his pollen crosses, as he sowed powder-fine seed on agar in an Erlenmeyer flask, as he transplanted tiny plants to a community pot, as he moved larger plants to individual pots, as he watched buds form. In all, it took from four to fifteen years for his plants to produce their first blooms. Whether caring for his orchids or developing a double agent or working out strategies for retribution, Mother was a patient man.

Mother sprayed a row of lady's-slipper orchids that he had planted the year John Kennedy entered the White House. They would be bearing their first blooms soon. Moving on, he busied himself culling retrograde hybrids. As he pulled the condemned plants, he amused himself by repeating over and over to himself: "And this is the director" . . . (yank) . . . "and this is the secretary" . . . (yank) . . . "and this is the director." . . .

Mother's taste in orchids had evolved over the years. In the beginning, his favorites had been the gaudier cattleyas, but he had ended up preferring the lady's-slippers, which were more understated and harder to grow. The flower's "slipper" was a large, protruding pouch that looked ugly to some but not to Mother. It was an acquired taste. He wanted his plot to be like the lady's-slipper—complex elements reduced to simple lines.

Once he had a plan, Mother began to feel better. He had been a strategist all his life and he was uncomfortable when he did not have some map for his actions. Now he began to relax and to sleep a little better. Mother was an orderly man who liked to know what was coming. He knew to the week when his orchids would bloom. And now he knew, as certainly as he knew which cattleyas would flower at Easter, that he would have his revenge.

The telephone rang in a suite in the Madison Hotel. The assassin answered it. The hotel operator informed him that it was 7:00 A.M. He thanked her, pulled himself wearily from the bed, and turned on the "CBS Morning News." Lesley Stahl was doing a stand-up in front of the Capitol. She said that the secretary of state and the director of the Central Intelligence Agency were both scheduled to testify before congressional committees that morning. The secretary was to be questioned by the Senate Foreign Relations Committee, the director by the special Senate committee that had been set up to investigate the CIA. While Hughes Rudd reported on further downturnings of more economic indicators, the assassin showered. While Roger Mudd was interviewing a Democrat who wanted to be president, there was a knock at the door. The eggs Benedict had arrived. The killer always liked to eat a good breakfast before going to work.

Dressed in a conservative blue suit, which made him feel uncomfortable, he descended to the hotel garage, where his rented Dodge Dart awaited him. Heading downtown, he turned on WTOP all-news radio. He heard once again that the secretary and the director would be testifying on the Hill. He groaned at the thought of all the TV cameramen, sound men, still photographers, and reporters who would be staking out the Old Senate Office Building that morning. And he winced at a vision of dozens of Secret Service agents running around wearing hearing aids.

When he reached Seventh and F Streets NW, he parked his Dart outside the Hecht Company building. Leaving the car unlocked, he hailed a cab. It dropped him at the Capitol on the Senate side, where he entered, nodding to the policeman at the door, who nodded back. The policeman checked briefcases and packages for weapons, but he did not check people, so the .44 caliber Magnum revolver, carried in a hired killer's belt, went unnoticed.

He took the elevator down to the basement, where he boarded the Capitol Hill subway for the short ride to the Old Senate Office Building. Then he made his way to an unmarked door that he knew led to the senators' underground parking garage. Inside the garage, he pulled a blue chauffeur's cap out of his pocket and put it on his head.

He walked over to a black Fleetwood limousine that belonged to one of the nation's most powerful senators. He happened to know that the senator was out of town. This was not the first time the assassin had seen this car. Several days earlier, armed with a locksmith's tool, he had visited the garage in order to make keys that would unlock and start the senator's limousine. He pulled on a pair of brown leather driving gloves, opened the door, crawled in behind the wheel, turned the ignition, and drove the black car up out of the garage into the daylight.

The man in the blue chauffeur's cap stopped the limousine on Delaware Avenue near the main entrance to the Old Senate Office Building. He kept the motor idling. There was a policeman wearing an orange vest directing traffic about twenty-five feet away, but he paid no attention to the throbbing black car. Through some perversion in the laws of protective coloration, a huge black limousine in front of a white government building is invisible.

It was 9:15. The man in the blue cap watched the white steps and waited. There were television crews camped on the steps and on the sidewalk. They waited and watched, too. It occurred to the killer that he and the TV crews were really in the same business: waiting. The actual time they spent practicing their crafts were infinitesimal compared with the time they spent loitering.

The man in the cap noticed a man in a business suit killing time in the park opposite the Old Senate Building. The wire leading from his ear made him look like a robot—he was definitely Secret Service. If a Secret Service agent was lucky, the assassin thought, he would spend his entire career waiting for some dreaded event that would never happen.

The counterfeit chauffeur turned on the car radio and kept punching buttons until he found WTOP. The State Department had just announced that the secretary of state would once again visit the Middle East. He planned to leave in two days.

The killer reached out and turned off the radio. He eased the .44 Magnum out of his belt. He touched a button and the glass on the passenger side sank out of sight. He saw his target approaching.

A man came up the sidewalk and mounted the marble steps. The assassin raised the revolver. He steadied the hand that held the gun on the edge of the open car window. He remembered shooting rabbits the same way when he was a kid. He would drive very slowly along country roads scanning the brush for cottontails. When he spotted one, he would stop and aim a rifle or a pistol out the car window. Rabbits would run from a man on foot, but they did not know to be afraid of a man in a car. They would just sit there while he knocked them over. Men, especially men who worked in government, were the same way about limousines. They did not expect assassins to arrive in long black Cadillac Fleetwoods.

The chauffeur sighted down the barrel of the .44 Magnum at the back of a long black coat. He squeezed the trigger. When the man pitched forward, his black homburg fell off and started rolling down the white steps.

The television cameramen, who had waited so long for something to photograph, dropped their equipment and ran. The chauffeur fired five more 240-grain slugs into the hunched, twisted back. Then he calmly drove the black car away down the avenue toward Union Station. The television cameramen picked up their cameras and stared through their viewfinders at a tall, crooked black corpse sprawled on the marble steps.

At about the time the chauffeur parked the senator's limousine in front of Hecht's, an ambulance pulled up in front of the Old Senate Office Building. While they loaded the body onto a stretcher, the killer, leaving his hat and gun on the front seat of the Fleetwood, got out of the car and walked into the department store. While the ambulance was speeding toward George Washington University Hospital, the killer left Hecht's, dropped his gloves in a street trash bin, got into the rented Dart, and drove away.

At the hospital, where the bullet-riddled man was pronounced dead on arrival, the police went through his clothing and found in the breast pocket of his suit coat the typed transcript of a taped telephone conversation. The typescript contained the following exchange:

THE SECRETARY OF STATE: Saxonton wants revenge. He's been in touch with that Senate committee that's investigating your agency. He told them he could destroy you.

THE CIA DIRECTOR: He's got to be stopped.

THE SECRETARY: Will you take care of it?

THE DIRECTOR: I will.

That conversation never took place. Mother had faked the transcript, but that would be hard to prove. The media played up the possibility of a conspiracy. In a sense, the story had been leaked by a dead man.

The senator whose limousine had been stolen could be counted on to pursue the targets of that leak vigorously. The appropriation of his car would not only make him mad, but it would also make him anxious to shift suspicion to others before it settled on him or his office. He would trail the putative killers into the highest reaches of our government.

Mother, who had plotted so many murders that looked like suicides, had at last plotted a suicide that looked like a murder.

At the requiem mass, in accordance with a provision in Mother's will, the only flowers allowed were white orchids.

◆　　◆　　◆

When my short story appeared in *New York* magazine—it was my first published fiction—a book editor called and asked if I would be interested in expanding it into a novel. I said I would like to try and went to work.

It was hard work. I soon learned that for me writing fiction is harder than writing journalism. The difficulty with fiction is that it gives you so many choices: Anything can happen. In journalism, only one thing can happen, and that is what actually did happen.

When you are doing journalism and don't know what happens next, you make some phone calls until you find out what did happen. When you don't know what happens next in a novel, you sit and talk it over with yourself until you figure it out. Or go crazy. Whichever comes first.

SEVEN DAYS IN
OCTOBER

• • •

Strangely enough, one of my most vivid memories of this investigative
piece has to do with the copy editing. I remember because it rained and
we were on the top floor of an aging brownstone and the roof leaked.
The copy editors held umbrellas in their left hands and pencils in the
right as they worked their way through the galleys of my story.

On that particular day, the office of *New York* magazine looked like
that wonderful umbrella scene in Alfred Hitchcock's *Foreign Correspondent*. For just a moment, I felt a little like Joel McCrea, the reporter
in the movie, who exposed villains and uncovered a vast conspiracy ...

• • •

New York, April 1974

*Impeachment and conviction of President Richard Nixon became
thinkable on October 20, 1973. On that day the president fired Archibald Cox, the special prosecutor, which led to the chain-reaction resignations of Elliot Richardson, the attorney general, and William
Ruckelshaus, the deputy attorney general. When Americans learned of
the "Saturday Night Massacre," they were badly shaken. Mail flooded
the capital demanding impeachment. The denouement of Nixon's presidency began with a seven-day struggle in October.*

◆

Attorney General Elliot Richardson was hungry. He owed his appetite, in part, to one of the most crucial press conferences of his career. He had gone before the television cameras to defend his handling of the investigation of Spiro Agnew, who, the day before, had resigned the vice-presidency and copped a plea in a Baltimore courtroom. For an hour, Richardson had fielded reporters' questions fairly well. By the time it was over, he was ready for a good lunch. He invited two of his closest aides to join him at one of his favorite restaurants, the Jean-Pierre. The three men from Justice sat down to their meal with a certain sense of relief. It was all over now. They could relax.

And yet Elliot Richardson was not altogether at ease. He knew that there would be more problems to come. When he glanced up, he noticed a painting of a Spanish *corrida* hanging on the wall. The picture seemed to fascinate him. He identified with the bullfighter.

"The trouble with being a matador," Richardson told his aides, "is that you have to face a new bull every Sunday."

The two men at the table with Richardson had been in the same ring with him for several years, moving with him as he held three cabinet jobs in succession, first serving as secretary of health, education, and welfare, then as secretary of defense, and now as the attorney general. One of the aides was J. T. Smith II, thirty, an alumnus of Yale College, Yale Law School, and the CIA, where he was a programs analyst; his patterns of speech and thought were as precise as the parallel lines in his pinstripe suit. The other aide was Richard Darman, also thirty, an alumnus of Harvard College and the Harvard Business School; he still looked somewhat collegiate and was one of the most articulate men in government. Smith and Darman not only liked working for Richardson, they liked working with each other. They had become best friends.

Appropriately, there was an empty chair at the table, for the third member of Richardson's palace guard had not been able to attend the lunch. He was Jonathan Moore, forty-one, an alumnus of the failed presidential campaigns of Nelson Rockefeller and George Romney; he bounced from scholarly repose to childlike animation and wore bow ties, like Cox. Around town, Smith, Darman, and Moore had earned the nickname, "Richardson's Mafia."

When the waiter appeared, the attorney general ordered quiche, mussels, salad, white wine, Brie, and espresso.*

* This is what it is like to be the aide of a "great man": In separate interviews, I asked Richardson's two aides what he had ordered. They recalled his meal in great detail. Then I asked what they had eaten. Neither could remember.

Returning to his metaphor, Richardson said that one attempted to concentrate on the bull of the moment but that one could not get complete satisfaction from having performed well because one was always conscious of the next bull and the next Sunday.

The three men from Justice sipped their espresso, happily oblivious of the precision of the implied prophecy. For it would be precisely the following Sunday that the next bull would come charging at them. The fatal *corrida* would be in large part the work of General Alexander Haig, who was himself as skilled as any matador when it came to manipulating the capes of deception. In the days that followed, Haig would lead Richardson to charge head-on into one phony crisis after another until the attorney general was worn out. Then the president and his general would spring the real crisis.

Sunday, October 14. Just four days after Spiro Agnew pleaded nolo contendere, Alexander Haig telephoned Elliot Richardson at his home in McLean, Virginia. Haig told Richardson that he would like to see him the next morning at the White House. The president's general implied that the president would like Richardson's help in solving the Middle East crisis.

All week, the White House would skillfully wave the Middle East war in front of Richardson to distract him from the crisis building over Nixon's tapes, which Cox had subpoenaed and which the Court of Appeals had ordered turned over to Judge John Sirica by October 19. It was typical of the men around Nixon that they trusted no one, not even their supposed friends, not even their own attorney general.

Elliot Richardson agreed to be at the White House the next morning at nine.

Monday, October 15. The attorney general went to the White House alone. All week he would go to the president's home alone. He had been requested to do so. General Haig, a talented tactician, knew the value of outnumbering and ouflanking the other side.

Richardson met not only with Haig but with Fred Buzhardt, who was then the president's chief Watergate lawyer. The conversation began with a Middle Eastern gambit. Haig said that the president feared that the Russians might be about to intervene in the so-called Yom Kippur War, which had been raging in the Middle East for a week with no end in sight. The general went on about the war for ten or fifteen minutes.

Richardson was flattered that the White House would turn to him for help with so serious a matter as the conflagration in the Middle East. And he was a man who enjoyed flattery. He often compared himself to an inflatable swimming-pool toy that had a slow leak—every so often he needed someone to come along and blow him up again. When Haig hinted that Richardson was to play a crucial role in restoring peace in the Holy Land, the attorney general almost swelled with pride.

Richardson said, "I'm ready. I'll go home and pack my bags. Where do you want me to go?"

Haig said. "Now, wait a minute. That's not exactly what I had in mind."

The attorney general could feel himself deflate. He soon perceived that the White House wanted him to deal not with Anwar Sadat, but with Cox, who was virtually painted as the man who had paved the way for the war by weakening the U.S. president.

Alexander Haig presented the attorney general with a bold initiative. Richardson later recalled the plan as follows: "The president would himself prepare an authenticated version of the nine subpoenaed tapes for presentation to the District Court [and] the president would fire Special Prosecutor Cox—as a way of mooting the case." This new offensive was to be the Watergate equivalent of the drive into Cambodia during the Southeast Asian war. The president was ready to attack.

Startled, Richardson said that such a course would be disastrous. The conversation turned to alternatives to the president's proposal. They discussed appealing the tapes case to the Supreme Court or finding a third party to review the presidential recordings. Richardson argued in favor of a third-party review.

Richardson told Haig that the bottom line was this: If the president went ahead with his plan to issue his own expurgated version of the tapes and to fire the special prosecutor, then he would resign as attorney general.*

When Richardson returned to the Justice Department, he asked to see Deputy Attorney General William Ruckelshaus, a tall, broad-shouldered man who almost dwarfed his superior at Justice. Where Rich-

---

* Before Richardson was sworn in as attorney general, he had promised the Senate Judiciary Committee he would abide by the following rules: "The attorney general will not countermand or interfere with the special prosecutor's decisions or actions. The special prosecutor will determine whether and to what extent he will inform or consult with the attorney general about the conduct of his duties and responsibilities. The special prosecutor will not be removed from his duties except for extraordinary improprieties on his part."

ardson's speech was often careful to the point of anemia, Ruckelshaus had a booming voice and outgoing personal style. One immediately respected Richardson but one immediately liked Ruckelshaus. Ruckelshaus's fourth-floor suite of offices was directly underneath Richardson's fifth-floor suite. The deputy attorney general rode up in a private elevator that connected the two offices.

The attorney general said, "We've got a real problem. It may be even worse than the vice-president."

The deputy attorney general said, "Good Lord, how could that be?"

In retrospect, it is unclear whether Haig's Monday morning proposal was genuine or whether it was just another cape waved in front of the attorney general to provoke a misdirected charge. Perhaps it was put on the table only to make any subsequent compromise seem welcome by comparison. Perhaps Alexander Haig learned this technique from Henry Kissinger during the Vietnam negotiations, for Kissinger was reportedly a master at offering disaster in the morning and compromise in the afternoon. It may well have been that these negotiating tools, which had been used to squeeze the North Vietnamese, were now being applied to the attorney general of the United States.

At 12:10 P.M., General Haig called Richardson to say that he would try to persuade the president to go along with a third-party review of the tapes. Haig proposed as the third party Senator John Stennis, who had recently advised the president to "tough it out."

Richardson endorsed the idea. If the morning proposition had been intended to set Richardson up for the afternoon proposition, then it worked well.

At 1:15, General Haig called back to say that he had been in to see the president. Haig made it sound as though he had been through the Oval Office equivalent of hand-to-hand combat. In the end, Haig said, he had convinced the president that he should allow John Stennis to review the tapes.

But it was not quite that simple. In return for going along with the "Stennis plan," the president wanted certain clear-cut understandings. The president stipulated that Cox must agree that "this was it." Moreover, the president wanted Richardson to promise in advance to fire the special prosecutor if he would not go along with the "compromise." The attorney general had until 2:30 to think it over.

Richardson called J. T. Smith and Jonathan Moore into his office. For the first time, he told his aides about the new bull that had entered their ring. He wanted their reaction.

While Richardson led a discussion of how to cope with the biggest crisis of his career, he doodled. He had done so for many years, turning out thousands of abstract ink sketches, some austere and modern, others as ornate as a baroque garden. One of his best doodles was a scowling portrait of Nixon.

Richardson called Haig back at 2:55, twenty-five minutes late, but the general could not take the call. Haig returned Richardson's call at 3:20 P.M. The attorney general told the White House chief of staff that he supported the idea of the Stennis review but that he would not agree to fire Cox if he resisted the compromise. Haig backed down on his insistence that Richardson promise to sack Cox. The general said he would make overtures to Stennis.

So far, Senator John Stennis had never heard of the "Stennis compromise." Haig and Buzhardt made an appointment to see him.

Haig and Buzhardt asked Stennis if he would do the president of the United States a favor. They went on to explain that the White House would like him to listen to some of the president's tapes and verify a transcript. They did not tell the senator that the transcripts he would verify would be presented to the court in lieu of the subpoenaed tapes. Nor did they suggest that the proposed Stennis transcript might be used as a lever to pry Archibald Cox out of office.

Stennis said that he would like to sleep on the proposal. He reminded Haig, however, that he was not in the best of health. The senator had not fully recovered his strength after being shot by a mugger who attacked him in front of his home. Stennis said that he did not feel that he could possibly undertake the task by himself. If he took on the assignment, he wanted someone to help him. The senator said that he would accept Fred Buzhardt as his assistant.

There must have been rejoicing at 1600 Pennsylvania Avenue.

Shortly after 4:00 P.M., Richardson returned to the White House to talk to Haig and Buzhardt. The attorney general agreed to meet with Cox as soon as possible and try to sell him what the White House called the "Stennis authentication proposal." (Around the attorney general's office the plan was referred to as the "Gospel According to St. John.") No one mentioned anything about any presidential proclamation that *this was it.*

Haig and Buzhardt went on to fill Richardson in on past negotiations with Cox to which the attorney general had not been a party. Richardson says: "I was given the impression that Cox had virtually agreed at an earlier stage to having a third party verify the tapes. It turned out later that that wasn't exactly the way it worked. They were going to use former Solicitor General James Lee Rankin as a kind of neutral arbiter with respect to claims of executive privilege or national security." It was either more confusion or more deception.

At 6:00 P.M., Elliot Richardson met with Archibald Cox in the attorney general's office at the Justice Department. Richardson undertook to sell the White House proposal of a Stennis review to the special prosecutor. Cox remembers sitting with his "antennae quivering" trying to read Richardson's signals.

One message was coming through loud and clear. Cox could see that the attorney general was in a hurry. He was expected at the White House that evening for dinner. While Richardson proceeded with his exposition of the Stennis proposal, he walked about his office getting dressed. Unlike Jerry Ford, who, according to Lyndon Johnson, could not chew gum and walk at the same time, Elliot Richardson could negotiate and knot his black tie at the same time.

By about 7:30 P.M., Richardson was shaking hands with the president at a White House dinner given to say good-bye to outgoing Secretary of State William Rogers. The occasion caused Nixon and Richardson to miss Spiro Agnew's pathetic denouement on national television, in which he protested what he called the unfairness of his "nightmare come true." Richardson, whose nightmare was just beginning, was surprised to be invited to the White House that evening. The attorney general suspected that Rogers himself had made up the guest list, for he could imagine no other reason for his inclusion. This was the first time that Richardson had been asked to the White House socially since he had taken over at the Justice Department. He had felt ostracized.

Tuesday, October 16. At 10:00 A.M., Elliot Richardson met with Archibald Cox, who said that it would be helpful to see the proposed Stennis plan in writing. After the meeting, Cox left Richardson's office and the two men did not see each other again until it was all over. Nor did Richardson meet face to face with several other important players who were eventually brought into the drama—Stennis, Ervin, Baker. They remained apart because the White House claimed to be afraid that the press would become suspicious if people started getting together. This White House insistence on absolute secrecy may have been yet another ploy, for if all the key figures in the supposed deal could have ever come together in the same room, they might have been able to piece together what the president and his men were up to.

At about 11:00 A.M., Richardson was driven across the Potomac to

National Airport, passing near the Pentagon, where a few months earlier he had led a relatively peaceful life as the head of the nation's war machine. The attorney general boarded American Airlines flight 358 to New York City, where he was to dedicate the new police headquarters and to see a parade.

In his speech to the policemen who were gathered for the opening ceremonies, Elliot Richardson, who always sprinkles his speeches with quotations, quoted from Gilbert and Sullivan's operetta *The Pirates of Penzance:*

> When constabulary duty's to be done,
> A policeman's lot is not a happy one.

Richardson, the country's chief law enforcement officer, realized that his lot was anything but happy and likely to get worse.

At 4:00 P.M., the attorney general boarded a police helicopter, which flew him to La Guardia Airport, where he boarded American Airlines flight 632. The visit to New York City had been a pleasant interlude, but once Richardson was seated in the plane's first-class compartment he could escape his "duty" no longer. During the flight back to troubled Washington, he opened his briefcase and labored over a draft of the proposal that he planned to submit to Cox. It began:

> The objective of this proposal is to provide a means of furnishing to the Court and the Grand Jury a complete and accurate record of the content of the tapes subpoenaed by the Special Prosecutor. . . .

As usual, the words came very slowly. Richardson wrote the way he dressed, very deliberately, very precisely, very conservatively, very formally, and a little dully.

The plane landed in Washington at about 5:30 P.M. and Richardson returned to this office during rush hour. He continued to struggle with his writing assignment on into the evening. When Richardson finally went home, the proposal remained unfinished.

Wednesday, October 17. Returning to the office early, the attorney general attacked his composition once again. When the proposal was completed shortly before lunch, it was only about two pages long.

Shortly after noon, Richardson was visited by Fred Buzhardt. The two men had known each other for some time. When Richardson had been secretary of defense, Buzhardt had been the Defense Department's general counsel. Back then a former presidential adviser had praised Buzhardt to Richardson in these terms: "If you ever need the dirtiest deed done without a trace, Fred's your man. He can bury a body six feet under without turning a shovelful of dirt." Now Buzhardt had come to read Richardson's proposal to Cox. He took it back to the White House with him because he wanted to show it to someone.

At 1:00 P.M., the attorney general went over to the State Department to have lunch with Secretary of State Henry Kissinger. They talked mostly about the Middle East, but they also touched on Watergate. While they were eating, Kissinger was interrupted by a call that he had to take. It was from the president of the United States.

Returning to the table, Kissinger said something like, "The president really does want to get rid of Cox. He started talking about it in the middle of our talk about the Middle East just now."

When the attorney general got back to the Justice Department, he told a Catholic assistant, "If you ever lighted candles, now is the time to do it."

At about 3:30 P.M., Buzhardt showed up at the Justice Department again. He suggested several changes in the proposal Richardson planned to submit to Cox. Richardson says, "I gathered that he had shown my draft to the president and that the revisions reflected his conversation with the president." Buzhardt wanted to cut entirely a section called "Other Tapes and Documents," which promised that the compromise would "cover only the tapes heretofore subpoenaed." The president's lawyer attempted to make his objection seem merely stylistic. Playing the English teacher, Buzhardt said that on its face the proposal dealt only with the nine subpoenaed tapes and that to spell it out in so many words was redundant. In retrospect, it seems clear that what bothered Buzhardt was not the redundancy. The habit of being devious came as naturally to the White House as doodling did to Richardson.

Late in the afternoon, Richardson dispatched the proposal to Cox and then called him for his reaction.

Cox said, "I think that I should respond to you in writing, because it would be more careful that way."

Once again, Richardson was in a hurry and once again Cox read the message clearly, but this time it had nothing to do with getting to the White House on time. Rather, it was now the White House itself that was running out of time since it only had until Friday midnight to turn over the tapes or appeal to the Supreme Court. Haig had told Richardson that the negotiations with Cox had to be concluded by the close of business on Thursday. Richardson says, "I tried to convey to Cox the sense of time pressure being communicated to me. I didn't want to do so starkly, because I didn't want him to feel that he was being delivered an ultimatum."

Cox thought the White House was making too much out of the Friday midnight deadline. After all, it could have simply asked Cox to agree to an extension of the deadline, a request it would have been hard for him to turn down. Instead, the White House seemed to want a High Noon.

Cox thought he knew what the White House might be up to, for, as he says, "I had already figured out for myself that, if I were the president and I were going to disobey a court decision, I would not take it to the Supreme Court. So it wasn't any great surprise to me that the showdown came at that stage."

That evening, Elliot Richardson gave an informal dinner in his home for William Ruckelshaus. The occasion for the dinner was a celebration of the rather tardy confirmation of Ruckelshaus as deputy attorney general. The man they toasted would remain in that high office for three more days.

The guests included David Broder, the *Washington Post*'s respected political writer, and his wife; Robert Bork, the solicitor general, who would later follow orders; and several politicians.

After dinner, Elliot Richardson turned philosophical and led a deep introspective discussion about government and morality. Richardson and Ruckelshaus both had some idea what lay ahead, but none of the others had any idea what lay behind all the soul-searching. The conversation went on and on and got deeper and deeper.

In the car on the way home, Broder turned to his wife and asked, "What the hell was going on back there?"

Thursday, October 18. At 9:50 A.M., Elliot Richardson telephoned United States Attorney George Beall—the leader of the Baltimore prosecution team who eight days earlier had destroyed a vice-president—to clear up a few loose ends pertaining to the Agnew investigation.

Beall said, "We are breathing a sigh of relief. I hope you have had a chance to unwind, too."

Richardson said, "No, we have another gigantic problem."

Meanwhile, William Ruckelshaus flew to Grand Rapids, Michigan, where, as a favor to Gerald Ford, he spoke to a Dutch organization.

Back at Justice, Cox's written response to the proposed compromise was delivered to the attorney general during the afternoon. In his comments, Cox never mentioned Stennis by name, and yet the senator had been very much on his mind as he wrote. Cox says, "The Stennis proposal was a damned ingenious thing. Senator Stennis is a demigod in Washington, particularly in any respect that involves personal integrity. On the other hand, in terms of anything that you would think of as Cox's natural constituency around the country, his reputation is certainly different. So it somewhat put me in a position where, if I bought it, I was dead with my natural constituency, whereas, if I rejected it, I was dead with a lot of people in Washington. Of this I was very aware. My responses were influenced by not wanting to get in a position of either buying or rejecting Senator Stennis, as such."

In his comments, Cox attempted to get around the Stennis matter by saying simply: "The public cannot be fairly asked to confide so difficult and responsible a task to any *one* man operating in secrecy, consulting only with the White House." Cox then went on to suggest that they explore the idea of asking the court to name a panel of "Special Masters" to verify a transcript of the relevant portions of the tapes. Taking care to leave the door open for further negotiations, Cox wrote, "I am glad to sit down with anyone in order to work out a solution if we can."

At 6:00 P.M., Elliot Richardson carried the special prosecutor's comments over to the White House, where this time he found himself not just outnumbered but completely surrounded. The attorney general was met not only by Haig and Buzhardt, but also by presidential lawyers Charles Alan Wright and Leonard Garment.

Richardson showed the president's men the comments, which Cox had written out. The White House team ignored Cox's suggestion of impaneling "Special Masters" and chose to see his comments as tantamount to a rejection of a compromise. Haig, Buzhardt, Garment, and Wright said that Cox should be fired. The only man opposed was Elliot Richardson.

The attorney general sank deeper and deeper into a depression. The White House team suggested that the Watergate Investigation be turned over to Richardson and Henry Petersen. Richardson protested that the public would not believe such an investigation.

Charles Alan Wright argued vigorously in support of executive privilege. He said that the president's offer to go along with the Stennis compromise was exceptionally generous.

Richardson said, "Charlie, you are very convincing. Why don't you talk to Archie? I've done all I can."

Wright agreed to try to persuade Cox. The president's lawyer said that he would call and try to arrange a face-to-face meeting with Cox. If Wright failed to persuade Cox, however, Richardson was told, Cox would be fired.

Richardson left the White House feeling the way Howard Hunt must have felt directly after the Bay of Pigs.

Charles Alan Wright was disappointed. The lawyer had been out of town all week, back home in Texas, working in seclusion on what he fully expected to be the greatest case he would ever argue before the Supreme Court. When he returned to the White House on Thursday, he was dismayed to learn that, in his absence, a plot had been hatched that would deny him his historic appearance before the high court. He found himself in the position of the star whose show is suddenly and unexpectedly closed out of town. Therefore, when Wright picked up the telephone to call Cox, he may have been suffering, in the words of one of Richardson's aides, from "a dangerous and tragic conceit."

But when the phone rang in Cox's office, the special prosecutor wasn't there.

At about 6:30 P.M., Cox had had to break off a conference in his office because he had an engagement. Normally, he made a point of not telling his office of any evening plans, but this time he felt he should offer some explanation for his rather abrupt departure.

Cox remarked quite casually to his deputy, Henry Ruth, "I guess I've got to go now. I've got to go to my brother's house for dinner."

Cox and his wife went to his brother Louis's home in McLean, Virginia, where they sat around a crowded dinner table. His brother had five children. In the middle of dinner, the telephone rang. It was Henry Ruth calling with a message for Cox: The special prosecutor was to call "Marshal Wright" at the White House. Perhaps his office had simply taken down the message wrong: On the other hand, perhaps Wright had been around the White House so long that he had been infected by the secret-agent atmosphere: Perhaps he was using phony names like a minor-league Tony Ulasewicz, alias Mr. Rivers. Sitting on the floor in the hall where the telephone was located, Cox called the White House and asked for "Marshal Wright." The White House operator rang an extension and a familiar voice answered.

Cox said, "Oh, it's you, Charlie."

Over the excited chatter of his nieces and nephews, Uncle Archie heard Charles Wright say, "Here are some conditions you can't accept."

The president's lawyer told the special prosecutor, in essence, that the tapes would be verified by only one man and that Cox would have to promise not to subpoena any more White House tapes, papers, or documents. Wright made no attempt to arrange a face-to-face meeting.

Cox remembers telling Wright, "The way it sounds to me, what you are insisting on is out of the question, but why don't you put it in writing."

The whole conversation—carried out with children clamoring in the background—had the air of a confrontation between an Allen Drury novel and "Sesame Street."

While Archibald Cox was eating dinner at his brother's house, Elliot Richardson was at home on Crest Lane laboriously composing a document that he titled "Why I Must Resign." Working over a yellow legal pad—the kind the president himself used when he had something important to write—Richardson wrote:

> I do not believe the president's attitude toward Cox's role is fundamentally valid: Many problems and headaches could have been avoided by cooperating with him more and fighting him less. . . . I cannot stay if he goes.

Richardson wrote as slowly and painfully as if he were carving his "reasons" in stone.

Friday, October 19. The Justice Department is a fairly lazy institution. It does not really begin to percolate until considerably past 9:00 A.M.—well after such departments as Defense and Health, Education, and Welfare have come to an energetic boil. On Friday morning, Richardson and his closest aides met at 8:00 A.M. At that hour, the halls of Justice were as quiet as a Sunday morning in Georgetown.

Richardson led his dawn patrol into the attorney general's inner office. The aides were Smith, Darman, and Moore. They had often met like this during the worst days of the Agnew crisis, but they sensed that this meeting would be even more serious. It was one thing to contemplate someone else's "execution"; it was another thing to contemplate your own.

The attorney general briefed his aides on what had happened at the White House the evening before. Then he took out of his pocket the reasons why he felt he had to resign and read them to his aides. The empty building felt even emptier than before.

Richardson asked a secretary to type up his reasons for resignation. He then passed out carbon copies of his reasons to his aides. It was an unhappy ritual.

At 9:15 A.M., as the Justice Department was just coming to life,

Richardson called Haig to see if Wright had made any headway with Cox. Haig said that the negotiations were continuing. Richardson said that if the negotiations reached an impasse, he would like to see the president as soon as possible. The request for an audience was a veiled threat to resign.

A messenger arrived at the special prosecutor's office that morning sometime after nine bearing a letter from Charles Alan Wright to Archibald Cox. The letter's scolding tone might have been more appropriate had Wright been addressing one of Cox's nieces or nephews. Rather than spelling out "conditions" for a compromise, Wright seemed to put an end to negotiations. The letter, which began "Dear Mr. Cox," called the Stennis plan a "very reasonable proposal" and went on to say:

> [Some of] your comments depart so far from that proposal and the purpose for which it was made that we could not accede to them in any form. If you think that there is any purpose in our talking further, my associates and I stand ready to do so. If not, we will have to follow the course of action that we think is in the best interest of the country.

Wright's letter to Cox arrived as Cox was drafting a letter to Wright. Cox's letter was primarily addressed to the points Wright had raised over the telephone the night before. Beginning "Dear Charlie," Cox went on to say that he could not accept the requirement that "I must categorically agree not to subpoena any other White House tape, paper, or document."

Cox dispatched his letter to Wright and then left his office to keep a 10:00 A.M. appointment in Judge John Sirica's court. When he arrived, the courtroom was jammed. The crowd had come to hear the following exchange:

JUDGE SIRICA: How do you plead?

JOHN DEAN: I plead guilty.

When the White House received the special prosecutor's letter, the president's men chose to interpret it as an outright rejection. At 9:55, Alexander Haig called Elliot Richardson and told him that a stalemate had been reached. Richardson reasserted his desire to see the president and was told to come to the White House as soon as possible. The attorney general folded the freshly typed reasons "Why I Must Resign" and put them in his pocket.

As Richardson was leaving his office, he told his aides, "Until this moment, I haven't been nervous. Now I am."

The aides could think of nothing to say. They all shook hands. The attorney general stepped into his private elevator and started down. The aides who were left behind sat around on couches in the attorney general's suite like anxious relatives gathered in a hospital waiting room. They thought the end had come.

When Richardson arrived at Haig's office at just after 10:00 A.M., a startling development awaited him.

The president's general told him, "Maybe we don't have to go down the road we talked about last night. Suppose we go ahead with the Stennis plan without firing Cox."

Perhaps the White House was using Vietnam negotiating tactics once again, offering disaster in the evening in order to offer compromise the next morning. The attorney general, who had come to the White House to resign his office, suddenly found that he might not have to quit, after all. Richardson had once again charged an empty cape.

The attorney general was disoriented. Wright, Buzhardt, and Garment dropped by Haig's office. Not only was Richardson off balance, he was once again outnumbered. Haig went in to see the president. His stated mission was to persuade Nixon not to fire Cox.

The attorney general and the three presidential lawyers discussed where they should go from here. During these deliberations, Richardson was handed a copy of Cox's "Dear Charlie" letter. Reading it, Richardson thought Cox was confused about something, for Richardson could not understand why Cox was objecting to a requirement that he agree not to subpoena any other White House material. The attorney general pointed out that *he* had never asked Cox to make such a promise. Richardson urged that a new letter be written to Cox setting the record straight. The White House team agreed.

(Charles Alan Wright did not bother to tell Elliot Richardson that when he had called Cox the night before he had attempted to saddle the special prosecutor with a promise to subpoena no more White House evidence.)

General Haig returned and announced that the president had agreed not to fire Cox. Richardson says that he thought he had won a significant victory and made the mistake of savoring that victory rather than attending closely to the rest of the deliberations.

They went on to discuss ways of preventing or containing future court battles over presidential tapes and documents. In this context, one of the bulls Richardson thought he had already killed was suddenly revived: The old idea of ordering Cox to seek no more White House material was once again put on the table. It is unclear just who reintroduced this concept. Richardson was asked what he thought Cox's reaction to such a limitation would be. The attorney general said that he thought the special prosecutor would resign.

All through the meeting, Richardson was at a disadvantage. He was trying to recover from the shock of not being out of a job. He liked his decision-making processes to be as orderly as his wardrobe, but the White House's sudden change of direction had left him mentally disheveled. He was in no condition to make any final decision, and so far as he was concerned, no final decisions were made. The meeting broke up and Richardson returned to Justice, where he hoped to button down his thoughts.

Elliot Richardson emerged from his private elevator shortly after 11:00 A.M. to find his aides holding what amounted to a wake. They summoned their reserves to face the inevitable bad news. Richardson wore an expression that seemed to say that they would never guess what had happened. He explained that he had lived to fight another day. As it turned out, exactly one more day.

Instead of cleaning out their desks, Richardson and his aides began another marathon meeting. The attorney general doodled as he led a discussion of what to do next. Near his desk stood a wastepaper basket with a miniature basketball goal attached. Five months earlier, when Richardson's confirmation hearings had hit a snag, he had crumpled dozens of his doodles into paper balls and fired them at that basket. Back then the problem had been that he wanted final authority to fire the special prosecutor, but the Senate Judiciary Committee did not want to give it to him. Richardson had been unwilling to compromise on this point; he had told his aides that, if he did not get his way, he would just go fishing; he did not have to be attorney general. At the height of the tension over whether the attorney general designate would resign before he was even confirmed, Richardson had hit four baskets in a row and had jumped into the air shouting, *"That's a record!"* Almost half a year later, the final authority that Richardson had held out for was coming home to roost. His fate had been inextricably tied to Cox's. Richardson was once again on the verge of resignation, and he was once again shooting baskets. While he debated his future with his staff, he crumpled his doodles and sent them arching through the air, but this time he set no records.

During the meeting, Haig called Richardson. The general in the White House reported that Senator Stennis was enthusiastic about going ahead—even without Cox. (Stennis would later dispute this.) General Haig said that the White House had also been in touch with Senators Howard Baker and Sam Ervin, which had not been easy. Evidently Nixon had concluded that he needed another lever to use on Cox and had decided to try to sell the "Stennis compromise" to the Watergate committee. So a harried and desperate White House tried to contact Senators Baker and Ervin, only to find that both men were out of town lecturing on Watergate. The president's men eventually located Baker at a symposium in Chicago and Ervin at the New Orleans airport. Both senators agreed to rush to Washington to meet with the president.

Over the phone, General Haig told Richardson that Senator Baker had agreed to the deal. Evidently Haig was too wily a general to attempt to take the committee by a frontal assault. Instead, he moved to win over Baker before making his pitch to Ervin. Perhaps Haig saw Baker as the committee's weaker flank. Or perhaps Baker—as some have suggested—had been serving as a fifth column inside the committee all along.

After the Haig phone call, Richardson and his aides decided to continue their discussions over lunch. Richardson, Moore, Smith, and Darman adjourned to the attorney general's dining room, which opened off his office. The wallpaper was a floral print that was as loud as the woman who had picked it out, Martha Mitchell. Over the flowers were hung Richardson's eighteenth- and nineteenth-century prints of Boston.

Meanwhile, William Ruckelshaus was on his way in from the airport with a lot on his mind. The night before he had called Jonathan Moore from Grand Rapids and learned that Richardson might possibly be on the brink of resignation. Ruckelshaus had caught a plane bound for Washington that morning. As he bore down on the Justice Department, he was worried. He was afraid that Richardson might already have quit. Ruckelshaus thought that *he* might already be the acting attorney general and not know it.

When he finally arrived at the Justice Department, Ruckelshaus found Richardson still on the job. The deputy attorney general joined the lunch in progress in the attorney general's suite.

During the luncheon discussion, Elliot Richardson came to the conclusion that he could not live with a presidential order to Cox to seek no further White House material.

At 2:25, Richardson called Haig. He tried to state his objections in terms of what was good for the president, arguing that the White House was in danger of undermining its own case. Richardson said that the "Stennis compromise" was reasonable, but that placing limitations on

Cox was unacceptable. Richardson said that an attempt to couple the two would make the unacceptable idea doom the reasonable one.

Haig said this argument seemed reasonable, never hinting that the White House had already set its course and was forging ahead on its own.

Richardson spent much of the afternoon on the telephone. When he was not on the phone to the White House, he was on the wire to public servants all over the government. His behavior reminded one of his aides of the way his wife had acted the day before she went to the hospital to go into labor. The attorney general seemed to be housecleaning as though he knew he was going to be away for a while.

At the White House, they were tidying up, too, brushing old promises under the rug.

Wright got busy and wrote the letter to Cox that he had promised Richardson he would write, this time beginning "Dear Archie." Referring to the prohibition on Cox, the president's lawyer wrote, "I had in mind only . . . private presidential papers and meetings, a category that I regard as much, much smaller than the great mass of White House documents with which the president has not personally been involved." Wright had agreed to write a letter and he had written it, but he had hardly changed his position. In fact, Wright closed his letter by asserting, "The differences between us remain so great that no purpose would be served by further discussion. . . ."

When Senator Sam Ervin arrived in Washington, he was hurried to the White House, where he was met by Haig, Wright, and Senator Baker. Evidently Baker did not tell Ervin that he had already agreed to go along with the White House deal.

They all went in to see the president. It was a particularly auspicious time to offer a deal to the Watergate committee, for two days earlier the committee had lost its court battle to obtain White House tapes. Therefore, the president's offer of evidence authenticated by Senator Stennis seemed attractive, especially when compared with being shut out altogether. When Ervin tried to ask about Cox, Nixon changed the subject.

The meeting in the Oval Office lasted forty minutes. At the end of it, Senators Ervin and Baker agreed to recommend the Stennis authentication plan to the Watergate committee. As it later developed, however, there was some confusion about what had been agreed to. Senator Ervin would say that he had been promised verbatim transcripts of relevant conversations. The White House would say that it planned to issue only third-person summaries. A lot of important people got confused that week. Either all of this simultaneous confusion was a coincidence, or else it was a part of the White House game plan. The president and his men seemed to specialize in the screen pass.

That afternoon, General Haig called Richardson and told him that the responsible leadership in the Senate on both sides of the aisle were not only in favor of the "Stennis compromise" but also in favor of the prohibition on Cox. That was a considerable exaggeration.

Haig went on to say, "This will help you with your constituency, Elliot."

The attorney general asked what constituency.

Haig said, "Republicans."

The general's arguments notwithstanding, Elliot Richardson continued to object to limiting Cox.

At 7:00 P.M., General Haig called Richardson to read him a letter. It was from the president and it was addressed to the attorney general. Haig said that the letter had already been dispatched by messenger and that he was only reading from a carbon, the implication being that the letter was final and not a draft that could be negotiated.

The president's letter said: "I am instructing you to direct Special Prosecutor Archibald Cox . . . that he is to make no further attempts by judicial process to obtain tapes, notes, or memoranda of presidential conversations. I regret the necessity of intruding, to this very limited extent, on the independence that I promised you with regard to Watergate when I announced your appointment."

When Haig had finished reading, Richardson said with understated fury, "Al, given the history of our relationship on this, I would have thought that you would have consulted me prior to sending any letter."

The attorney general's aides, who overheard his end of the conversation, knew right away that something was seriously wrong, because, for Richardson, this was strong language.

Richardson went on to say that, indeed, he had thought that there was to have been further discussion involving him before any action was taken. He said that he did not understand how such a letter could have been written given his objections.

General Haig said that he had twice carried Richardson's objections into the Oval Office but that the president had rebuffed him.

Richardson said, "I never understood that there was to be any order to me."

About 7:20 the president's letter was delivered by messenger. Richardson was furious.

Archibald Cox had spent most of his day waiting. As the hours went by, he even grew a little impatient for the showdown. He had expected the courtesy of a reply to his letter, but it had not come. All day long, the White House had been announcing an important press briefing, but at each announcement the time of the briefing was set later, at, say, 3:00 P.M., then 4:00 P.M., then 5:00 P.M. . . . By 6:30 P.M., Cox decided, in his words, "The hell with this," and went home. He had not much more than walked through the door when the phone rang. It was Elliot Richardson.

The attorney general said, "I have a letter. I am going to read it to you. It is for your information. . . ." Richardson was clearly signaling that he was not issuing the order, just bringing Cox up to date.

That evening, the attorney general was once again confused. He once again channeled his energy into charging the wrong cape. And for once, the slowness of his writing was a real liability, costing him precious reaction time. The confusion was over whether the president's letter to Richardson ordering him to place limitations on Cox was to be made public. Richardson thought that he had understood from the White House that it was to be. He therefore began composing a press release that he planned to issue in answer to the president's letter. Richardson agonized over the release for two vital hours.

While the attorney general was pinned down at his writing desk, the White House was busy launching a public-relations offensive. For the first time, Haig briefed special presidential assistants Melvin Laird and Bryce Harlow, who in turn called all of the cabinet secretaries and told them of the president's "generous offer." It was an exercise in attempting to create an ex-post-facto consensus.

At 8:30 P.M., Harlow called Elliot Richardson to see how he was taking the president's order. Richardson told Harlow that he felt he had been "shabbily treated" by the White House.

Sometime after 9:00 P.M., Elliot Richardson and Archibald Cox talked by phone. Cox was back at his office by then. The attorney general asked the special prosecutor if he had any idea what was going on.

Cox said that his office had managed to get a copy of a press release put out by the president. They had not gotten it from the White House. They had gotten it from the *Los Angeles Times*. Cox had been expecting a message from Nixon or at least from Wright, but, instead, the president, who hated the news media, had chosen to communicate with the special prosecutor through the press.

Richardson knew even less than Cox. The White House had ignored him. And he had not been in contact with the press. He asked Cox what the press release said.

Cox read him the president's words: ". . . Though I have not wished to intrude upon the independence of the special prosecutor, I have felt it necessary to direct him, as an employee of the executive branch, to make no further attempts by judicial process to obtain tapes, notes, or memoranda of presidential conversations. . . ."

Richardson asked if the president's letter to him was attached to the press release.

Cox said no, and pointed out that the president said *he* was issuing the order to Cox. Richardson had been left out of it.

Richardson, who had in front of him Nixon's letter ordering him to limit—to handcuff—Cox, asked, "Well, have I got this letter or haven't I got this letter?"

Cox suggested that he ask the White House.

Directly after the Cox call, Richardson got a call from Solicitor General Robert Bork, who was at home, where he had just heard television reports of the "Stennis compromise."

Bork exclaimed, "God, I've just heard the news, Elliot! It's great!"

Richardson was less enthusiastic.

At about 10:00 P.M., the attorney general left the Justice Department and went home. He left behind him on his desk the unissued press release that had cost him so much futile time.

Late that evening, General Haig called Richardson at home to say that he had heard that the attorney general felt shabbily treated.

Richardson said, "Well, I'm home now. I've had a drink. Things look a little better and we'll see where we go from here."

He was not a screamer.

It was an evening for warning wives that some sort of shootout was coming at Justice. When William Ruckelshaus reached his home, he told his wife, "We have a very serious problem brewing." Jill Ruckelshaus did not seem unduly concerned because she had heard that one before.

A more somber mood settled over the Richardson household that evening as Anne and Elliot Richardson discussed the day's events and what might happen the next day. Once again, the attorney general labored over his yellow pad. He was making notes for the letter that he would write the president the next morning. At the top of the first page, Richardson printed an unusual title, one suggested by his wife to connote going out in style: THE MAHOGANY COFFIN.

Saturday, October 20. On his last day as attorney general, Elliot Richardson arrived at his office at 10:00 A.M. His first task was a painful one: writing.

The attorney general carefully composed a letter to the president based on "The Mahogany Coffin." Richard Darman, who was angry, had worked up a draft of a letter that he thought his boss should send to the president. Darman's draft began: "I am returning herewith your letter of October 19 . . ." Richardson read the draft but rejected it. He could no more begin a letter without a formal "thank you" than he could come to the office without a necktie. Consequently, he opened his letter somewhat oddly:

"Dear Mr. President: Thank you for your letter of October 19, 1973, instructing me to direct Mr. Cox that he is to make no further attempts by judicial process to obtain tapes, notes, or memoranda of presidential conversations." In spite of the "thanks," Richardson went on to say that he disagreed with that order. He suggested that the Stennis authentication model might be used if and when future tapes were subpoenaed. Richardson says of the letter, "I was trying to clarify my position even though it might be too late."

When Richardson finally completed his letter to the president, he wanted to read it to Cox before the special prosecutor held his press conference. Jonathan Moore called the special prosecutor's office, but Cox had already left for the National Press Building. Moore finally reached Cox just before he went onstage to face reporters. Richardson came on the line and started reading his letter and Cox started getting nervous. This time *he* was the one in a hurry. Cox remembers, "It was getting awfully tense, getting up to air time, and Elliot was on the phone." Richardson finished reading and then Cox went out before the microphones and the cameras for his finest hour.

Richardson and his aides went into a small study that opened off the attorney general's office to watch Cox's press conference. On the wall of the study was hung a comic telegram received months earlier that said:

YOUR CHOICE OF COX
WAS THAT OF A FOX.

During the press conference, there was a lot of eye contact between the men in the attorney general's study, but few words were spoken.

They heard Cox say: "Now, eventually, a president can always work his will. You remember when Andrew Jackson wanted to take the deposits from the Bank of the United States and his secretary of the treasury wouldn't do it. He fired him and then he appointed a new secretary of the treasury and he wouldn't do it, and he fired him. And finally he got a third who would. That's one way of proceeding."

There was a lot of eye contact at that point. When it was over,

Richardson said that he thought Cox had done a good job. Lunch was wheeled in.

At 2:07 P.M., Leonard Garment called Elliot Richardson—and once again the Middle East was waved in front of the attorney general. Garment said that, because of the Middle East crisis, the president wanted to avoid a chain of resignations. Garment asked if Richardson would agree to fire Cox and then resign if he must. Richardson refused.

At 2:20, General Haig called Richardson and ordered him to fire Cox.

Richardson remembers saying, "Well, I can't do that. I guess I'd better come over and resign."

While Richardson waited for an audience with Nixon to be arranged, he presided over another meeting to discuss what would happen next. The meeting was attended by Deputy Attorney General William Ruckelshaus and by Solicitor General Robert Bork. Richardson showed Bork, who had just arrived at the Justice Department, the president's letter of the night before.

Bork said, "Who would write a dumb letter like this?"

Richardson called Robert Dixon and Sol Lindenbaum, both assistant attorneys general, to ask them to do a little research for him. Richardson had never bothered to learn the line of succession at the Justice Department. He knew that the deputy attorney general was second in line, but he did not know who came after that. A few minutes later, the report came back: The solicitor general was third in line but beyond that no provision had been made. No one had thought that it would ever come up.

Richardson turned to Ruckelshaus and asked him what he would do if the White House ordered him to fire Cox.

Ruckelshaus said that he had given the matter a lot of thought and had concluded that he would refuse.

Richardson turned to the red-bearded Bork and asked him what he would do.

Bork had obviously not given the matter any thought at all. His expression seemed to ask how he had gotten himself into something like this.

Bork eventually replied, "Somebody has to carry out the commander-in-chief's order." After firing Cox, however, Bork said he would resign, asking, "How could I stay on and be regarded as an apparatchik?" (An apparatchik, of course, is a functionary who implements the will of an executive in a totalitarian state.) Bork called his plan to fire the special prosecutor and then to resign a "murder-suicide."

Richardson urged Bork not to resign. He did not want to see the Justice Department decimated.

There was little more to be said or done. Months earlier, during the Agnew investigation, Richard Darman had said that he thought Richard Nixon might be trying for a "hat trick," a hockey expression for three goals in one game. The "hat trick" that Darman had in mind was Agnew, Cox, and Richardson—he suspected the president of wanting to get rid of them all. Richardson had dismissed the idea out of hand. But now, whether by design or more probably by accident, the "hat trick" was about to be accomplished.

Just before leaving for the White House, Richardson said, "This is like a Greek tragedy we are going through."

Richard Darman said, "It seems to me to be more Shakespearean." He did not believe that the king had the redeeming heroic qualities of a Greek tragic hero.

At 3:20 P.M., Alexander Haig called to invite Elliot Richardson to the White House. When the attorney general arrived at 1600 Pennsylvania Avenue, the president's men worked him over with the Middle East crisis one last time and then ushered him in to see the president.

Richardson once again faced the broad presidential desk. Two chairs for visitors waited, one at either end. Richardson sat in the chair at the president's right hand as he always had whenever he visited the Oval Office. Haig sat at the president's left.

Nixon stared at Richardson and said, "Brezhnev wouldn't understand it if I didn't fire Cox after all this."

Unswayed by this argument, the attorney general told the president that he had come to resign. The president did not try to dissuade him, but he did try to convince him to defer his resignation because of its potential effect on the Middle East situation. Richardson declined.

Richardson remembers Nixon's saying, "I wish you could see it not in terms of your personal commitments but rather in terms of the national interest."

Richardson remembers replying, "Mr. President, we may not see the national interest in exactly the same terms, but I would like at least to be understood as acting in the light of what I think is the national interest."

Resigning as attorney general proved to be even more difficult than Richardson had imagined. The president made sure of that. He pulled out all the stops.

Richardson says, "It is fair to say that I have never had a harder moment than when the president put it on me in terms of the potential repercussion of my resignation on the Middle East situation. I remember a long moment when the president looked me steadily in the eye and I said: 'Mr. President, I feel that I have no choice but to go forward with this.' I had the feeling, God, maybe the bombs are going to drop!"

•

As Richardson left the White House, he did not have the feeling that the president had been sorry to lose him. He returned to the Justice Department shortly after five o'clock. Richardson's first words were a paraphrase of those spoken by Macbeth when he killed the king: "The deed is done."

A secretary announced that Haig was calling. Richarad Darman naturally assumed that he wanted to talk to Richardson. When the secretary said that Haig had asked to speak to Ruckelshaus, it suddenly hit Darman that Richardson was now just a private citizen. Ruckelshaus was swallowed up by the attorney general's elevator. Richardson and his aides heard the car purr down to the floor below.

When Ruckelshaus reached his office, he heard what he had expected to hear: Haig wanted him to fire Cox.

Ruckelshaus remembers, "Haig talked about the Middle East situation and how difficult that was. He said the Middle East hangs in the balance on the basis of your decision. I said, if it is that ticklish, why don't you put off firing Cox? Why do you have to do it right now? I'll still be here in a week."

But Haig was in a hurry.

The general said, "Your commander-in-chief has given you an order. You have no alternative."

Ruckelshaus said, "Other than to resign."

Haig asked Ruckelshaus to fire Cox and then resign.

Ruckelshaus again refused, but suggested, "If you really are determined to get rid of Cox, I think Bork may be your man."

Richardson and his entourage heard the elevator purring once again as it rose toward them. Smith turned to Bork and said, "You're next, Bob."

The elevator door opened and Ruckelshaus said, "Bob, Haig wants to talk to you."

The elevator purred again as it carried Bork down to his dubious place in history. The solicitor general took the call on Ruckelshaus's phone; Haig had been holding on rather than place another call. It seemed a little strange that the general had not called Bork back on his own line. It almost seemed that Haig was trying to save another message unit. When Bork took the elevator back up, he announced that the White House was sending a limousine for him.

When the car arrived, it bore two escorts, Fred Buzhardt and Leonard Garment. The White House lawyers climbed in on either side of Bork like marshals escorting a prisoner. Haig had sent them along to make sure that Bork did not bolt.

The changing of command at Richardson's old headquarters, the Pentagon, had been accompanied by a reviewing of troops, a nineteen-gun salute, cannon firing on the Potomac, a sense of ritual and continuity. And now the command at the Justice Department had been changed three times in a matter of minutes with no ceremony other than the ringing of a telephone.

William Ruckelshaus sat down in front of the attorney general's office and dashed off a letter of resignation. Inside the office, Elliot Richardson was also attempting to write his resignation, but it was slow going.

Ruckelshaus kept waiting for Richardson to finish, but eventually he gave up and decided to go home. While Richardson continued to labor in his office, Ruckelshaus left the Justice Department and went out to his car, pursued by a pack of reporters. One newsman asked him if the activity at Justice that evening had anything to do with anyone's getting fired.

Ruckelshaus, wanting to be honest without volunteering too much information, said, "It might."

Sometime after 7:00 P.M., word reached the attorney general's office that the wire services were carrying a story quoting Ruckelshaus. Richard Darman went down the hall to the press office to read the wires. When he located the proper story, he discovered that it had one of those omnipresent wire-service typos in it. The Ruckelshaus quote had been rendered: "It night."

On his way back to the attorney general's suite, Darman met a band of reporters who asked if he could confirm what Ruckelshaus had said. Darman said he could confirm it completely.

"Look outside," he said. "It night."

The sun had gone down and Darman felt a darkening all across the republic.

J. T. Smith received a call from Fred Buzhardt. The president's lawyer asked if several sheets of Justice Department stationery could be sent to the White House. Smith immediately realized that they wanted Robert Bork to write the letter firing Cox before he left the custody of the White House and had a chance to change his mind. John Scott, the attorney general's chauffeur, carried the stationery over to the White House in the same package with Richardson's and Ruckelshaus's letters of resignation.

Shortly after Scott left, J. T. Smith received another telephone call. This one was from a friend on the staff of the Senate Armed Services Committee. He told Smith that Senator Stennis had evidently been misled, for the Senator had never understood that his authenticated transcripts were to be presented to the courts in lieu of the subpoenaed tapes. It was clear to Smith that Stennis had been conned, but the call had come too late. The letters of resignation were already en route to the president.

Richardson called Cox to tell him that he had resigned. Since both men had clerked for Judge Learned Hand, Richardson read a quotation from *The Iliad* that the judge had inscribed on a picture of himself. The inscription was in Greek but Richardson translated: "Now, though numberless fates of death beset us which no mortal can escape or avoid, let us go forward together, and either we shall give honor to one another, or another to us."

At the White House, they were busy composing a less flowery message for the special prosecutor. Bork wrote a two-paragraph letter faster than Richardson could have written "Dear Archie," and he was more brusque than Richardson could ever have been. When Cox answered the door to receive his unemployment notice, two questions occurred to him: Why had it taken the messenger three hours to make the trip from the White House to his home? And why couldn't they find a messenger who wore a necktie?

The White House called Richardson to say that it was accepting his resignation but that it had decided not to allow Ruckelshaus the dignity of resigning. He would be fired.

When he got off the phone, Richardson said, "That's pretty low."

Ruckelshaus had gone to a friend's house, where he and his family had been invited to dinner. He told his wife that he had resigned. Then he explained it to his five children, who ranged in age from five to twelve. They seemed to take the news pretty well until they heard a broadcast that reported that their father had been "fired."

Elliot Richardson went home at about 8:45 P.M. A few minutes later, the aides who still remained in the attorney general's suite learned that FBI agents had sealed off the special prosecutor's office.

At 9:35 P.M., Assistant Attorney General Stan Pottinger walked up to Richard Darman and tried to tell him something. At first, Darman could not understand why Pottinger was talking like a ventriloquist, without moving his lips. Then he realized what Pottinger was saying: "The FBI is here!"

Darman's first impulse was a milder version of what Clyde Barrow's might have been. He wanted to avoid the G-men if he could, and started walking toward the door with an FBI man right behind him. In

the middle of the reception area Darman met Smith walking in the opposite direction. Also talking like a ventriloquist, without moving his
lips, Darman said that he was being followed by an FBI agent. Smith,
talking like a ventriloquist, said that he was being followed by an FBI
agent, too.

The federal agents had burst through the front and back doors simultaneously. The G-men had obviously been interrupted in the middle of their day off and ordered to rush immediately to the attorney
general's office. The tallest of the agents was wearing a T-shirt and
looked terribly embarrassed.

The federal agents said that they were under orders from the president of the United States. They told the aides and secretaries that they
would not be frisked but that they could take no papers out with them.
A black secretary gathered up her personal papers and stormed out of
the office, defying anyone to stop her. In the hallway, she found a dozen
blue-uniformed policemen who were fully armed, but none of them
dared bar her way.

Near tears, Concetta Leonardi, Richardson's secretary, called her
boss at home to tell him what was happening.

Richardson was silent for a while and then said, "Oh, no, how
awful."

Concetta Leonardi handed the telephone to J. T. Smith, who described for Richardson the occupation of the attorney general's office by
the Federal Bureau of Investigation. At the end of his report, Smith said:
"About all I can tell you is they don't have high-topped boots on."

◆　◆　◆

Richard Darman, whom I first met when doing this story, has done
well—and gotten even. A few years after his confrontation with the
White House, he wound up working in the White House. When Ronald
Reagan became president, he hired Darman to be a presidential assistant. The former Richardson aide quickly became one of the most powerful men in the Reagan administration. And then, using his White
House office the way another kind of warrior would have used a camp in
the jungle, Darman began fighting a "guerrilla war" (his words) against
his old nemesis, Alexander Haig, who was Reagan's first secretary of
state.

Darman was determined to turn the tables. During the Saturday
Night Massacre, Haig had passed along the orders that forced Darman
and the others to resign their jobs. During the early years of Reagan's
presidency, Darman worked hard to force Haig to resign his position.
And he succeeded.

On the day Haig submitted his resignation as secretary of state, Darman had a little party at the Palm restaurant to celebrate. My wife, Lesley, and I were among the guests.

"This is the second happiest day of my life," Darman announced. He did not say what the first happiest was.

THE TRIAL OF RICHARD NIXON: WHAT IF HE HADN'T BEEN PARDONED?

•　　•　　•

It started with an interview. A reporter for *Regardie's* magazine in Washington did a Q&A story—with me on the A end of the matter.

Q: You write magazine stories that are dramatic, almost like short stories. Why not take the next step and write short stories?

A: There's no market. If I decided to write a short story, I could mail it to my mother, but that's about all I could do with it.

The owner of *Regardie's*—a man named William Regardie—read the interview and decided to ask me to write fiction for his magazine. Evidently he wanted to put my mother out of business.

•　　•　　•

Regardie's, July 1986

Richard Nixon could not help taking the historical view. He had added one more first to the record of his administration. He was the first president of the United States ever to be tried for his crimes.

While his attorney and the special prosecutor argued a motion at the bench, Nixon remembered the dream he had dreamed again last night. In the dream, he had been able to play one last trick, to make one last deal, to exchange his resignation for a pardon. But then, as always, he had awakened from this dream to the reality of his living nightmare: That last dirty trick had misfired and he had been forced to resign the presidency with no hope of being treated any differently from anyone else who broke the law. Making tight fists, the disgraced president desperately wished he could rewrite history.

Even inside the sealed courtroom, the former president could still hear the honking of the cars as they passed the John Marshall Federal Courthouse, where he was standing trial. He couldn't help remembering all the bumper stickers that said HONK FOR CONVICTION. He wanted to put his fingers in his ears, but at the same time he didn't want to give his enemies the satisfaction of knowing they had upset him.

In spite of how miserable he was, Nixon couldn't help feeling a certain sense of anticipation about what was going to happen today. It was almost as though he were looking forward to it. How could he help it? How could anyone help it? A man who for all practical purposes had been dead for many years was about to come back to life.

The catch was that this dead man was going to rise from the dead in order to testify against the former president of the United States. So Nixon's fear and dread mingled with anticipation. Why couldn't the dead stay dead?

Still, the former president couldn't help being curious. What would he look like? What would he sound like? Would his fingernails really be a foot long?

The witness who was to appear that day had not wanted to come back to life, had not wanted to testify. At first he had defied the government's efforts to compel him to do so. He had even laughed off a fine of $1 million a day for every day he didn't appear. Feeling safe in his hideaway in the Bahamas, he had been content to continue playing dead. But then the U.S. government had grounded all U.S. flights to the Bahamas until the Bahamian government agreed to extradite the witness. Since the Bahamas depended on American tourists to remain solvent, it had quickly agreed to extradition.

Then the witness had been faced with two choices: the courtroom or a cell. Prisons were dirty. Prisons meant all kinds of contacts with other human beings. Sometimes intimate contacts. The witness considered a courtroom unsafe and germ-ridden, but it was better than getting raped in jail. Rape was so unsanitary.

Howard Hughes entered the courtroom in a wheelchair and a borrowed suit. He didn't own any clothes of his own. He hadn't needed any for years. Hughes spent his days and nights in a darkened hotel bedroom, wearing custom-made undershorts or nothing at all. But now he had been flushed out into open court. Now he needed to cover his nakedness. Now he had to put on the mask of sanity. So Hughes, who stood six feet four inches tall, had accepted the loan of a suit of clothes from one of his Mormon attendants, who was both shorter and fatter than his boss. The suit looked baggy on the skeletal Hughes. It looked even worse because his bony wrists and ankles stuck too far out of the too-short sleeves and legs. Since he was so concerned about germs, Hughes had, of course, insisted that the suit be boiled for hours and hours and hours—which hadn't improved its appearance any. The richest man in the world was the worst-dressed man in the courthouse.

Although the spectators in the courtroom were expecting Hughes's entrance, they still reacted as if they had witnessed the miracle of Lazarus. At first no one said anything. The courtroom was as quiet as Lazarus's tomb. Then the whispering started, getting louder and louder, crescendoing into a shout. Everyone described Hughes to everyone else.

"Look how thin he is."

"I bet he doesn't weigh 100 pounds."

"That suit looks like it's hung on a coat hanger."

Hughes looked neither to the left nor to the right. As he rolled down the center aisle, he kept his eyes on the floor.

"I expected his fingernails to be a foot long."

"Me too."

Hughes's Mormon keepers had manicured his curling claws early that morning. He hated to see them go. It depressed him to see any part of himself perish. In a sense, Hughes had let his fingernails grow for the same reason Nixon had not destroyed the White House tapes: because they were a part of him. The former president considered the tapes not an arm or a leg but a lobe of his brain, his memory.

"Where's the foot-long hair?"

"I never believed that story anyway."

An hour earlier Mel Stewart, the billionaire's resident barber, had finished trimming Hughes's shoulder-length locks. And the witness's Father Time beard had been reduced to a neat Vandyke. Stewart had been Hughes's full-time barber since 1961, but in all that time he had cut his employer's hair less than a half dozen times. The haircut made the sixty-eight-year-old Hughes look younger but feel older, because again he was losing a part of himself.

"Why's he in a wheelchair?"

"I dunno. I expected him to be in a basket."

Hughes had suffered a crippling fall in London two years earlier. At the time he was hiding out in the Inn on the Park, a hotel owned by the Rothschilds. While he was being helped into the bathroom one day, he fell and broke his right hip. A surgical pin was inserted in the hip, but he never did the prescribed exercises that would have put him back on his feet, so he never walked again. The man who found it difficult to part with his fingernails and his hair had given up his legs without a struggle.

Seeing the witness, Richard Nixon was simply terrified. His whole face was moist with fear. He mopped his forehead with a big handkerchief that looked like the white flag of surrender. (It was a special handkerchief, not only because it bore an RMN monogram but because it was soaked with aluminum chloride, a chemical that fought perspiration.) In the former president's eyes, Hughes was no Lazarus. Nixon beheld a much less friendly ghost. It was a though Banquo were about to testify for the prosecution.

A Mormon attendant wheeled Hughes to the brink of the witness stand. Rather than mounting the stand, the witness remained in his wheelchair, facing the stunned audience. Hughes appeared fairly tranquil, thanks in large part to a heavy dose of barbiturates.

Mortimer Gray was an old-fashioned judge who ran an old-fashioned courtroom. Unlike most modern judges, he still believed in witnesses swearing on the Holy Bible, since he considered the Good Book to be an old-fashioned polygraph.

"Please place your left hand on the Bible," instructed the clerk of the court, "and raise your right hand."

Howard Hughes was stunned. He sat paralyzed in his wheelchair, trying to think the problem through. He had not been aware that he would have to touch anything. His fear of germs filled his consciousness, crowding out everything else.

"Excuse me, Mr. Hughes," Judge Gray said. "Is anything wrong?"

"No, no."

"Then would you place your hand on the Bible?"

Hughes hesitated a moment longer, then placed his hand not on the book but inside his borrowed suit coat. When his hand reappeared, it trailed a Kleenex, which he carefully draped over the Bible. Then, raising his right hand, he rested his left on the tissue. He didn't want to catch anything from the Holy Scripture.

"Do you swear to tell the truth, the whole truth, and nothing but the truth, so help you God?"

"I do."

Special prosecutor Grant Barrington rose and advanced slowly toward the richest man in the world. The government's lawyer looked as if his head belonged on a dollar bill. His face had the patrician expression that the Founding Fathers usually assumed when they posed for their paper-money portraits. The perfect nose and the wavy hair added a classical touch, so the face wouldn't have looked out of place stamped on a Roman coin. At any rate, when you looked at him, you thought of money—old money, new money, but mainly lots of money.

Whenever he looked at Barrington, Nixon couldn't help feeling waves of hatred. For Barrington had everything that not even the White House had been able to bestow upon Nixon: looks, an aristocratic bearing, acceptance, confidence, grace, fluid speech that coordinated with fluid movement, and bottomless money. Nixon had had political power, but he had always wanted social power too—drawing-room power, dinner-party power, Georgetown power. Yet the socially powerful had always treated him as part enemy and part clown. They preferred a perfect package, a Grant Barrington.

Barrington's nickname was the Rainmaker because his clients' businesses tended to grow green and lush when he interceded on their behalf with the gods of government. But as far as Nixon was concerned, the Rainmaker was simply an ominous cloud.

The Rainmaker had numbered the Hughes Tool Company among his clients for many years, but he had never met his client face to face. He had never even heard his client's voice. And now he was about to interrogate him.

"For the record," intoned the special prosecutor, "would you tell the jury your name?"

"Howard Robard Hughes," the witness said in a reedy voice with a hint of a Texas twang.

"Mr. Hughes, what is your present residence?"

"The Xanadu—"

"Excuse me, Mr. Hughes," the judge interjected. "Could you speak directly into the microphone?"

The witness experienced a momentary burst of reflex anger. He hated being told what to do. In his own very small world, he never allowed it. With an effort, he reminded himself where he was and acquiesced.

"Of course, Your Honor," Hughes said into the mike. "My current residence is the Xanadu Princess Hotel in the town of Freeport on Grand Bahama Island. I live on the top floor."

"And, Mr. Hughes," the prosecutor continued, "for the record, what is your current occupation?"

"I'm self-employed," Howard Hughes said.

The whole courtroom burst out laughing. Hughes recoiled. He was afraid the laughter was stirring up the germs.

"Could you be a little more specific?" the prosecutor crooned.

"I'm the head of the Summa Corporation. I mean, I own all the stock. But I didn't think up the name. So don't blame me. I never liked it."

Again the courtroom audience laughed and again the witness recoiled.

"Mr. Hughes," the prosecutor asked, "are you acquainted with the defendant?"

"Could you talk a little louder?" Hughes asked. "I'm a little hard of hearing. Not as young as I used to be." He paused and looked around. "Course, I'm in tolerable condition," he rambled. "I keep in fair shape. Not great. Not as good as I should, I can tell you that. I certainly am not happy about my condition. I mean, I'm not seriously disparaging—oh, that's not the word. What the hell is the word I'm looking for? I'm not seriously derogatory—oh, that's not the word either. I'm not seriously deficient—now, there's the word. I'm not seriously in a deficient condition."

"Mr. Hughes," Judge Gray said, "we are all relieved to hear that you are in fair health, but in the future would you please confine yourself to answering the questions asked you?"

Again the witness experienced a flush of anger. Feeling that he couldn't stand being told what to do, Hughes wanted to get up and walk out of the courtroom. But he couldn't walk.

"Mr. Hughes," the special prosecutor tried again, speaking louder, "are you acquainted with the defendant?"

The special prosecutor made a point of always referring to Nixon as "the defendant" rather than "the president" or even "the former president." He didn't want to keep reminding the jury that a president was on trial.

"I've talked to him on the phone," answered the witness, "but I've never actually met him."

The witness thought: When people talk to you on the telephone, they don't breathe on you. They don't get their germs on you. Why couldn't all human communications be by phone? Why couldn't you testify by phone?

"When did you first speak to the defendant on the phone?"

Normally the special prosecutor talked to his witnesses at length before puting them on the stand, but Hughes had refused to be interviewed. Proceeding this way made the prosecutor extremely apprehensive, although no one could see that he was. He was always careful about that. The prosecutor hid behind his perfect composure the way Hughes hid in a darkened hotel bedroom.

"In 1956," answered Hughes. "You may be surprised that I remember the year so well after all this time. But you don't forget giving somebody $205,000. Least I don't."

"Objection, move to strike," called the defense attorney, Benjamin

Wells, rising to his feet. "The witness's reference to a sum of money is irrelevant."

Wells was the leading defense counsel in Washington and perhaps in the whole country. Like the prosecutor, he had a nickname. In and around courthouses he was known as Big Jesus because he could save you.

"Your Honor," said the Rainmaker, "this testimony is relevant to the issue of motive. Its relevancy will become clear during the course of my examination of this witness." He paused, studying the judge. "May I approach the bench, Your Honor?"

Nixon watched as the special prosecutor, followed closely by Big Jesus, moved forward for a conference with the judge. The defendant hated these moments when he couldn't hear what was going on. He felt so helpless, so powerless.

Soon the conference at the bench was over. The defense attorney returned to the defense table and sat down next to his client. And the prosecutor once again took up his position in front of the witness.

"Motion to strike denied," ruled Judge Gray. "You may continue, Mr. Barrington."

"Mr. Hughes, directing your attention once again to that 1956 conversation," the Rainmaker intoned, "can you tell us where you were at that time?"

Hughes hesitated.

"If you recall," added the prosecutor.

"I'm sorry," the witness said. "I'm not sure I can help you there. That was back before I . . . well, before I . . . before I settled down."

Again the courtroom audience aimed a volley of laughter—and germs—at the witness.

"I was sort of a gypsy back then. I moved from hotel to hotel. But I always kept in touch with Romaine . . ."

"Romaine?" asked the special prosecutor.

"My headquarters are at 7000 Romaine Street in Hollywood. It's two stories. Sort of art deco. I got it back when I thought I was going to stay in the movie business the rest of my life. It didn't work out, but I still like movies, you know. I keep a projector beside my bed to watch my favorite movie whenever I want, you know, *Ice Station Zebra*." He looked confused. "Now, what were we talking about?"

"Your business headquarters at 7000 Romaine Street," prompted the special prosecutor.

"Right," the witness said. "I'd call Romaine for messages. I wouldn't let them call me, but I'd call them from time to time when I got a chance. I'd call from whatever hotel I was in. And one day Ro-

maine told me the vice-president—that's what he was then—was trying
to get in touch with me. He'd called from Washington."

"Objection," Big Jesus said in a strong voice. "Hearsay."

"Your Honor," responded the prosecutor, "I'm merely trying to
establish a foundation for my questioning of the witness."

"I'll overrule the objection," rumbled the judge. "You may continue, Mr. Hughes."

"So I called him back," Hughes said. "Not that day, but a couple of
days later. His secretary put me right through."

The defendant mopped his face with the aluminum chloride handkerchief again. He felt threatened by the witness in a way he didn't fully
understand. Somehow Hughes represented not only a legal but a psychic threat. Without really thinking it through, Nixon was aware that
Hughes was, in a sense, his double, his secret sharer, his doppelganger.
They both had an overdeveloped need for isolation. They both had an
exaggerated fear of other people. The defendant's fear of the billionaire
was in part a fear of himself.

And a fear of Mom. For some reason Hughes had always reminded
him of his mother. Hannah and Howard—they were married in his
mind. Mom and the billionaire—they were both secretive. Hannah
withdrew emotionally, while Howard withdrew physically. They were
both boundlessly stubborn. Nixon even thought the two looked alike.
At least pictures of the young Hannah looked like pictures of the young
Howard.

"All right, Mr. Hughes," the special prosecutor said. "Do you recall what was said in that conversation?"

"You mean word for word? That was almost twenty years ago. I
don't remember it word for word. I didn't tape it, you know."

Again the audience aimed its unhealthy laughter at the witness.

"Your Honor," Big Jesus said as he rose to address the court, "will
you please instruct the witness to answer the questions and not to edito-
rialize?"

"Mr. Hughes," the judge said, "just answer the questions."

"Your Honor, I smell smoke," Hughes said. "I was promised that
smoking wasn't allowed in the courtroom."

The judge looked over his domain and saw no one smoking. He
sniffed the air and smelled no smoke.

Nonetheless, he cleared his throat and said, "Ladies and gentlemen,
if anyone is smoking, please stop. Smoking is forbidden in my courtroom. Put out your cigarette or you will be put out."

"Thank you, Your Honor," the witness said.

"Mr. Hughes, if you don't remember the conversation word for word," said the prosecutor, "do you at least remember the substance of what was said?"

"Yes."

"Then could you tell us the substance of that conversation?"

"The substance was he asked me if I would help his little brother, Donnie. Said his brother needed dough, a loan. Said his brother was always getting in trouble. I got the idea he wanted me to help his brother but couldn't stand him."

"Objection." Big Jesus stood up. "Speculation. I move to strike the witness's testimony relative to the defendant's feelings regarding his brother."

"I'll sustain the objection and grant the motion," said His Honor. "Mr. Hughes, please confine yourself to matters of your own personal knowledge."

As he listened to this lecture, Hughes told himself he had been right to go to any lengths to avoid courtrooms for so many years. Appearing in court was like living with your parents again. Don't do this, don't do that. He had never liked his father.

Neither had Nixon. He hated the way his old man had always ordered him around. Maybe that was why he always needed to be in control. In fact, his need for control had come to control his whole life. That was finally why he wanted—why he needed—to be president. But all his attempts to gain control had led him into this courtroom, where he was totally in the control of other people. Where he controlled no one and nothing. He couldn't control the judge, he couldn't control the prosecutor, he couldn't control the witness.

Why, he couldn't even control his own defense attorney. And that made him the maddest of all. Why wouldn't his own lawyer listen to him? The defendant found himself hating his lawyer. Big Jesus reminded him of his father.

"Did you agree to make this loan?" asked the Rainmaker.

"You bet," the witness answered, "$205,000. Of course, I never expected to get it back. I knew Donnie'd blow it on his burger business. That's what he was doing back then." He paused and added with a billionaire's condescension, "Donnie wasn't much of a businessman."

Listening helplessly, the former president frowned. In a feeble effort to exert some minimal control, he leaned over and placed his mouth near his lawyer's ear.

"Can't you stop him?" whispered the man on trial. "Object or something. Don't let him keep talking about my brother."

Big Jesus gave his client a stern, fatherly look—and did nothing.

Irritated, the defendant reached out and tore off a piece of the front page of the *New York Times*. Without realizing it, he'd torn off a fragment of a headline that contained his own name. He began feeding the ragged-edged morsel into his mouth, eating NIXON one letter at a time.

"I warned him," continued the witness. "I told him it would be political dynamite if it came out. But he said it wouldn't come out. Obviously he didn't know his brother very well."

The former president couldn't stand what his brother was doing to him. That was how he looked at it—his brother was once again trying to drag him under.

He ate another bite of the *Times*.

The defendant caught himself wishing his brother were dead. After all, he told himself, Donald had hurt him so many times that he deserved to be punished. Especially for what had happened in 1960. During that campaign the Hughes loan had become a scandal. Big Brother blamed Little Brother for losing him the election. In other words, Donald had betrayed Richard to Jack Kennedy.

So Donald deserved to die. But what if he did die? Wouldn't Richard be overwhelmed with guilt, the way he had been when his other brothers died? After all, hadn't he wanted Arthur to die? And hadn't he died? And hadn't he wanted Harold to die too? And hadn't he also died? And hadn't he wonderd if he had killed them?

The former president bit off another piece of newspaper.

Hughes turned to face the judge. "Excuse me, Your Honor. Could I have a drink of water?"

"Of course," Judge Gray said. "Bailiff, please bring Mr. Hughes a glass of water."

"No, no," the witness protested. "I brought my own. My man has it. Would it be all right if he brought it up to me?"

"I suppose," His Honor said.

In the audience, one of the billionaire's Mormon handlers opened a thermos and poured something into a Styrofoam cup. In the press section, the reporters began to whisper their speculations about what Hughes wanted to drink. "Vodka." "Glucose." "Holy water." "Geritol." But actually it was Poland water. For over twenty years it had been the only water he would drink. Moreover, he would only drink Poland water bottled at the company's original plant in Maine. And he insisted on quart bottles. He liked his water as cold as it could get without freezing, which explained the thermos. Since he considered regular glasses unhygienic, he insisted on drinking out of Styrofoam. The Mormon handler carried the Poland water to the witness, who sipped from the white container and handed it back. His throat needed lubricating. He hadn't talked so much at one time in years.

"Thank you, Your Honor," the witness said.

When he had first been rolled into the courtroom, Hughes had scowled angrily at everyone, but now he was smiling ever so faintly. His eyes were brighter. It was as if he was beginning to enjoy testifying.

It was a paradox. Total freedom based on unlimited wealth had made a prisoner of Hughes, but a court subpoena was beginning to set him free. Or so it seemed. When Hughes could do anything he wanted, he didn't want to do anything. But now that he had been compelled to testify, he seemed to want to talk. When he could go anywhere in the world, he went nowhere at all. But now that he had been forced to go to court, he seemed to be enjoying the outing. When he could have been a citizen of the world, he chose to be a citizen of a dark bedroom. But now that he had no choice but to do his duty as an American citizen, his world had been infinitely expanded. And he was surprised by how much he liked this world beyond the bedroom door.

"Donald Nixon is about the only person I ever heard of," Hughes testifed, "who ever went broke selling hamburgers in California."

The defendant returned to his room on the top floor of the Madison Hotel during the lunch recess. His lawyer accompanied him.

"You should read *Six Crises* again," the former president said. "You haven't read it lately, have you?"

"Not lately," Big Jesus admitted.

"See, it explains the whole thing. How the best defense is an attack. Like when they accused me of having a slush fund. And when I went on TV and said they all had their relatives on their payrolls. It's worth reading. You know, I still get royalty checks from that book."

"I'll look at it again."

"See, I think you have to be more aggressive in the courtroom. Attack more."

Big Jesus was someone else who hated being told what to do. Especially by a client. In fact, he simply wouldn't allow it.

"You want me to stand up in the courtroom and push around that sick old man? You think that's the way to win the jury's sympathy?"

"That sick old man can take care of himself. What I'm saying is you don't object enough. You should always be interrupting them. Breaking their concentration."

"I'm not so sure. If you protest too much, you look like you're trying to hide something."

"I think we should work out a set of hand signals so I can tell you when I want you to object. Maybe we could—"

"No." Big Jesus cut him off. "No signals. Remember, I agreed to defend you on one condition: I had to be in total control. That's the only way I can work. I've got to be the dictator in the case."

"But I'm the one on trial," the client protested. "And I'm the one who'll have to go to jail if we lose. So don't I get some say?"

"Of course," Big Jesus said, getting angry too. "The final say always rests with the client because the client can always fire me or keep me. But if he keeps me, he keeps me on my terms. Fair enough?"

But the client was no longer listening. His mind was lurching from subject to subject. He thought: I wonder what jail is like, where you have no control at all. No, I don't want to think about that. He thought: I wonder what Mao thinks of me now. No, I don't want to think about that, either. He thought: I wish I'd destroyed the tapes.

"I wish I'd burned them," the client said, as though his lawyer had been following his train of thought.

It took Big Jesus a moment to puzzle out what his client was talking about.

"You mean the tapes?"

"Sure. I knew I should have burned them, but I didn't want to. I needed them. I . . ."

The former president didn't finish his thought but simply sat there, musing. He was vaguely aware that his need to record White House conversations had somehow been connected to his need to control. He had supposed that the possession of verbatim transcripts of meetings would give him some control over those who had only their memories of what had been said. But that wasn't all. Nixon had wanted to control not just other people but also something much, much bigger.

Time.

The former president had sought to somehow capture his presidential years. He wanted to be able to hold those years in his hands. He planned to listen to and relive those years over and over again. He wanted to wind up time on spools of tape, to master time. He couldn't destroy the tapes because that would have been destroying his presidency; his years in office were on those reels. And yet, strangely, since the president couldn't destroy the tapes, the tapes destroyed the president—taking away presidential time he would otherwise have had.

"Let's order a bottle of wine," the former president suggested.

"I don't think that's such a good idea," said Big Jesus.

"You're not my mother, you know," said Hannah's boy.

A short distance across town, Howard Hughes sat atop another hotel, the L'Enfant Plaza. He had rented the top floor. Hidden away in a bedroom with the shades pulled, he was eating his standard lunch, a Swanson's TV dinner.

Turkey.

"Good," he proclaimed.

His Mormon handlers were surprised. Normally the billionaire seemed to regard food as a necessary evil. But testifying had given him an appetite. His body was coming back to life.

The French chef in the hotel's kitchen had labored over Hughes's TV dinner before it was served. Acting on instructions from Hughes's staff, he had removed all the dark meat from the aluminum tray because the billionaire ate only white meat.

The chef had also tampered with the tray's dessert compartment. The Swanson turkey dinner came with apple cobbler, but Hughes preferred peach, which graced several other Swanson dinners. So the chef cooked a second TV dinner just for the peach cobbler. Then he switched the desserts. By the time he finished his labors, the French chef wasn't in a very good mood.

"I think I'd like to have another one," a hungry Howard Hughes said.

None of his staff could remember anything like this ever happening before.

Hearing a mild stir of voices, Big Jesus looked up. Howard Hughes was once again being wheeled down the aisle of the courtroom toward the witness stand. His second entrance didn't provoke half the response that his first entrance had. It occurred to Big Jesus that people quickly become accustomed to even the most extraordinary events. Already Hughes had lost much of his novelty. What if Lazarus had risen from the dead a second time? Would he have been able to draw a crowd?

Hughes still looked unhealthy, but he appeared more at ease. He was becoming accustomed to the world, just as the world was becoming accustomed to him. He even nodded to the judge as if he were an old friend.

"Let me remind you, Mr. Hughes," Judge Gray told the witness, "that you are still under oath."

"Thank you, Your Honor," the witness said because he couldn't think of anything else to say.

Hughes looked out at the courtroom audience rather benignly. Human beings seemed more presentable—less rowdy and insufferable and germ-ridden—than he had remembered.

Special prosecutor Barrington rose and approached the witness in the wheelchair. The prosecutor was old and somewhat feeble himself, but the witness made him look young and robust—and even more dap-per than usual. Hughes's borrowed suit was as drab and ordinary as the rented rooms in which he had spent so much of his life.

"Good afternoon, Mr. Hughes," said the prosecutor, limbering up his Stradavarius voice.

"Good afternoon," responded the witness in a voice that was dis-proportionately stronger than his body.

"As you recall, this morning we were discussing the various con-tacts you've had with the defendant," Barrington said by way of preface. "In this context, I would direct your attention to 1969. That was the first year of the defendant's presidency. Did you have any contact with him during that calendar year?"

"Yes, I did. Several times. He'd call up my Romaine headquarters, just like before. And then I'd call in and they'd tell me I had a message to call the president. And I'd call back when I got around to it."

The courtroom audience chuckled, but the witness didn't mind their laughter quite so much this afternoon. He was warming up to the human race.

"Do you recall when you received your first telephone call from the defendant that year, 1969?"

"It was right after his inauguration. When would that have been? When do they swear presidents in?"

"January 21."

"Okay. So a little after that. I remember because I thought, 'He's just moved in and he's already got his hand out.' I figured he wanted dough."

The audience laughed. Hughes was beginning to sense that he could make them laugh almost at will. It was a good feeling.

"Objection," shouted Big Jesus. "Speculation. I move to strike the witness's characterization of the defendant's motives."

"Sustained," ruled Judge Gray. "The jury is instructed not to con-sider the witness's last comment. Mr. Hughes, let me remind you again that we are not interested in what you thought, only in what you saw and heard."

"Yes, Your Honor."

The special prosecutor put his hands behind his back and paced as he questioned the witness.

"Mr. Hughes, do you recall where you were when you had this conversation with the defendant?"

"I was staying on the top floor of the Desert Inn in Las Vegas. And he said he was at Camp David."

"Do you recall what was said—what was the general thrust—of that telephone conversation?"

"Sure. He told me to keep away from his brother."

This answer puzzled the press corps. The idea of telling Howard Hughes to keep away from anybody struck them as being odd, since he kept away from everybody.

"Did he tell you what he meant?"

"Well, his brother Donnie had just moved to Las Vegas. And he figured I'd enticed him there. Or not me, really. Some of my guys. He acted like we were trying to seduce Donnie. See, he was always his brother's keeper. Not because he liked him but because he was always afraid Donnie was going to embarrass him. I guess a psychiatrist would say it had something to do with sibling rivalry, you know."

The former president hunched his head even more deeply between his shoulders. Was this trial going to turn into a psychological examination? The playing of the White House tapes had been bad enough. The tapes had allowed his enemies to invade his Oval Office, but what if they found a way of boring even deeper into his secret life? Of invading not only the presidential office but also the presidential head? He was afraid his foes might possess the psychological equivalent of microphones embedded in the mind. What if they could actually hear him think?

"Objection," Big Jesus said. "This is pure, unbridled speculation, Your Honor. I move to strike the witness's psychoanalysis of my client. The witness is not a doctor."

"Sustained," ruled the judge. "I'll grant the motion."

"And would you please direct the witness once again to answer the questions from his personal knowledge?"

"Mr. Hughes, let me—"

"I know, I know," the witness said.

"Mr. Hughes," intoned the special prosecutor, "how did you respond to the defendant's concern about his brother?"

"I told him his brother's a big boy now," the witness said. "He could live anywhere he wanted to. My boys hadn't made him move to Las Vegas. And they couldn't make him get out of town either. That sort of thing."

"And how did he respond to 'that sort of thing'?"

"He said he *knew* some of my boys were trying to cozy up to his brother. I guess he'd had Donnie followed."

"Objection. More speculation."

"Sustained. The jury will disregard the witness's guesses about what may or may not have happened. Now, Mr. Hughes—"

"I know. Guesses aren't evidence."

"That is correct, Mr. Hughes."

"Anyway, I told him I'd look into it and if any of my boys were meddling with Donnie, I'd call them off. And he said I'd better or my problem with the Justice Department was going to get a lot worse. And I—"

"Just a moment, Mr. Hughes," interrupted the special prosecutor. "For the benefit of the ladies and gentlemen of the jury, could you elaborate on your problem with the Justice Department? I don't believe you've mentioned it before."

"Well, I wanted more hotels, you know, in Vegas, but Justice thought I already had too many. So they wouldn't let me buy any more."

Pausing for a moment, the witness scratched his nose with a rather curious thumbnail. It was long and cut straight across so that it looked remarkably like a screwdriver. Seeing it, the former president wondered: Why was the nail trimmed in this fashion? And then he answered his own question: He probably used it for something perverted. Actually, Hughes's thumbnail was used for just what it looked like it would be used for: He turned screws with it. The billionaire found this unlosable screwdriver especially handy when it came to tinkering with his motion picture projector.

"See, my guys were dumb," the witness continued. "They thought the way to get close to the president was to get close to his brother. But I knew better. I knew the more the president's brother liked you, the more the president would hate you."

This was what the former president had been afraid of: Howard Hughes knew him too well because they were too much alike. It wasn't fair, putting someone's secret sharer on the stand. It was practically like forcing someone to testify against himself. It should have been covered by the Fifth Amendment.

"Objection," Big Jesus said. "I'm sorry, Your Honor. I hate to keep interrupting these proceedings. But Mr. Hughes's continued speculation about my client is just that. Speculation. Not evidence. I move to strike the witness's last response in its entirety."

"Sustained," said Judge Gray. "Motion granted."

As usual, the witness's ramblings were stricken from the record of the trial but not from the defendant's or the jury's memory.

"When did you next speak to the defendant?" asked the Rainmaker.

"Must have been a couple of weeks later."

"And where were you at the time?"

"Desert Inn."

"And do you recall that conversation?"

"Well, he phoned to see if his little brother was behaving. Funny, huh? First he tells me to stay away from Donnie, then he expects me to baby-sit him. So I said Little Brother was keeping his nose clean. Not that he really was. I just wanted to tell the president what he wanted to hear. And since that seemed to put him in a pretty good mood, I thought it might be a pretty good time to ask him about the atomic tests."

"You mean the underground testing program in Nevada?"

"That's it. They were poisoning the state. The government figured it was okay to blow up Nevada because nobody lived there. Well, I lived there. So I told the president I wanted the tests stopped. That I'd pay any price. A million dollars. A million in cash. What's your health worth, after all?"

"What reply did the defendant give you?"

"He said he'd look into it. See what could be done. Said as far as he was concerned, he'd like to hold the tests in New York City, right under the CBS building."

The audience laughed loudly at the courtroom jester. He was a kind of baggy-pants Yorick, a jester reduced to a skeleton.

"Did the defendant say anything else?"

"Yes. He said he'd have Kissinger talk to the Atomic Energy Commission and try to work something out."

"Objection. Hearsay . . ."

"Overruled. Continue."

And the Rainmaker did so.

"Do you recall anything else that was said in that conversation?"

"Not really."

"Then when was your next contact with the defendant?"

"It gets kind of hard to keep the calls straight, but sometime that summer he called up madder'n hell. Said, 'As long as I'm president, you'll never buy another hotel anywhere. Not if I can help it.' And I said, 'Hold your horses. What's eating you?' And he said, 'Some of your blankety-blank boys and my blankety-blank brother have slipped off to the Dominican Republic together. And they've got some blankety-blank Mafioso with them.' Only he didn't say blankety-blank. I'm deleting the expletives, as they say."

The audience laughed, as he had known they would, and he smiled back at them.

"He said, 'They're meeting with President What's His Name right now.' He knew the name, but I can't remember it. Sorry."

"President Joaquin Balaguer?" suggested the Rainmaker.

"That sounds about right. Anyway, the president said everybody down there wanted to put over a fast one. Donnie wanted to build a building on land owned by the Dominican Republic. And that president—whatever you said his name was—wanted a bigger sugar quota. See, President What's His Name made the same mistake my boys did.

He thought the way to get to Richard Nixon was through his brother. Dumb."

"Objection," said Big Jesus. "I move to strike the witness's last answer. It's both hearsay and speculation, Your Honor."

"Sustained," ruled the judge. "I'll grant the motion."

"I don't know how he knew this," Hughes continued, unfazed, "but I guess he had the president's house down there bugged."

"Objection. Speculation. Move to strike."

"Sustained. Motion granted."

"Do you know what made Nixon the maddest?" the witness asked the prosecutor.

"No, Mr. Hughes, I don't."

"What made him the maddest was a present Donnie gave to President Who's It. He gave him a bronze bust of President John Kennedy."

The audience smiled.

"So to get the president off my back, I had to promise to fire the boys who'd run off down there with Donnie. Poor guys. They thought Donnie was going to make their fortunes for them, but he just ended up losing them their jobs. I guess Donnie's good at losing things for people, huh?"

"Objection. Speculation. Move to strike."

"Sustained. Motion granted."

"Now were you going to ask me about the next phone call?" asked the witness, taking over the prosecutor's job.

"Yes, Mr. Hughes, I was," said the Rainmaker with a smile.

"Well, the next call, the next one I remember, he finally got around to what I always knew he'd get around to. Money."

"Objection," Big Jesus said. "Your Honor, may I approach the bench?"

"Of course," Judge Gray consented.

The defense attorney and the prosecuting attorney marched forward together and spoke to the judge in low voices.

"Your Honor," Big Jesus argued in a near whisper to keep the jury from overhearing, "my client is charged with obstruction of justice, not taking bribes. I suggest that this line of questioning is irrelevant and immaterial."

The witness, waiting in his wheelchair, felt peculiarly euphoric. He was practically drunk on public exposure. Almost giddy, he began to sing softly to himself.

Hey! Ba-ba-re-bop. Hey! Ba-ba-re-bop. Hey! Ba-ba-re-bop.

Big Jesus lost the verbal skirmish in front of the judge's bench and retreated to the defense table.

"Let me refresh your memory." The Rainmaker addressed his witness soothingly. "You were telling us about a discussion you had with the defendant concerning money. Could you please continue?"

As he waited for an answer, the prosecutor's perfect head, fit for a bronze statue, smiled benevolently at the witness's shrunken head, fit for a mummy.

"Like I was saying," the wraith said, "he finally got around to money. He wanted a campaign contribution. A big one. All in $100 bills. I told him he liked those bills so much he should put his picture on them."

The audience interrupted the witness with appreciative, warming laughter. And the billionaire smiled back at his people.

"Well, we negotiated back and forth over several weeks. He wanted more than I wanted to give. But I wanted more hotels, so I stuck with it."

"Did your monetary negotiations with the White House ever reach any sort of consummation?" asked the special prosecutor, whose rich voice seemed to harmonize with his rich vocabulary.

"You mean, did money change hands?"

"That is correct, Mr. Hughes."

"A hundred thousand dollars. In cash."

"And after you made this contribution, Mr. Hughes, were you allowed to buy more hotels?"

"Sure. The president called and told me it was okay. But he said if he ever heard about any more contact with Donnie, he'd bring an antitrust suit. My hotels were hostages. He'd keep his hands off them if I'd keep my hands off Donnie. He'd do anything to keep his brother from embarrassing him."

"Objection. This is the worst kind of speculation."

"Sustained."

"He was more afraid of his brother than the law."

"Objection! Your Honor!"

"Sustained! Mr. Hughes, please. We will take a short recess."

After the recess, when the witness was wheeled back into the courtroom, he held his head more erect than before. And when he resumed his testimony, his voice was stronger than it had been before. His ear was becoming used to the sound of living voices, including his own.

The courtroom audience was witnessing its second Lazarus miracle. When Hughes had first been rolled into court, it had seemed as though Lazarus had been raised from his tomb; but upon closer examination, Hughes appeared to be more dead than alive. Now, after hours on the stand, Lazarus actually seemed to be coming back to life.

"Mr. Hughes, in your conversations with the defendant," the Rainmaker intoned, "did he ever mention Mr. Lawrence O'Brien, the chairman of the Democratic National Committee?"

Since O'Brien's telephone had been bugged in the Watergate break-in, the prosecutor hoped Hughes could tell the jury how the former president felt about the DNC chairman.

The witness spoke right up. "Sure, we talked about him."

"Do you recall when the defendant first mentioned Mr. O'Brien to you?"

"Must've been in '71. January of '71. I remember because I'd just fired Larry. The president called to congratulate me." Hughes already had his audience laughing again. "He said Larry'd never been worth the money I paid him anyway. He always talked a lot about money."

Again the billionaire's audience responded.

"And how much did you pay him?"

"Let's see. Something like $15,000 a month. He drove a pretty hard bargain."

"And what service was he supposed to perform for this handsome remuneration?"

"Oh, you know, PR. Lobbying."

"Why did you sever your relationship with Mr. O'Brien?"

"Well, see, he was a Democrat, and the Republicans were in power, so he wasn't really much good. I decided I could live without him."

"I see."

"And that's when the president called. He asked me if I had anything on Larry. Anything he could use."

"Use in what manner?"

"Hell, he wanted something to blackmail him with."

At the defense table, Big Jesus was beginning to rise, his objection already in his throat, when he heard his client whisper, "Object, for God's sake!" Glaring at his client, the lawyer sat back down.

"Did he say why he wanted something of that sort?"

"To make Larry keep his mouth shut."

"About what particular subject, if any?"

"About Donnie, of course. See, Nixon was sure his brother was up to no good. Probably involved in something shady with some of my boys. And he figured a guy like Larry, who'd worked for me, would know all about it. Have the goods on Donnie."

The defendant stared with a new expression at the wheeled witness. He seemed to have recognized the other man at last. He was not simply his double. He was the part of himself that he had always hated. The part of himself he couldn't control. The part of himself that made sure his secrets were always found out. The part of himself that always ruined things just when they were going well. The part of himself that wanted to testify against himself and convict himself. The part of himself that thought he should be punished for committing the unforgivable crime of doing so well in this world when his brothers had done so poorly—one a failure and two in their graves.

And hadn't his father failed too? Wasn't failure a family tradition? And if it was, what right had he to succeed? Wasn't it natural that a part of him should keep trying to pull himself back down to where he had begun, back down to his family's level, back down to where a part of him thought he belonged? Didn't a part of him want to fail?

And didn't another part want to destroy that part? Obliterate it? Reduce it to rubble?

Staring at the witness was like looking into a mirror and seeing a man whom he had been trying to kill for sixty years. But the recognition had come too late. The former president had telephoned the witness too many times and told him too much. Nixon had talked to Hughes so often and so freely because it had been like talking to himself. It had been a dialogue of one. But now he realized that the last person on earth he should have trusted was himself. He was his oldest enemy.

"He wanted something on Larry," the witness continued, "to cancel out what Larry had on Donnie. Because he was afraid that Larry would make Donnie a campaign issue again. Just like in 1960."

Big Jesus looked at his client, who said nothing. So the lawyer rose to his feet.

"Objection. Speculation. I'm going to move to strike the witness's entire last response. Mr. Hughes's theories are not evidence."

"Sustained. Motion granted."

"Anyway," the witness forged ahead, undaunted, "he was scared to death of Larry."

"Objection. Spec—"

"Sustained."

"All right, Your Honor, he *said* he was scared of Larry. Is that better?"

Judge Gray nodded.

"And he *said* that's why he wanted something on him. But I told him I couldn't help him there."

The prosecutor stood head down like an elegant old man lining up a shuffleboard shot.

"So you were unable to help the defendant?"

"I didn't say that. I just said I didn't help him blackmail Larry."

"Are you implying that you helped the defendant with something else?"

"Sure. I told him some people to talk to."

"Who?"

"Well, Bob Bennett, for one."

"Could you identify Mr. Bennett for the record?"

"Oh, he runs that PR outfit. Mullen and Company. You know, it's here in Washington. After O'Brien left, I hired Bennett to take his place."

"Do you know of your own knowledge whether the defendant followed up on your suggestion?"

"Sure, I know. Pretty soon Howard Hunt was working for Bennett. You know, as a cover, because he was really working for the White House. I'd say I did the president a big favor."

The audience's amusement surprised the witness. It took him a moment to puzzle out the reason for their laughter.

"Some favors don't turn out to be favors, do they?" he added.

The former president almost laughed, but he stopped himself just in time, realizing the joke was on him. Since he had almost chuckled, he now exaggerated his frown. His gloom deepened.

"Mr. Hughes," the Rainmaker said, "do you recall any other conversations in which Mr. O'Brien's name was mentioned?"

"Well, there was one other call that stands out in my memory," the witness responded. "He said something I didn't understand at the time. But maybe I get it now."

"And what was it that he said?"

"He said he'd figured out what to do about O'Brien. Said he was going to handle him in the same way he'd handled Donnie."

Hughes smiled at Nixon.

"See, he'd been bugging his brother for years."

The richest man in the world was hungry. After a Rip van Winkle nap, his appetite was waking up and stretching. He hungered not only for food but for company. He was tired of being alone all the time. Howard Hughes wanted to go to a party.

One of his aides called up a leading Washington hostess and asked her, "Would you like to give a party for Howard Hughes?"

Not unexpectedly, the hostess agreed. She was informed that her guest of honor would prefer a small dinner party. The guest list would generally be left to her, for the richest man in the world didn't know anybody, not anymore.

But there was one man the billionaire wanted to meet: Senator John Glenn. Since aviation had been his lifelong obsession, Hughes wanted to get to know America's most famous space hero. The hostess had always considered John Glenn to be too dull for her parties, but she agreed to invite him anyway.

The aide also insisted that turkey be served. Hughes wanted a familiar dish to keep him company among all the strangers.

The fortunate hostess was Courtney Sutton, who had only a few hours to put together her party. When Howard Hughes wanted to go somewhere, he wanted to go right now. He had waited twenty years to go to a party, but he didn't want to wait a minute longer.

"Are we late?" Hughes asked one of his aides.

He never wore a watch. It was as though he thought he could escape from time if he didn't pay any attention to it. Perhaps that was partly why he chose to live in a darkened bedroom, where he could ignore not only the clock but the motion of the clockwork universe. He was never forced to see the sun ticking its way across the sky.

"No, we're on time," said the aide.

The rich man and his helpers rode in the back of a dark green Chevrolet. Hughes knew that Chevys were better protection than armored limousines because they drew no one's attention. His car was followed by two more Chevys bearing bodyguards. This plebeian parade pulled into the Suttons' stately driveway.

A wheelchair that had been sent ahead was waiting for the guest of honor. He was, by design, the first to arrive.

"How do you do?" the host greeted his guest of honor. "I'm Alistair Sutton."

The tall former ambassador did not bend down to offer his hand, for he had been warned not to. Hughes did not shake hands. He suffered no direct human contact whatsoever.

The other guests arrived a few minutes after Hughes. Senator John Glenn, who came with his wife, had canceled a speech in Ohio in order to attend. The other guests included Dan Rather and his wife, Secretary of State Henry Kissinger and his wife, Senator Barry Goldwater, and Barbara Howar. That was all.

The guests sat in an irregular circle in the living room, drinking and nibbling on cheese and paté. While the guests studied the guest of honor, he studied the women. After living for so many years in a dark room where he was visited only by men, he stared at the opposite sex as if it were a new invention. He had always been fascinated by inventions.

Without warning, the latest model of this particular invention came bouncing into the room. She was the Suttons' nine-year-old daughter, who was either a mistake or a miracle or both. Her mother was only in her late forties, but her father was in his seventies. This little sandy-haired girl stopped, stared at the man in the wheelchair, and then started toward him.

"No," her mother said.

Moving quickly, she wrapped her arms around her daughter and stopped the child's progress. It was a kind of tackle but a gentle, loving one.

"I thought you were going to play in your room with Carmen," Courtney Sutton said.

"I got bored," the little girl said.

"Well, darling, run along now. This party is just for grown-ups."

"Oh, Mommy!"

The little girl looked around the room as if appealing her mother's decision.

"Let her stay," said the old man in the wheelchair.

It sounded like an order.

"Well, all right," the hostess said, surprised and confused. "For a little while." She had supposed that children would be anathema to her guest of honor. "Mr. Hughes, let me introduce my daughter, Amanda."

"Hello, Amanda," said the guest of honor. "You can call me Howard."

When the drinks were finished, Courtney pushed the guest of honor into the dining room. Soon the guests were ranged around the candlelit table. An extra place had been set for little Amanda because the guest of honor had insisted.

As the dinner progressed, Hughes kept staring at Senator Glenn, expecting him to speak. But the senator from outer space said very little. John Glenn was more impressive in the history books than he was at the dinner table.

Senator Goldwater was more affable. He managed to draw Hughes into a conversation about aircraft. Since both of them had been pilots, they compared notes on which planes were the most maneuverable.

"While you're in town, you really should take time to see the Air and Space Museum," Senator Goldwater said, as if Hughes had come to Washington to see the sights.

"I'd like that," the guest of honor said, surprising the table.

Secretary of State Kissinger was quieter than usual. He wasn't fond of being upstaged by anyone, even Howard Hughes. And yet from time to time he did manage to give off little bursts of charm and humor.

"If there's anything I hate, it's false modesty," Kissinger said. "And so far that's the only thing I haven't been accused of in this town. So when the press asked me what I was doing this evening, I told them,

'The smartest man in the world is having dinner with the richest man in the world.' "

And Barbara Howar recited a medley of some of the lines that had made her a favorite extra woman over the years. "I stopped dating younger men because I got tired of explaining the Korean War." "The thing to remember about Washington is that the politicians fuck beneath themselves." And so on into the night.

Even little Amanda joined in, telling a joke.

"Why did the chicken cross the road? To get the Chinese newspaper. Do you get it?"

"No," said Howard Hughes.

"I don't either. I get the *Washington Post*."

Hughes laughed.

Unfortunately, age and inactivity had rendered the billionaire clumsy. He had trouble cutting his turkey, but he worked at it doggedly. The hostess had a chronic impulse to reach over and cut up his turkey for him. She often performed this service for her aged husband when they dined alone. But in this instance she resisted.

"Could you please pass the wine?" Courtney Sutton asked her guest of honor without thinking.

If she had paused to reflect, it might have occurred to her that the fragile cadaver might object to touching the wine bottle, for it was the dirtiest object on the table. It had been in a wine cellar collecting dust and germs for a couple of decades. He wished people washed their wine before they put it on the table.

The guest of honor hesitated for a moment, but he finally reached out for the dusty bottle. The billionaire's atrophied hand quivered as it lifted the wine. Then halfway through his errand, the richest man in the world panicked. Sudenly it seemed to him that he was clutching not the neck of a wine bottle but death itself by the throat. His bony hand shook violently, churning up a wine storm inside the bottle. If he didn't let go, he felt, he would die. He held his own mortality in his hand.

When the bottle started to shake, the other guests looked up, startled, and their stares frightened the shy billionaire even more. Now his fear of germs was coupled with his fear of appearing absurd. He felt as if he were on the verge of not only dying—but dying a fool. At first his grip on the bottle tightened, as if he were trying to choke it to death. But then his hand sprang open, and the wine bottle dropped with a crash. It hit the table, bounced, and fell on its side. The tablecloth was discolored by a widening stain like the white shirt of a man who had just been shot in the stomach. Then the wine spilled over the edge of the table and dribbled into the lap of the guest of honor.

"Oh!" Courtney Sutton gasped.

Then the hostess made her second mistake. Acting on impulse once again, without foreseeing the consequences, she grabbed the napkin out of her lap and began blotting the wine in the lap of Howard Hughes. The emergency had made her forget his fear of being touched.

"*No!*" the guest of honor screamed. "Stop it! Don't!"

He was quivering all over, as if an invisible hand were shaking him the way he had shaken the bottle. And a terrible storm was churning inside him, too. His fear of touching the wine bottle was mild compared to his horror at his hostess's touching him. The wine bottle was dusty, but Courtney wore makeup. The bottle was a dead receptacle of germs, but she was a live breeder of diseases. On top of all that, the bottle had no sex, but she was a woman. He hadn't been touched by a woman in many, many years.

"Don't touch me! Don't touch me!"

Now it was Courtney's turn to be horrified. Her hand retreated in confusion. Her face lost color as her tablecloth gained more and more. Her guest's shudders set up a sympathetic quiver in her.

"Leave me alone! Just leave me alone!"

The hostess felt helpless, unable to aid her guest of honor, her other guests, or even herself. She was as afraid of embarrassing scenes as he was afraid of dirt. The hostess could feel her party dying, and she was unable to save it.

Courtney Sutton foresaw it all: Howard Hughes rushing angrily out of her home. The other guests lingering at the scene of the accident. Then everyone dispersing nervously into the night.

"It's all right," said a soft voice.

The startled hostess looked around to see if her eyes would confirm what her ears had heard. Yes, there she was, standing beside the wheelchair.

Amanda.

"Everything's going to be all right," the child soothed. "It was just an accident. It's over now. Everything's okay."

The little girl reached over and touched the back of the terrified old man's right hand. He flinched—but then his hand grew quieter and quieter.

"See, it's all right. It's okay. Don't worry."

The guest of honor slowly turned his hand over, then gently closed his skeletal fingers. The old cadaver and the little girl huddled together, holding hands.

◆

That evening, atop the Madison Hotel, the former president studied a menu at length and then called room service. As if attempting to prove that he still retained some power, he placed both orders without so much as consulting with his guest. Then he leaned back in his chair and scowled.

"Did you hear about Hughes?" asked Big Jesus.

"What about him?" asked Nixon, startled, perhaps even frightened.

"He's going to a party tonight."

"What?"

"That's right. He's stepping out. Kind of funny, isn't it?"

"Funny?" The former president thought it over. "No, not really." He frowned. "Where's the party?"

"The Suttons are giving it."

"Where do they live?"

"Someplace in Georgetown."

"I might have known," Nixon said angrily.

By the time room service arrived, the lawyer and his client welcomed the interruption. All that menu studying had produced fairly conventional results: sirloin steaks, salads, and mashed potatoes. Perhaps Nixon's instincts were so in tune with the Silent Majority's that he simply ordered what they would have ordered. He balanced a plate the way he balanced a ticket. The most popular entrée: steak. The most popular running mate: potato.

Of course he had ordered wine, a bottle of Chateau Ansone 1964. It might have been a little too good for his constituency, but they didn't have his troubles.

The former president tried the mashed potatoes first, savoring them carefully, like a connoisseur testing a wine. Then he frowned.

"Lumps," pronounced the former president of the United States. "I hate mashed potatoes with lumps. It's just a matter of caring. That's all it is. Potatoes don't have to have lumps. When I used to help my mother in the kitchen, she let me beat the potatoes. And they never had lumps. Never. I used a whipping motion to make them smooth instead of just going up and down the way my brothers did."

As he stared down into his potatoes, the former president smiled weakly in spite of the lumps, for he was remembering those days in the kitchen with his mom. Once more he seemed to feel the metal masher in his hands. Again he relished the way the potatoes crumbled beneath his weapon. If only his enemies could have been crushed as easily and as completely.

"I'm going to the bathroom," Nixon announced abruptly.

He rose awkwardly from his chair and moved stiffly toward relief.

Reaching his destination, he closed the door behind him, but he had trouble bolting it. Big Jesus heard him fumbling with the lock.

The lawyer was happy to be relieved of his client's oppressive presence for a moment. He leaned back and tried to gather his nerves and energy. He heard the president peeing and was embarrassed.

Then Big Jesus heard his client fumbling with the lock on the bathroom door again. The bolt rattled but wouldn't let go. The lawyer remembered a story he had heard about his client. The president had once called an aide into the Oval Office because he was utterly unable to remove a childproof cap from a bottle of medicine. Now the former commander in chief was having the same trouble with the bathroom door, finding it an inscrutable puzzle, like the medicine bottle. Perhaps the wine was in part to blame. At any rate, the former president of the United States had locked himself in the bathroom and couldn't get out.

On the other side of the door, Nixon was sweating uncontrollably. He was trapped, and he knew it. Trapped by a stubborn lock that he couldn't release. Trapped by past mistakes that he couldn't undo. Trapped by family ties that he could never unknot. Trapped by Howard Hughes's testimony in open court, which could not be erased the way so many White House tapes had been erased.

Trapped.

Locked up.

Imprisoned in the bathroom.

Rattling the doorknob, Richard Nixon heard Hughes's voice rattling on inside his head. He knew how damaging the testimony had been. He realized that the motive for the Watergate break-in had finally been placed on the record.

Howard Hughes had told the whole world: Watergate had been a Cain and Abel crime. One brother had been trying to protect himself from the other brother, who was always trying to pull him down. Trying too hard to fend off danger, the frightened brother had broken the law—had bugged the Democrats—but only to keep them from talking about the brother who constantly threatened him. Of course, the crime had been found out, and the presidency had been lost. Cain had gotten Abel. Again.

The former president already knew what was going to happen to him. He would be convicted, thanks in large part to Hughes's testimony, and end up a prisoner in a cell not much larger than this claustrophobic little room. The panic he felt now was a preview of the panic he would feel then. He started pounding on the locked bathroom door.

"Let me out!" Richard Nixon screamed. "Let me out! Let me out of here!"

But he knew no one would. No one could. He was a prisoner, and he was his own jailer. Tears mixed with perspiration on his slippery face.

"I'm sorry. I didn't mean to do it."

Imagining himself already in jail, the former president writhed in pain—hurting all the more because the man who had cost him his freedom was out having a good time.

"Help me! Please!"

Nixon felt that he had traded places with Hughes. Now the former president, who had once gone all the way to China, couldn't go more than a few feet in any direction. And the eccentric billionaire, who had imprisoned himself in a small room for decades, had finally been released into the wide, living world.

"Get me out! I can't stand it! I'm really sorry! Forgive me! Just let me out!"

He kept on banging on the locked door of his cell.

♦ ♦ ♦

When I turned in this story, the magazine's lawyer tried to persuade the editors to change Nixon's name. They refused.

SPIRO AGNEW LOOKS FOR A GOOD TIME

. . .

I was in Rome doing research for my novel *Orchids for Mother*. My wife, Lesley, joined me there. I would call up sources, tell them I was working on my first novel, and invite them to lunch or dinner. Hearing the words *first novel*, they would assume I was broke—not a bad assumption—and graciously take us to the cheapest restaurants in town. We ate a lot of tripe. My wallet didn't suffer, but our palates did. After a week in Rome, we still had not eaten a good meal. So we decided to splurge and go to Passetto's . . .

. . .

Playboy, August 1977

The Roman restaurant was as empty as political rhetoric. At first we thought Passetto's dining room was closed, but by Italian standards, we were simply too early for dinner. It was 8:30 P.M., a June evening in 1975. The maître d' seated us at the end of a long row of deserted tables. When a man in a tuxedo finally condescended to take our order, we asked for two veal dishes, which came after a long wait. We two barbarous early diners were hungrily sacking our table when another customer entered to help dispel the loneliness. Naturally, at that hour, he was another American.

My wife, Lesley Stahl, announced: "As I live and breathe, it's Spiro T. Agnew."

Agnew was alone. With a restaurant of empty tables to choose from, the maître d' seated the former vice-president at the table next to ours. Lesley and I started to giggle. Ever since Spiro Agnew had resigned the vice-presidency twenty months earlier, every reporter in Washington had been looking for him. And here we were, sitting by sheer accident at his well-tailored elbow. I challenged Lesley to speak to him.

Lesley replied, "You say something."

I said, "You're more aggressive; you say something."

Grown-up, intrepid journalists both, we were afraid to say anything. Here was a man who made a career of attacking the press and who was certainly sick of being pursued by the press. We could not bring ourselves to ruin the evening of a ruined man. We resigned ourselves to returning home to tell our friends we had had dinner with Agnew—then admitting he had been at the next table and we hadn't said a word.

"You're Americans, aren't you?" Agnew asked suddenly.

"It's worse than that," Lesley said.

"What do you mean?" Agnew wanted to know.

"We're reporters," she explained. "But it's even worse than that."

"What could be worse than that?" he asked.

"I work for CBS," she admitted.

I started to tell Agnew that I worked for *New York* magazine, a liberal bastion, but I was drowned out by his laughter. He could not believe he had come all the way to Rome to sit next to Lesley Stahl of CBS, the network that was his particular nemesis during his Washington years. He was on his way to Saudi Arabia on business.

"Well, Aaron, what's your background?" Agnew asked.

"I was born and grew up in Texas," I said. I was flattered by his interest.

"Aaron, what's your *family* background?"

"My father used to be a high school football coach," I said. "The family's lived in Texas for years."

"But what's your *background?*"

I gave him my whole curriculum vitae. Undergraduate at Amherst College. Grad school at Princeton. I was amazed that he wanted to know so much about me.

Exasperated, Agnew asked, "Aaron, what's your religion?"

"I was brought up a Methodist," I said.

Agnew looked relieved.

Turning to Lesley, he said, "You may not believe this, but some of my best friends aren't Jews."

We sat there wondering whether he was trying to be funny, serious, or both. We could not think of anything to say. We later heard that Agnew often uses that line in Arab countries where he goes to do business. He reportedly points out that many of those who gave evidence against him, as well as those who prosecuted him, were Jewish.

He tells the Arabs he knows how they feel.

Not knowing any of this, Lesley and I were simply puzzled. We turned to less sensitive topics. Agnew said he would never regret having been vice-president of the United States, because it had given him a chance to meet so many world leaders, many of whom he had studied when he was in school. Lesley asked how the older generation of world leaders had treated him as a member of the younger generation. He said that the older leaders had been through those largely ceremonial meetings so many times that they often seemed half asleep. He considered it a challenge to wake them up and make them remember which American vice-president he was. I searched my memory for the oldest leader I could think of. Then I asked him how he had tried to get the attention of a man like Haile Selassie of Ethiopia.

Agnew's eyes sparkled and he said, "I told him I had a great admiration for the Italians."

We liked Spiro Agnew at that moment as much as we would ever like him. The evening had a curve to it, beginning with a poised Agnew with a sense of humor and sloping to a bitter Agnew possessed by self-pity. We went downhill literally, ending up, appropriately, underground.

In the beginning, Lesley and I were being careful with the former vice-president. Afraid tough questions might frighten him off, we led the conversation down a banal path. I said I was in Rome researching a novel: He said he was writing a novel, too, so we compared experiences.

He said that by then he had written about 250 pages and really knew his characters. I said I kept forgetting my characters' names. I asked which novelists he read and admired. He said his favorite was James Michener. I thought: I might have known. I told him that Lesley was reading my novel as I wrote and asked if his wife did the same. He said, no, he wouldn't let her, because the vice-president in his story had an affair with a member of the cabinet.

An Italian woman in black pants as tight as an olive's skin passed in front of us. She was so beautiful she momentarily stopped conversation. Agnew broke the silence by saying he couldn't stand women in pants. He couldn't see what Lesley was wearing under the table. Pants.

Lesley and I shied away from political questions the way one avoids mentioning sight around blind people. But our artsy-craftsy talk about the novel business eventually bored him. A curious role reversal developed: He became the reporter and we became the elusive politicians. Agnew started interviewing *New York* and CBS.

"Who do you think the Democratic presidential nominee will be?" the former vice-president asked, looking ahead one year to the 1976 convention.

We waffled.

"It might be Teddy Kennedy," I said. "On the other hand, it might be somebody else. It's too early to tell."

Agnew said, "I think Lloyd Bentsen will be the next president of the United States."

We naturally asked how he had come to that conclusion. He said the so-called Silent Majority wanted to vote for a conservative, but they didn't want to vote for a Republican. We asked: Why not?

"Because they feel they were betrayed by Nixon and Agnew," said Agnew.

As it turned out, of course, Agnew had the right idea but the wrong candidate. The American people were ready for a Democrat with a conservative image. Agnew's only problem was that he knew who Lloyd Bentsen was. The former vice-president, who was once headlined as Spiro Who, had very likely never heard of Jimmy Who.

"What do you think of Kissinger?" Agnew asked, continuing the interview.

I said, "On the one hand, he's very smart. On the other hand, Vietnam didn't work out very well. Still, he can be very funny. . . ."

Agnew said, "I think he's a disaster."

The former vice-president said that Kissinger used his academic credentials to pass himself off as an intellectual—but he really wasn't one. Agnew complained that Kissinger had no overall plan but just dealt with each crisis as it came along, like a fire fighter.

Another American—naturally, at that hour—came into the restaurant. He came over and shook Agnew's hand. Lesley said she supposed that must happen to him a lot. Agnew said it did. Lesley said people respected him because he resigned when he got into trouble, whereas Nixon put the country through a terrible ordeal by trying to hang on to power for so long.

Agnew said, "Nixon's a bastard."

He did not elaborate.

Lesley and I finished our main course and Agnew insisted on buying us capuccinos. We reflexively declined. He accused us of not trusting him. Rather than admit to not trusting the least trustworthy vice-president in American history, we accepted his largess. Agnew told the waiter to bring us some good capuccino and, if the restaurant didn't have any, to send out for some.

The former vice-president said he had been in Rome all day but had seen none of the city. He asked us to show it to him. Agnew said he wanted to see Rome because he was on his way to Riyadh, "where they roll up the sidewalks at 4:00 P.M. and all the women wear veils." We agreed to a tour.

Agnew skipped dessert and coffee in order to finish his meal at the same time we finished ours. We walked to the door with a man who had been complaining all evening about how poor he was, who claimed he had not brought his wife along on this trip because he couldn't afford it, who said he had "never planned to work this hard at this age." Stepping out of the restaurant, we were confronted with a limousine built on the scale of Cleopatra's barge.

"Well, in Riyadh they roll up the sidewalks at 4:00 P.M.," Agnew said. "Where'll we go?"

"Piazza Navona," we said. It was our favorite piazza in all Rome. We loved the church and the fountain.

Agnew told us to tell the driver, Carlos, where to go.

"Carlos, take us to Piazza Navona," we said knowingly.

Carlos stepped on the gas; the long car pulled ahead 100 feet and stopped.

"What's the matter?" I asked.

"You're there," Carlos announced.

We had eaten dinner across the street from the Piazza Navona. Now Agnew knew he was in the hands of competent guides.

Leading the former vice-president into the piazza, we explained to him that those two Baroque giants, Bernini and Borromini, had fought it out architecturally in the square. Bernini got his licks in first by building a fountain adorned with a figure who covered his face in anticipation of confronting the yet-to-be-built Borromini church. Then Borromini got in his licks. He constructed a beautiful domed—

We never finished the story. Agnew was bored. This charming piazza was not exactly what he had in mind when he asked us to show him Rome. This moment was a turning point for us. We liked Agnew less for not liking our piazza.

As we were leaving the square, I tried to think of a topic of conversation that might interest the former vice-president. I finally asked him if he had been in Riyadh since King Faisal died. He said he hadn't and so was anxious to see how much had changed. I asked him what he thought of the new leaders of Saudi Arabia. Agnew said he had serious misgivings, because the new king was a sick man and the crown prince was corrupt. There was an embarrassing silence.

"It may sound funny to hear Agnew talk about corruption," he said at last, "but I think the crown prince is a dangerously corrupt man."

Lesley, who felt a need to be nice to this wounded man, said she imagined he dwelled upon the accusations made against him more than other people did.

"I think about corruption all the time," Agnew said. "I wake up at four o'clock in the morning in a cold sweat thinking about corruption."

We left the Piazza Navona and returned to poor Agnew's rich car.

"Well, in Riyadh they roll up the sidewalks at four o'clock and all the women wear veils," the former vice-president said. "Where'll we go now?"

"Saint Peter's," we said.

At least the pope's church was more than a block away. When we arrived, we walked around the huge square, telling the former vice-president all about the fountains. He was bored. This wasn't what he had in mind, either. Carlos pointed to a lighted window in the Vatican Palace and said, "The pope is still awake." And at that very moment, the light went out. Even Agnew, who had once met world leaders face to face but was now on the outside looking in like the rest of us, seemed amazed.

We got back in the long black limousine.

"Well, in Riyadh all the women wear veils," Agnew said. "Where to now?"

"The Colosseum," replied his guides.

On the drive over, Lesley asked Agnew how he thought Nelson Rockefeller was doing in Agnew's old job. The former vice-president said he had only one complaint: Right after he resigned, Agnew had approached Rockefeller to ask his help in securing a foundation grant for a legal study he wanted to undertake. What subject did he want to look into at the expense of the Rockefeller family? One very dear to his heart, one on which he was already something of an expert: plea bargaining.

Agnew said he thought prosecutors abused their powers when they resorted to offers of immunity to put pressure on witnesses. He told us that using plea bargaining to get dope pushers was all right, but using it against politicians was a crime. He called the practice a form of "corruption." Supported by a Rockefeller grant, Agnew had hoped to become a well-paid expert on this type of corruption.

Rockefeller got in touch with him and said the foundation's board members were concerned about funding Agnew. There wouldn't be any grant. That was bad enough, according to Agnew, but even worse was the disclosure made at Rockefeller's confirmation hearings. Rocky told the senators that Agnew had come to him with a request for money. Agnew thought Rockefeller made it sound as if he were looking for a handout. Driving along the Tiber, Agnew complained about how the press had played up the story. Lesley and I both said we hadn't read, seen, or heard anything about it. Agnew seemed disappointed.

When we got to the Colosseum, we drove around it but didn't stop. This wasn't quite what Agnew had in mind, either. Despairing that Lesley and I would never catch on to his hints about all the women in Riyadh wearing veils, the former vice-president took charge of the tour.

"Carlos, we'd like something to drink," he said.

Driving toward refreshment, Agnew finally showed an interest in Rome's ancient heritage. Lesley and I had been asking Carlos tourist questions all evening, but the former vice-president had remained dumb. Now, at last, he asked his first question: "What do you know about Caligula's horse? The *Washington Post* once compared me to him."

Carlos pleaded ignorance. Lesley diplomatically said nothing. I, on the other hand, rushed in to tell him that Caligula had appointed his horse consul. Then I remembered the context of the *Washington Post* comparison: When Nixon named Agnew his vice-presidential candidate, the paper compared the choice of running mate to Caligula's choice of consul—implying an insult to the nation. Lesley later upbraided me for that one.

We drove up Via Veneto and stopped in front of a charming sidewalk café.

Agnew said, "This isn't what I had in mind."

Carlos stepped on the gas, turned a couple of corners and halted in front of the Jicky Club at the foot of the Via Veneto. We walked down a flight of stairs that twisted and turned as they led us deeper and deeper into the ground, like entering the catacombs. On the way down, we passed the door to the men's room.

"Due to my age and infirmity, I have to stop here," said Agnew.

Lesley and I finished our descent alone. At the bottom of the stairs, we found an incredibly seedy bar with loud music and a mirror ball with a spotlight on it. Looking around, we were embarrassed for Agnew: Imagine how he would feel when he discovered what sort of dive he had led us into! The maître d' tried to lead us to a table up front near the stage. We insisted on being seated in a dark corner as far away from the stage as possible. A few minutes later, we saw the former vice-president of the United States stumbling around in front of the stage, looking for us.

As I led him to our distant table, Agnew said, "It's OK. We'll move up when the show starts."

In the dark corner, the former vice-president opened up a new theme: how many big people still treated him the same, in spite of his "trauma." The big people included Milton Berle, Frank Sinatra, and the late King Faisal.

Agnew said when he had visited Faisal officially as vice-president, he wanted to take him a present, but choosing one was a terrible problem.

"What do you get a king?" Agnew asked.

At last, he chose a book of contemporary American art, which he apprehensively presented to Faisal. While he was talking to the king, he slowly realized that the old ruler was not paying any attention to him. But this time it was not because Agnew was just another interchangeable American vice-president. Rather, the ancient desert monarch was lost deep in the bizarre labyrinth of the modern American art world. He was like an American kid discovering camels.

After his resignation, Agnew had returned to Riyadh on business. A limousine met him and drove him to the guest palace. Agnew told Faisal that he was no longer in office, that this was not an official visit, and that he should therefore stay at a hotel. Faisal would not hear of it. The king said, "You are our friend and that does not change." Agnew said that the only favor he sought was permission to call upon some of Faisal's ministers. The king said that permission was denied. "You will not call on my ministers," Faisal ordered. "My ministers will call on you." Spiro Agnew held profitable court in the guest palace.

Frank Sinatra, the monarch of the Palm Springs desert, also treated Agnew as if he were still in office. The former vice-president told us that the guesthouse in the Sinatra compound was still called the Agnew House, in spite of everything.

Up onstage, a female vocalist started singing Sinatra's hit, "My Way." Agnew asked me if I wasn't offended to hear a woman sing that song. I said no.

After the vocalist stopped singing, she was replaced by a Sinatra album. Agnew went on and on about what a great singer and a great friend Sinatra was.

Then the music changed and a woman came onstage and started dancing. In the middle of one of Agnew's stories echoing with self-pity, Lesley announced: "I don't want to interrupt, but do you realize there's a striptease show going on?"

She might just as well have said, *Eyes right,* for Agnew immediately turned toward the stage. And he almost never looked back. The show reminded the former vice-president of the ones he used to see at the old Gayety Theater in Baltimore. He recalled that he was thirteen years old when he started going to the Gayety to stare up at the naked ladies. He said the Roman strippers were better looking than the Baltimore strippers.

Another woman came onstage and took her clothes off. Her act involved a round table on which she rotated like a Lazy Susan. As Agnew watched her turn, he complained once more that there would be no night life in Riyadh.

At 1:30 A.M., Lesley and I said we had to go. I paid the bill, which came to 20,000 lire—or about $34—for four scotches and a Coke.

As we were getting up to leave, Agnew said, "Before you go, I've got to dance with CBS."

And he did. Lesley and Spiro danced two slow dances, the strippers by then having vacated the dance floor to make room for amateurs.

Finally, we left Spiro Agnew sitting in the Jicky Club deep in the ancient Roman earth.